SONGPA

compiled and arranged by

IAN BUTLER

CONTENTS

*(For an **Index of First Lines,** please see back page)*

AUTHOR'S NOTE

Many friends and colleagues have generously given of their time and expertise in the preparation of this book. Amongst them I would like to acknowledge David Joyner and Stephen Richards — who stimulated my thoughts into action, Naomi Saxl at Chester Music, and particularly Colin Evans for his advice and encouragement.

Ian Butler
Autumn 1985

CHESTER MUSIC

USING SONGPACK

SONGPACK consists of three elements; this **Teacher's Book,** a **Pupil's Book** and an **Instrumental Pack** which contains Melody in B♭, Easy Recorder and Tuned Percussion parts.

TEACHER'S BOOK

In this book each song is presented in full score, including a simple keyboard accompaniment which may be developed as required. The chords in bold type may be used to provide alternative accompaniments, while those chords in light type show which guitar chords are indicated in the Pupil's Book when a Capo is needed.

Adjacent to each song a page of teacher's notes appears in four sections: **Performing;** ideas and suggestions about the rehearsal and performance of the song: **Listening;** a list of pieces of music on subjects and in styles similar to or derived from the song: **Ideas;** (the main part of which is reproduced in the Pupil's Book), suggestions for untuned percussion riffs, and **Inventing;** ideas for the class to use as they invent their own music, alone or in groups, using the type or the subject matter of the song as a starting point. **Acknowledgements,** an **Index of First Lines** and a **Glossary** are to be found at the back of the book.

PUPIL'S BOOK

The **Pupil's Book** contains the melody line and the optional subsidiary vocal part for each song. The melody always appears in large notation, though it does not always stay with the upper part. (Stems of notes up indicates the upper vocal part, and stems of notes down indicates the lower vocal part). Where the words for the subsidiary part differ from the melody line they appear in italics. Guitar chords are shown above the stave, and where the use of a Capo is required, those chords only are indicated.

INSTRUMENTAL PACK

Melody in B♭ : This part consists of transpositions of the melody line and the optional subsidiary vocal line. (The number of verses contained in each song is noted beneath the last bar of music in all parts in this pack).

Easy Recorder: This part is designed for in-experienced recorder players. More advanced players should play with the upper vocal part, along with other concert pitch instruments. Unless indicated, the lower vocal part cannot be played on the recorder or flute.

Tuned Percussion: Most of these parts are simple, and require only a diatonic instrument with F sharp and B flat bars. Many need to be played with two beaters.

GENERAL HINTS

Singing in two parts takes care and practice. The exercises that are suggested for some songs will be useful for all!

Vocal improvisation, encouraged in the teacher's notes to many of the songs, should be attempted regularly. Do not be discouraged by early results, which will probably sound less than attractive! They will improve dramatically with confidence; and that comes with practice.

Hum with the lips slightly parted to reduce headaches!

Expect pupils to sing alone or in pairs to vary the performances.

Be careful not to "drown" the singers! Restrict the number of instruments used, to *balance* and accompany the singers, who will *always* be in the majority.

All the instrumental parts need not be played for every verse. Vary their usage to add to the interest.

Use one *instrumental verse* as an introduction, interlude or postlude.

Take the notes you do not require off the tuned percussion instruments for ease of performance.

Vary the texture and the volume of the tuned percussion instruments by varying the type of beater used.

Invent games and exercises to help pupils to learn to count rests.

When sounds are on the *off beat,* encourage the pupils to make a silent physical action on the beat to help remember it.

Do not merely copy the melody rhythm on untuned percussion instruments.

Bass instruments could be accommodated by either playing the bass line of the keyboard part, or inventing a part from the guitar chord symbols in the Teacher's Book.

Make the performance as *musical* as possible.

Most importantly, enjoy using **SONGPACK!**

TEACHER'S NOTES 1

THE BARE NECESSITIES

PERFORMING

Sing this song with a great sense of fun! The Tuned Percussion part would sound good on a Xylophone. Use hard felt beaters.

At *"wherever I wander . . ."* the second part has the tune and should predominate. Keep the first part light.

Start by practising the rhythm: 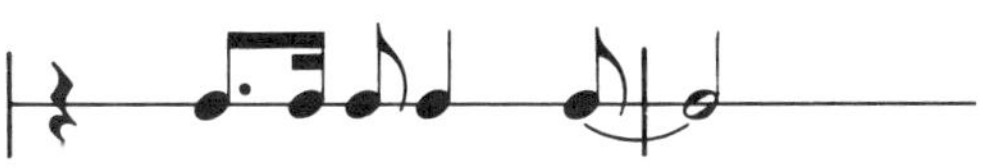 alone.

Vary the verses or sections by altering the number of voices singing.

LISTENING

Music about Animals:
Babar the Little Elephant – Poulenc
Jumbo's Lullaby, from *Children's Corner* – Debussy
Jungle Book Soundtrack
Oiseaux Exotiques – Messiaen
Poisson d'Or from *Images* – Debussy
Tales of Beatrix Potter (ballet)
The Bear from *Wand of Youth* – Elgar
The Carnival of the Animals – Saint-Saëns
The Cuckoo – Daquin
The Night of the Electric Insects – Crumb

IDEAS

Tambourine in lap

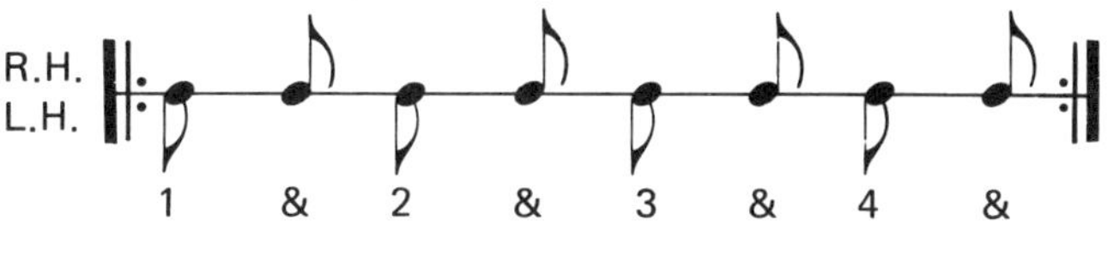

Woodblock

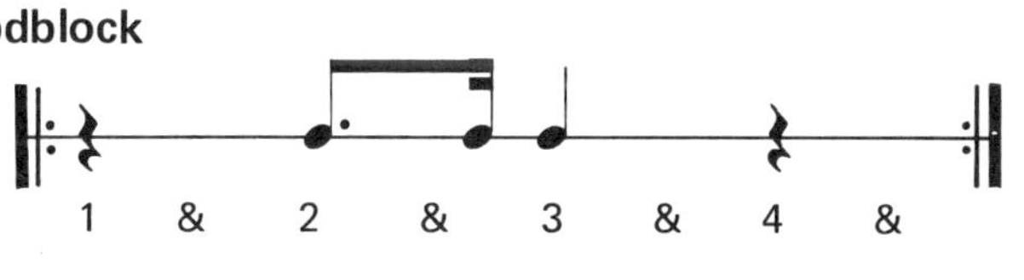

INVENTING

Make up a piece which reflects the character and mood of an animal, bird or insect. Choose an obvious example like elephant, snake, plaice, frog or bee! The piece might reflect the animal's movements, shape or speed of movement; or it might concern itself with some anecdote, myth or fable about the animal. Try to encourage invention which goes beyond the imitation stage, and becomes musical; really developing the sounds through repetition, sequence, metamorphosis. Alternatively the piece might be developed by changing the dynamic, speed, pitch, or tone colours used. The animals might be human animals! The piece may use voices exclusively, or in conjunction with all kinds of instruments.

1 THE BARE NECESSITIES

Words and music: Terry Gilkyson
Arr. Ian Butler

With a bounce (𝅗𝅥 = c.90)

14
ces - si - ties or Moth - er Na - ture's re - ci - pes that bring the bare ne - ces - si - ties of
F7 D7 Bb G F D D7 B7 G7 E7 C7 A7
19
mp
life.
Bare ne-ces-si - ties
Bare ne-ces-si - ties
Wher-ev - er I wan - der,
Wher - ev - er I roam,
F D Bb G F D C A F D
24
mf
Bare ne-ces-si - ties
Bare ne-ces-si - ties
The bees are
I could-n't be fon - der
of my big home.
The bees are
C A C7 A7 F D

29
buzz-ing in the tree to make some ho-ney just for me
buzz – ing for me
You look un-der the
mf
B♭ B♭ m F G7 Dm
G Gm D E7 Bm
34
rocks and plants and take a glance at the fan-cy ants and may - be try a few.
D Gm Tacet F D7
B7 Em D B7
39 Chorus
f
The bare ne - ces-si-ties of life will come to you, they'll come to
Chorus
Gm C7 F Dm Gm C7
Em A7 D Bm Em A7

2. Look for the bare necessities, the simple bare necessities;
Forget about your worries and your strife.
I mean the bare necessities,
That's why a bear can rest at ease
With just the bare necessities of life.
When you pick a paw-paw, or prickly pear,
And you prick a raw paw, next time beware!
Don't pick the prickly pear by paw,
When you pick a pear, try to use the claw.
But you don't need to use the claw when you pick a pear of the big paw-paw.
Have you observed a clue?

Chorus

3. Look for the bare necessities, the simple bare necessities;
Forget about your worries and your strife.
I mean the bare necessities,
Or Mother Nature's recipes
That bring the bare necessities of life.
Just try to relax in my back yard.
You act like that bee acts, you work too hard!
Don't spend your time just lookin' round for something which cannot be found,
You'll find out you can live without,
And go along without thinkin' 'bout it.
Tell you something true!

Chorus

2 TEACHER'S NOTES

BLOWIN' IN THE WIND

PERFORMING

When preparing your interpretation of this song, it is useful to bear in mind that it is accompanied by guitar alone in the original version; it might therefore benefit from a *sparing* but varied use of the tone colours available in this arrangement.

The Tuned Percussion part would sound good on either Glockenspiels, Chime Bars or Xylophones with medium to soft beaters.

Further variety might be added by dividing the class into three groups. Each group sings in turn: Bars 5-12; 12-20; 20-28, and then everyone sings in the Chorus.

Both Vocal parts can be doubled by Recorder and Flute.

LISTENING

*Compare Bob Dylan's performance with that by Peter, Paul and Mary

*Compare this song with *Where have all the Flowers gone?*

Music to do with the pity of War:
Children's Crusade — Britten
Give Peace a Chance — Lennon
In Paradisum, from *Requiem* — Fauré
Mars (middle section), from *The Planets Suite* — Holst
Memorial to Lidice in Bohemia — Martinů
Threnody — Penderecki
War Requiem — Britten

IDEAS

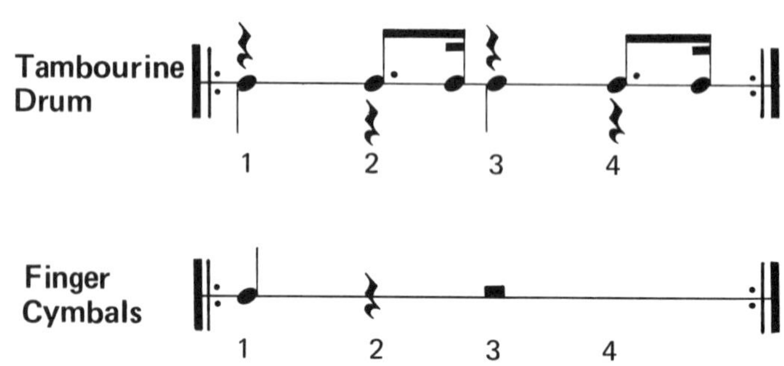

INVENTING

Improvise a musical collage contrasting war and peace (the pity of war; sadness at the loss of life; joy of peace; parting; reunion . . .)
Perhaps use the words of this song as a basis.

The piece could have words invented by the pupils.
It might be a song; it might be instrumental with spoken words.
Pictures might be shown with the performance.

2 BLOWIN' IN THE WIND

Words & Music : Bob Dylan
Arr. Ian Butler

14
mf
seas must a white dove_ sail be-fore_ she sleeps in the
ears must_ one man_ have, be-fore he can hear peo-ple
years can some peo-ple ex-ist, be-fore they're al-lowed to be
Bb F Dm Am Bb
19
f
sand?_ Yes 'n' How ma-ny times must the can-non balls_
cry?_ Yes 'n' How ma-ny deaths will it take till he
free?_ Yes 'n' How ma-ny times can a man turn his
C7 F Bb F
24
mf
fly, be-fore they're for ev-er banned?_)
knows that too ma-ny peo-ple have died?_) The
head pre-ten-ding he just does-n't see?_)
Dm Am Bb F F7

29
Chorus
mp
mp
mp
an — swer, my friend, is blo-win' in the wind, the an — swer is
Chorus
p
B♭ C F Dm B♭
34
1. and 2.
Last time
mp
mp
mp
blo-win' in the wind.
The an — swer is
C7 F B♭ C7 Dm B♭
39
pp
pp
p
blo - win' in the wind.
p
rit
pp
C7 F

3 TEACHER'S NOTES

'TIS THE GIFT

PERFORMING

This song originates from the Shaker sect (an austere branch of the Quakers).
It will benefit from a straightforward, simple performance.
Do not be tempted to take it too fast, or to clutter the performance with too many instruments; one to a part is probably enough.

The Tuned Percussion part is meant for Glockenspiel or Metallophone. Use soft beaters. Practise this part alone, and practise counting the rests with care.

LISTENING

This song is used in:
Appalachian Spring – Copland
Old American Folksongs – Copland

Move on to other music from specific areas of the USA:
Big Country film score
El Salon Mexico – Copland
Grand Canyon Suite – Grofe
Rodeo – Copland
West Side Story – (Symphonic Dances)
– Bernstein

IDEAS

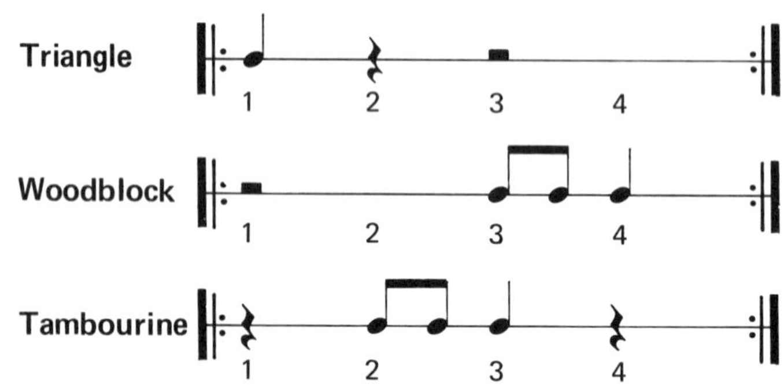

INVENTING

Improvise vocally to the chord sequence which is used for much of this song: **F Dm Gm C^7** (finishing on a chord of F after the last time through). Try using other pulses from $\frac{4}{4}$
With confident singers experiment with a 5 pulse, and a variety of syncopated rhythms. Start with a very slow tempo, then increase the speed as confidence builds up.

However, it should be remembered that some slow pieces are very beautiful in their own right, and are more than just a preliminary to faster pieces!

Some of the earlier sequences in No. 40 may prove useful as starting points for this activity.

3 'TIS THE GIFT

Words & Music : Anonymous
Arr. Ian Butler

9
be in the val - ley of love and de - light. When true sim - pli - ci - ty is gained, To
Gm C7 F B♭ F Dm Am Dm
13
bow and to bend we shan't be_ a — shamed; To turn turn will be
F Dm Gm C7 F Dm
16
our_ de - light, Till by turn - ing, turn - ing we come round right.
poco rit.
Am Dm7 Gm C7 F B♭ F

LITTLE BROWN JUG

PERFORMING

It is vital that this piece should be performed with a bounce.

The parts, for absolute simplicity, could be learnt in 4-bar chunks, each of which may then be repeated as an ostinato throughout the song.

Notice that the second vocal part in the chorus has different words!

The Tuned Percussion (probably Xylophones with hard sticks) can, if played with two sticks, tremolo on the single notes.

LISTENING

The arrangement of this number by Glen Miller

Drinking songs:
Auld Lang Syne — Traditional
Drink to me only with thine eyes — Traditional
In Cellar Cool — Traditional
Student Prince — Sigmund Romberg
Wine, Women and Song Op. 333
— Johann Strauss

Similar type chorus words:
It was a Lover and his Lass — Morley
Now is the Month of Maying — Morley

IDEAS

Tambourine in lap or Woodblock

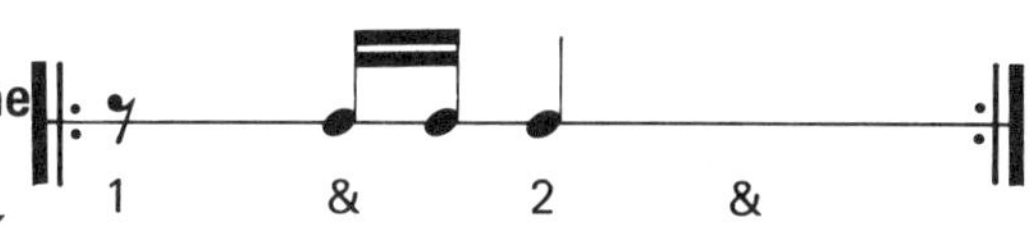

Claves
Bass Drum

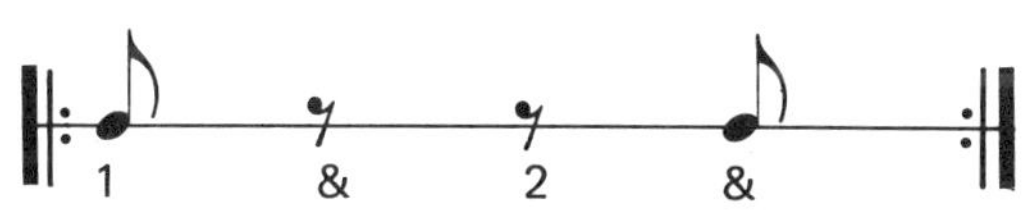

INVENTING

Invent a 4 bar ostinato to the following chord sequence:

$\frac{2}{4}$ B♭ / E♭ / F^7 / B♭ F^7 B♭–//

In an easier key this becomes:

$\frac{2}{4}$ C / F / G^7 / C G^7 C–//

This could then (if in the same key as the song!) be used as an alternative ostinato accompaniment to the song.

Write a nonsense poem, similar to Verse Three of the song, and then write a tune to fit it. Try accompanying it with the alternative ostinato accompaniment.

4 LITTLE BROWN JUG

Traditional
Arr. Ian Butler

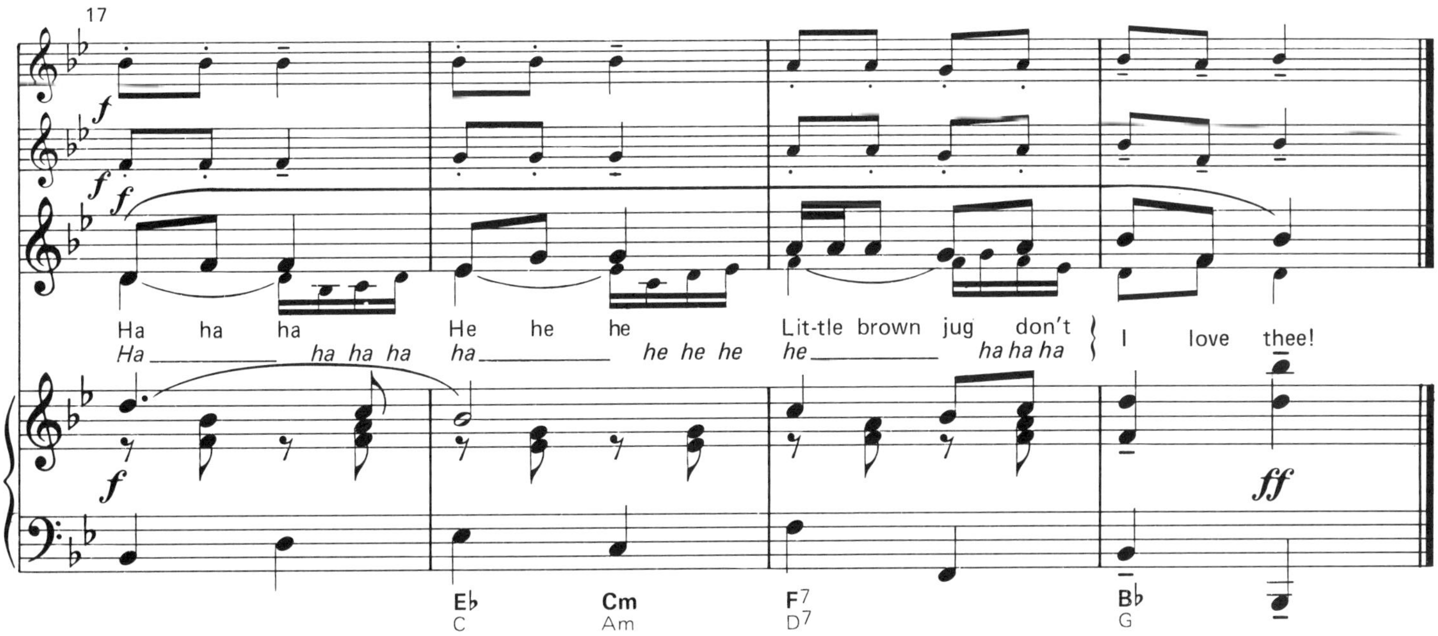

2. 'Tis you who makes my friends and foes,
'Tis you who makes me wear old clothes.
Here you are so near my nose,
So tip her up and down she goes!

Chorus

3. The rose is red, my nose is too,
The violet's blue, and so are you.
Yet I guess, before we stop,
We'd better take another drop!

Chorus

5 TEACHER'S NOTES

MORNING HAS BROKEN

PERFORMING

The feeling of this song should be one in a bar, but not too fast.
The song should flow smoothly. Arch the phrases.

Vary each verse by using different elements of the accompanying parts. E.g. Verse1: Tuned Percussion (metal), Verse 2: Easy and Advanced Recorder, Verse 3: Orchestral Instruments.
In addition, Verse 2 might be sung by two soloists or a small group.

LISTENING

Pieces to do with morning, dawn and daybreak:
Dawn, from *Grand Canyon Suite* – Grofe
Dawn, from *Sea Interludes* in *Peter Grimes* – Britten
Lever du Jour, from *Daphnis and Chloé* – Ravel
Morning, from *Peer Gynt* – Grieg
Night on a bare Mountain (last section) – Mussorgsky
Oh, what a beautiful Morning, from *Oklahoma* – Rodgers
Song before Sunrise – Delius
The great Discovery – Elton John

IDEAS

Tambourine in lap

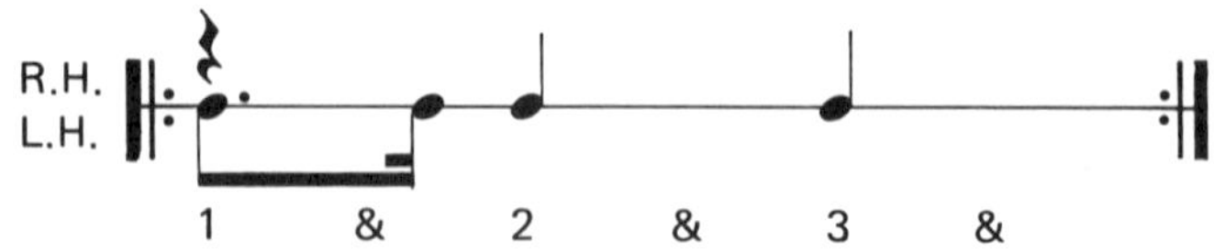

Invent a Triangle or Finger Cymbal part.

Bass Xylophone, if available, could play the left hand of the Keyboard part.

INVENTING

Using only the first four notes of this song (C E G C'), make a new melody. Sing it over a drone bass of C and G.

Improvise a piece entitled *Daybreak*. Perhaps the sequence of events could be: stillness and darkness; the early bird; light comes; more birds; movement of people; the day begins.

Take an individual word from the song and invent a piece which explores it. E.g. rain; dewfall; recreation; blackbird; etc. . .

5 MORNING HAS BROKEN

Words: Eleanor Farjeon
Music: Traditional Arr. Ian Butler

16
bird. Praise for the sing - ing!
grass. Praise for the sweet - ness
play! Praise with e — la - tion,
C7
F maj7
21 G7
Praise for the mor - ning! Praise for them, spring -
of the wet gar - den, Sprung in com - plete -
Praise ev - 'ry morn - ing, God's re - cre - a -
Em (C bass)
Am
D7
G13
C
26
1. and 2.
Last time
ing fresh from the word.
ness where His feet pass.
tion of the new day.
rit.
Dm (C bass)
Em (C bass)
Dm (C bass)
C
C

TEACHER'S NOTES 6

MICHAEL FINNIGIN

PERFORMING

Try performing this piece at a variety of speeds! It works very well really fast, but requires lots of practice with the diction. Start slowly!

Get the players of the Easy Recorder and Tuned Percussion parts to sense the question and answer in their rhythm:

The second vocal part words *"There was an old man"* are the same for every verse.

LISTENING

The idea of perpetuum mobile (continuous movement):

Bolero — Ravel
Flight of the Bumble Bee — Rimsky-Korsakov
Perpetuum Mobile, from *Mikrokosmos* — Bartok
Perpetuum Mobile — Johann Strauss
Ritual Fire Dance, from *El Amor Brujo* — de Falla
Sabre Dance, from *Gayaneh Suite* — Khachaturian
Scherzo, from *Octet* — Mendelssohn

IDEAS

Claves or Woodblock

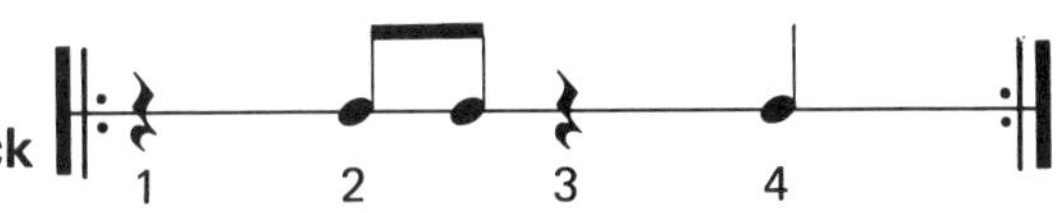

Tambourine in lap

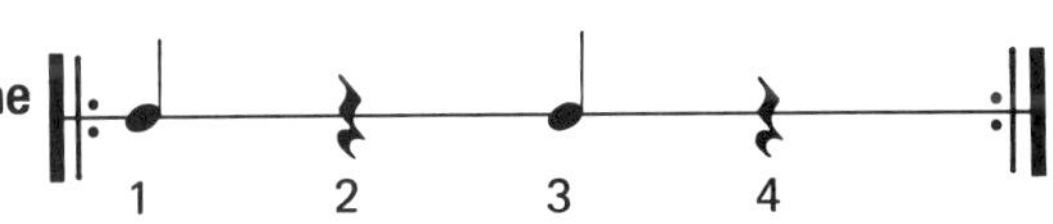

INVENTING

Invent a question and answer melody to the rhythm:

Make up a melody which has a repeated note pattern as in this song, see: *"was an old man"* and *"Finnigin beginigin!"*

Make up a repeated note ostinato, which could be a rhythmic drone over which you could sing or play your 'question and answer' melody.

6 MICHAEL FINNIGIN

Traditional
Arr. Ian Butler

2. There was an old man called Michael Finnigin,
He kicked up an awful din-i-gin,
Because they said he must not sing-i-gin,
Poor old Michael Finnigin (begin-i-gin).

3. There was an old man called Michael Finnigin,
He went fishing with a pin-i-gin,
Caught a fish but dropped it in-i-gin,
Poor old Michael Finnigin (begin-i-gin).

4. There was an old man called Michael Finnigin,
Climbed a tree and barked his shin-i-gin,
Took off several yards of skin-i-gin,
Poor old Michael Finnigin (begin-i-gin).

5. There was an old man called Michael Finnigin,
He grew fat and then grew thin-i-gin,
Then he died and had to begin-i-gin,
Poor old Michael Finnigin. STOP!

7 TEACHER'S NOTES

HUSH LITTLE BABY

PERFORMING

This lullaby needs sensitive handling in order that it doesn't sound too cloying. Don't be tempted to take it too slowly!

Great variation in the accompanying forces (always to be small and played gently) will keep the interest through the eight verses. (The vocal parts will work without accompaniment if desired).

In the third and fourth verses, the melody is split between the second vocal part (first two bars) and the first vocal part (second two bars).

LISTENING

Lullabies:
Berceuse – Fauré
Charm of Lullabies – Britten
Evening Primrose – Britten
Hush Little Baby – sung by Joan Baez
Jumbo's Lullaby, from *Children's Corner* – Debussy
Rock a bye your Baby – Schwarz
Sea Slumber Song, from *Sea Pictures* – Elgar
Wiegenlied – Brahms
Wiegenlied – Richard Strauss (Op 41)

Quiet Evenings:
Evening Song – Kodaly
Summer Night on a River – Delius

IDEAS

Cabassa

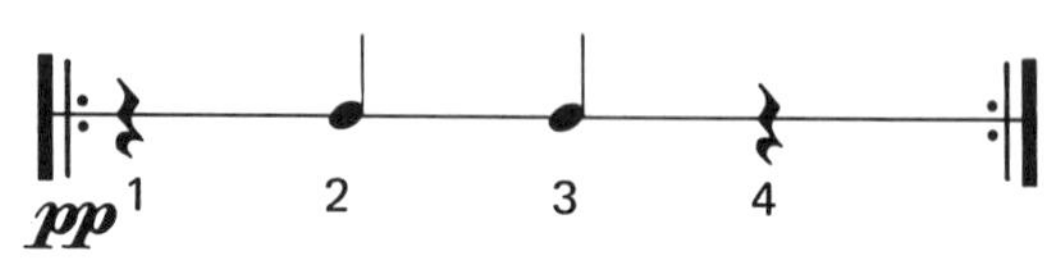

The chime bars playing the note of the guitar chord, could play the first beat of each bar.

INVENTING

This is a two-chord song! It uses the tonic and the dominant seventh chords (**G** and **D**^{7}, **C** and **G**^{7}, and **F** and **C**^{7}).

Using **C** and **G**^{7}, invent a chord sequence. Then add one or more improvised melodies for voice and instruments to fit this.

If you have access to an electronic keyboard with chord accompaniment, this will be very useful for those whose keyboard skills are limited!

7 HUSH LITTLE BABY

Traditional
Arr. Ian Butler

10
mp
mf
3. If that dia - mond ring is brass, Ma - ma's gon-na buy you a
4. If that look - ing glass gets broke, Pa - pa's gon-na buy you a
mp
C
G7
13
1.
2.
mf
mf
look - ing glass.
bil - ly goat.
5. If that bil - ly
6. If that cart and
mp
C
C
C7
F
16
(2. = ♪♩.)
goat don't pull, Ma - ma's gon-na buy you a cart and bull.
bull turn over, Pa - pa's gon-na buy you a
1.
C7
F

19 2.
dog named Ro - ver. 7. If that dog named Ro - ver don't bark,
F D7 G D7
22
Ma - ma's gon - na buy you a horse and cart. 8. If that horse and
G
25
cart fall down You are still the best lit - tle ba - by in town!
rit.
molto rit.
D7 G

8 TEACHER'S NOTES

A WINDMILL IN OLD AMSTERDAM

PERFORMING

Sing this song with a swing, keeping a feeling of one beat to a bar. Don't let it drag!
There are opportunities for solos, either as a narrator, or the various characters in the story. The rest of the singers could act as the chorus. Add *"mouse sounds"* ad lib, perhaps in the gaps between the lines.

The Tuned Percussion part is intended for the Xylophone.

Neither vocal part can be played on Flute, Recorder, or Oboe.

LISTENING

Recordings of this song.

Pieces with mice:
Mouse Dance, from *The Nutcracker* – Tchaikovsky
Of Mice and Men – Copland
Scherzo Humoristique, from *Cat and Mouse* – Copland
The Fieldmouse – Martinů

Holland and Windmills:
Dutch Street Organs
Windmills of your Mind – Michel Legrand

IDEAS

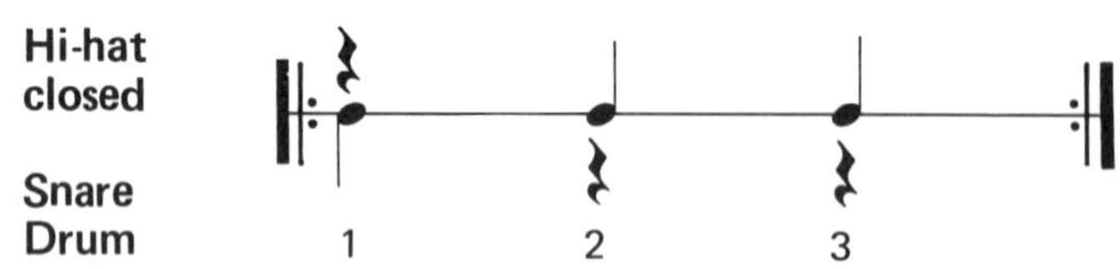

INVENTING

Improvise a piece about groups of small animals. Use the characteristics of the animals' behaviour or movement to suggest the character of the music. E.g. Ants – fast, scurrying; Caterpillar – slow, 'up and down' movement of body; Worm – wiggling and twisting, etc.

Work out the melody to *Three Blind Mice*. Make up some variations on this tune. Try altering the speed, the pulse, the rhythm, the instruments you use, the key, the mode . . .

8 A WINDMILL IN OLD AMSTERDAM

Words & Music by
Ted Dicks and Myles Rudge
Arr. Ian Butler

14 Chorus
f
I saw a mouse. Where? There on the stair. Where on the
Chorus
mf
F E
B♭ A
F E
C7 B7
20
stair? Right there. A lit-tle mouse with clogs on. Well, I de-
F E
F+
B♭ A
F E
26
– clare, go - ing clip clip-pe-ty clop on the stair. Oh yeah!
G7 F♯7
C7 B7
F E
B♭ A
C7 B7
F E

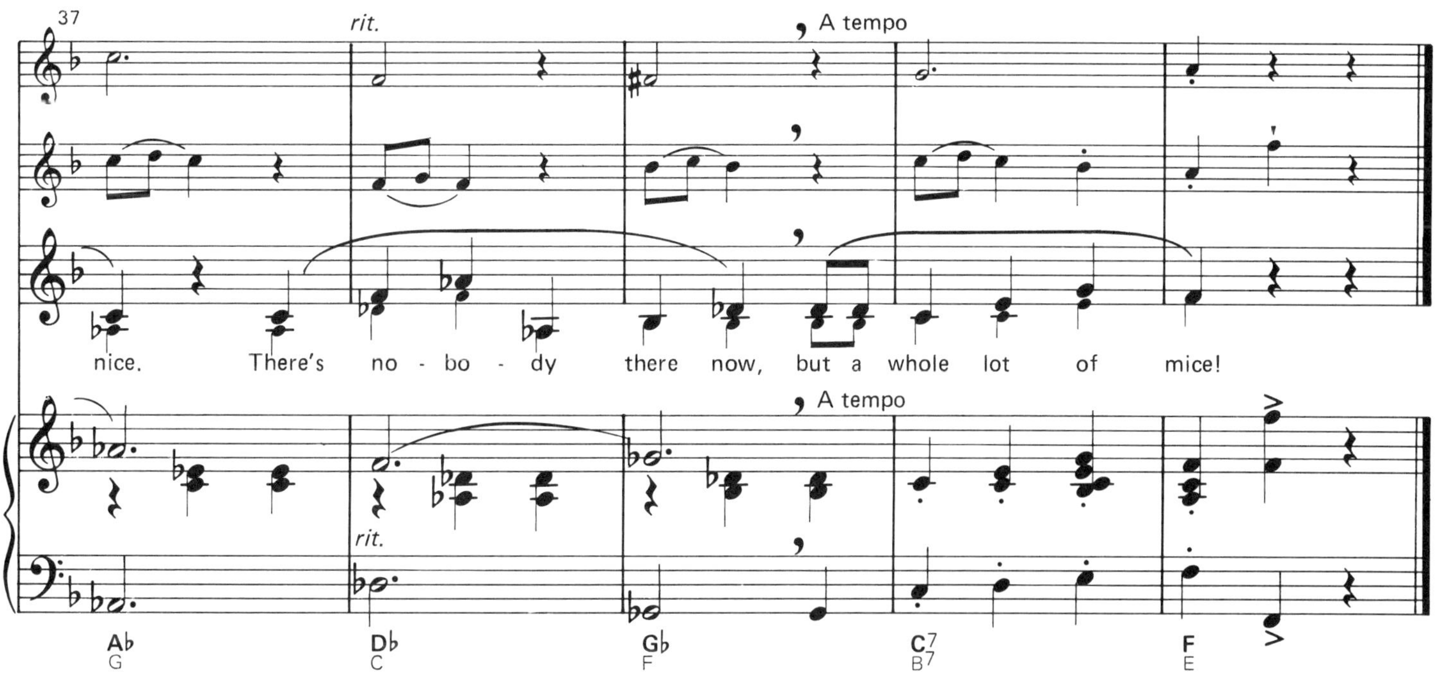

2. The mouse he got lonesome, he took him a wife.
A windmill with mice in it's hardly surprisin'
She sang ev'ry morning, How lucky I am,
Living in a windmill in old Amsterdam.

Chorus

3. First they had triplets and then they had twins,
A windmill with quins in, triplets and twins in,
They sang ev'ry morning, How lucky we are,
Living in a windmill in Amsterdam, ya!

Chorus

4. The daughters got married and so did the sons,
The windmill had chris'nings when no-one was lis'ning.
They all sang in chorus, How lucky we am,
Living in a windmill in old Amsterdam!

Chorus

A mouse lived in a windmill so snug and so nice,
There's nobody there now, but a whole lot of mice!

9 TEACHER'S NOTES

SUMMER IS A COMING IN

PERFORMING

This is one of the most famous rounds ever written. However it also works as a straight song. The words have been slightly adapted.

The more bucolic the performance, the more enjoyable and probably more authentic it will be! The round works at a two bar interval, in up to 12 parts.

The instrumental parts are written in two-bar phrases too. These may be played in order, repeated as ostinati or in any combination. Alternatively further accompaniment figures invented by teachers or pupils can be added.

The vocal part cannot be doubled on Flute or Recorder.

LISTENING

A Summer Day, from *Children's Suite* — Prokofiev
It fell upon a Summer's Day — Holborne
Midsummer Nocturne — Copland
Music for a Summer's Evening — Delius
Nuits d'Eté — Berlioz
Pastorale d'Eté — Honegger
Spring Symphony — Britten (last movement)
Summer, from the *Four Seasons* — Vivaldi
Summer Holiday (film score) — Welch/Bennett
Summer, from the *Seasons* — Glazunov
Summertime Blues — Cochran/Capehart
Summertime, from *Porgy and Bess* — George Gershwin

IDEAS

Various tambours, tambourines, woodblocks, shakers, etc. can play one or more of the following:

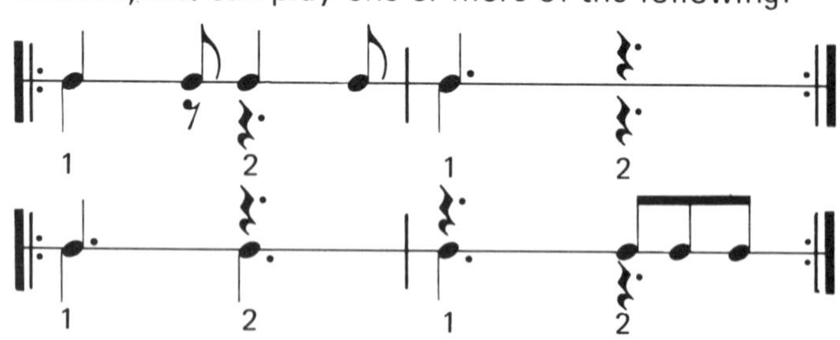

Play the drone (left hand of piano part) on bass wind instruments

INVENTING

Using this song's predominent rhythmic pattern:

plus occasional variations, invent a dance piece that will work, like this one, over a drone bass.

9 SUMMER IS A COMING IN

Anon. c.1250
Arr. Ian Butler

13
af - ter calf the cow. Bul - lock start - eth, buck de - part - eth,
f
17
Mer - ry sing cuck - oo! Cuck — oo! Cuck — oo!
21
Well sing - est thou cuck — oo, nor cease to sing it now!

I KNOW WHERE I'M GOING

PERFORMING

This lovely song sounds best if not taken too fast. Aim for a really smooth supported sound. Since much of the part writing is in thirds and sixths, practise the following exercise before attempting the song:

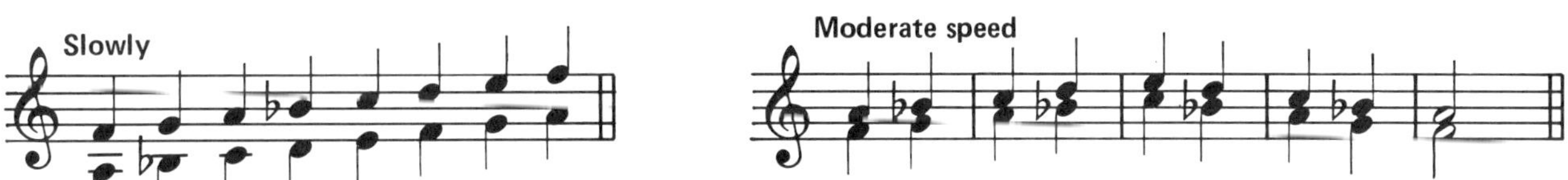

This can also be used to prepare for other songs in the book.

LISTENING

Pieces using rounds, fugue or imitation:

Chichester Psalms (choral section, last movement) – Bernstein
Chiome d'oro (violin parts) – Monteverdi
Old Joe has gone Fishing, from *Peter Grimes* – Britten
Symphony No. 1 (slow movement) – Mahler
Toccata and Fugue in D minor – J.S. Bach

IDEAS

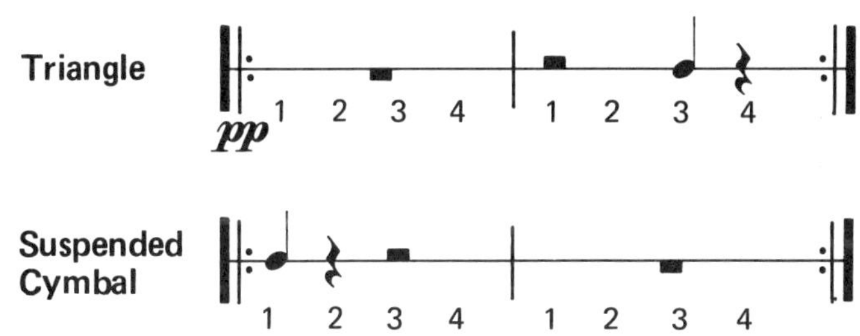

INVENTING

The opening section of this arrangement is like a round or canon.

Try inventing a round for voices and instruments. Give clues that it should be short; that each bar or section should have the same chords to accompany it; and that thirds and sixths work well.
Take *Frère Jacques* to pieces, to see how it works!

If this proves difficult to start with, suggest that the round is a rhythmic one, either to be chanted to one note or spoken, or to be played on one note or on instruments which do not have a fixed pitch (i.e. Drums, Triangle, Tambourine, Guiro etc.)

10 I KNOW WHERE I'M GOING

Traditional
Arr. Ian Butler

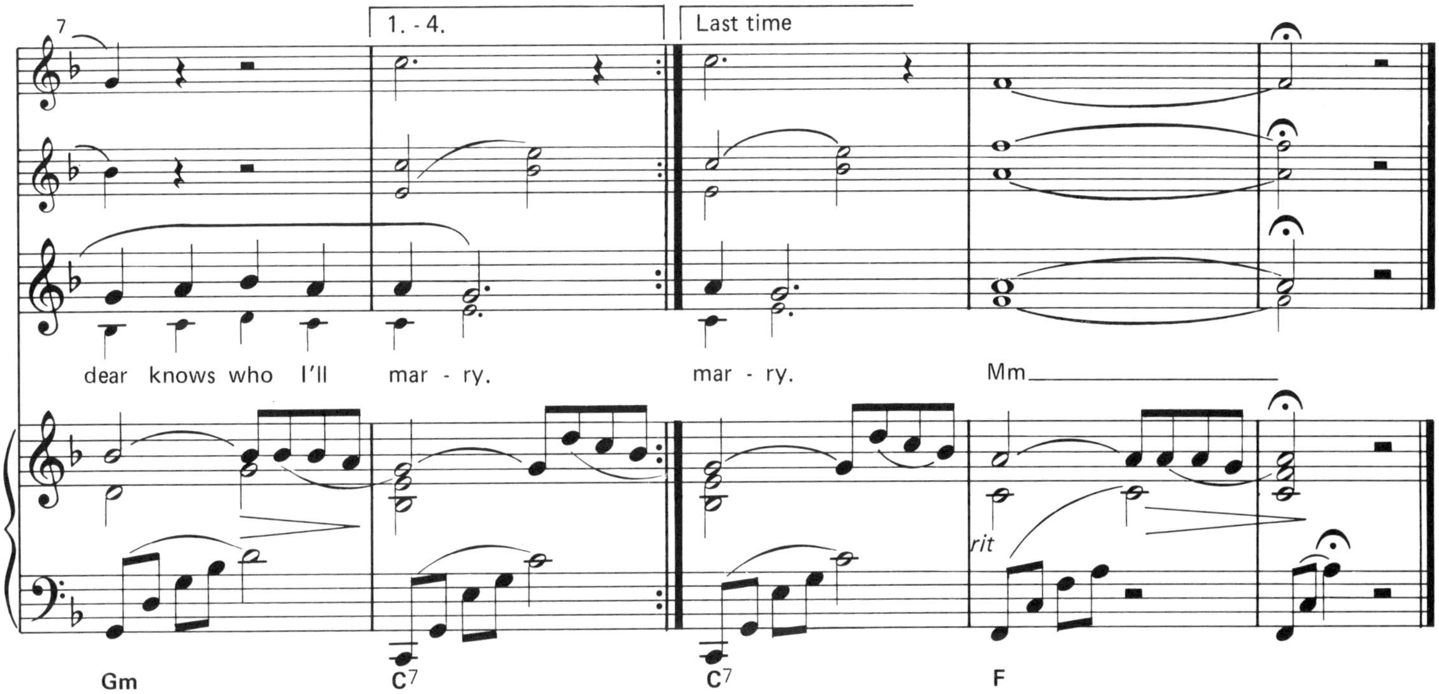

2. I have (she has) stockings of silk,
And shoes of fine green leather,
Combs to buckle my (her) hair,
And a ring for every finger.

3. Some folks say he's bad,
And some folks say he's bonny,
Some folks know him well,
My (her) handsome winsome Johnny.

4. Feather beds are soft,
And painted rooms are bonny,
But I (she) would leave them all,
To go with my (her) love Johnny.

5. I know where I'm going,
And I know who's going with me,
I know who I love,
But the dear knows who I'll marry.

11 TEACHER'S NOTES

MY GRANDFATHER'S CLOCK

PERFORMING

This song should swing along like clockwork! Feel the quaver between each beat.

Make sure that the melody, which is often in the second vocal part, is never obscured by the first vocal part.

Practise the intervals A – D (*"the"* and *"shelf"*) and C – A (*"born"* and *"and"*) separately to be certain of the intonation.

Neither vocal part can be played on Flute or Recorder.

LISTENING

Clockwork:
Boutique Fantasque – Rossini/Respighi
Coppelia – Delibes
L'Heure Espagnole (opening) – Ravel
Music for Musical Clocks – Haydn and Beethoven
Petrushka – Stravinsky

Bells:
Cinderella (midnight) – Prokofiev
Clock Symphony – Haydn
La Vallée des Cloches, from *Miroirs* – Ravel
Time Piece – Paul Patterson

IDEAS

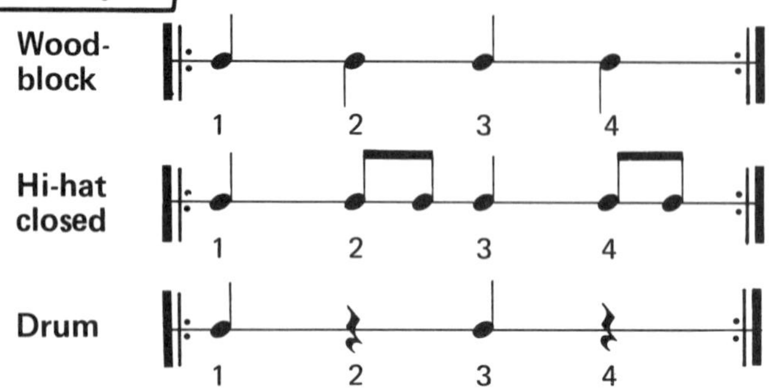

Wind up the *"clock"* on the Guiro before the song starts, in addition to the *"alarm clock"* percussion suggested at the beginning of the score!

INVENTING

Invent a *Clock Piece* based on various types of clock. The size, character, or use of the clock may suggest the type of music which develops. In addition to clockwork clocks and watches, there are electric and electronic time pieces these days!

Develop the idea of clockwork, with regular interacting sounds and actions reflecting the cogs, wheels and springs.

This subject provides countless opportunities for defining and developing the following musical concepts: speed, volume, length, pulse, etc. . .

11 MY GRANDFATHER'S CLOCK

Traditional
Arr. Ian Butler

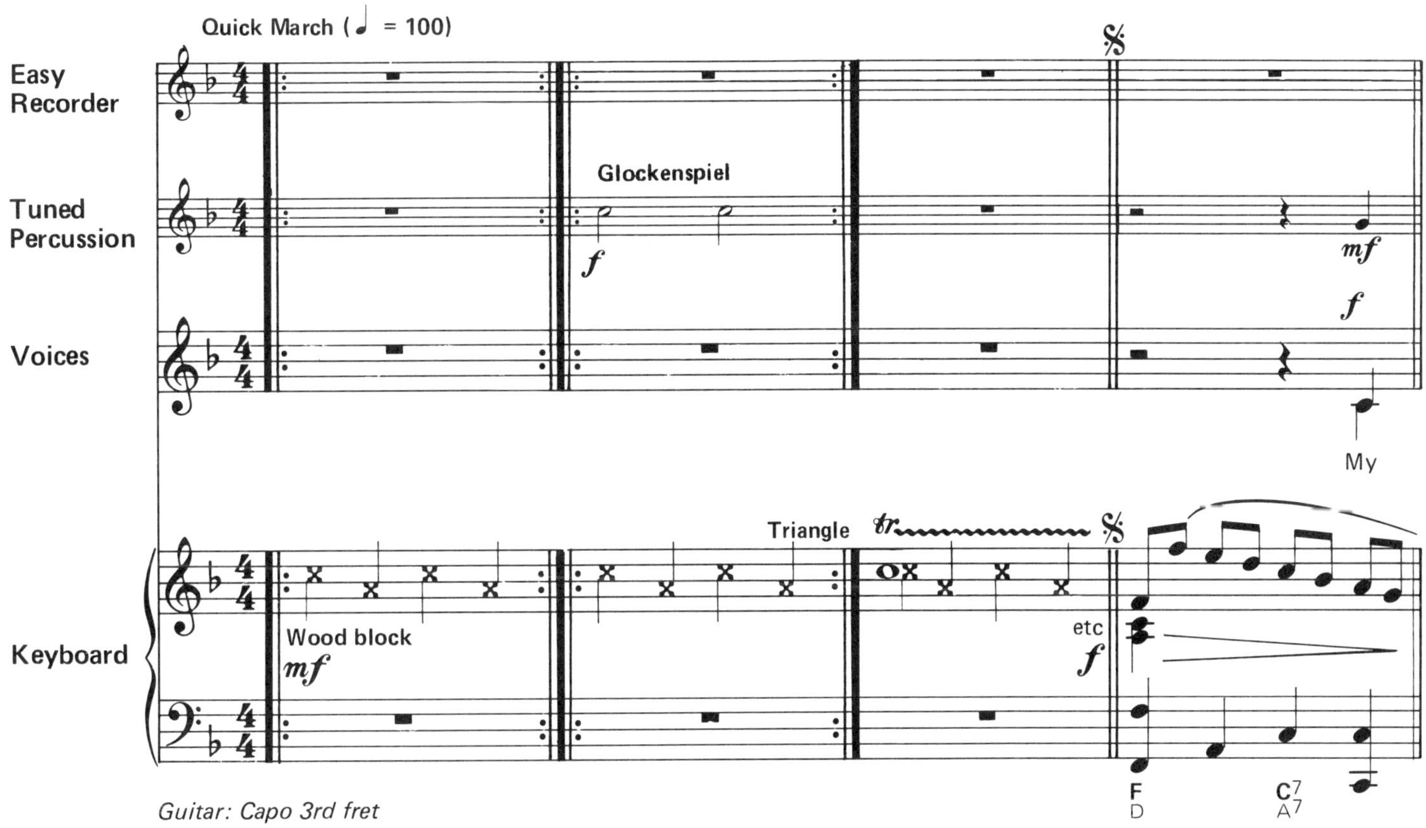

9
bought on the morn of the day that he was born and was al - ways his plea - sure and pride. But it
F D Dm Bm G7 E7 C A G E C7 A7 F D Dm Bm G E C A C7 A7
13
Voice 1 only
stopped short, ne-ver to go a - gain, when the old man died. Nine-ty
F D C A F D B♭ G Gm Em F (C bass) D C7 A7 F D
17 Chorus
+ V. 2
years with-out slum-ber-ing, Tick tock, Tick tock, his life's sec-onds num-ber-ing, Tick tock, Tick tock, But it
Chorus
F D

2. In watching the pendulum swing to and fro
Many hours had he spent while a boy.
And in childhood and manhood the clock seemed to know,
And to share both his trouble and his joy.
For it struck twenty-four when he opened up the door,
With a blooming and beautiful bride.
But it stopped short, never to go again
When the old man died.

Chorus

3. My grandfather said that of those he could hire,
Not a servant so faithful he found,
For it wasted no time and had but one desire
At the end of each week, to be wound.
And it kept in its place, not a frown upon its face,
And its hands never hung by its side.
But it stopped short, never to go again
When the old man died.

Chorus

12 TEACHER'S NOTES

CUSHY BUTTERFIELD

PERFORMING

Full *'music hall'* treatment is really needed for this song! Plenty of punch and swing is the order of the day, and there should be a strong feeling of one in a bar. Emphasize the first beat of each bar.

However don't let the singers *shout*. There is a world of difference between singing loudly, with the voice supported on the body, and *shouting*, where the voice is all in the throat.

LISTENING

Northumbrian songs:
Blaydon Races – G. Ridley
Waters of Tyne – Traditional
When the Boat comes in – Traditional

Street cries:
London Symphony (second movement) – Vaughan Williams
Street Corner Overture – Rawsthorne
The Cryes of London – Gibbons
The Cryes of London – Weelkes
Who will Buy?, from *Oliver* – Bart

IDEAS

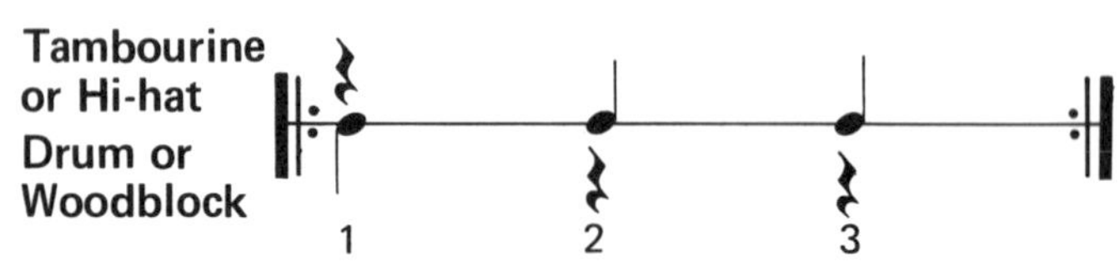

INVENTING

Invent a piece which uses a street cry like *"Will you buy any Clay?"* There are many others, particularly London cries.

Make a collage of sounds from the street. Either use voices and instruments alone, or research and record the actual sounds of today's streets. These could then be edited and used to make a taped collage with or without live or recorded voices and instruments playing alongside.

12 CUSHY BUTTERFIELD

Traditional
Arr. Ian Butler

call her my dove! And her name is Cu — shy
fright — en a cow. And when - ev - er she starts
B♭ F (C Bass) C7 F F7 B♭
G D A7 D D7 G
But - ter - field and she sells yel — low clay. And her
hol - ler - ing, Will you buy an — y clay? Like a
Cm F7
Am D7
ol - der cou - sin is a muck - man and they call him Tom Grey!
can — dy — man's — trum - pet it will steal my heart a — way.
She's a
B♭ Cm F F7 B♭ F F7
G Am D D7 G D D7

3. You can see her down at Sandgate when the herring's brought in.
   Like a bag full of sawdust, she's tied round with string!
   And she wears big galoshes too, and her hose once was white,
   And her petticoat is lilac, and her hat's never straight!

   Chorus

4. When I asked her to wed me, then she started to laugh.
   Are you pulling my leg? That's a long downhill path!
   Then she started on a-blubbering, and she roared like a bull.
   And the fellas down there on the quayside say I'm nowt but a fool!

   Chorus

13 TEACHER'S NOTES

MICHAEL ROW THE BOAT ASHORE

PERFORMING

The mood of this song is gentle.
The long notes need strong support to keep both tone and pitch secure.
Keep the *"oo"* sound of Alleluia very deep.

The *"alleluias"* could be sung by everyone, and the rest of the song by one or more small groups. The first verse could be treated as a refrain between the other verses, to extend the song.

The Tuned Percussion part is intended for Xylophones.
Their rhythm might be remembered with the words *"sausage and chips"*.

Both vocal parts can be doubled by Recorder and Flute.

LISTENING

Rivers:

Bridge over Troubled Waters — Simon and Garfunkel
Moon River — Mancini
Old Man River — Kern
On Banks of Green Willow — Butterworth
Reflets dans l'eau, from *Images* — Debussy
Sweet Thames flow softly — McColl
Vltava, from *Ma Vlast* — Smetana

IDEAS

Tambourine in lap

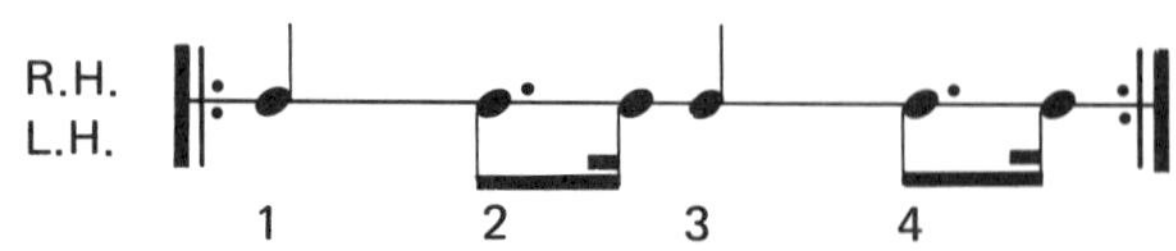

Add further improvised ideas. Think about the words, and the feeling of the music, to help you decide what is appropriate.

INVENTING

Invent a piece of your own to describe the course of a river from its source to the sea. In this way a series of sections could be linked together. Perhaps each section could be made up by a different group or person.

One group could provide the link passages between the sections. These sections might describe the mood of the river and the people using it, or might act as a river boat carrying the listener from one section to another like the *Promenade* in *Pictures at an Exhibition*, by Mussorgsky.

13 MICHAEL ROW THE BOAT ASHORE

Traditional
Arr. Ian Butler

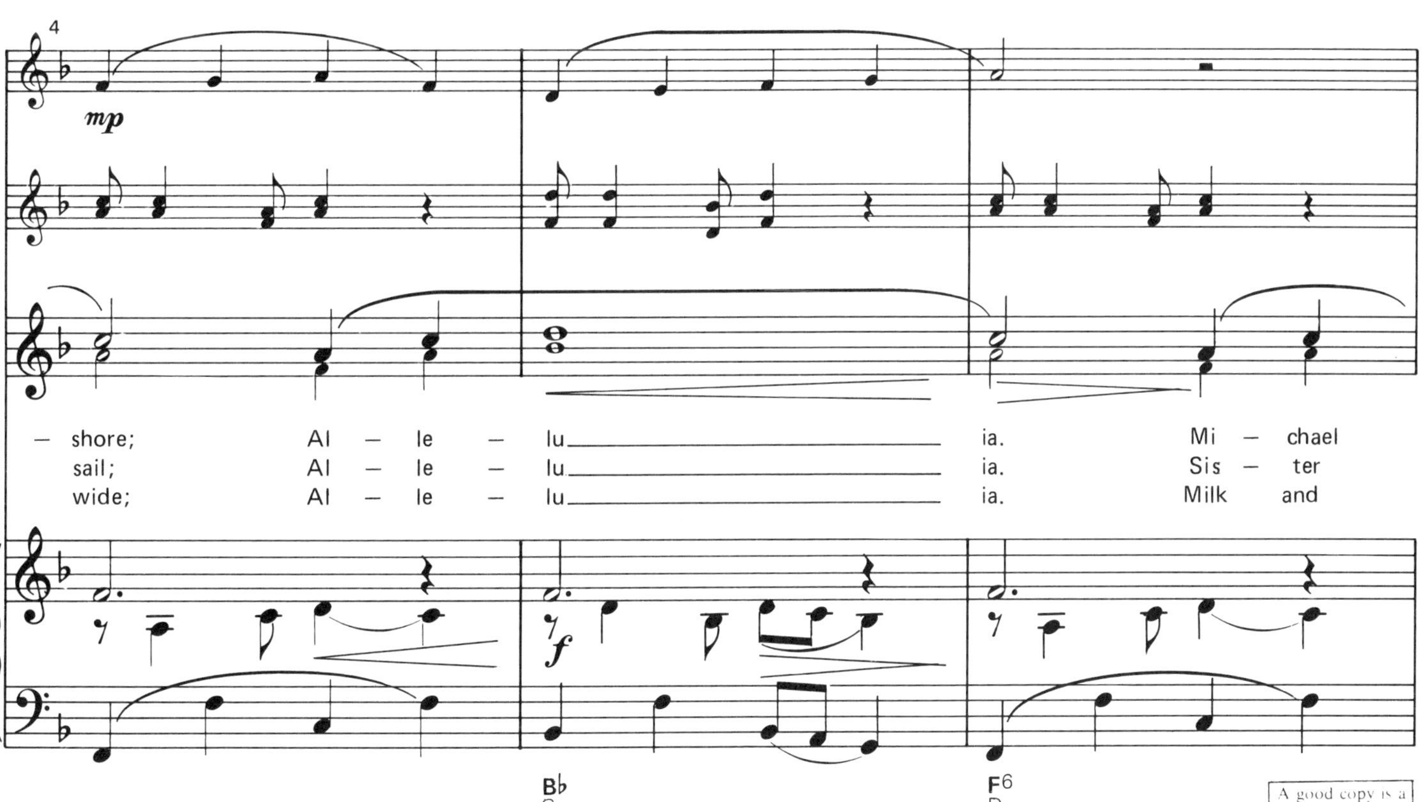

7
mp
row the boat a – shore; Al – le – lu –
help to trim the sail; Al – le – lu –
ho - ney on the oth – er side; Al – le – lu –
rit. (last time)
F (A bass) Gm F C7 F C7
D Em D A7 D A7

10
1. 2. and 3.
Last time
p
– ia!
– ia!
– ia!
F6 F6 F6
D D D

SWEET GINGERBREAD MAN

PERFORMING

Perform this song at a brisk speed.
Practise the exercise for singing in thirds from Song No. 10.

The Tuned Percussion part needs Xylophones for the short notes in bars 6-12, Glockenspiels or Metallophones for bars 13-18, Xylophones for bars 19-20, metal instruments for bars 21-22, and finally Xylophones again for bars 22-24 and the Coda.

Much of the writing in this arrangement is more complex than the rest of the songs.

Neither vocal part can be played on Flute or Recorder.

LISTENING

On the subject of sweets . . .
Gingerbread Children, from *Hansel and Gretel* – Humperdinck
Sugar Plum Fairy, from *The Nutcracker* – Tchaikovsky

Antiphonal writing (Uh huh, etc):
El Grillo – Josquin des Pres
The Echo – Lassus

IDEAS

Brushes on Hi-hat

Drum

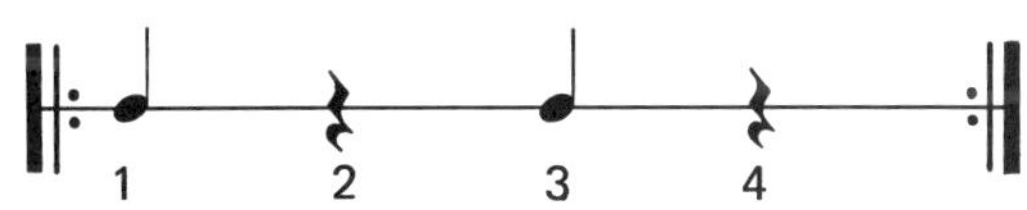

INVENTING

Use the chord sequence of bars 5-8 of *Sweet Gingerbread Man*, with the bass line of the Keyboard Part to improvise a piece. This piece could end with two bars: **F / B♭ / F / / 𝄽 //**

The piece might be antiphonal, or make use of echoes, since the chord sequence is the same for each four bars. The echoes could involve differences in pitch, volume, tone colour or even length.

14 SWEET GINGERBREAD MAN

Lyrics: A. & M. Bergman
Music: Michel Legrand
Arr. Ian Butler

13
Can't think a-bout rai — ny weather now, I've fi-nal-ly got my-self to-ge-ther now!
Spun su-gar-y cloud I'm float-in' on, sun's spread-in' my suit o' su-gar coat-in' on.
Am7 Dm7 Am7 Dm7 Dm7 (C bass)
17
Last time to CODA
Fresh out of the pan, sweet gin-ger-bread man!
All tas-ty and tan sweet gin-ger-bread man!
Last time to CODA
B♭ F (A bass) Gm7 A A4 A
21
Fresh out of the pan, sweet gin-ger-bread man!
Fresh out of the pan, sweet gin-ger-bread man!
B♭ F (A bass) Gm7 F Gm7 F

25
Voice 1 only
I got a feel-in' wouldn't trade for a-ny-thing, for all the beans, for all the greens,
Am7 Dm7 B♭ E♭ (G bass) A♭ Cm Fm G7
30
for all the world! Oh!
f
Cm E♭ A♭ E♭ C Gm7 C Gm7 C Gm7
35
Dal Segno CODA
Fresh out of the pan sweet gin-ger-bread man!
Dal Segno CODA
f
C7 B♭ F (A bass) Gm7 F Gm7 F

TEACHER'S NOTES 15
IMAGINE

PERFORMING

Sincerity is the quality which young people will bring to this song, so read the words and talk about them first.

Sing the song gently, with smooth lines and phrases. Don't hit the syncopations, but sing them accurately.

One Glockenspiel or Metallophone with a soft beater should play the Tuned Percussion part. A word pattern may help that player to keep time:

The Easy Recorder part may need adapting — play crotchet E instead of the semiquavers if they cause problems!

Neither vocal part can be played on Flute or Recorder.

LISTENING

Lennon's own recording of the song

Imaginative use of voices:

Cry — Giles Swayne
Stimmung — Stockhausen

and instruments:

String Quartet — Penderecki

IDEAS

Sparing and quiet addition of less usual percussion instruments:

Bell Tree, Wind Chimes, Bells, Gong, Suspended Cymbal, Vibra-slap, etc.

Try to add short sounds which will resonate. Add them at significant places. To decide where these might be, look at the meaning of the words, and reflect them.

Be imaginative!

INVENTING

Make up an abstract piece — all the sounds must be new — nothing imitating or reminding you of anything. Use not only voices and instruments, but other methods of creating sounds as well.

Invent a piece which sums up your feelings about Peace. Use sounds and combinations of sounds and textures which reflect those feelings. Words could be used, either spoken or sung.

15 IMAGINE

Words & Music: John Lennon
Arr. Ian Butler

9
No hell below us.
Nothing to kill for.
Above us only sky.
And no religion too.
G9
C6
G9
C6
13
mf
Im-a-gine all the peo-ple
Im-a-gine all the peo-ple
Li-ving for to-day
Li-ving life in peace
Ah!
Ah!
C
Em (B bass)
Am7
Am7 (G bass)
D
D7
17
1.
2. & 3.
mp
p
I-ma-gine there's no cou
You may say I'm a drea-mer.
But I'm not the on-ly one.
G9
C
D
G
B7
Em
D7

2. Imagine no possessions. I wonder if you can.
No need for hunger; a brotherhood of man.
Imagine all the people sharing all the world.
Ah!
You may say I'm a dreamer.
But I'm not the only one.
I hope some day you'll join us,
And the world will live as one.

TEACHER'S NOTES 16

THE MERMAID

PERFORMING

Performances of this song should retain the strong element of satire!

The melody in the chorus is always in the second vocal part and this should predominate.

The word *"mermaid"* often needs three syllables in this setting:
"mer-mai-aid" is the nearest phonetic setting.

LISTENING

Fantasia on Sea Songs — H. Wood
Journey to the Centre of the Earth
— Mike Oldfield
Rule Britannia (last night of the Proms)
Sirenes, from *Nocturnes* — Debussy
20,000 leagues under the Sea (film score)

Fantastic Creatures:
Dance of the Water Sprites — Catalani
Hall of the Mountain King, from *Peer Gynt*
— Grieg
Where the Wild Things are — Knussen

IDEAS

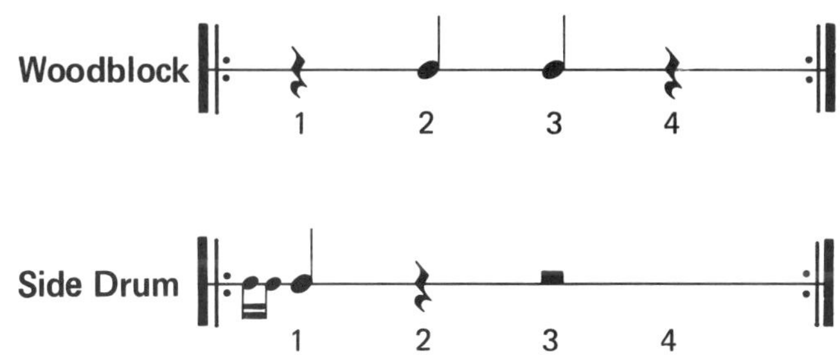

INVENTING

Make up a musical sequence depicting a journey to a fantastic world under the sea. It might follow a story, or become a related sequence of atmospheric sections, with water as the common element.

Encourage the children to experiment with all sorts of sound sources which may evoke these elements. Here is an opportunity to explore the musical concept of timbre and tone colour.

16 THE MERMAID

Traditional
Arr. Ian Butler

young fel — low fell o — ver — board a — mong the sharks and
— til he came to a mer — ma — id at the bot-tom of the deep blue
C C7 (B♭ Bass) F Dm G7
1. 2. Chorus
whales And Rule Brit — ta — nia
sea. Sing - ing Rule Brit — ta — nia, Brit —
Chorus
C C F
Yes Brit — tan — ia rules the waves, Yes she does! Bri - tons
— tan — ia rules the waves Bri — tons
Dm (C G7 Am) G7 (F Em Dm) C G7

2. She raised herself on her beautiful tail,
And gave him her soft white hand;
I've long been waiting for you, my dear,
Now welcome safe to land.
Go back to your mess-mates for the last time,
And tell them all from me
That you're married to a mermaid
At the bottom of the deep blue sea.

Chorus

3. We sent a boat to look for him,
Expecting to find his corpse,
When up he came with a bang and a shout,
And a voice sepulchrally hoarse!
My comrades and my mess-mates,
O do not look for me.
For I'm married to a mermaid
At the bottom of the deep blue sea.

Chorus

4. The anchor was weighed and the sails unfurled,
And the ship was sailing free;
When the bosun said to the Captain,
Sir, we have to put to sea.
The Captain went to the old ship's side,
And out loud bellowed he:
Be happy as you can with your wife, my man,
At the bottom of the deep blue sea.

Chorus

TEACHER'S NOTES 17
WHERE HAVE ALL THE FLOWERS GONE?

PERFORMING

Avoid the temptation of taking this song too slowly, but do give the long notes at the ends of phrases their full value. The voice needs to be supported for this to happen.

The questions and answers could be sung by two different groups or by soloists and the whole class.

The Tuned Percussion part is intended for Glockenspiel, Metallophone or Chime Bars using medium felt beaters.

Untuned Percussion parts on Side Drum and Suspended Cymbal could be invented by the children.

LISTENING

Chord sequence:
Cello Concerto (bridge passage, last movement) — Elgar
Piano Concerto No. 2 (second subject of last movement) — Saint Saëns

Songs with same sequence:
Diana — Paul Anka
La Mer — Charles Trenet

War theme:
Music from *Oh What a Lovely War*

IDEAS

Bells or Finger Cymbals or Triangle

Invent a *"lazy"* accompaniment on Side Drum and Suspended Cymbal.

Use brushes instead of drum sticks.

INVENTING

Most of this song uses the famous I VI IV V chord pattern.

Starting with 4/4 ||: C / C / G^7 / G^7 :|| as a straight vamp, encourage firstly everyone, then small groups, and finally individuals to improvise on the notes of these chords. When this has been successfully coped with, work on: 4/4 ||: C / F / G^7 / C :||; 4/4 ||: C / Am / F / G^7 :|| and then try moving on to the inventing activities in Song No. 34.

Some of the earlier sequences in No. 40 might prove useful as starting points for this activity.

17 WHERE HAVE ALL THE FLOWERS GONE?

Words & Music: Pete Seeger
Arr. Ian Butler

2. Where have all the young girls gone?
 Long time passing.
 Where have all the young girls gone?
 Long time ago.
 Where have all the young girls gone?
 Gone to young men, every one.
 When will they ever learn,
 O when will they ever learn?

3. Where have all the young men gone?
 Long time passing.
 Where have all the young men gone?
 Long time ago.
 Where have all the young men gone?
 Gone for soldiers, every one.
 When will they ever learn,
 O when will they ever learn?

4. Where have all the soldiers gone?
 Long time passing.
 Where have all the soldiers gone?
 Long time ago.
 Where have all the soldiers gone?
 Gone to graveyards, every one.
 When will they ever learn,
 O when will they ever learn?

5. Where have all the graveyards gone?
 Long time passing.
 Where have all the graveyards gone?
 Long time ago.
 Where have all the graveyards gone?
 Gone to flowers, every one.
 When will they ever learn,
 O when will they ever learn?

18 TEACHER'S NOTES
RAINDROPS KEEP FALLIN' ON MY HEAD

PERFORMING

This song needs rather 'laid-back' treatment. Don't let it get too fast!

The second vocal part in bars 3-6 should be practised separately to check intonation. The following exercise might be an amusing way of getting a chromatic scale accurate!

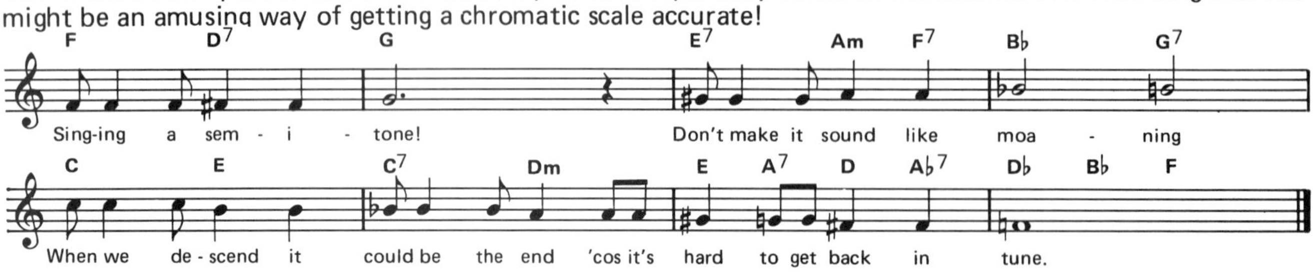

The Tuned Percussion part is intended for Xylophone with soft beaters. Words to help the rhythm for the Xylophones in bars 17-20 are:

Both vocal parts can be doubled by Recorder and Flute.

LISTENING

A recording of this song!
It might as well rain until September — Carol King
Jardins sous la Pluie, from *Estampes* — Debussy
Pastoral Symphony end of Fourth Movement) — Beethoven
Raindrop Prelude — Chopin
Raining in my Heart — Buddy Holly
Rainy Days and Mondays — Carpenters
The Rain in Spain, from *My Fair Lady* — Loesser
William Tell Overture (start of storm) — Rossini

IDEAS

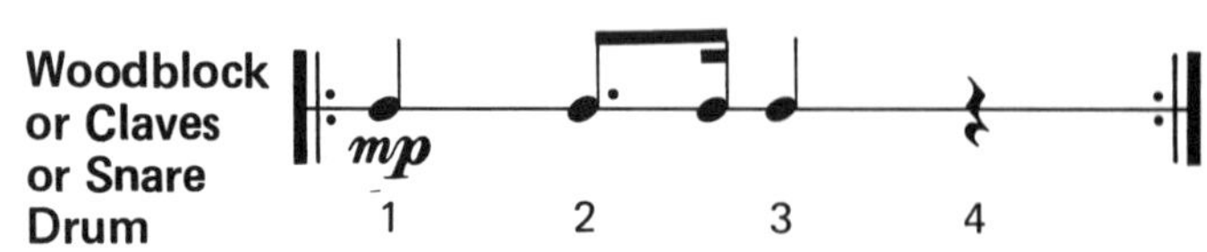

INVENTING

Explore the chromatic scale; there are several ways to begin. Use short scraps of chromatic scale within a melody; or invent a piece which uses lots of semitone trills.

Improvise a group piece entitled *"Rain"* or *"After the Rain Shower"*.
Explore the idea of a-rhythmic sounds like rain falling. Imagine the dripping of water from eaves, leaves, petals; and drops caught in spiders' webs.

18 RAINDROPS KEEP FALLIN' ON MY HEAD

Words & Music: Hal David & Burt Bacharach
Arr. Ian Butler

12
mp
unis.
thing I know. The blues they sent to meet me won't de-feat
F
D
F maj7
D
B♭
G
C
A
C7
A7
16
f
me. It won't be long till hap-pi-ness steps up to greet me.
f
Am7
F♯m7
D9
B7
Gm7
Em7
20
mf
f
mf
f
4. Rain-drops keep fal-lin' on my head, but
Doo be doo be
mp
C7
A7
F
D
F maj7
D

24
that doesn't mean my eyes will soon be turn - in' red, cry - in's not for me, 'cause
doo be doo be doo be doo be doo be doo be
F7 D7 B♭ G Am7 A D7 B7 Am7 A D7 B7
28
mp
I'm ne - ver gon-na stop the rain bycom-plainin': Be - cause I'm free,
doo be doo Be - cause those Rain - drops keep fal-lin' on my
f
rit. al fine
Gm7 Em7 C7 A7 F D F maj7 D
32
p
pp
nothin's worryin' me, noth-in's worry-in' me!
head Rain-drops keep fal-lin' on my head
Gm Em C7 A7 F D F maj7 D Gm Em C7 A7 F D

19 TEACHER'S NOTES
KUM BAYA

PERFORMING

This famous song sounds very good with a guitar accompaniment.
It has a very small range (only a sixth, middle C to the A above).

Most of the second vocal part is written in thirds with the melody.
Practise singing a scale in thirds before teaching the second vocal part:

The Tuned Percussion is meant to be played on Glockenspiels or Chime Bars with medium to soft beaters.

LISTENING

Compare the recordings of this song by Bob Dylan, Joan Baez, Peter, Paul and Mary, the Seekers, etc.

Doh Me Soh openings:
Blue Danube Waltz – Johann Strauss
Fifth Symphony (last movement) – Beethoven
Piano Sonata in C – Mozart
Surprise Symphony (slow movement) – Haydn

IDEAS

Invent a simple triangle part.
e.g. "Kum baya, my Lord, Kum baya" for each line.

INVENTING

Examine the shape and structure of the song. There are four sections. Rhythmically the first three are the same, and melodically they are very similar. The last section is a conclusion.

Invent a new piece which makes use of the same pattern.

19 KUM BAYA

Traditional
Arr. Ian Butler

3. Someone's crying Lord, Kum baya.
Someone's crying Lord, Kum baya.
Someone's crying Lord, Kum baya.
Oh Lord, Kum baya.

4. Someone's praying Lord, Kum baya.
Someone's praying Lord, Kum baya.
Someone's praying Lord, Kum baya.
Oh Lord, Kum baya.

WHEN I'M SIXTY-FOUR

PERFORMING

Sing this song with a swing. The humour then comes out!

The first part of the verse section is instrumental the first time round. The second time it is vocal.

The Tuned Percussion part is written for Xylophone with hard beaters.

Both vocal parts can be doubled by Recorder and Flute.

LISTENING

The original recording by the Beatles, and other versions.

Age:

Cortege, from *Petite Suite* – Debussy
Evening Song – Kodaly
Fanfare for the Coming of Age – Bliss
Forty Years On – Eton Songbook
Les Quatre Ages – Alkan
Saturn, the Bringer of Old Age, from *The Planets* – Holst
Sixty Years On – Elton John
When I'm Dead and Gone – Gallagher and Lyle

IDEAS

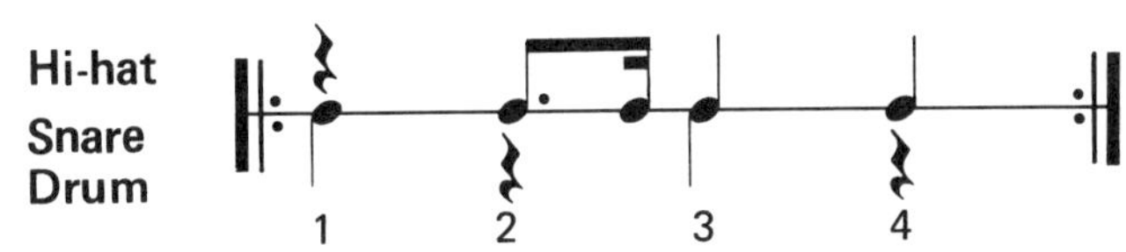

From bar 1 - 18 the woodblock could play the same rhythm as the Tuned Percussion part.

INVENTING

Find an amusing or satirical poem about growing old. Set this to music; either as a song, or as a sequence of musical events which could be both vocal and instrumental.

Use the opening rhythm of the melody of this song as the basis of a new piece for untuned percussion instruments. Explore the textures and tone colours of different combinations of instruments.

20 WHEN I'M SIXTY-FOUR

Words & Music: Lennon & McCartney
Arr. Ian Butler

9
birth-day greet-ings bot-tle of wine?
Sun-day mor-nings, go for a ride.
Yours sin-cere-ly wast-ing a-way.
If I'd been out till quar-ter to three,
Do-ing the gar-den dig-ging the weeds;
Give me your an-swer, fill in a form,
sfz
8va
sf
mf
F7 D7
B♭ G
13
would you lock the door?
Who could ask for more?
Mine for ev-er more.
Will you still need me, Will you still feed me, When I'm six-ty-
Need me! Feed me! Six-ty-
f
sfz
B♭7 G7
E♭ C
G♭ E♭
B♭ G
G7 E7
C9 A
F13 D
18
Third time Fine
four?
four!
Play first time only
Sing second time only
(Voice 1 only)
1. Tacet
2. Ev'-ry summer we can rent a cot-tage in the Isle of Wight if it's not too dear.
mf
mp
sfz
B♭ G
Gm Em
E♭ C
F D
Gm Em

23
1. You'll be old – er too
2. We shall scrimp and save
Gm Em Dm7 Bm Gm Em B♭ G D B7 Gm Em D B7 Gm Em D B7
27
Ah! And, if you say the word
Ah! Grand – chil - dren on your knee
Gm Em F D Gm Em Cm Am
31
I could stay with you.
Ve – ra, Chuck, and Dave.
E♭ C F D F9 D7 B♭ G

TEACHER'S NOTES 21

SAILING

PERFORMING

Sing this song smoothly, with broad phrases. It should be strong but not sentimental, with room to let the melody breathe.

The voices need to be firmly supported to sustain the long notes to their full length.

Build up the volume to Verse 4, and use the Coda as a fade out.

The left hand of the Keyboard part will make a good bass guitar part.

LISTENING

Rod Stewart's and the Ark Royal Band's versions on record.

Transport:
En Bateau, from *Petite Suite* – Debussy
Going Home, from the *New World Symphony* – Dvořák
Homeward Bound – Simon and Garfunkel
Trains and Boats and Planes – Bacharach/David
24 Hours from Tulsa – Gene Pitney

IDEAS

Invent sounds that may be appropriate to the words in this song. Suspended cymbal with brushes may suggest waves; others may involve the "bird", "clouds" and the dark night. Use all the sounds sparingly, otherwise they might spoil the song.

INVENTING

Using the words in the song that are related to movement, make up a piece of music. Either make sections which reflect the characteristics of the movements (e.g. flying) or combine the diverse movements together into a more complex and contrasting piece.

It is difficult, but not impossible, to relate the movements musically, whilst retaining their individual characters. Each movement could be represented by a variation of the same original theme. The theme could be part of the song!

21 SAILING

Words & Music: Gavin Sutherland
Arr. Ian Butler

10
1.
mp
wa - ters, to be near you to be free.
high clouds, to be with you to be
2. I am
Dm
Gm
F
13
2.
mf
(f 2nd time)
3. Can you hear me? Can you hear me? Thro' the
free sail - ing, we are sail - ing, Home a -
F
C7
F
Dm
16
dark night far a - way I am dy - ing for-ev - er
gain 'cross the sea. We are sail - ing stor-my
B♭
F
G7

19
1.
try – ing, to be with_ you who can say?
wa – ters, to be with_ you to be
Dm
Gm
F C7
22
2.
mf
mf
f
4. We are free. Oh Lord to be with_ you to be
f
F C7
F C7
Gm
25
dim
dim
dim
p
p
mp
free. Oh Lord to be with_ you to be free.
dim
rit.
p
F C7
Gm
F

TEACHER'S NOTES 22

O SOLDIER, SOLDIER

PERFORMING

A jaunty song! The verses are a dialogue, the chorus a narration.
Obviously parts may be allocated accordingly.
Make no breaks between the verses please!

Variety of instrumentation will add interest to the performance, and could grow in strength through the song.

Neither vocal part can be played on Flute or Recorder.

LISTENING

Marches and Soldiers:

Carmen (March, Act I) – Bizet
Faust (Soldiers' Chorus) – Gounod
Jeux d'Enfants (March) – Bizet
Lt. Kije – Prokofiev
Marching thro' Georgia – Miller
March of the Little Tin Soldiers – Gabriel Pierné
Scottish Soldier
Soldier's Tale – Stravinsky
The Minstrel Boy – Traditional

IDEAS

Introduction and Verse:

Woodblock
Drum

Chorus:
Snare Drum
& Cymbal

INVENTING

Try inventing a dialogue song to words made up by pupils.

At first it may be helpful to improvise an instrumental or wordless dialogue, to get the idea of taking turns! Vamp one chord for one of the participants, and change to another when the second's turn comes. Try both major and minor keys.

22 O SOLDIER, SOLDIER

Traditional
Arr. Ian Butler

4. O soldier, soldier, won't you marry me,
With your musket, fife and drum?
O no, sweet maid, I cannot marry thee,
For I have no hat to put on.

Chorus

Then up she went to her grandfather's chest,
And brought him a hat of the very, very best,
She brought him a hat of the very, very best,
And the soldier put it on.

5. O soldier, soldier, won't you marry me,
With your musket, fife and drum?
O no, sweet maid, I cannot marry thee,
With a wife and baby at home!

23 TEACHER'S NOTES

TRY TO REMEMBER

PERFORMING

This song should not be allowed to become sentimental.

It needs supported legato singing. The breathing should follow the four bar phrase length! Keep the melody prominent when the second part goes above it.

The Tuned Percussion part should be played on Glockenspiels or Metallophones with medium felt beaters.

The first beat of the left hand of the Keyboard part could be used for double bass, cello or bass guitar.

Try playing an instrumental verse as an interlude between vocal verses.

LISTENING

Ebb Tide — Maxwell/Sigman
Farewell Symphony — Haydn
Memory, from *Cats* — A. Lloyd Webber
Nocturne, from *Quartet No. 2* — Borodin
Now, O now I needs must part — Dowland
September Song — Weill
The Way we were — Hamlisch/Bergman
Yesterday — Lennon & McCartney

IDEAS

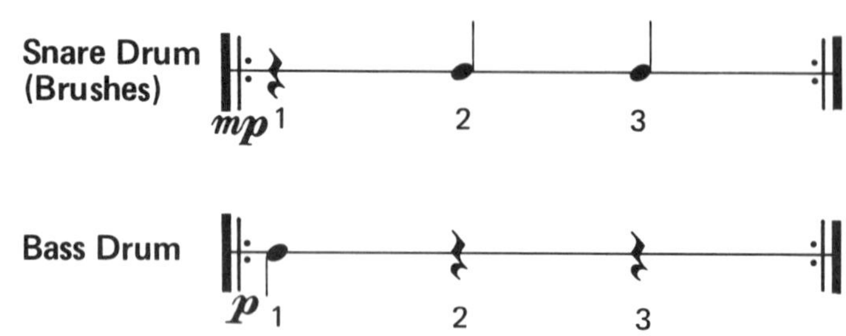

INVENTING

Make up a piece which captures the mood and character of September.
It could be to do with Autumn in general: Leaves, mists, harvest, browns, golds.

Or September could be thought of as a beginning: New school year, new experiences, remembering the summer.

Think about the nature of the sounds that are used, the pulse chosen, and the pitch used. Make sure they are all appropriate.

23 TRY TO REMEMBER

by Tom Jones & Harvey Schmidt
Arr. Ian Butler

13
mf
Try to re — mem — ber the kind of Sep — tem — ber when you were a
Am7 Dm7 Gm7 C7 F maj7
18
p
ten - der and cal — low fel - low. Try to re — mem — ber, and
B♭ maj7 E♭ C7 F maj7
23
if you re — mem — ber, then fol - low. Fol-low, fol-low, fol-low, fol-low, fol-low,
Gm7 C7 F maj7 B♭ Gm7

2. Try to remember when life was so tender
That no-one wept except the willow.
Try to remember when life was so tender
That dreams were kept beside your pillow.
Try to remember when life was so tender
That love was an ember about to billow.
Try to remember, and if you remember,
Then follow.

3. Deep in December it's nice to remember
Altho' you know the snow will follow.
Deep in December it's nice to remember
Without a hurt the heart is hollow.
Deep in December, it's nice to remember
The fire of September that made us mellow.
Deep in December our hearts should remember
And follow.
Follow,follow, follow, follow

24 TEACHER'S NOTES

RIVERS OF BABYLON

PERFORMING

The main part of this song should be sung with a swing and a sense of enjoyment and commitment.

The opening unaccompanied voices could be doubled by clarinets or treble recorders, but why not make the effort to prove that unaccompanied singing can sound really successful? Smiling always helps to keep the pitch more accurate!

The whole song, in structure, is a huge arch shape, beginning and ending with the unaccompanied passage.

LISTENING

Belshazzar's Feast — Walton
Gospel songs
Music from *'Godspell'* — Schwartz

Rivers:
Lazy River —Carmichael/Arodin
Vltava, from *Ma Vlast* — Smetana

IDEAS

Improvise around this riff using various instruments

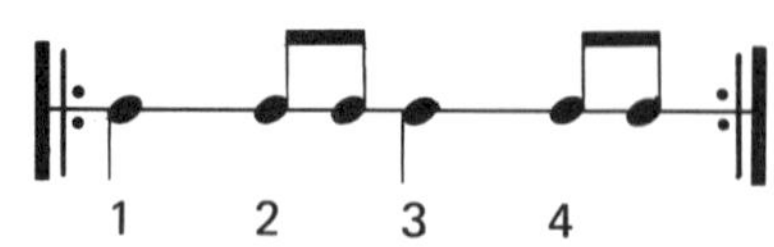

INVENTING

This is one of many songs which only uses three chords in the accompaniment. They are F, B♭ and C^7. In an easier key, they would be C, F and G^7. Using just these chords make up a tune.

An electronic keyboard with an automatic accompaniment facility will make playing the chords much simpler.

Some of the earlier sequences in No. 40 may prove useful as starting points for this activity.

24 RIVERS OF BABYLON

Words & Music: Farian, Reyam, Dowe & McNaughton
Arr. Ian Butler

car-ried us a-way in cap - ti - vi - ty, re - qui - ring of us a song. Now
F E
B♭ A
F E
how shall we sing the Lord's song in a strange land?
For there they that
C7 B7
F E
2.
Let the words of our mouths and the med - i - ta - tions of our
C7 B7
F E
C7 B7
F E

40
hearts be ac – cep – ta – ble in thy_ sight here to – night.
C7 B7 F E C7 B7 F E
44 1. 2.
_ Let the _ By the ri-vers of Ba - by-lon_ there we sat down
C7 B7 F E
49
Da Capo al Fine
Yeah_ we wept When we re - mem - bered Zi - on.
C7 B7 F E

25 TEACHER'S NOTES
GREENSLEEVES

PERFORMING

This should be a very gentle piece, but not sentimental.
Try some verses solo, or with small groups. Others could hum.

The Guitar part sounds good imitating a lute by picking the chords, or alternatively strumming to the rhythm: ♩. ♩.

The Tuned Percussion part should use just a single Glockenspiel with medium to soft beaters.

Neither vocal part can be played on Flute or Recorder.

LISTENING

England:
English Dances — Malcolm Arnold
English Folksong Suite — Vaughan Williams
Fantasia on Greensleeves — Vaughan Williams
Introduction and Allegro — Elgar
Merrie England — German
Walk to the Paradise Garden — Delius

Music by:
Lindisfarne
Steeleye Span
Pentangle

IDEAS

Using tambour, tambourine, finger cymbals or triangle play a simple accompaniment, for example:

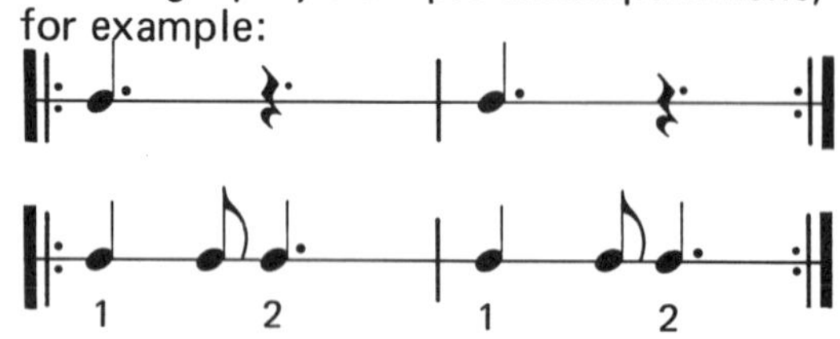

Don't make the rhythm sound too heavy!

INVENTING

Invent a melody in a minor key.

Improvise on the sequence $\frac{6}{8}$ ||: Em / Am | Em / B^7 :||

using rhythm patterns from this song.

Further work could be done on Elizabethan styles and dances.

Some of the earlier sequences in No. 40 may prove useful as starting points for this activity.

25 GREENSLEEVES

Traditional
Arr. Ian Butler

3. Your smock of silk, both fair and white,
   With gold embroidered gorgeously;
   Thy petticoat of sendal right;
   And these I bought you gladly.

   Chorus

4. Well, I will pray to God on high,
   That you my constancy may see,
   And that yet once before I die
   Thou wilt vouchsafe to love me.

   Chorus

TEACHER'S NOTES 26

TOP OF THE WORLD

PERFORMING

Sing this song with a light bounce, and don't take it too slowly.

Practise the thirds and sixths exercise in song No. 10 to help with the vocal parts.

Vary the verses by the instrumentation and perhaps with an instrumental verse between vocal verses.

The Tuned Percussion part should be played on a Xylophone with hard beaters.

The left hand of the Keyboard part will make a good bass line.

LISTENING

The Carpenters' recording of the song.

Revolving:
Also sprach Zarathustra (opening) – Strauss
Carousel Waltz – Rodgers
La Valse (opening) – Ravel
The World is a Circle – Bacharach
Windmills of your Mind – Michel Legrand

IDEAS

Tambourine (shaken)

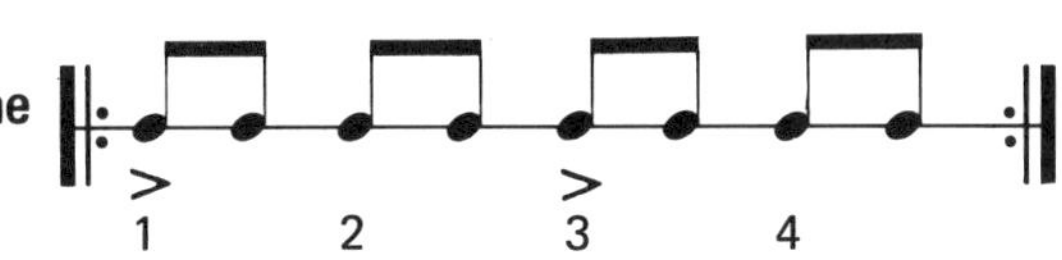

INVENTING

Make up a short melody for voices (it doesn't have to have words), which will work with a second part in thirds above or below. Decide what instruments might accompany it, or if it is to be unaccompanied.

Invent a rhythmic ostinato to fit with it. What will it be played on?

26 TOP OF THE WORLD

Lyrics: John Bettis
Music: Richard Carpenter
Arr. Ian Butler

11
see. Not a cloud in the sky, got the sun in my
me, And the rea – son is clear, it's be – cause you are
F Bb C7 Am
16
1.
eye, and I would-n't be sur - prised if it's a dream!
here, you're the near-est thing to hea-ven that I've seen.
D7 Gm C7
21
2.
Chorus
f
I'm on the top of the world, look-ing down on cre - a - tion, and the
Chorus
f
C7 F Bb

2. Something in the wind has learned my name,
And it's telling me that things are not the same
In the leaves on the trees, and the touch of the breeze,
There's a pleasing sense of happiness for me.
There is only one wish on my mind,
When this day is through, I hope that I will find
That tomorrow will be just the same, you and me;
All I've wanted will be mine if you are here.

Chorus

TEACHER'S NOTES 27

AMAZING GRACE

PERFORMING

An accompaniment on guitar alone works well with this famous song, but other versions give a variety of effects. Try changing the instrumentation for each verse. Don't sing the song too slowly!

The right hand counter melody in the Keyboard part of Verse Four could be played upon a solo instrument, or sung by a chorus (to *Aah . . .*). It is a type of descant.

The Tuned Percussion part is intended for Glockenspiel, Chime Bars or Metallophone.

LISTENING

Descants:

Any of the well-known carols recorded by Kings College Chapel Choir, among others.

Fantasia on a Theme by Thomas Tallis
 – Vaughan Williams

The Trout Quintet (variation movement)
 – Schubert

Ground Bass:

Dido's Lament, from *Dido and Aeneas*
 – Purcell

IDEAS

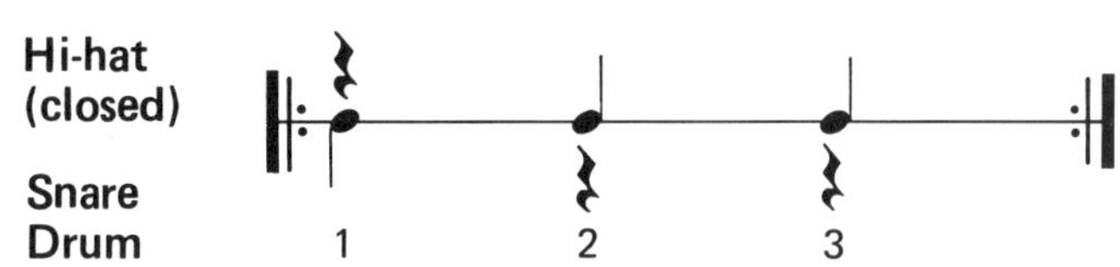

INVENTING

Use the chord sequence of this song, perhaps with a different time signature, to improvise a new melody:

F / F / B♭ / F **/** F / F / C^7 / C^7 **/** F / F / B♭ / F **/** F / C^7 / F / F **//**

Easier key:

C / C / F / C **/** C / C / G^7 / G^7 **/** C / C / F / C **/** C / G^7 / C / C **//**

Invent a descant for a well-known melody. Choose one with a simple chord sequence.

27 AMAZING GRACE

Traditional
Arr. Ian Butler

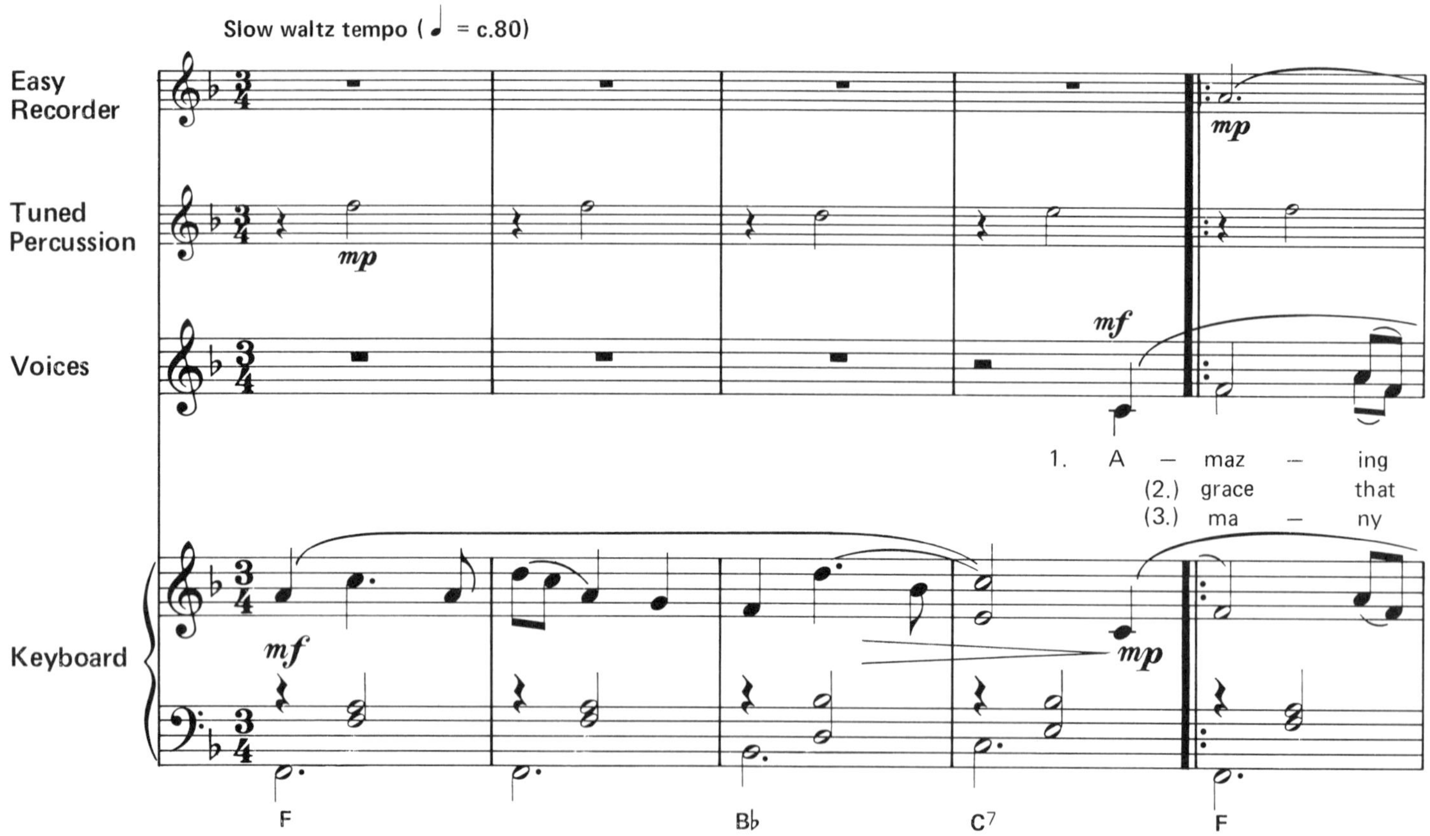

11
me. I once was lost, but now am
— lieved; How pre — cious did that grace ap —
come; 'Tis grace that brought me safe thus
C7
F
F7
B♭
16
1. & 2.
found, was blind but now I see. 2. 'Twas
— pear, the hour I first be — lieved. 3. Thro'
far, And grace will bring me home.
F
C7
F
21
3rd time
f
mf
mf
mf
4. A — maz — ing grace, how sweet the sound, That
D7
G
G
C
G

26
saved a wretch like me. I
G D7
30
once was lost, but now am found, Was
G G7 C G
34
mp
mp
mp
blind, but now I see.
p
D7 G

PASS THE DUTCHIE

PERFORMING

There are elements of *rapping* about this song. It requires great freedom in performance. Because of its repetitive nature, variety must be created by altering the forces used at each repetition.

One way to do this might be to start with very few performers, and gradually add to the numbers. The fade-out at the end could be achieved by the performers dropping out group by group.

If you have access to these, electric instruments and a drum kit in the accompaniment, will give a more authentic sound.

LISTENING

The recording by **Musical Youth** of this song.

Records of songs in reggae style and other pop styles which have strong West Indian influence.

Though different in style, an investigation into the sound and timbre of the steel band.

IDEAS

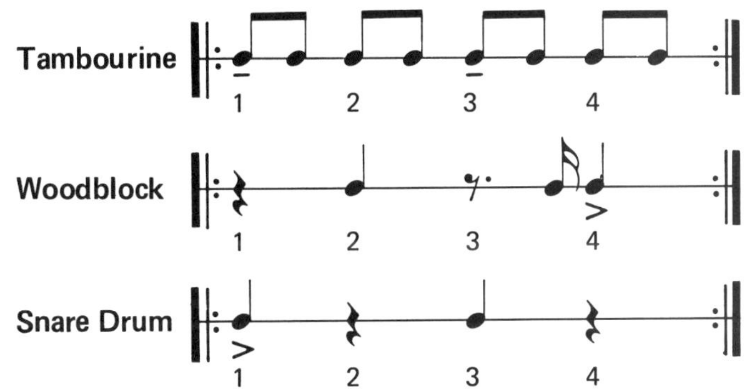

INVENTING

Invent a piece which is spoken rhythmically against a rhythmic or melodic ostinato. These might be invented, or taken from a pre-programmed electronic keyboard rhythm section.

Encourage the children to think carefully about the words they use. They could value their meaning, or their sound, or both.

Listen to the original version of *Facade* by Walton to show the potential of this idea in the hands of the master!

This could be an opportunity to link with the Drama or English areas of the curriculum.

28 PASS THE DUTCHIE

Words & Music: Jackie Mittoo, Lloyd Ferguson
and Fitzroy Simpson
Arr. Ian Butler

12
jump and prance It a go done gim-me the mu-sic, make me rock-in' at the dance. It was a
rock-in' at the dance and so I
F7 E7
B♭6 A
F7 E7
15
mp
mf
cool and love-ly bree-zy af-ter-noon
stop to find out what was go-ing on
Pass the dutch-ie on the
B♭6 A
F7 E7
B♭6 A
18
left hand side
You could feel it 'cause it was the month of
'cos the spir-it of Jah you know he leads you
F7 E7
B♭6 A
F7 E7

21
June
Pass the dutch-ie on the left hand side
on
so I leave my gate and
There's a ring of dreads whose
Bb6
A
F7
E7
Bb6
A
24
went out for a walk
ses - sion was in swing
Pass the dutch-ie on the left hand side
As I
You could
F7
E7
Bb6
A
F7
E7
27
pass the dread - locks' camp I heard them say
feel the chill as I seen and heard them say
Pass the dutch-ie on the
Bb6
A
F7
E7
Bb6
A

30
mp
left hand side Pass the dutch-ie on the left hand side,
F7 E7
B♭6 A
F7 E7
33
Pass the dutch-ie on the left hand side Gim - me the mu-sic make me
B♭ 6 A
F7 E7
B♭ 6 A
36
jump and prance Gim–me the mu-sic make me rock-in' at the dance 'cos me say
F7 E7
B♭ 6 A
F7 E7

39
cresc.
cresc.
cresc.
lis - ten to the drum-mer, Me say lis - ten to the bass Gim-me lit - tle mu-sic, make me
boom boom boom
cresc.
poco
B♭6 A
F7 E7
B♭6 A
42
f
f
f
wind up me waist. Me say lis - ten to the drum-mer, me say lis - ten to the ba, ba, ba,
3
3
f
F7 E7
B♭6 A
F7 E7
45
mp
mp
mp
3 3
ba, ba, ba, ba, ba, ba, bass Pass the dutch-ie on the
boom boom boom
3 3
mp
3
B♭6 A
F7 E7
B♭6 A

48
left hand side, Pass the dutch-ie on the left hand side
F7
E7
Bb6
A
F7
E7
51
Gim-me the mu-sic make me jump and prance Gim-me the mu-sic make me
Bb6
A
F7
E7
Bb6
A
54
(Repeat ad lib. and fade)
unis.
rock-in' at the dance Pass the dutch-ie on the left hand side.
(Repeat ad lib. and fade)
F7
E7
Bb6
A
F7
E7

29 TEACHER'S NOTES

A WINTER'S TALE

PERFORMING

This is rather a sad song. Don't let that put you off though and don't compromise by trying to sing it too fast.

Sustained voice production, with sound use of support, and legato phrasing are essential. Hold the long notes at the ends of phrases for their full length and balance the level of the accompaniment.

Encourage the children to think about the words. Present them with care.

LISTENING

David Essex's recording of this song.

Winter:

Lara's Theme, from *Dr Zhivago* — M. Jarré
November Woods — Bax
Snow is dancing, from *Children's Corner* — Debussy
Winter, from *The Four Seasons* — Vivaldi

IDEAS

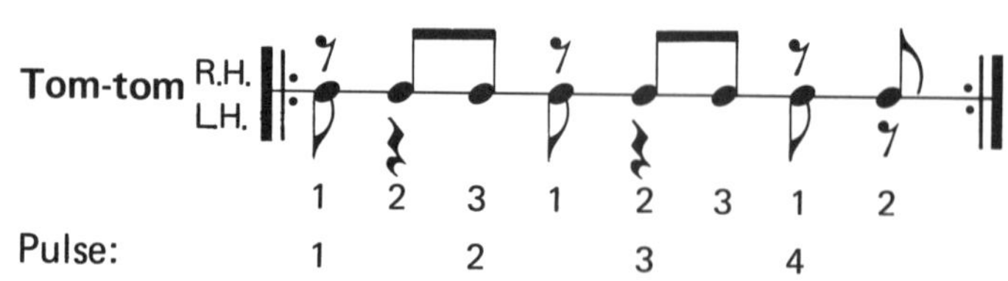

Invent some gentle sounds. Look at the meaning of the words to decide what the sounds might be and where it might be appropriate to use them. A rhythmic ostinato might work well!

INVENTING

Make up a song about some aspect of winter, which could be a personal *Winter's Tale*. It might be a story; the description of a picture; a photograph taken; a myth; a fairy tale.

Alternatively it might just be thoughts and feelings about winter. It might be concerned with sleeping (hibernation); or death; coldness; ice; snow; whiteness, etc.

Take great care to choose the right combination of instruments and voice sounds; the exact speed and volume you mean, and the words you choose or invent.

29 A WINTER'S TALE

Words & Music: Mike Batt & Tim Rice
Arr. Ian Butler

2.
Chorus
cresc.
-lone at this time of_ year. It was on - ly a win-ter's tale,
Chorus
B♭ C7 F B♭ F
— just a - no-ther win-ter's tale,_ and why should the world take
C7 F Gm F B♭ F B♭ F
no — tice of one more love that's failed? It's a love that can ne-ver be,
B♭ F C F

2. And while I stand alone,
Bells are ringing far away;
I wonder if you hear, I wonder if you're listening,
I wonder where you are today.
Good luck! I wish you well,
For all that wishes may be worth;
I hope that love and strength
Are with you for the length of your time on earth.

Chorus

30 TEACHER'S NOTES

THE RIDDLE SONG

PERFORMING

The verses of this song are questions and answers. This could give a hint on its performance — antiphonally, contrasting solo voice and chorus, or various small groups. The words should be very clear.

The Tuned Percussion part is intended to be played on Metallophone or Chime Bars. It could be played by one person playing both notes, or divided between two players.

The Easy Recorder part should be carefully phrased.

LISTENING

Riddles in music:

Enigma Variations — Elgar
Hidden Melodies — arr. J. Cooper

Melodies opening on one note:
Chanson Triste — Tchaikovsky
Mars, from *The Planets* — Holst
Raindrop Prelude — Chopin
Symphony No. 2 (Trio) — Sibelius
Symphony No. 7 (slow movement)
— Beethoven

IDEAS

Triangle or Finger Cymbals:

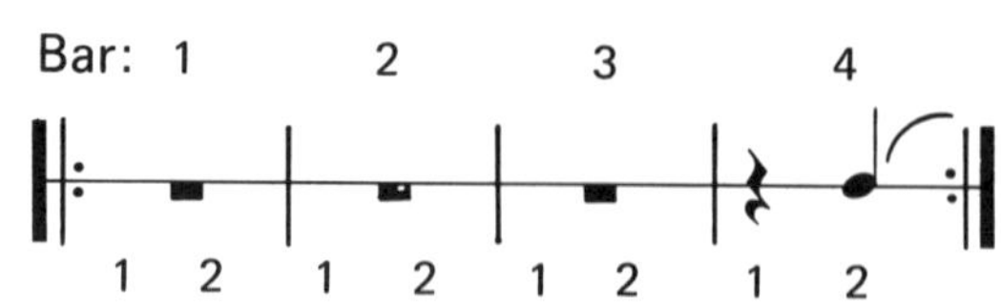

INVENTING

Using a pentatonic scale (as this song does) i.e. C D F G A, get the children to improvise vocally, or on Tuned Percussion instruments. Take off the E and B bars to avoid "wrong notes"! If required, the chord progression: F F Gm C^7 will help. Vary the time signature and speed from time to time.

Make up a piece that consists of questions and answers. See if these can be musical rather than verbal questions. E.g. rising and falling phrases; melodies which are completed by the second performer; rhythms which are complemented by other rhythms.

Introduce the idea of musical development, and the ways in which this can be achieved (i.e. augmentation, inversion, diminution, sequence, etc.) Perhaps this could be described as a question and answer discussion in music!

30 THE RIDDLE SONG

Traditional
Arr. Ian Butler

9
gave my love a chick - en that had no bone; I gave my love a
can there be a chick - en, that has no bone? How can there be a
chick-en when it's pip - ping, it has no bone, A ring when it is
C7 F B♭ F C Gm
14
ring that had no end; I gave my love a ba - by with
ring that has no end? How can there be a ba - by, with
rol - ling, it has no end, A ba - by when it's sleep-ing, there's
Dm7 Am Gm C7 F B♭
19
1. & 2.
Last time
p
pp
no cry – ing. 2. How
no cry – ing? 3. A
no cry – – ing.
dim
Gm7 C9 F F

TEACHER'S NOTES 31
WHAT SHALL WE DO WITH THE DRUNKEN SAILOR?

PERFORMING

This is a happy song; sing it with gusto!

Take care that the melody remains prominent when the parts cross in bars 6 and 8. Verses can be varied by changing the instrumentation of the accompaniment, or by different vocal forces singing each verse. *"Early"* in this song is pronounced *"Er-lie"*

The Tuned Percussion part is intended to be played by chromatic Xylophone with medium to hard beaters.

The Easy Recorder part should be played legato in contrast with everything else.

LISTENING

Sailors:

Fantasia on British Sea Songs
arr. Henry Wood
Hornpipe, from *The Water Music* — Handel
The Sailors' Hornpipe — C. Neil
Three Shanties — arr. for wind quintet by
Malcolm Arnold

Sea:

Fingal's Cave — Mendelssohn
Sea Interludes, from *Peter Grimes* — Britten

IDEAS

Tambourine

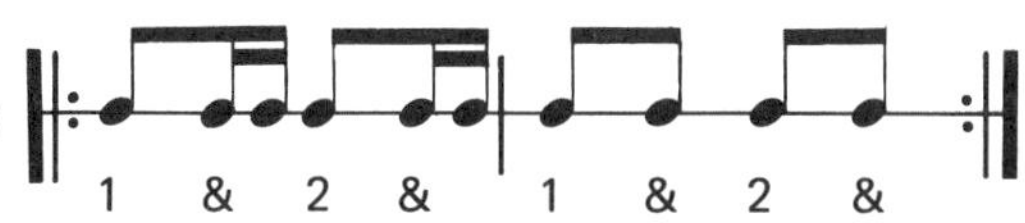

Woodblock

Make up words for extra verses!

INVENTING

Invent spoken ostinati to accompany the song. Use words associated with the sea.

Improvise a piece about the sea for voices and instruments. It might be a storm at sea; sailing ships running before the wind; a calm moonlit night; toy ships on the lake, etc. Think about the mood of the scene, and see how that can be created in music. Don't just make a sequence of sound effects, although some might be included.

Make up a work song that sailors might have used on board sailing ships a long time ago. First attempts at this might be based on an existing children's singing game chant, with new words, and then developed from there. *"The big ship sails on the alley-alley-oo"* might provide a suitable model.

31 WHAT SHALL WE DO WITH THE DRUNKEN SAILOR?

Traditional
Arr. Ian Butler

2. Down in the longboat until he's sober,
Down in the longboat until he's sober,
Down in the longboat until he's sober,
Early in the morning.
Chorus

3. Pull out the plug and he'll get a dousing,
Pull out the plug and he'll get a dousing,
Pull out the plug and he'll get a dousing,
Early in the morning.
Chorus

4. Down in the hold with a hosepipe on him,
Down in the hold with a hosepipe on him,
Down in the hold with a hosepipe on him,
Early in the morning.
Chorus

32 TEACHER'S NOTES

SCARBOROUGH FAIR

PERFORMING

A gentle song, which sounds best when performed smoothly and with a legato tone.
The singers will need to have the voice well supported.
The parts cross at bar 19. Make sure that the melody retains its prominence.

Take care not to overload the accompaniment with too many instruments.

The Tuned Percussion part is intended for Glockenspiel or Chime Bars.

Both vocal parts can be doubled by Recorder and Flute.

LISTENING

Simon and Garfunkel's arrangement and recording of the song.

Fairs:
Brigg Fair – Delius
Market Place at Limoges, from *Pictures at an Exhibition* – Mussorgsky
Romeo and Juliet (opening) – Prokofiev
Shrovetide Fair, from *Petrouchka* – Stravinsky
Strawberry Fair – Traditional
The Floral Dance – Traditional
Widdicombe Fair – Traditional
Yarmouth Fair – Warlock

IDEAS

Suspended Cymbal or Triangle

Tambourine

or

Hi-hat (closed) Drum

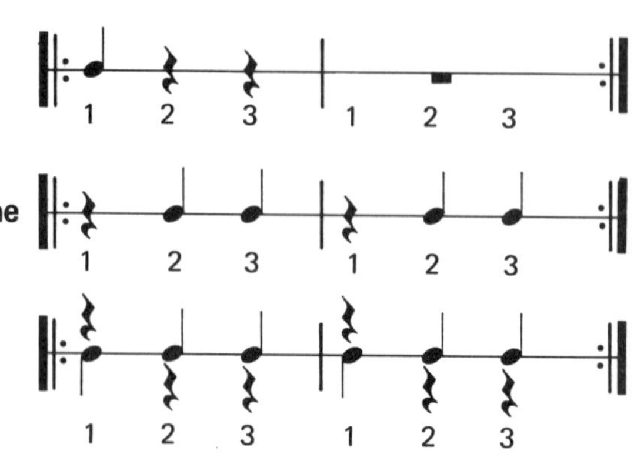

INVENTING

Find out about the herbs mentioned in the song, and about others too.

See if a piece suggests itself based on the properties or myths about the herbs.

E.g. Parsley was awarded to Greek athletes as a mark of great distinction.
Sage is the symbol of virtue, and is often used to soothe.
Rosemary is the dew of the sea; the wood from the plant is used for making lutes.
Thyme is a strong, sweet aromatic herb.

32 SCARBOROUGH FAIR

Traditional
Arr. Ian Butler

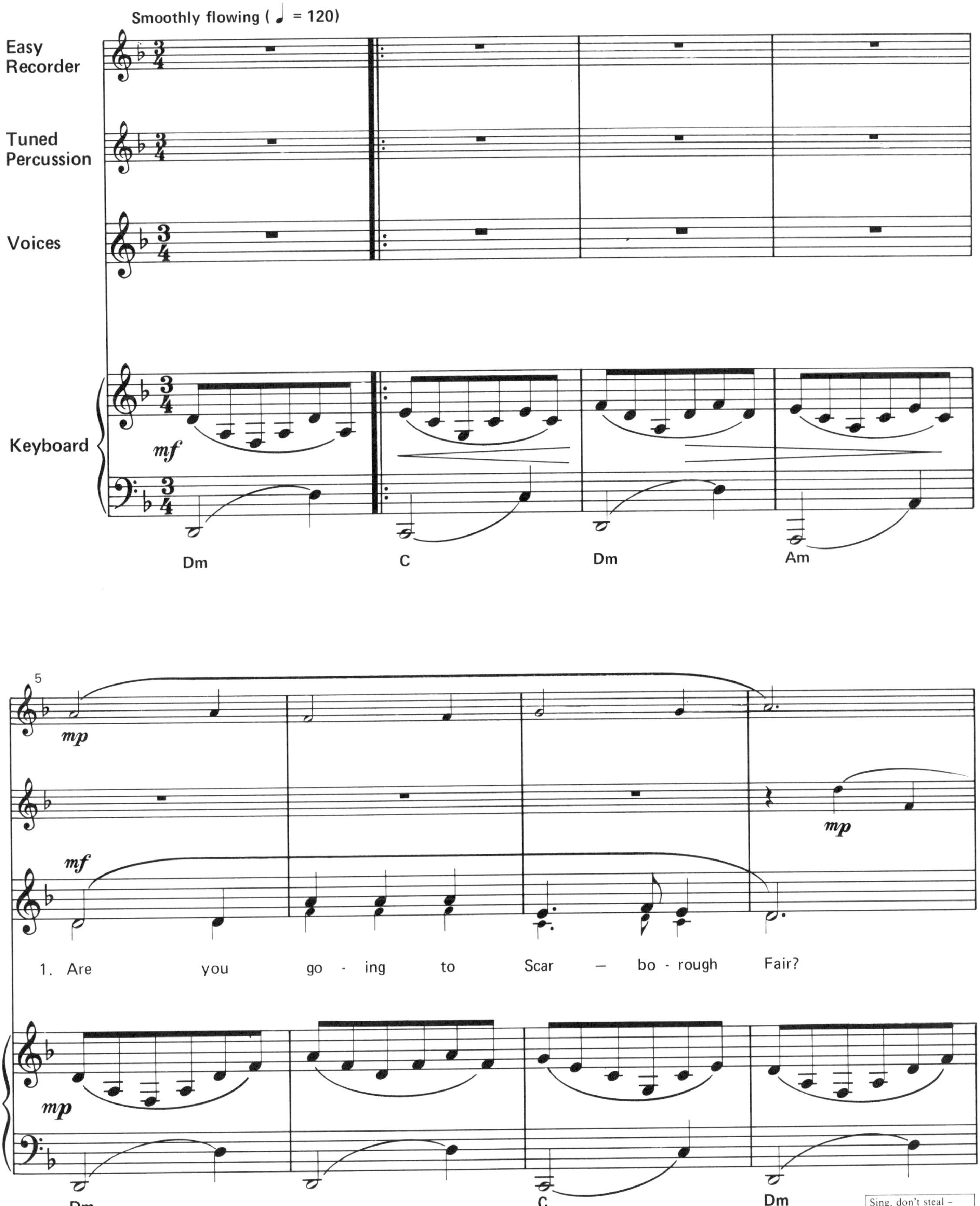

9
mp
Pars - ley, sage, rose - ma - ry and thyme; Re –
F Dm Am F G Dm
13
mp
– mem – ber me to one who lives there
B♭ F F Em Dm C Am
17
1. – 5.
dim.
She once was a true love of mine.
dim.
Dm C Am Dm

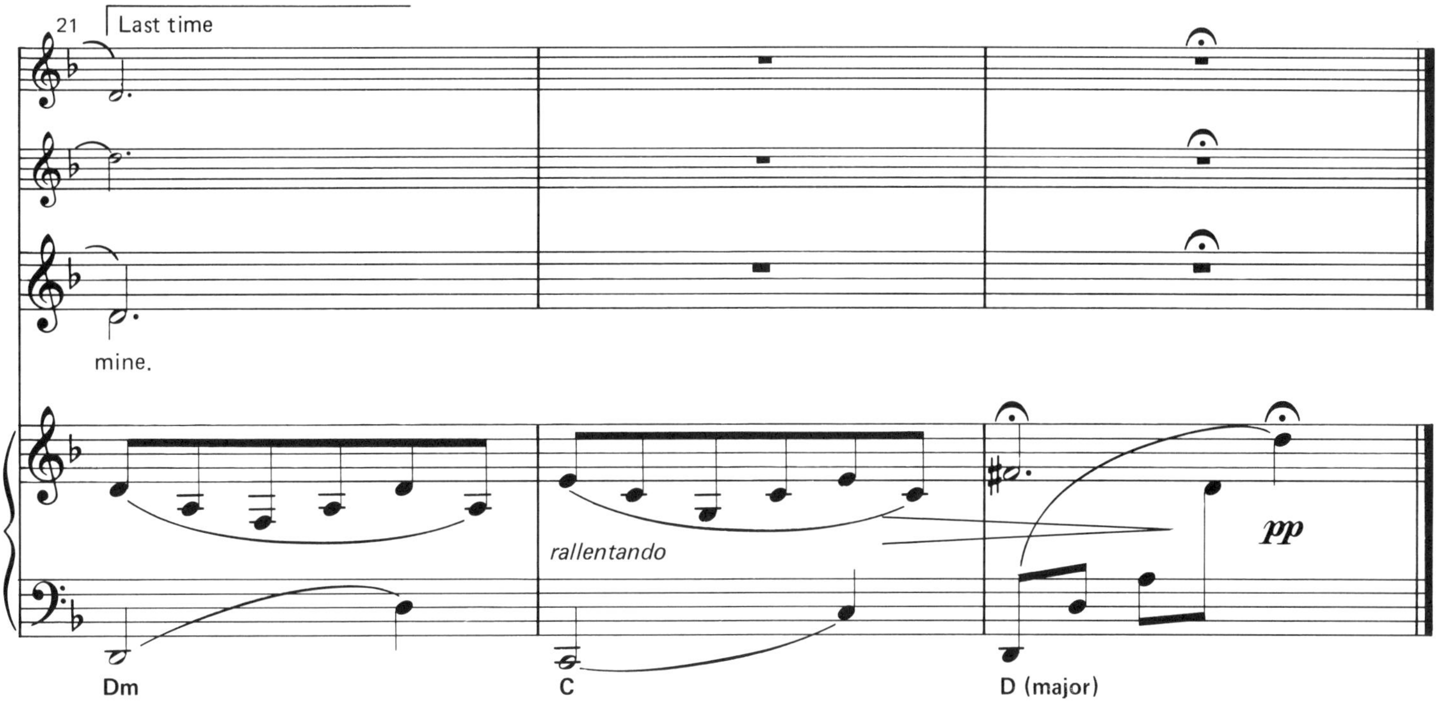

2. Tell her to make me a cambric shirt,
   Parsley, sage, rosemary and thyme;
   Without a seam or needlework,
   Then she'll be a true love of mine.

3. Will you find me an acre of land,
   Parsley, sage, rosemary and thyme;
   Between the sea foam and the sea sand,
   Or never be a true love of mine?

4. Will you plough it with one lamb's horn,
   Parsley, sage, rosemary and thyme;
   And sow it all over with one peppercorn,
   Or never be a true love of mine?

5. Will you reap it with sickle of leather,
   Parsley, sage, rosemary and thyme;
   And tie it all up with a peacock's feather,
   Or never be a true love of mine?

6. When you have done and finished your work,
   Parsley, sage, rosemary and thyme;
   Then come to me for your cambric shirt,
   Then you'll be a true love of mine.

33 TEACHER'S NOTES

LITTLE BOXES

PERFORMING

There is a mechanical feeling behind the words and music of this song which could be reflected in the performance.

The Tuned Percussion part is for Xylophone, with a variety of beaters. Give each colour in the verses a different sound, by adding other instruments.

Apart from the introduction, only two chords are used in the song. Put the bass notes (or *roots*) of these chords on cello, double bass, or bass guitar. If necessary re-tune the strings to the notes C and G.

LISTENING

Triple time:
La Valse – Ravel
Romeo and Juliet (Waltz scene) – Berlioz
Symphony No. 5 ($\frac{5}{4}$ 'waltz' movement) – Tchaikovsky
Minuets, Scherzos, Viennese waltzes, etc.

Similar message:
Plastic Spoon in my Mouth – Rolling Stones

IDEAS

Hi-hat or Woodblock

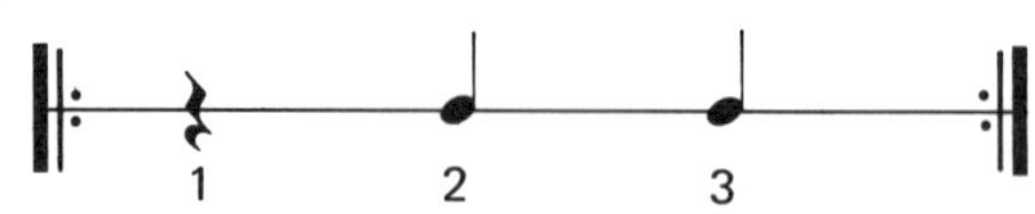

Snare Drum

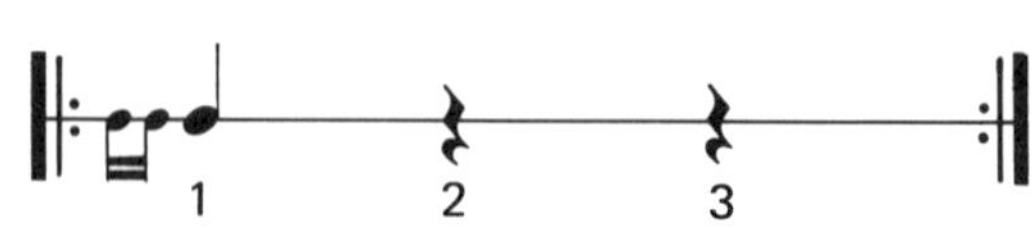

Improvise parts for guiro, cabassa and other instruments. Don't play too much and make sure that you don't copy the rhythm of the tune.

INVENTING

Improvise on the notes of the two chords that accompany the song.

Use chime bars, glockenspiels and xylophones with:

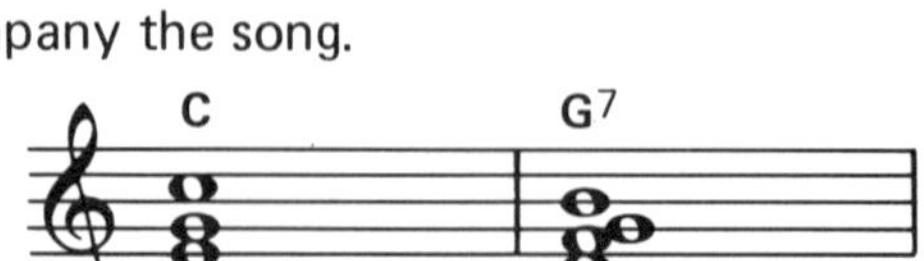

Don't always play together. Vary the texture and tone colour with your choice of instruments.

If desired the following chord sequence might provide a framework for such an improvisation.

$\frac{4}{4}$ C / C / C / G^7 / G^7 / G^7 / G^7 / C // Start slowly; vary the rhythm.

An electronic keyboard might provide this sequence if the automatic accompaniment chords or arpeggios are used.

33 LITTLE BOXES

Words & Music: Malvina Reynolds
Arr. Ian Butler

2. And the people in the houses all went to the university,
   Where they were put into boxes, little boxes, all the same.
   And there's doctors and there's lawyers and there's business executives,
   And they're all made out of ticky tacky and they all look just the same.

3. And they all play on the golf course and drink their martini dry,
   And they all have pretty children and the children go to school,
   And the children go to summer camp, and then to the university,
   Where they all get put in boxes and they all come out the same.

4. And the boys go into business and marry and raise a family,
   In boxes, little boxes, little boxes all the same,
   There's a green one and a pink one and a blue one and a yellow one,
   And they're all made out of ticky tacky and they all look just the same.

STREETS OF LONDON

PERFORMING

A song where the guitar accompaniment is authentic! Sparing use of all other accompaniment instruments is recommended.

In the verses the lower part has the melody. Where the first part fits the words, these should be sung. Otherwise, it is intended that this part should sing wordlessly to a vowel such as *"ah"*. Both parts sing the words in the Chorus. Variety might be achieved by small groups or soloists singing the verses and everyone singing the Chorus. Try one verse unaccompanied for a change!

The Tuned Percussion part is intended for Glockenspiels.

Both vocal parts can be doubled by Recorder and Flute.

LISTENING

Ralph McTell's recording of the song.

London streets and people:
City Lights – Alan Price
Cockaigne Overture – Elgar
Feed the Birds, from *Mary Poppins* – Sherman
Knightsbridge March – Coates
London Overture – Ireland
London Pride – Coward
London Symphony – Vaughan Williams
Morning, from *Cats* – A. Lloyd Webber
Where is love, from *Oliver* – Bart
Wouldn't it be loverly, from *My Fair Lady* – Lerner & Lowe

IDEAS

The Untuned Percussion in this song needs to be very discreet. (It could be performed without any.) If you think you can invent something very quiet and gentle, which may fit in with the mood or meaning of the words or enhance the music, have a go! Perhaps sounds made with things other than conventional instruments, or tape recordings of real street sounds might be the answer?

INVENTING

The opening chord sequence in this song is the same as that used in the famous *Canon* by Pachelbel. Starting with the ideas presented in No. 40, and working through the *Inventing* ideas in No. 17, try vocal improvisations on this sequence.

In an easier key, the chords are:

‖: C / G^7 / Am / Em / F / C / Dm / G^7 :‖ End on C.

Choose your own time signature and speed. Encourage a variety of rhythm patterns. Let the pupils work in large and small groups, and, when they gain confidence, alone!

34 STREETS OF LONDON

Words & Music: Ralph McTell
Arr. Ian Butler

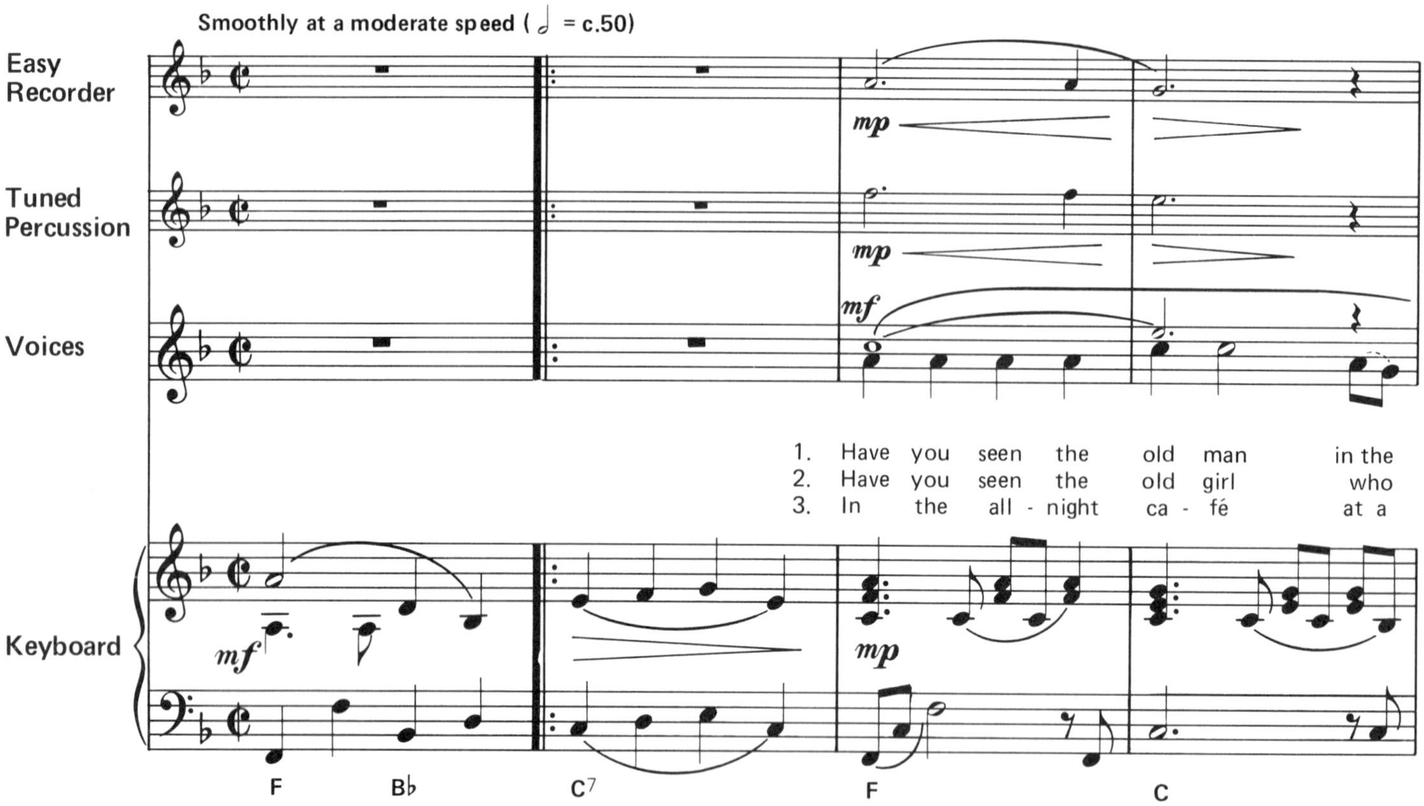

...Soon the music has to go out of print...

20 Chorus
mf
how can you tell me you're lone - ly.
B♭ F F maj7 C9 Dm7
24
And say for you that the sun don't shine?
G7 C C7
28
mp
mf
Let me take you by the hand and lead you through the
F C Dm

4. Have you seen the old man outside the seaman's mission,
Memory fading with the medal ribbons that he wears?
In our winter city the rain cries a little pity
For one more forgotten hero and a world that doesn't care.

35 TEACHER'S NOTES
JOHNNY TODD

PERFORMING

This is a story song, or ballad. Parts could be allocated either to individuals or groups. Don't let the pace drag. Keep a light tone and lilt to the music.

The Tuned Percussion part is intended for Xylophones with medium to soft beaters. Teach this part separately. The players will need two beaters to play the repeated semiquavers.

LISTENING

Z Cars — signature tune

Liverpool:
Ferry across the Mersey — Jerry and the Pacemakers
Liver Birds — Pentangle
Liverpool Lass — Traditional
The Leaving of Liverpool — Traditional
Songs by the Spinners

Doh me soh:
Sunset — Royal Marines Band
(See also Song No. 19)

IDEAS

Tambourine in lap

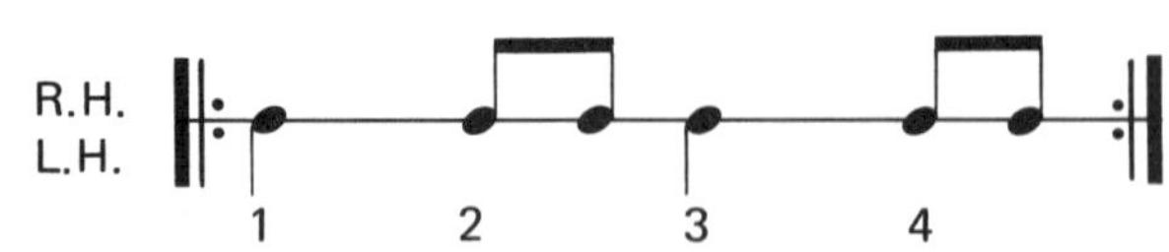

INVENTING

The song opens with the *doh me soh* triad. This could be a good opportunity to develop some concept of chords and chord sequences.

A melody could be invented that only used the notes doh, me and soh. Illustrate these by listening to bugle calls first. If a class member plays in a bugle band, the successful melodies might be performed on the bugle(s).

This is a **nine** bar song. Perhaps children who produce pieces of unusual length, or phrases which work even though they are longer or shorter than four bars, should be encouraged!

35 JOHNNY TODD

Traditional
Arr. Ian Butler

2. For a week she wept full sorely,
Tore her hair and wrung her hands,
Till she met with another sailor,
Walking on the Liverpool sands!

3. Why, fair maid, are you weeping,
For your Johnny gone to sea?
If you'll wed with me tomorrow,
I will kind and constant be!

4. I will buy you sheets and blankets,
I'll buy you a wedding ring,
You shall have a gilded cradle
For to rock your baby in.

5. Johnny Todd came back from sailing,
Sailing o'er the ocean wide;
But he found that his fair and false one,
Was another sailor's bride.

6. All you men who go sailing,
For to fight the foreign foe,
Don't you leave your young love like Johnny,
Marry her before you go!

TEACHER'S NOTES 36

MR TAMBOURINE MAN

PERFORMING

This song needs to be felt in two beats to the bar. Don't sing it too slowly, or the repetitions will become boring! Vary the sound through instrumentation. Cumulative use of voices could also add interest. Start with two voices to each part. At each new **phrase** or line add extra voices.

Alternatively, perform the song antiphonally, with alternate phrases being sung by different groups. It might be exciting to space six or eight groups of singers around the classroom and spread the sound.

LISTENING

Bob Dylan singing this song.

Tambourines:

Carmen — Bizet

L'Arlésienne Suite — Bizet

Spanish music

The Troubadour singer:

The old Castle, from *Pictures at an Exhibition* — Mussorgsky

Serenades, Minstrel songs, court musicians

IDEAS

Tambourine (Feel in 2)

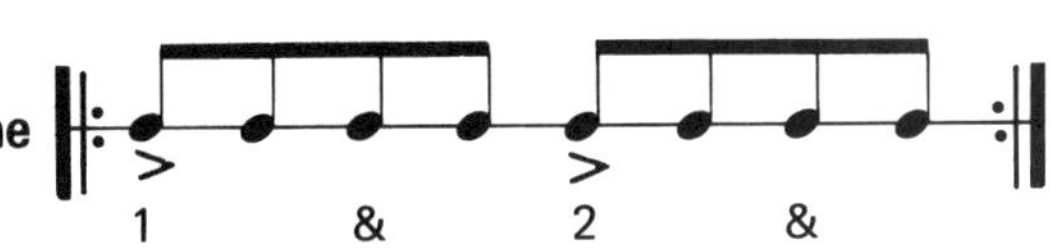

INVENTING

Experiment with the sounds that can be made using one or more tambourines. There are many ways in which a tambourine can be played. Try using a jingle-ring (a tambourine without a head). Show how the sound changes the more jingles there are on the instrument. Invest in a 24 or 36 jingle jingle-ring!

Record the sound of tambourines. Replay at different speeds, and through a reverb unit. Record them in resonant and dry acoustics; close to or at a distance.

Experiment to see which instruments or voices might successfully be added to your tambourine extravaganza!

36 MR TAMBOURINE MAN

Words & Music: Bob Dylan
Adapted and arr. Ian Butler

11
mp
mp
mf
go - ing to.
Hey Mis - ter Tam - bou - rine Man
G
E
F
D
G
E
15
play a song for me in the jin - gle, jan - gle morn - ing I'll come
C
A
F
D
C
A
F
D
19
1. 2. and 3. to verse
Last time
Fine
fol - low-ing you
1. Tho' I
rit.
p
G
E
C
A

24 Verse
mf
know that eve - ning's Em - pire has re - turned in - to sand
Take me on a trip up - on your ma - gic swirl - ing ship, My
Verse
F D
G E
C A
F D
28
Van - ished from my hand left me blind - ly here to stand but still not
toes too numb to step, wait on - ly for my boot heels to be wan –
C A
F D
C A
F D
32
slee - ping My wear - ri - ness a - maz - es me, I'm
- der - ring. I'm rea - dy to go an - y - where, I'm
G E
F D
G E

3. Then take me disappearing through the smoke-rings of my mind,
The haunted frightened trees, far from the twisted reach of crazy sorrow.
Yes, dance beneath the diamond sky
With one hand waving free,
Silhouetted by the sea,
Circled by the circus sands.
Forget today, til tomorrow.

Chorus

37 TEACHER'S NOTES

O WALY WALY

PERFORMING

A smooth, legato sound is required for this beautiful song.

Each verse should be shaped like a long smooth arch. The voices will need to be well supported. Practise the breathing – one breath to a line. The melody in bar 4 moves to the second vocal part, and back to the first vocal part in bar 7. Ensure that it remains prominent.

Vary the number of singers and the instrumentation to add further interest to the verses.

The Tuned Percussion part is intended for Glockenspiel or Chime Bars. Use medium beaters.

LISTENING

Britten's arrangement of this song.

Eriskay Love Lilt – Arr. Kennedy-Fraser

Skye Boat Song – Traditional

The Bluebird – Stanford

The Road to the Isles – Arr. Kennedy-Fraser

IDEAS

Suspended Cymbal with brushes

INVENTING

Improvise a piece which describes reflections in still water. Imagine a rowing boat, for example, as it glides slowly across the water, leaving ripples in its wake which dissolve into the calm surface as it passes.

Choose the instruments that you use carefully. Experiment with instruments. There may be unusual ways in which the instruments can be played to get unexpected and appropriate sounds out of them. Take great care to listen to others in the group, and use your sounds to fit in with everybody else.

Think about speed and tone colour in particular for such a piece.

37 O WALY WALY

Traditional (Somerset folk song)
Arr. Ian Butler

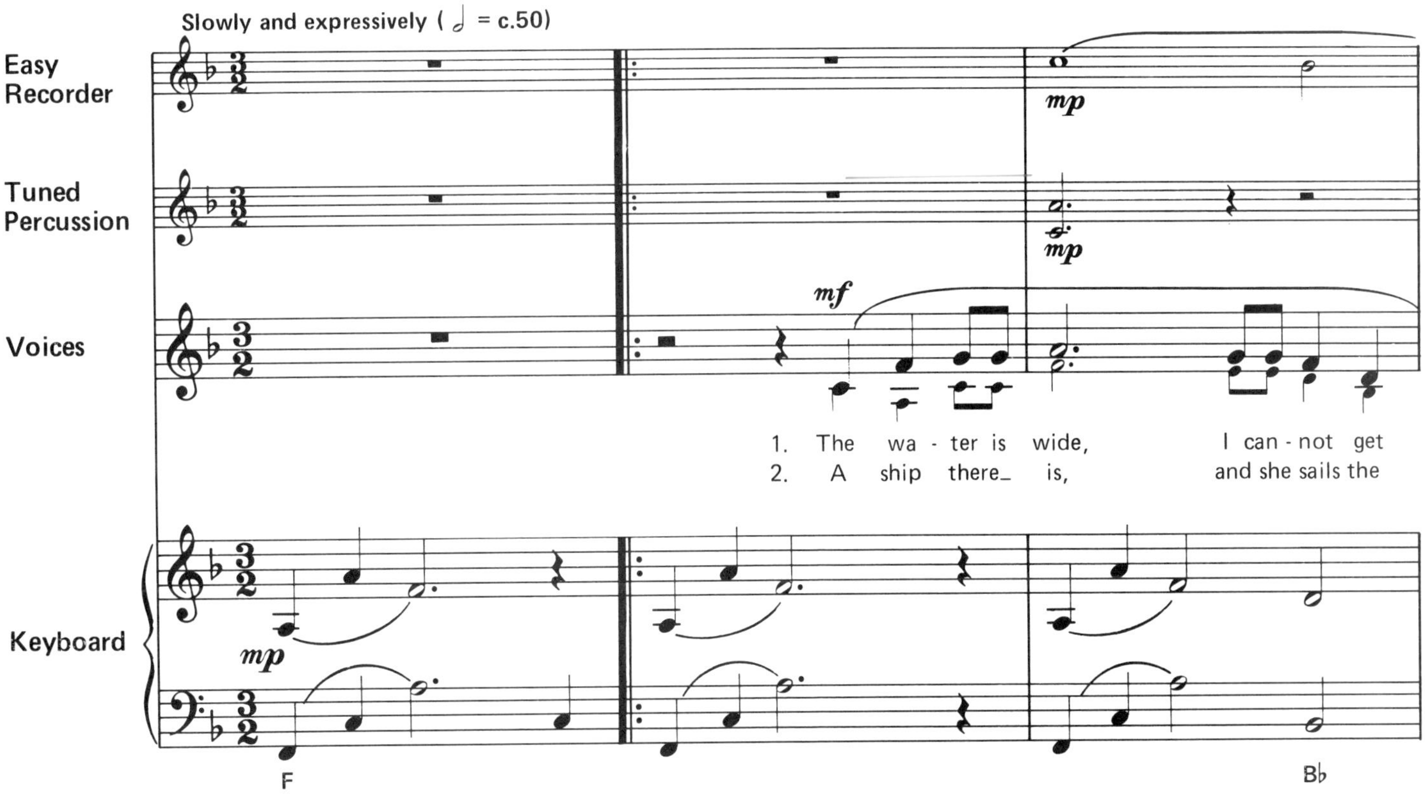

3. I leaned my back up against some oak
   Thinking that he was a trusty tree;
   But first he bended and then he broke;
   And so did my false love to me.

4. O, love is handsome and love is fine
   And love's a jewel while it is new,
   But when it is old, it groweth cold,
   And fades away like morning dew.

TEACHER'S NOTES 38

THIS OLD MAN

PERFORMING

The correct tempo for this song gives it a real swagger! Feel the semiquavers between the beats.

Vary the verses by using different elements of the arrangement for different verses. Ask the singers to suggest percussion instruments to fit the words (See Ideas Box).

For an experiment add *Skip to my Lou*, *Bobby Shaftoe*, *Michael Finnigin* or *Little Red Wagon* to *This Old Man*. Don't let them drown the main song though!

Try adjusting the instrumental parts to fit.

Both vocal parts can be doubled by Recorder and Flute.

LISTENING

The sound track from the film *Inn of the Sixth Happiness* — M. Arnold

Nonsense songs:
by Seiber and Copland

Marches:
Colonel Bogey — Alford
Elephant, from *Jungle Book* — Gilkyson
March of the Siamese Children, from *King and I* — Rodgers
Men of Harlech — Bonniseau
Oh, When the Saints — Traditional
Radetzky March — Strauss
Wedding March — Mendelssohn

IDEAS

Woodblock

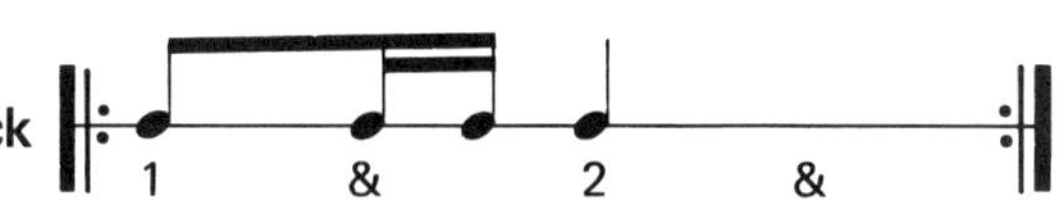

Choose instruments to match the words of each verse: e.g. "hive" could be maraccas to suggest the buzzing of bees; "sticks" could be castanets — dry and brittle. Get thinking!

INVENTING

Make up a march. It must have a regular even-numbered pulse. It might have as its main rhythmic interest one of the rhythms from the song, such as;

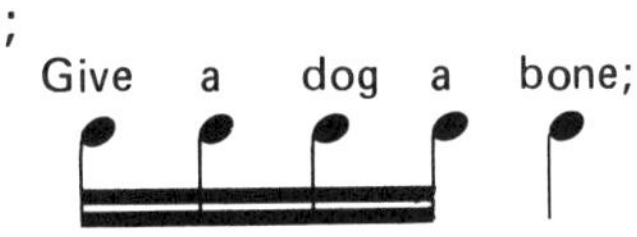

or a predominant interval such as: *"This old man; he played one"*; or it might be totally original. But try to get the feeling of marching, swinging along!

38 THIS OLD MAN

Traditional
Arr. Ian Butler

4. This old man, he played four,
He played knick-knack on my door,
With a knick-knack paddy-wack,
Give a dog a bone, this old man came rolling home.

5. This old man, he played five,
He played knick-knack on my hive,
With a knick-knack paddy-wack,
Give a dog a bone, this old man came rolling home.

6. This old man, he played six,
He played knick-knack on my sticks,
With a knick-knack paddy-wack,
Give a dog a bone, this old man came rolling home.

7. This old man, he played seven,
He played knick-knack up in heaven,
With a knick-knack paddy-wack,
Give a dog a bone, this old man came rolling home.

8. This old man, he played eight,
He played knick-knack on my gate,
With a knick-knack paddy-wack,
Give a dog a bone, this old man came rolling home.

9. This old man, he played nine,
He played knick-knack on my vine,
With a knick-knack paddy-wack,
Give a dog a bone, this old man came rolling home.

39 TEACHER'S NOTES

EBONY AND IVORY

PERFORMING

This is a lovely song. Make sure that the words are clearly understood before singing it.

The first and second vocal parts sing alternately in bars 5 and 6 and from 17-20. Ensure that the singers listen to each other and follow carefully.

It may prove valuable to use some exercises from No. 10 to practise singing in thirds.

Extend the piece by performing it three times, second time with instruments alone.

LISTENING

The McCartney recording of the song.

Black and Blue — Ellington
Black and White Rag — Botsford

Antiphonal music:
Gabrieli, the Venetian School . . .

Concerto Grosso:
Brandenburg Concertos — Bach
Concerto Grossi — Corelli, Handel

IDEAS

To decide whether this song needs any untuned percussion:

* Think about the words and the mood and speed of the music.

* If you can then think of a way of complementing these with an accompaniment, do so.

* Otherwise, decide to leave these instruments out this time, and enjoy singing the song!

INVENTING

Make up a piece with short questions and answers, which can be played or sung by different groups.

The groups could be similar, or provide great contrast.

The *"questions"* and *"answers"* may be melodic, rhythmic or both.
Think about the size, tone quality, pitch, volume, and position of the groups. Then decide whether this fits the music that you have made up, and whether the pairs of groups go together.

Remember it is not necessary to be the same to fit together!

39 EBONY AND IVORY

Words & Music: Paul McCartney
Arr. Ian Butler

At a steady, moderate speed (♩ = c.100)

We all know that peo-ple are the same wher - ev - er you go. There is good and bad in ev - 'ry - one we learn to live we learn to give each o-ther what we need to sur-vive to - ge - ther, a - live
E - bo - ny and iv - o - ry live to -
C Am G7 F C
G7 B♭6 A7 Dm F
F (G bass) G7 C Dm7 G

24
— ge - ther in per - fect har - mo - ny __ side by side on my pia - no
C Dm7 G C
27
molto rit.
key - board, oh __ Lord, why don't we?
f
molto rit.
L.H.
F G G7 G7 (C bass) C

40 TEACHER'S NOTES

IT'S YOUR TURN NOW

PERFORMING

These are five graded chord sequences which can be used as a basis for vocal improvisation. All of them can be taken at a variety of speeds. It may be best to start each one slowly.

At first try with all the pupils together, reducing down to solo gradually, in order to retain their confidence. Some suggestions are given in the Pupil's Book for the more timid.

The vocal part can be doubled by Recorder or Flute.

LISTENING

Listen to some examples of the more accessible traditional, mainstream or dixieland jazz.

Point out when a particular instrument has a *"break"*, (i.e. improvises alone)

Some contemporary "classical" music also used the device in places. For most young people it is often difficult to hear this without a score. But try!

IDEAS

INVENTING

A sort of Rondo form of performance helps to keep everyone's attention, once confidence has been gained and some ideas have been worked out (perhaps in groups). The whole class sings a melody, preferably invented by one of the pupils; then one or more improvise alone; then the whole class joins in again as a Chorus. Each section could be one or more playings of the chord sequence, but once it has been chosen, it is helpful to keep the length constant.

There are a number of songs in the book where vocal improvisation is suggested in the *"Inventing"* notes. These sequences will hopefully provide a starting point for such activities.

Remember, the whole technique of improvisation is based on listening, and being prepared to have a go. Most people need a lot of encouragement to get started. Once they have however, it can be quite a problem to stop them!

40 IT'S YOUR TURN NOW

Ian Butler

Five graded sequences for vocal improvisation

1.

At a moderate speed (♩ = c.100)

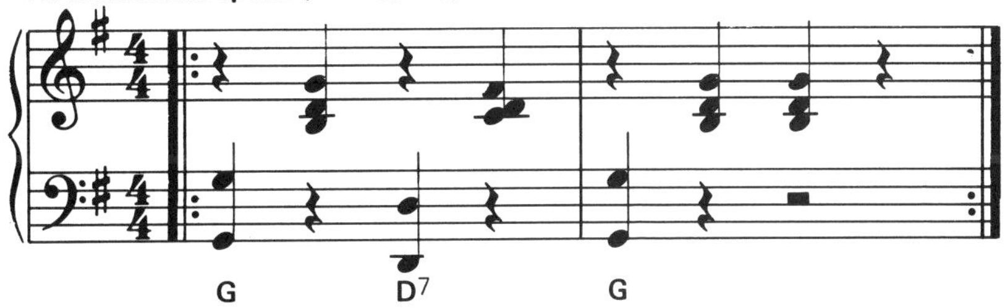

2.

With a sense of fun! (♩ = c.120)

3.

Slowly (♩ = c.80)

4.

March (♩ = c.120)

OH WHEN THE SAINTS

ACKNOWLEDGEMENTS

1 **THE BARE NECESSITIES** (from the motion picture *Jungle Book*) Words and Music by Terry Gilkyson © 1964 by Wonderland Music Company, California, USA. International Copyright Secured. All Rights Reserved.

F.B. Music Ltd. 14 New Burlington Street, London W1X 2LR for the British Commonwealth (including Canada & Australasia), the Republic of Ireland and South Africa.

2 **BLOWIN' IN THE WIND** © Warner Brothers Music Ltd. Reproduced by permission.

3 **'TIS THE GIFT** © This arrangement copyright for all Countries 1985 J. & W. Chester/Edition Wilhelm Hansen London Ltd.

4 **LITTLE BROWN JUG** © This arrangement copyright for all Countries 1985 J. & W. Chester/Edition Wilhelm Hansen London Ltd.

5 **MORNING HAS BROKEN** Copyright words by Eleanor Farjeon from *The Children's Bells,* published by OUP. This arrangement copyright © for all countries 1985 J. & W. Chester/Edition Wilhelm Hansen London Ltd.

6 **MICHAEL FINNIGIN** © This arrangement copyright for all countries 1985 J. & W. Chester/Edition Wilhelm Hansen London Ltd.

7 **HUSH LITTLE BABY** © This arrangement copyright for all countries 1985 J. & W. Chester/Edition Wilhelm Hansen London Ltd.

8 **A WINDMILL IN OLD AMSTERDAM** Words and Music © Ted Dicks & Miles Rudge. Used by permission of Westminster Music Ltd.

9 **SUMMER IS A COMING IN** © This arrangement copyright for all countries 1985 J. & W. Chester/Edition Wilhelm Hansen London Ltd.

10 **I KNOW WHERE I'M GOING** © This arrangement copyright for all countries 1985 J. & W. Chester/Edition Wilhelm Hansen London Ltd.

11 **MY GRANDFATHER'S CLOCK** © This arrangement copyright for all countries 1985 J. & W. Chester/Edition Wilhelm Hansen London Ltd.

12 **CUSHY BUTTERFIELD** © This arrangement copyright for all countries 1985 J. & W. Chester/Edition Wilhelm Hansen London Ltd.

13 **MICHAEL ROW THE BOAT ASHORE** © This arrangement copyright for all countries 1985 J. & W. Chester/Edition Wilhelm Hansen London Ltd.

14 **SWEET GINGERBREAD MAN** © 1970 Metro-Goldwyn-Mayer Inc. Rights throughout the world controlled by Leo Feist, Inc. All Rights of Leo Feist, Inc. assigned to CBS Catalogue Partnership. All Rights controlled by CBS Feist Catalog. International Copyright Secured. All Rights Reserved.

15 **IMAGINE** Words and Music by John Lennon © 1971 by Lenono Music. This arrangement © 1985 by Lenono Music. Published by J. & W. Chester/Edition Wilhelm Hansen London Ltd. by kind permission of the copyright owners.

16 **THE MERMAID** © This arrangement copyright for all countries 1985 J. & W. Chester/Edition Wilhelm Hansen London Ltd.

17 **WHERE HAVE ALL THE FLOWERS GONE?** Words & Music by Peter Seeger. Copyright © Harmony Music Ltd. Used by permission.

18 **RAINDROPS KEEP FALLIN' ON MY HEAD** Reproduced by kind permission of the copyright owners, Carlin Music Corporation, 14 New Burlington Street, London W1X 2LR.

19 **KUM BAYA** © This arrangement copyright for all countries 1985 J. & W. Chester/Edition Wilhelm Hansen London Ltd.

20 **WHEN I'M SIXTY-FOUR** by Lennon & McCartney © 1967 Northern Songs Ltd., 19 Upper Brook Street, London W1. All rights for Canada controlled by Maclen Music of Canada, Toronto. All Rights Reserved. Used by permission.

21 **SAILING** by Gavin Sutherland. © Island Music Ltd. Reproduced by permission.

22 **O SOLDIER, SOLDIER** © This arrangement copyright for all countries 1985 J. & W. Chester/Edition Wilhelm Hansen London Ltd.

23 **TRY TO REMEMBER** © 1960 Tom Jones & Harvey Schmidt, Chappell & Co. Inc. New York, owner of publication and allied rights. Reproduced by permission of Chappell Music Ltd. and International Music Publications.

24 **RIVERS OF BABYLON** by McNaughton/Dowe/Farian/Reyam. © Blue Mountain Music Ltd. Reproduced by permission.

25 **GREENSLEEVES** © This arrangement copyright for all countries 1985 J. & W. Chester/Edition Wilhelm Hansen London Ltd.

26 **TOP OF THE WORLD** by Richard Carpenter & John Bettis. © 1972 by Almo Music Corporation/Hammer & Nails Music. Reproduced by permission of Rondor Music (London) Ltd.

27 **AMAZING GRACE** © This arrangement copyright for all countries 1985 J. & W. Chester/Edition Wilhelm Hansen London Ltd.

28 **PASS THE DUTCHIE** © 1967 by Jackie Mittoo Music © 1982 Assigned to Sparta Florida Music Group Ltd., Suite 4, Carlton Tower Place, London SW1 for the World. International copyright secured. All Rights Reserved.

29 **A WINTER'S TALE** Music by Mike Batt/Lyrics by Tim Rice and Mike Batt. Lyrics reproduced by permission of the copyright owners, 64 Squares Music Ltd./Warner Brothers Music Ltd. Music reproduced by permission of the copyright owners, CBS Songs Ltd./Batt Songs Ltd.

30 **THE RIDDLE SONG** © This arrangement copyright for all countries 1985 J. & W. Chester/Edition Wilhelm Hansen London Ltd.

31 **WHAT SHALL WE DO WITH THE DRUNKEN SAILOR?** © This arrangement copyright for all countries 1985 J. & W. Chester/Edition Wilhelm Hansen London Ltd.

32 **SCARBOROUGH FAIR** © This arrangement copyright for all countries 1985 J. & W. Chester/Edition Wilhelm Hansen London Ltd.

33 **LITTLE BOXES** Words & Music by Malvina Reynolds © copyright 1962 Schroder Music Co. (ASCAP). Used by permission. All Rights Reserved.

34 **STREETS OF LONDON** Words & Music by Ralph McTell. © Westminster Music Ltd. Used by permission.

35 **JOHNNY TODD** © This arrangement copyright for all countries 1985 J. & W. Chester/Edition Wilhelm Hansen London Ltd.

36 **MR TAMBOURINE MAN** © Warner Brothers Music Ltd. Reproduced by permission.

37 **O WALY WALY** © This arrangement copyright for all countries 1985 J. & W. Chester/Edition Wilhelm Hansen London Ltd.

38 **THIS OLD MAN** © This arrangement copyright for all countries 1985 J. & W. Chester/Edition Wilhelm Hansen London Ltd.

39 **EBONY AND IVORY** Words and Music by Paul McCartney © 1982 MPL Communications Ltd. Reproduced by permission.

40 **IT'S YOUR TURN NOW** © This arrangement copyright for all countries 1985 J. & W. Chester/Edition Wilhelm Hansen London Ltd.

INDEX OF FIRST LINES

GLOSSARY

Ad lib. an abbreviation for *ad libitum* — as you like, if you wish

Arpeggiando to spread a chord, starting with the lowest note

Augmentation increasing the length of each note of a melodic figure, while retaining their rhythmic relationship

Cabassa a Latin American instrument with a serrated cylinder surrounded by metal beads

Descant a second melodic part above the tune

Diminution the opposite of augmentation (see above)

Drone a single note, usually in the bass, sounded throughout the piece

Glockenspiel melodic percussion instrument with chrome bars

Imitation a contrapuntal device where the parts begin one after another in a similar melodic way, thus imitating each other

Inversion to turn a melodic phrase upside down

Metallophone melodic percussion instrument with grey metal bars

Rapping a technique of Caribbean derivation involving rhythmically spoken, rhyming words

Riff. a short repeated rhythmic phrase

Sequence a repeated rhythmic and melodic pattern, altering the pitch by step

Tacet keep silent

Timbre tone colour or quality

Unis. short for *unison* — all parts perform the same notes

Xylophone melodic percussion instrument with wood or fibreglass bars

Printed and bound in Great Britain by
Caligraving Limited Thetford Norfolk

10/95 (22607)

KEY [illegible] HY

Lower Ability Support Pack

Mike Clinch – has taught geography for 16 years in schools in Sussex and South Wales. Throughout his teaching career, he has taught mixed ability classes and has extensive experience producing differentiated worksheets for less able pupils. As head of department he has worked closely with Mid Glamorgan Advisory Staff for Special Needs developing suitable teaching strategies for use with lower ability classes. He is an established author, having published other material for KS3. He is currently Deputy Headteacher at St Richard Gwyn R.C. High School, Barry.

Peter Goatley – has taught geography in the West Indies and Britain for over 20 years. He is currently Head of Geography at Longdean School, Hemel Hempstead. He has taught lower ability pupils within both mixed ability and setted groups and is currently running a basic literacy course within schools.

Phil Gordon – has taught geography at Walker School, an inner city comprehensive, in Newcastle upon Tyne for 21 years. As classroom teacher, head of department and assistant head, making the subject accessible to students with typical language difficulties, has been the major aim in response to the National Curriculum.

KEY GEOGRAPHY

Lower Ability Support Pack

Key Stage 3
Book 1

Mike Clinch Peter Goatley Phil Gordon

Adviser: Tony Bushell

STANLEY THORNES

First published in 1996 by:
Stanley Thornes (Publishers) Ltd
Ellenborough House
Wellington Street
CHELTENHAM GL50 1YW
England

96 97 98 99 00 / 10 9 8 7 6 5 4 3 2 1

A catalogue record for this book is available from the British Library.

ISBN 0–7487–2784–1

Acknowledgements

Illustrations by Nick Hawken, Angela Lumley and Barking Dog Art.

Cartoons by Harry Venning.

The authors and publishers are grateful to the following for permission to reproduce photographs and logos in this book:

Panos Pictures (p. 8); Tony Stone Images (p. 7); MetroCentre (p.165); Nissan Product & Corporate Affairs (p.165)

Typeset by Raynor Design

Printed and bound in Great Britain at Ashford Colour Press, Hampshire

Contents

Introduction

Teachers of geography are very fortunate. Everyone is interested, to a greater or lesser degree in the issues that affect our lives. We are constantly asking ourselves questions of a geographical nature – what is the weather like today? Where shall we go on holiday this year? Where has all this traffic come from? Everyone, therefore, is a geographer. It is the job of the geography teacher to tease out this latent interest and to develop in their pupils an awareness of their surroundings. Geography is a fun subject that can inspire and excite pupils when presented in an interesting and enjoyable way.

Aims

The aim of this pack is to make teaching and learning of geography fun for lower ability pupils. We aim to provide pupils with a range of activities that will help to develop their knowledge and understanding and for them to learn and practice new skills. It will allow such pupils to work alongside more able students, allowing them to progress at their own pace.

This is 'real geography' using relevant themes and topics. The pack will enable teachers to spend more time identifying the needs of each individual rather than spend the time creating their own support material.

What do we mean by lower ability?

Lower ability pupils differ enormously. Variations can occur, not only between schools, but also between classes in the same school and even within classes. In some schools less able pupils are fully integrated into mixed ability groups. In others, slow learners are taught in separate special needs' classes. There can be considerable variation in even the smallest of classes. A teacher may be presented with difficulties ranging from an inability to read English to dyslexia. The problems faced can be as many as the pupils in the class. Some pupils may present behavioural problems. This pack is aimed at pupils who, for whatever reason, find the traditional geography textbook too demanding. The structure of the pack and the range of material on offer, will provide the teacher with a flexible resource to be used as a 'stand alone' or in conjunction with 'Foundations'.

Why is this material needed?

As teachers we are required to make our subject accessible to all irrespective of ability. This task becomes increasingly more difficult given the range of abilities that many of us encounter in our schools. To date, in many cases, traditional textbooks have proved inappropriate for slow learners. Language levels may be too high, the tasks set can be far too demanding and expectations are beyond their capabilities. Even where attempts have been made to rectify the problem the tasks set are frequently repetitive and unchallenging. Pupils quickly become demotivated, lose interest and fail to make progress at the desired rate. As classroom teachers we all face the increasing pressure of having to maximise the progress of every individual pupil. Adapting material, preparing separate worksheets and developing individual learning programmes can take an inordinate amount of time. Many of us face the constant battle with our own conscience of how much time do we spend with each individual at the expense of the rest of the class or other teaching groups. It is hoped that this resource pack will ease some of the burden.

Features of the scheme

Having recognised the need for a series of resource materials for pupils of lower ability, we identified the essential features that such a series would require.

The needs of lower-ability pupils

These pupils have a wide range of problems which can limit their progress. These may include slow and laborious writing, a low reading age, limited memory, teachers' low expectations and, perhaps most commonly, a limited concentration span.

As practising, and practical, teachers of such pupils, we decided that the worksheets should exhibit the following features:

- Focus on geographical skills and concepts rather than on reading, writing and time-filling activities.
- Feature activities which are simple enough to be realistic for pupils of lower ability and which involve sufficient repetition and practice of the necessary skills.
- Contain activities which can be completed in twenty to thirty minutes by even very low ability pupils so that the frustration of unfinished work is avoided.
- Involve a wide variety of activities.
- Reinforce understanding of key words and specific geographical terminology.
- Focus on the explanation or practice of only one key theme, geographical concept or skill on each worksheet.
- Be self-contained so that they can be used for homework or by specialist teachers removed from the geography department.
- Avoid too many 'glue-and-stick' exercises or games with complex rules which seem attractive but which often lead to difficulties in practice.
- Include a 'recap' of the main concept or skill.

Reading level

Many textbooks contain difficult words in long sentences. They include words or information which give valuable further explanation or detail to the sophisticated reader, but which confuse or intimidate the less competent reader. We have attempted, therefore, to make the reading level of these materials as simple as possible whilst adhering to correct grammar and including accurate geographical terminology. The instructions for the activities are as clear and simple as we can possibly make them. We are assuming, of course, that there will be a teacher present to explain ideas and instructions further!

Written work

Many lower-ability pupils are slow writers so we have attempted to limit the amount of writing required. The activities often require pupils to fill in the gaps, match 'heads' and 'tails' by drawing lines or by colour-coding, underline the correct alternative answer or answer 'true' or 'false'. Base-maps, partially-completed diagrams and crossword blanks are provided so that pupils can concentrate on the geography. Relatively few activities require free-response writing.

Some of the worksheets require pupils to use coloured pencils or pens – this is always to make written work or concepts clearer rather than as a time-filling activity.

Star-coding

We recognise that lower-ability pupils vary enormously. Some can read well and copy neatly but have very limited reasoning abilities. Others can grasp concepts quickly but lack basic literacy skills. Many may lack the concentration required to complete work set in the main-stream classroom and so experience the frustration of always being behind and rarely completing work.

We therefore decided to differentiate these lower-ability materials; for most of the key themes there are three worksheets, graded by difficulty:

- 'One-star' (✪) sheets are aimed at very low ability pupils. They use very simple language, large type and often involve minimal writing.

- 'Two-star' (✪✪) sheets generally contain two or three different activities which require a wider variety of skills. All activities on the one-star and two-star sheets are designed to be completed on the worksheet itself.
- 'Three-star' (✪✪✪) sheets usually include slightly more text and require higher-level skills, including some free-response writing. The three-star sheets sometimes include some extension activities which are to be completed on file-paper or in exercise books.

Progression. motivation and flexibility

The materials are designed to be as flexible in use as possible. Lower-ability pupils vary enormously as do the pupil groupings in which they are taught.

These materials may be used by only a few pupils within a mixed-ability class (with or without in-class support) or they may be used by all the pupils in a 'sheltered' lower-ability set. In either case, these worksheets allow such pupils to gain access to the geographical themes, concepts and skills which are being addressed, albeit at a more basic level than the majority of pupils.

Each pupil may use only one of the two or three worksheets for each theme; they may use one in class and another (either simpler or harder) at home, reinforcing or practising the classwork. Alternatively, sometimes pupils may work through the series of sheets for a particular key theme from one-star to three-star. The worksheets progress both in difficulty and in the amount of work required for completion. In classroom trials of these materials we have witnessed pupils galvanised into action, really concentrating on the activities, motivated to try and get as far as they can through the series of worksheets in the time available.

The following diagram illustrates how the materials may be used in practice. It is based on the first five themes of the Map skills section.

Topic	**Pupil 1 (very low-ability)**	**Pupil 2 (more able but with poor basic skills)**
Direction	Lesson ✪ ✪✪ (start) Homework ✪✪ (finish)	✪ ✪✪✪ ✪✪
Scale	Lesson ✪ (activities 1 and 2) Homework ✪ (activity 3)	✪✪✪ ✪✪
Symbols	Lesson ✪✪ Homework ✪	✪✪ ✪✪✪
Four figure Grid References	Lesson ✪ (teacher explains the skill)	✪ (oral) ✪✪ ✪✪✪
Six figure Grid References	Lesson ✪ (teacher explains the skill)	✪ ✪✪ ✪✪✪ (finish at home)

Thus the star-coding and differentiation allows for progression, extension, homework activities (which are often very difficult to set for lower-ability pupils), reinforcement of key points and terms, practice of key skills and target-setting.

Page features

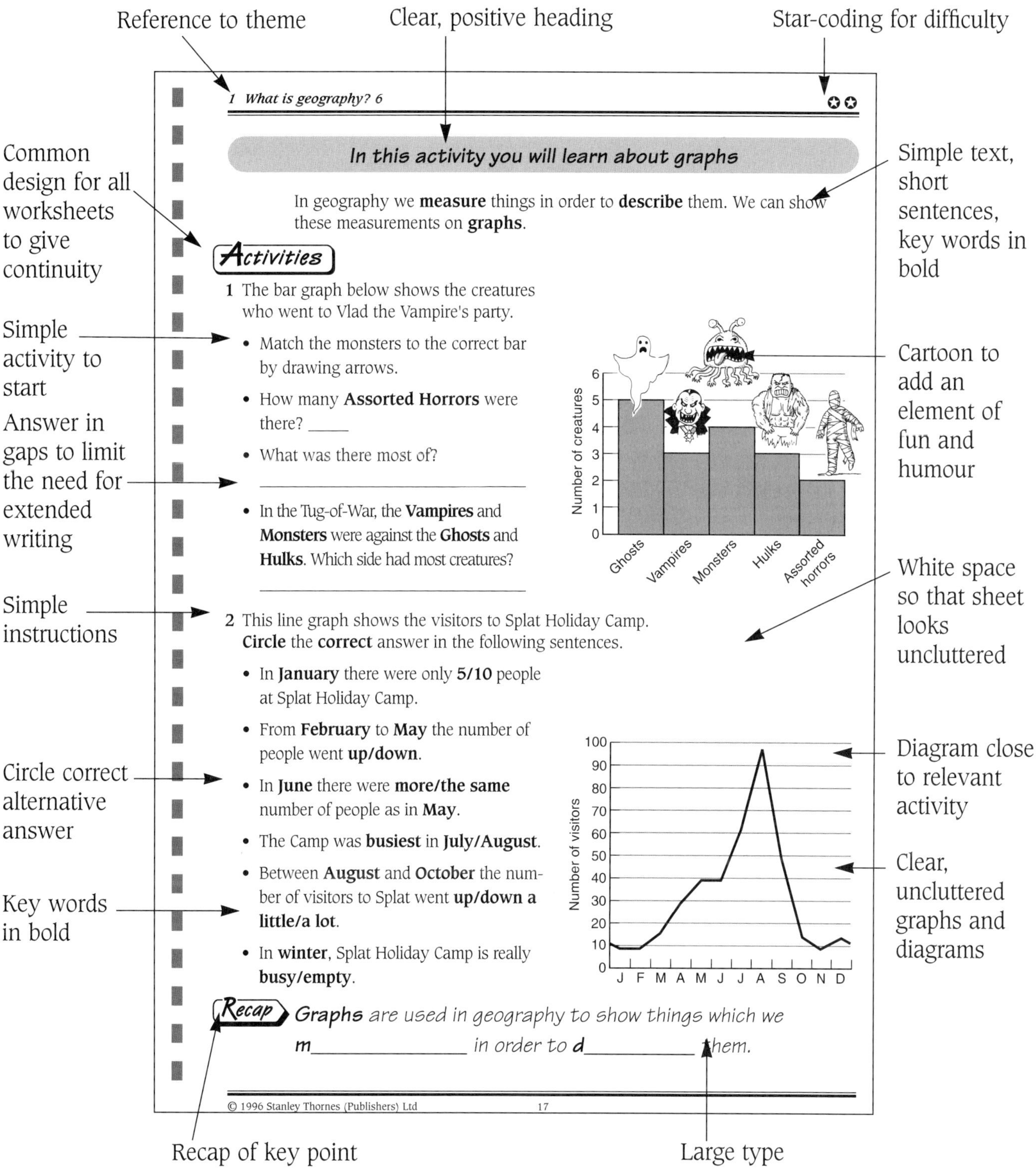

1 What is geography? 6

In this activity you will learn about graphs

In geography we **measure** things in order to **describe** them. We can show these measurements on **graphs**.

Activities

1 The bar graph below shows the creatures who went to Vlad the Vampire's party.

- Match the monsters to the correct bar by drawing arrows.
- How many **Assorted Horrors** were there? _____
- What was there most of?

  ____

- In the Tug-of-War, the **Vampires** and **Monsters** were against the **Ghosts** and **Hulks**. Which side had most creatures?

  ____

2 This line graph shows the visitors to Splat Holiday Camp. **Circle** the **correct** answer in the following sentences.

- In **January** there were only **5/10** people at Splat Holiday Camp.
- From **February** to **May** the number of people went **up/down**.
- In **June** there were **more/the same** number of people as in **May**.
- The Camp was **busiest** in **July/August**.
- Between **August** and **October** the number of visitors to Splat went **up/down a little/a lot**.
- In **winter**, Splat Holiday Camp is really **busy/empty**.

Recap *Graphs are used in geography to show things which we m______________ in order to d__________ them.*

© 1996 Stanley Thornes (Publishers) Ltd 17

Theme matrix

Page in resource pack	Theme	1 star	2 star	3 star
	What is geography?			
29, 30	What geography is about	✔	✔	✘
31, 32, 33	About the environment	✘	✔	✔✔
34, 35, 36	How to describe places	✔	✔	✔
37, 38, 39	About plans and maps	✔	✔	✔
40, 41, 42, 43	Latitude and longitude	✔	✔	✔✔
44, 45, 46	About graphs	✔	✔	✔
	Weather and climate			
47, 48, 49	How to describe the weather	✔	✔	✔
50	Weather diary	✘	✔✔	✘
51, 52, 53, 54	Microclimates	✔	✔	✔
55, 56, 57, 58	The climate of Britain	✔	✔	✔✔
59, 60 61	How it rains	✔	✔	✔
62, 63, 64, 65	Weather associated with an anticyclone	✔	✔	✔✔
66, 67, 68	Weather associated with a depression	✔	✔	✔
69	How the weather works summary	✘	✔	✘
	River basins			
70, 71,	What happens when water falls onto the land	✔	✘	✔
72, 73, 74	The parts of a river basin	✔	✔	✔
75, 76, 77	About some famous rivers	✔	✔	✔
78, 79, 80	Flooding in Bangladesh	✔	✔	✔
81, 82, 83	Causes and prevention of floods	✔	✔	✔
84, 85, 86	The water cycle	✔	✔	✔
87, 88, 89	Water supply	✔	✔	✔
90, 91, 92	The use of the River Nile	✔	✔	✔
	Settlement			
93, 94, 95	The function of settlements	✔	✔	✔
96, 97, 98	The site of settlements	✔	✔	✔
99	Settlement patterns	✘	✔	✘
100, 101, 102	The good and bad points about living in cities	✔	✔	✔
103, 104, 105	How settlements have changed through time	✔	✔	✔
106, 107, 108	Land use patterns	✔	✔	✔
109, 110, 111	Size of settlement	✔	✔	✔
112, 113, 114	Shopping	✔	✔	✔
115, 116, 117	Out-of-town shopping	✔	✔	✔
118, 119, 120	Land use change in towns	✔	✔	✔

Page in resource pack	Theme	1 star	2 star	3 star
	Transport			
121, 122, 123	Different types	✔	✔	✔
124, 125, 126	Different routes	✔	✔	✔
127, 128, 129	Networks	✔	✔	✔
130, 131, 132	Developments	✔	✔	✔
133, 134, 135	Problems in towns	✔	✔	✔
136, 137, 138	Building a by-pass	✔	✔	✔
139	Transport game	✔	✘	✘
140, 141	Channel Tunnel	✘	✔	✔
	The home region			
	North-east			
160, 161, 162	Places in North England	✔	✔	✔
163, 164, 165	What is the region like?	✔	✔	✔
166, 167, 168	The climate of the region	✔	✔	✔
169, 170	Changes in industry in the region	✔	✔	✘
171, 172	Transport links with the region	✔	✔	✘
	Wales			
173, 174, 175	What is the region like?	✔	✔	✔
176, 177, 178	The climate of the region	✔	✔	✔
179, 180, 181	Changes in industry	✔	✔	✔
182, 183	Transport links with the region	✘	✔	✔
	Greater London			
142, 143, 144	What is the region like?	✔	✔	✔
145, 146, 147	The climate and landscape of the region	✔	✔	✔
148, 149, 150	Development of the region	✔	✔	✔
151, 152, 153	Transport in London and the south-east	✔	✔	✔
154, 155, 156	Pressures on the region	✔	✔	✔
157, 158, 159	Changes in the south-east	✔	✔	✔
	Map skills			
184. 185. 186	Direction	✔	✔	✔
187, 188, 189	Scale	✔	✔	✔
190, 191, 192	Symbols	✔	✔	✔
193, 194, 195	Four figure grid references	✔	✔	✔
196, 197, 198	Six figure grid references	✔	✔	✔
199, 200, 201	How height is shown on a map	✔	✔	✔
202, 203, 204	Contours	✔	✔	✔
205, 206, 207	Describing routes	✔	✔	✔

Skills matrix

		What is geography?	Weather and climate	River basins	Settlements	Transport	North-east England	Wales	Greater London	Map skills
Geographical skills	Rank ordering						✔			
	Recognising cause and effect	✔	✔	✔		✔	✔	✔		
	Recognising advantages and disadvantages		✔		✔	✔		✔		
	Recognising good and bad points		✔	✔	✔	✔	✔	✔		
	Classification and categorisation	✔	✔	✔	✔	✔	✔	✔	✔	✔
	Map skills (OS)									✔
	Map skills (general)	✔	✔	✔	✔	✔	✔	✔	✔	✔
	Graph skills	✔	✔	✔	✔	✔	✔	✔		
	Sequencing events		✔				✔			
	Tabulation			✔	✔	✔	✔		✔	✔
	Geographical vocabulary	✔	✔	✔	✔	✔	✔	✔	✔	✔
	Explaining patterns		✔			✔				
	Photograph interpretation	✔								
	Sketching	✔		✔						
	Locational knowledge	✔	✔	✔	✔	✔	✔	✔	✔	✔
Techniques list	Underlining		✔	✔		✔	✔	✔		✔
	Concept mapping		✔							
	Picture and text matching	✔	✔	✔			✔	✔	✔	✔
	Filling in gaps in text	✔	✔	✔	✔	✔		✔	✔	✔
	Spider (star) diagram		✔			✔			✔	
	Cut and paste	✔	✔							✔
	Heads and tails	✔	✔	✔	✔	✔	✔	✔		✔
	Multiple choice		✔		✔	✔		✔	✔	✔
	Crosswords	✔	✔	✔	✔	✔	✔	✔	✔	
	Wordsearches	✔	✔	✔	✔	✔		✔		✔
	Word games		✔	✔	✔	✔			✔	
	Dot to dot		✔	✔						✔
	True, false, not enough evidence (T, F, NEE)	✔	✔	✔	✔	✔	✔	✔	✔	
	Labelling	✔	✔	✔				✔		✔
	Time lines						✔			
	Map completion	✔	✔	✔	✔	✔	✔	✔		✔
	Model making									✔
	Games					✔				✔

Links with *Key Geography Foundations*

Foundations pupils' book	Page	Lower Ability Support Pack	Page
What is geography?			
What is geography: Human and physical	4, 5, 6, 7	...What is geography about?	29
What is environmental geography?	8, 9	...about the environment	31
How do we study geography?	10, 11	...how to describe places	34
How do we find out where places are?	10, 11, 12, 13	...about plans and maps ...latitude and longitude	37 40
Why do we use graphs in geography?	14, 15	...about graphs	44
Weather and climate			
How might you observe and record weather?	16, 17	...how to describe weather Weather diary	47
Local features affect temperature and wind	18, 19	...about microclimates	50
What is Britain's weather like?	20, 21	...about the climate of Great Britain	55
How does it rain?	22, 23	...about how it rains	59
Forecasting the weather – anticyclones	24, 25	...about anticyclones	62
Forecasting the weather – depressions	26, 27	...about depressions How the weather works	66 69
River basins			
What happens when rain reaches the ground?	28, 29	...what happens when rain falls onto the land	70
What is a river basin?	30	...river basins	72
Where are the world's most important rivers?	31	...rivers in Great Britain ...rivers of the world ...the longest rivers in continents	75
What are the results of a flood?	32	...floods in Bangladesh	78
What causes flooding in Bangladesh?	33		
What causes floods?	34	...why floods happen	81
How can the risk of flooding be reduced?	35		
How does the water cycle work?	36, 37	...the water cycle	84
How can supplies of fresh water be obtained?	38, 39	...water supply	87
How can providing reliable water supply create other problems?	40, 41, 42, 43	...using water from the River Nile	90

Foundations pupils' book	Page	Lower Ability Support Pack	Page
Settlement			
What are settlements and why do they grow?	44, 45	...the function of a settlement	93
How were the sites for early settlements chosen?	46	...the site of a settlement	96
What do we mean by settlement patterns?	47	...settlement patterns	99
What are the benefits and problems of settlement growth?	48, 49	...the good and bad points of living in a town	100
How do settlements change with time?	50, 51		
Why are there different land use patterns in towns?	52, 53	...land use patterns in towns	106
Why does land use in towns change?	54	...how settlements change over time	103
How does this change affect people	55		
What is a settlement hierarchy?	56, 57	...the size of settlements	109
Is there a shopping hierarchy?	58, 59	...shopping	112
Why are shops and offices found in city centres?	60	...out-of-town shopping	115
Why are shops and offices moving to out-of-town sites?	61	...out-of-town shops and offices	117
Transport			
Which transport to use?	62, 63	...different types of transport	121
Which route to take?	64, 65	...different routes	124
What is a network?	66, 67	...transport networks	127
Developments in transport – the good news	68	...transport developments	130
Developments in transport – the bad news	69		
Traffic in urban areas – why is it a problem?	70, 71	...problems of traffic in towns	133
Where should the by-pass go?	72, 73	...building a by-pass	136
		Transport game	139
Eurotunnel – the new way to Europe	74, 75	...the Channel Tunnel	140

Foundations pupils' book	Page	Lower Ability Support Pack	Page
The home region			
What is your image of a region?	76	...Wales	173
		...North-east England	160
		...Greater London	142
What is the climate and landscape of the region?	78	...the climate of Wales	176
		...the climate of NE England	166
		...the climate and landscape of Greater London	145
How has the region developed?	80	...developments in Wales	179
		...how NE England has developed	169
		...how Greater London developed	148
What is the settlement pattern in the region?	82	...places in NE England	160
Why are there so many roads and railways in the region?	84		
		...transport in Wales	182
		...transport in NE England	171
		...transport in Greater London and south-east England	151
What pressures do we put on the countryside?	86, 87	...pressures on the area around Greater London	154
Why do people have different views on changes in their local region?	88, 89	...different views on change in the south-east	157
Map skills			
How can we show direction?	92, 93	...direction	184
How can we measure distance?	94, 95	...scale	187
How do we use map symbols?	96, 97	...map symbols	190
What are grid references?	98, 99	...four figure grid references	193
How do we use six figure grid references?	100, 101	...six figure grid references	196
How is height shown on a map?	102, 103	...how height is shown on a map	199
How do contours show height and relief?	104, 105	...how contours show the shape of the land	202
How can we describe routes?	106, 107	...how to describe routes on maps	205

Suggestions for use

As a free standing resource

The lower ability support materials in this pack have been designed to fit the National Curriculum and to make the content and skills of the National Curriculum accessible to students with a range of learning difficulties. Some or all of the sheets in each unit can fit into any programme of study devised by any geography department in any school which answers many of the questions posed by the need for **differentiation**. Whilst most teachers might feel confident in developing additional resources for the more able, many find it more difficult to adapt material for the less able, particularly in schools where there are small numbers of such low ability students.

With a set text

Most geography departments will base their courses on a set text. All set texts will cover the major themes which these resources can fit into. Most set texts and related resources aim at the average or above average students at KS3. These resources can be fitted into any organisation provided by any set text and scheme of work.

For example **School A** might cover rainfall in a unit in Year 7 and climate in another unit in Year 8. **School B** might cover all aspects of weather and climate in a single unit in Year 9. These support materials can be adapted to fit both scenarios either by selecting certain sections e.g. the ones on rainfall in School A, or by having all the sheets on weather and climate available at the same time for students to be guided along a particular path through a topic in School B.

None of the sheets in this pack refer to any single text and are all completely self contained. There is no need for any additional resources although the stimulus of a text book, the teacher, related audio visual aids are assumed to be available as well. The most the students will need is an atlas and we assume all geography classrooms to have atlases.

Through appropriate techniques

We have utilised a wide variety of techniques which provide access to lower ability students (in particular those with reading and writing difficulties) constantly ensuring that students complete real tasks which cover important geographical content and skills. We provide differentiation by task and the opportunity for all students to achieve success whilst they are participating in the mainstream work done by their peers.

With mixed ability sets or groups

For schools which teach in sets, the sheets might mainly be used for the lower groups in which further differentiation is available by the star system. The variety and high expectations of the methods used mean that lower ability students are given respectable tasks and are doing the same content as the rest but at a more appropriate level. Some of the 3 star sheets might be adapted for higher sets.

The resources can be adapted to mixed ability situations in which one level of work is aimed at the higher ability children and the support material is available for the less able. We are confident that many of the techniques will also stimulate teachers to develop exercises for all levels based on the sheets in this pack and gain confidence in producing their own resources in the future.

In some inner city schools, in which language problems might be concentrated, these resources could form the basis of programmes of study which a large proportion of students use and more complex work developed on top.

Relations with the National Curriculum

One of the main aims of the National Curriculum is 'to make geography accessible to as wide a range of pupils as possible'. This pack, specifically written for pupils at the lower end of the ability range, helps to fufil that aim. It makes geography interesting, relevant and above all, enjoyable for less able pupils.

The themes throughout the book are closely linked to *Key Geography Foundations*.

The Key Geography series was originally designed to provide a complete, yet flexible, teaching resource. In practice, many teachers use *Foundations* as a core text for Year 7. This is because *Foundations* provides an excellent grounding in the basics of geography. A variety of themes are studied across the whole spectrum of the subject: physical geography, human geography, the environment, places and skills. Pupil interest is maintained by using a range of different approaches and a variety of meaningful activities.

Assessment

Assessment is an integral part of the teaching and learning process. It is of value to both the teacher and the pupil. It's purpose may be:

- formative: identifying what each pupil has understood to date
- diagnostic: identifying strengths and weaknesses which can be worked on so improvement can be made
- evaluation: appraise the progress that is being made
- summative: identifying what each pupil knows, understands and can do on completion of the Key Stage. It determines the final level of achievement in geography.

The material in this pack is aimed at pupils working at or about levels 3 and 4, although some topics, through their very nature, involve working at levels above 4. This is because National Curriculum Geography has to be accessible to all and some topics and issues are quite complex and require a significant depth of understanding.

As geography is not part of the National Curriculum 'core', final assessment is teacher-based. The level descriptors published in the National Curriculum document are there to help teachers differentiate between pupils. Sometimes this is a difficult task as pupils may struggle to understand some aspects of the course but excel in others. A basic guide to the difference between levels 3 and 4 is in the use of the words 'some' and 'range'. At level 3 pupils are expected 'to offer explanations for *some* geographical features…' whereas at level 4 pupils must demonstrate a knowledge, understanding and skill in relation to studies 'of a *range* of places and themes…'. It is important to remember that it is the performance over the whole Key Stage that determines the level of attainment.

Variety of approach

Many less able pupils have a very short attention span. They can quickly lose interest and easily become demotivated. One way of easing the problem is by using a variety of approaches during classroom teaching. Fotunately, there are a number of options open to teachers.

- There are many excellent video films and software packages commercially available covering a wide range of topics. Some television programmes are a valuable source of geographical information. Information technology is an excellent tool and is particularly conducive to the development of skills and broadening knowledge and understanding.
- Fieldwork is an essential part of geopgraphy. The less able have as much of an entitlement to fieldwork as mainstream pupils. This pack contains a range of ideas for fieldwork which are designed to enhance and support classroom learning.
- The National Curriculum places significant emphasis on Enquiry Based Learning. Pupils are being asked to apply the knowledge they have gained to real life situations. Pupils are being encouraged to investigate issues and play an active role in decision making. Trying to predict and justify changes is particularly significant.

A text book, no matter how good, can provide only part of the learning strategy for geography. It is strongly recommended that a broad and balanced approach is used when developing a scheme of work.

Themes in the Lower Ability Support Pack

What is geography?

Theme 1 What is geography?

Aims

- to introduce the main areas of study in geography
- to distinguish between human and physical features.

There are only two worksheets as this key theme is very basic. The ✪✪ sheet includes more difficult words and classification.

Extension work could involve identifying human and physical features on photographs and postcards.

Resources: blue and red colours for ✪✪.

Theme 2 The human and physical environment

Aims

- to distinguish between human and physical environments
- for pupils to understand that we can harm or improve the environment.

✪ is a basic 'heads' and 'tails' exercise. ✪✪ requires pupils to work out missing words and to categorise. ✪✪✪ includes a Close (fill gaps) exercise, categorisation and a word puzzle.

Pupils might be extended by asking them to draw a poster to show how the environment might be improved.

Resources: red and green colours for ✪✪.

Theme 3 Describing places

Aims

- to explain how places may be described
- to interpret field-sketches and photographs.

✪ uses a simple line drawing with features labelled. ✪✪ requires pupils to complete a field-sketch from a photograph and locate features. ✪✪✪ requires a higher level of drawing ability and guided response writing.

Pupils might extend this work by taking a postcard or photograph from a magazine and doing their own labelled field-sketch.

Resources: colours.

Theme 4 Maps and plans

Aims

- to introduce the concept of maps and plans being viewed from above
- for pupils to visualise left, right and simple locations on a map.

✪ involves identifying aerial views. ✪✪ requires interpretation of a plan. ✪✪✪ involves a comparison of an oblique view and a complex map.

This work could be extended by asking pupils to draw a sketch plan of some everyday objects or their bedroom.

Resources: red, yellow and blue colours for ✪✪. Light green, dark green, red blue, orange and yellow colours for ✪✪✪.

Theme 5 Latitude and longitude

Aim

- for pupils to understand the concepts of latitude and longitude.

It is intended that the teacher will introduce and explain the idea of lines of latitude and longitude. ✪ concentrates on the major lines of latitude and longitude; ✪✪ involves pupils in plotting points on a world map whereas ✪✪✪ gives instructions on how to make a simple 'globe' to show the major lines.

This work could be extended by simple exercises looking up places in an atlas or on a world map.

Resources: purple, dark blue, green, red, blue and yellow colours for ✪. ✪✪✪ requires purple, red, orange, brown, green and blue colours, scissors, glue and tissues for padding. It is preferable to photocopy the world map template on to card to make the finished globe more robust. (Light blue card saves colouring!) Some pupils will find the flaps a bit tricky to cut out and it may be preferable to cut the shape out if there is preparation time.

Theme 6 Graphs

Aims

- to introduce the idea of showing information on graphs
- to interpret information shown on different types of graphs.

From ✪ to ✪✪✪ the worksheets require pupils to interpret increasingly complex questions from a wider variety of graphs (bar, line, pie chart, scattergraph).

This work could be extended by pupils plotting data on to their own graphs, or by collecting their own data and then plotting it. IT may be involved here, plotting graphs from data on a spreadsheet.

Resources: none required.

Weather and climate

Theme 1 How we can describe the weather

Aim

- to provide language to be able to describe elements of weather.

✪ involves matching terms to pictures and cartoons and drawing lines between them. The ✪✪ sheet asks pupils to categorise terms before matching them to the pictures. ✪✪✪ comprises of a word game which develops pupils' language and vocabulary.

Pupils may develop the elements of these sheets by completing the weather diary every day either in the lesson or as homework. This involves simple observation or using instruments. Students could tell the rest of the class the weather formally as a weather forecast.

Boxes can be ticked or extended verbally or in written form. Pupils could display their findings and summarise their data at the end of the unit.

Resources: red and blue colours for ✪✪✪.

Theme 2 Microclimates

Aim

- to show how temperature can differ over short distances. Could relate to a simple enquiry in the playground or in the school grounds.

Pupils acquire information from the diagrams in the ✪ and complete sentences and multiple choice questions. Pupils can then shade the diagrams. The two ✪✪ sheets ask pupils to consider more aspects of temperature difference as they fill in the gaps. The ✪✪✪ could be used as a summary exercise requiring pupils to complete the crossword and label diagrams.

Resources: red and blue colours for ✪✪ and ✪✪✪.

Theme 3 Climate of Britain

Aim

- to show major aspects of temperature and rainfall differences in Britain.

✪ requires no writing, pupils identify which cartoon is linked to the correct area of the country. ✪✪ contains two maps showing temperature and rainfall in three locations, pupils are to match the heads and tails. The two ✪✪✪ sheets contain more detail of differences for the pupils to interpret with True, False and NEE exercises.

Resources: red and blue colours for ✪✪. Brown, blue and 3 other colours for ✪✪✪.

Theme 4 How it rains?

Aim

- to show how air rises causing condensation and rainfall.

✪ considers only relief rainfall, pupils are to complete the diagram and multiple choice exercise. The ✪✪ involves a sequencing exercise. Pupils cut out strips and order them. They can either stick them in order or copy them out into correct order. The letters spell RAINSHADOW but do not tell the students! These letters then complete the diagram below. The ✪✪✪ involves a labelling exercise of diagrams portraying frontal and relief rain. Pupils can also complete the paragraph.

Resources: coloured pencils. Scissors and glue optional.

Theme 5 Weather systems: anticyclones

Aim

- to show the major features of the weather and enable comparisons between them.

✪ requires pupils to study the picture showing an area experiencing an anticyclone and complete the True, False and NEE exercise. Pupils may also wish to label/colour the important elements. ✪✪ diagrams help to show the differences between the weather system in winter and summer. A variety of pupil activities are contained in the two ✪✪✪ sheets. These include a crossword, multiple choice exercise, sentence completion and True, False NEE exercise.

Resources: red and blue colours for ✪✪.

Theme 6 Weather systems: depressions

Aim

- to show the major features of the weather and enable comparison between them.

✪ shows a picture of an area experiencing a depression and complete the True, False NEE exercise. Pupils may also wish to label/colour the important elements. Depressions are complex, therefore, no attempt has been made to go into detail. Only simple language and main features have been highlighted. Pupils can complete the diagram and shade the warm and cool air to differentiate. Wordsearch develops language. Star diagrams on ✪✪ help to show the differences between the weather system in winter and summer. ✪✪✪ tries to show the sequence of the passage of the depression. Pupils could draw lines to each soccer club to identify different stages of weather system. Shading warm and cool air will help.

Resources: red and blue colours for ✪✪ and ✪✪✪.

Theme 7 Concept map showing how weather works

(To be done at the end of the unit)

Aim

- to allow students to make connections between the concepts in the bubbles.

This fits all levels (including the very able) and is an excellent differentiated exercise. Students try to make as many connections between as many pairs as they can. Whatever they think is the reason for a link is written along the line. Always encourage pupils to write the reason immediately as they will forget why they drew a connection.

Not all pairs can be linked and some pairs will have many links.

This can be a useful summary exercise or even an assessment.

It can be useful display material if done on a large scale and enhances group skills.

Resources: none required.

River basins

Theme 1 What happens when rain falls onto the land?

Aim

- to show that water sinks into the ground at different rates and flows down hill (run off) at different rates.

There are only two levels in this section. It is a limited key question , but nevertheless important to flooding. ✪ asks whether water will sink in or stand on the ground. Pupils match picture to text and answer True, False or NEE exercise. ✪✪✪ considers the slope aspect and the type of vegetation/features on it and their influence on the rate of run off.

Resources: none required.

Theme 2 What is a river basin?

Aim

- to examine the main features of a river basin. Source, tributary, mouth, watershed, river basin.

✪ involves a heads and tails and labelling exercise. ✪✪ requires pupils to complete a word game. The ✪✪✪ uses an actual river to show the main features of a river basin. All the information is on the map although pupils could refer to an atlas map.

Resources: red and blue colours for ✪✪✪.

Theme 3 Famous rivers

Aim

- to look at names and locations of major rivers.

✪ involves a crossword based on the map of Britain. Pupils are asked to fill in the gaps of world rivers in the ✪✪. ✪✪✪ requires pupils to underline the longest rivers found in each continent and then use this data to complete graphs.

Extension: The ✪✪✪ could be extended to create a piece of display work and identify additional major rivers.

Resources: three colours and a ruler for ✪✪✪.

Theme 4 Flooding in Bangladesh

Aim

- to show the main causes and effects of flooding in Bangladesh.

✪ asks pupils to match the heads and tails and consider human responses to flooding, e.g. what do the people need, causes and effects of flooding. The ✪✪ concentrates on the causes and effects of flooding. Pupils complete shading exercise and write in some of the causes. In the ✪✪✪ pupils are required to underline the effects of floods.

Extension: This work can be developed into producing the front page of a newspaper, display work, cartoons of effects etc.

Resources: coloured pencils.

Theme 5 Causes of floods and methods of reducing floods

Aim

- to show the main causes and solutions to flooding.

✪ has a similar activity to the heads and tails. Pupils follow the rivers from head to tail showing the reasons for four floods. Reasons can then be entered in activity 2. ✪✪ requires pupils to tick boxes showing causes or prevention of floods. Wordsearch develops vocabulary. ✪✪✪ develops further details about causes of river floods and coastal floods. Pupils can shade each type (involving them in classification) and write two causes for each.

Resources: green, red and blue colours for ✪✪ and ✪✪✪.

Theme 6 The water cycle

Aim

- to show the main features of the water cycle.

✪ consists of a wordsearch emphasising major vocabulary and pupils can classify terms. The word game on ✪✪ sheet also uses major vocabulary. Pupils arc to use these terms in completing the flow diagram. Pupils can complete the diagram of the water cycle on ✪✪✪ sheet and fill in the gaps in the text using the main terms.

Resources: coloured pencils for ✪✪✪.

Theme 7 Supply and demand for water

Aim

- to show the uses (demand) and sources (supply) of water in Britain.

✪ uses a picture to show how we use water in the home. ✪✪ illustrates supply and demand of water in Britain locating which side of the country has the greatest demand and supply. Pupils are to complete the map. A crossword on the ✪✪✪ uses vocabulary related to the water cycle and sources.

Resources: blue and green colours for ✪✪.

Theme 8 The River Nile and Aswan Dam. Using a river for water supply

Aim

- to show how we can use a river to irrigate crops in desert areas.

✪ involves a dot to dot drawing of shaduf followed by a heads and tails exercise. Pupils complete a crossword about the River Nile and the use of its water. ✪✪✪ shows the good and bad aspects of using the river. Pupils shade and choose two of each to write advantages and disadvantages.

Extension: A further sheet showing a map of the Nile can be used at all levels. Either drawing arrows to the relevant locations or writing the names on the map. Use an atlas to help.

Resources: red and green colours for ✪✪ and ✪✪✪.

Settlement

Theme 1 The function of settlements

Aims

- to show that there is a reason for each settlement being built
- to show a settlement may have more than one function.

✪ asks pupils to fill in speech bubbles to identify different types of settlement and complete sentences. ✪✪ involves completing a table by ticking boxes, pupils complete basic descriptions. Pupils are to interpret maps on the ✪✪✪ and complete sentences. There is also an opportunity for extended writing.

Resources: exercise book or folder for ✪✪✪.

Theme 2 The site of a settlement

Aim

- to show how the surrounding area influenced the location of early settlements.

✪ requires pupils to complete sentences. ✪✪ has a heads and tails activity along with a decision making exercise. ✪✪✪ presents pupils with another decision making exercise with an opportunity for extended writing.

Resources: exercise book or folder for ✪✪✪.

Theme 3 Settlement patterns

Aim

- to show how the shape of a settlement can vary.

There is only one worksheet in this section as the theme is quite basic. This ✪✪ consists of a multiple choice exercise.

Resources: none required.

Theme 4 Benefits and problems of living in a town

Aims

- to show that living in a town brings many benefits
- to show that every day life in a town creates problems.

Pupils complete a wordsearch for ✪ and add correct words to the table. ✪✪ requires pupils to complete a crossword. ✪✪✪ presents pupils with a word puzzle and a table to fill in. There is an opportunity for extended writing.

Resources: exercise book or folder for ✪✪✪.

Theme 5 How settlements change over time

Aims

- to show that settlements do not remain the same over time
- to show that settlements change in a variety of ways.

✪ pupils study a map showing the growth of Cardiff and complete a line graph. ✪✪ shows a comparative diagram of a village at different times. Pupils complete a table and may also wish to construct sentences. ✪✪✪ demonstrates changes in a street. There is a paragraph for pupils to complete and an opportunity for extended writing.

Resources: coloured pencils for ✪, exercise or folder for ✪✪✪.

Theme 6 Land use patterns in towns

Aim

- to show how land use in a town changes as you move away from the town centre.

✪ activities include sentences for pupils to finish and a table to complete. ✪✪ involves a sequencing exercise and a True, False or NEE exercise. ✪✪✪ pupils underline multiple choice sentences and there is an opportunity for extended writing.

Resources: exercise book or folder for ✪✪✪.

Theme 7 Settlement hierarchies

Aims

- to show that settlements vary in size
- to show that there are many small settlements and few large settlements
- to show the larger the settlements the greater the range of services on offer.

✪ requires pupils to interpret a table and a map with sentences to complete. ✪✪ is an underlining exercise with a table to interpret. Pupils tick true or false boxes for ✪✪✪ sheet and interpret a map.

Resources: none required.

Theme 8 Shopping patterns

Aims

- to show that some goods are bought more frequently than others
- to show that some types of shops are visited more frequently then others
- to show that certain types of shops are located in different areas of the town.

✪ involves a wordsearch and a crossword. ✪✪ requires pupils to complete a table and match the correct sentence endings. ✪✪✪ involves pupils in a questionnaire survey with bar charts and multiple choice sentences to complete.

Resources: coloured pencils for ✪✪✪.

Theme 9 Comparing town centres and out-of-town sites

Aim

- to show towns centres are different from out-of-town sites

✪ consists of 'The Shopping Game'. ✪✪ requires pupils to add words to sentences and match the heads and tails. ✪✪✪ asks pupils to complete a table and a paragraph with an opportunity for extended writing.

Resources: dice and counters for ✪. Exercise book or folder for ✪✪✪.

Theme 10 Changing land use in towns – case study London Docklands

Aims

- to show land use in towns changes over time
- to show that when land use change occurs there are 'winners' and 'losers'.

✪ involves a map colouring exercise and a paragraph to complete. ✪✪ pupils complete the speech bubbles and table. ✪✪✪ requires pupils to fill in tables and there is an opportunity for extended writing.

Resources: coloured pencils for ✪ and ✪✪✪. Exercise book or folder for ✪✪✪.

Transport

Theme 1 Types of transport

Aims

- to show that transport is a very important activity
- to show that there are many types of transport
- to show the advantages and disadvantages of each type of transport.

✪ presents pupils with a wordsearch and a table to complete. ✪✪ has a variety of exercises involving a crossword, boxes to tick and sentences to complete. ✪✪✪ has a decision making exercise.

Resources: none required.

Theme 2 Different routes

Aim

- to show that the route taken for a journey depends on many things.

✪ involves planning a journey home from school with sentences to complete and pupils to add to map. ✪✪ shows the influences on transport routes. Pupils are to complete map labels, a table and sentences. ✪✪✪ has a decision making exercise involving pupils in deciding a route for a road.

Resources: coloured pencils for ✪✪✪.

Theme 3 Transport networks

Aims

- to show that roads (and railways) are linked together to form a network
- to show that high density networks have many links and low density networks have few links.

✪ presents pupils with diagrams to complete and a decision making exercise. ✪✪ pupils are to complete a network diagram, add numbers to a table and complete sentences. For the ✪✪✪ sheet pupils compare the networks of London and South Wales and label maps. There is also a table and a network diagram to complete.

Resources: none required.

Theme 4 Transport developments

Aims

- to show how developments in transport have cut travelling times
- to show that technological change leads to developments in transport
- to show how changes in transport can affect the environment.

✪ pupils are to tick correct boxes and interpret a map. ✪✪ includes tick boxes with a table and spider diagram to complete. ✪✪✪ pupils tick correct boxes and complete a table. There is an opportunity for extended writing.

Resources: none required.

Theme 5 Traffic in towns

Aims

- to show that the amount of traffic in towns has increased in recent years
- to show that the growth in traffic in towns has created many problems
- to outline the alternative approaches to easing the problem of traffic in towns.

For the ✪ pupils complete a crossword and match the heads and tails. ✪✪ presents pupils with a spider diagram, a decision making exercise (tick boxes) and a sentence to complete. ✪✪✪ shows a line graph, pupils are to complete a table and sentences.

Resources: none required.

Theme 6 Building a by-pass

Aims

- to show that deciding on a route for a by-pass is never easy
- to show that when a by-pass is built there are 'winners' and 'losers'.

✪ pupils tick boxes and interpret a map. ✪✪ pupils match the heads and tails and complete sentences. ✪✪✪ involves a decision making exercise with a table to complete.

Resources: none required.

Theme 7 The Channel Tunnel

Aim

- to show how the building of the Channel Tunnel has affected travelling to and from the continent.

✪ consists of the 'Transport Game'. ✪✪ pupils complete a paragraph and label a map of Europe. For the ✪✪✪ pupils complete a table and there is an opportunity to justify a decision.

Resources: coloured pencils for ✪✪.

The home region

North-east

Theme 1 The image of a region

Aim

- to show the main features (historical and social) of the region.

✪ pupils decide whether elements of the region are good, bad or neither. ✪✪ pupils match up the heads and tails. ✪✪✪ requires pupils to link cartoons of locations with their descriptions.

Resources: blue and green colours for ✪✪✪.

Theme 2 The climate of the north-east

Aims

- to show the main features of the climate. This can be compared with other areas in the country and relate to the work on British climate in Weather and Climate.

✪ relates brief descriptions of climatic information to particular months, involves climate statistics to help. ✪✪ pupils complete the climate graph. ✪✪✪ pupils complete climate graph and True, False or NEE questions follow.

Resources: coloured pencils.

Theme 3 Changes in employment in the region

Aim

- to demonstrate closure of old established work in coal mines and opening of new factories, particularly Japanese investments in the region.

There are two sheets in this section, ✪ asks pupils to sequence and complete time line showing coalmining. ✪ pupils underline reasons for Nissan locating in the region from the conversation between Mr Newburn and Mr Yokama.

Resources: scissors, glue and coloured pencils.

Theme 4 Places in the region

Aim

- to show location and size of towns and cities in the region.

✪ pupils underline (classify) towns, rivers and counties. They can then tabulate this information. For the ✪✪ sheet pupils place the settlements in the region, based on the map, in rank order of size. ✪✪✪ pupils complete the crossword about towns in the region.

Resources: coloured pencils, an atlas or local map might be useful for ✪✪✪ exercise.

Theme 5 Transport links with the region and other regions

Aim

- to show road, air, rail and sea links with the region.

There are only two worksheets for this section. ✪ pupils use information from the map to answer true, false questions. Additional exercises related to journey times could be done (e.g. ranking journey times, etc.) ✪✪ shows the major roads leading to and from Newcastle and places which can be reached along them. This work could be extended by adding other places along the roads.

Resources: coloured pencils.

Wales

Theme 1 Wales

Aims

- to identify the characteristics of Wales
- to identify the main towns and features of Wales
- to show the importance of Cardiff.

✪ pupils are to label a map of Wales. ✪✪ presents pupils with a wordsearch, sentences to underline and true, false boxes to tick. ✪✪✪ consists of a crossword and a map of Cardiff to label.

Resources: atlas and coloured pencils for ✪.

Theme 2 The climate of Wales

Aims

- to the show the variability in the climate of Wales
- to identify reasons for the variability of the climate of Wales.

✪ requires pupils to complete climate graphs of Cardiff and underline sentences. ✪✪ shows temperature and rainfall maps of Wales with tick box exercises. ✪✪✪ pupils match up the heads and tails, study the cross section of North Wales and complete sentences.

Resources: coloured pencils.

Theme 3 Transport in Wales

Aim

- to show that travelling from North Wales to South Wales is not easy.

There are only two worksheets to this section. ✪✪ is a stimulation exercise, pupils are to tick boxes and complete sentences. ✪✪✪ involves completing a line graph, matching up heads and tails and completing a written exercise.

Resources: none required.

Theme 4 Development in Wales

Aims

- to show how industry in South Wales has developed in recent years
- to show how the Welsh countryside has changed in recent years.

✪ shows comparative maps of industry in South Wales with a table and paragraph to complete. ✪✪ illustrates changes in Welsh countryside by showing comparative diagrams of a farm. Pupils are to complete sentences. ✪✪✪ involves a case study on Sony in Wales with a table and sentences to complete.

Resources: none required.

Greater London

Theme 1 Image of Greater London

Aim

- to give pupils an idea about the image of Greater London.

The materials increase in complexity and use a variety of different skills and puzzles. ✪✪✪ includes some free-response writing.

This work could be extended by using a whole range of resources such as pictures, maps, CD ROM and video. London Underground maps can be obtained and used to plan 'a day out in London'.

Resources: none required.

Theme 2 Climate and landscape of Greater London

Aims

- to recap human and physical features
- to learn that human factors can have more influence on a place than physical factors.

✪ provides the main human and physical features and requires pupils to classify them. ✪✪ involves studying the features on a map. ✪✪✪ requires pupils to classify several features into spaces in a matrix. It would be valid for pupils to work through these sheets from the first to last (or as far as they can).

Resources: blue and red colours for ✪; brown, green, red, dark blue and light blue colours for ✪✪.

Theme 3 The development of Greater London

Aim

- to learn the reasons for the growth and development of London.

These sheets cover slightly different aspects of the development of London: ✪ is concerned with the site and functions whereas ✪✪ studies the physical growth and population and ✪✪✪ gives reasons for and consequences of the growth. They could be used in sequence as far as the individual pupils' abilities allow.

Extension work could compare London's growth with another settlement, perhaps in the home region.

Resources: yellow, orange, red, green, blue and black colours.

Theme 4 Transport in London and the South-east

Aims

- to understand that London has a dense transport network
- to learn that this brings benefits and problems.

✪ studies the benefits and drawbacks of transport at the personal level. ✪✪ uses a map and graph to learn about transport in the area. ✪✪✪ uses higher level reading skills and a word puzzle to practise following instructions.

This work links in with general transport themes such as the Channel Tunnel.

Resources: red and blue colours for ✪. Red, blue, green and black colours for ✪✪✪.

Theme 5 Pressure on the area around Greater London

Aims

- for pupils to learn about the green belt
- to evaluate the advantages and disadvantages of building in the green belt.

The simplest worksheet lists the types of development which may be built in the region; the second investigates the different views of different people towards these. The third requires pupils to judge which kinds of development would be allowed in the green belt.

There is scope here for oral work such as role-playing and for display work.

Resources: green and red colours for ✪✪✪.

Theme 6 Different views on changes in the South-east

Aims

- for pupils to realise that different people have different views
- for pupils to consider their own views on developments.

These materials are concerned with the idea of differing viewpoints at three different levels of complexity. ✪ chooses a theme park and simple reactions to it. ✪✪ looks at the various reactions to a new by-pass. ✪✪✪ requires pupils to work out the sequence of events resulting from the opening of a shopping mall and its wider repercussions.

Extension work could involve the discussion/investigation of a similar issue in the local area.

Resources: none necessary. Scissors and glue optional for ✪✪✪.

Map skills

Theme 1 Direction

Aim

- to learn and practise the principal compass directions.

✪ involves practice of the four cardinal directions. ✪✪ involves north-east, south-east, north-west and south-west as well. ✪✪✪ involves a simple dice game for two players – this is only more difficult in that the pupils will be working more independently and carrying out more activities including addition.

Resources: two dice and two counters for ✪✪✪. It may be advisable to enlarge the 'game-board' to A4 size.

Theme 2 Scale

Aims

- for pupils to understand the concept of scale
- to practise using a simple linear scale.

✪ introduces the idea of drawing a map at a larger scale and some very simple measuring. ✪✪ requires pupils to follow instructions and plot a route using the scale-line. ✪✪✪ involves more complex measuring and adding a simple scale drawing.

The work might be extended by taking measurements (e.g. of the room) and drawing a scale-plan.

Resources: a ruler will be useful, especially for ✪✪✪.

Theme 3 Symbols

Aim

- to introduce the concept of map symbols.

The worksheets are graded in length and difficulty from chiefly reading the symbols on ✪ to following instructions and plotting symbols on ✪✪✪.

The work could be extended by asking pupils to produce their own map. An 'old' treasure map is always popular, giving scope for the paper to be crumpled, stained with tea-bags and singed around the edges!

Resources: blue and red colours on ✪; a variety of colours for ✪✪ and ✪✪✪ will make the finished maps clearer.

Theme 4 Four figure grid references

Aim

- for pupils to understand and practise the use of four figure grid references.

It is intended that the teacher will undertake the initial explanation of the technique as it would be too lengthy to explain on a worksheet of this type. Many teachers explain the idea using the board or an O.H.P. and then use oral questioning around the class. These activities vary in the amount of practice they afford rather than in the difficulty of the exercises, as once the technique is understood it is understood! Many pupils find satisfaction in undertaking and completing quite a lengthy task if the skill is well-understood.

The work could be extended with a variety of questions based around map extracts. Pupils enjoy making up their own coded messages using the grid on ✪✪.

Resources: orange, brown, yellow, red and green colours for ✪✪✪.

Theme 5 Six figure grid references

Aim

- for pupils to understand and practise using six figure grid references.

Again, it is intended that the teacher explains the technique first. As with the four figure grid references, these activities are designed as a 'fun' way of practising the skill. Pupils do not find difficulty in transferring this to a map extract. Maps have been avoided here as they are too cluttered with detail. It is intended that the pupils will apply the technique to the particular maps available in class.

The activities progress in length rather than in difficulty, as with the four figure grid reference materials.

Remind the pupils to count the lines not the spaces on ✪✪ and ✪✪✪.

Again, extension exercises involving map extracts are available in many other books.

Resources: a clear plastic ruler is very useful to enable pupils to plot the points accurately.

Theme 6 Height on maps

Aim

- for pupils to understand how height may be shown on a flat map.

✪ involves spot-heights and layer colouring only. ✪✪ introduces the idea of contours. ✪✪✪ requires pupils to draw contour lines.

Resources: blue, light green, dark green, yellow, orange and brown colours.

Theme 7 Contours

Aim

- for pupils to learn how contours may be used to show height and relief.

✪ concentrates on how contours show steep or gentle slopes. ✪✪ introduces the way different contour patterns show different landforms. This is studied in a more abstract form on ✪✪✪. Some pupils with low writing skills can visualise contours well.

This work could be extended by the use of O.S. map extracts to study relief.

Resources: dark green and light green colours for ✪. Scissors and glue for ✪✪✪.

Theme 8 Describing routes on maps

Aim

- for pupils to be able to follow and give route directions on maps.

These activities use very simple maps with most of the irrelevant and therefore confusing detail removed. They each involve visualising moving along increasingly complex routes on maps and the ✪✪✪ activities involve writing directions.

Resources: none required.

In this activity you will learn what geography is about

Geography is about the world around us.

- **Human geography** is about things which have been made by people, such as roads.
- **Physical geography** is about natural things such as rivers. These things were **not** made by people.

Activity

Use the words in the Word box to label the picture below.

Word box

sea • lake • shop • river
farm • sun • airport
bridge • cliff • road

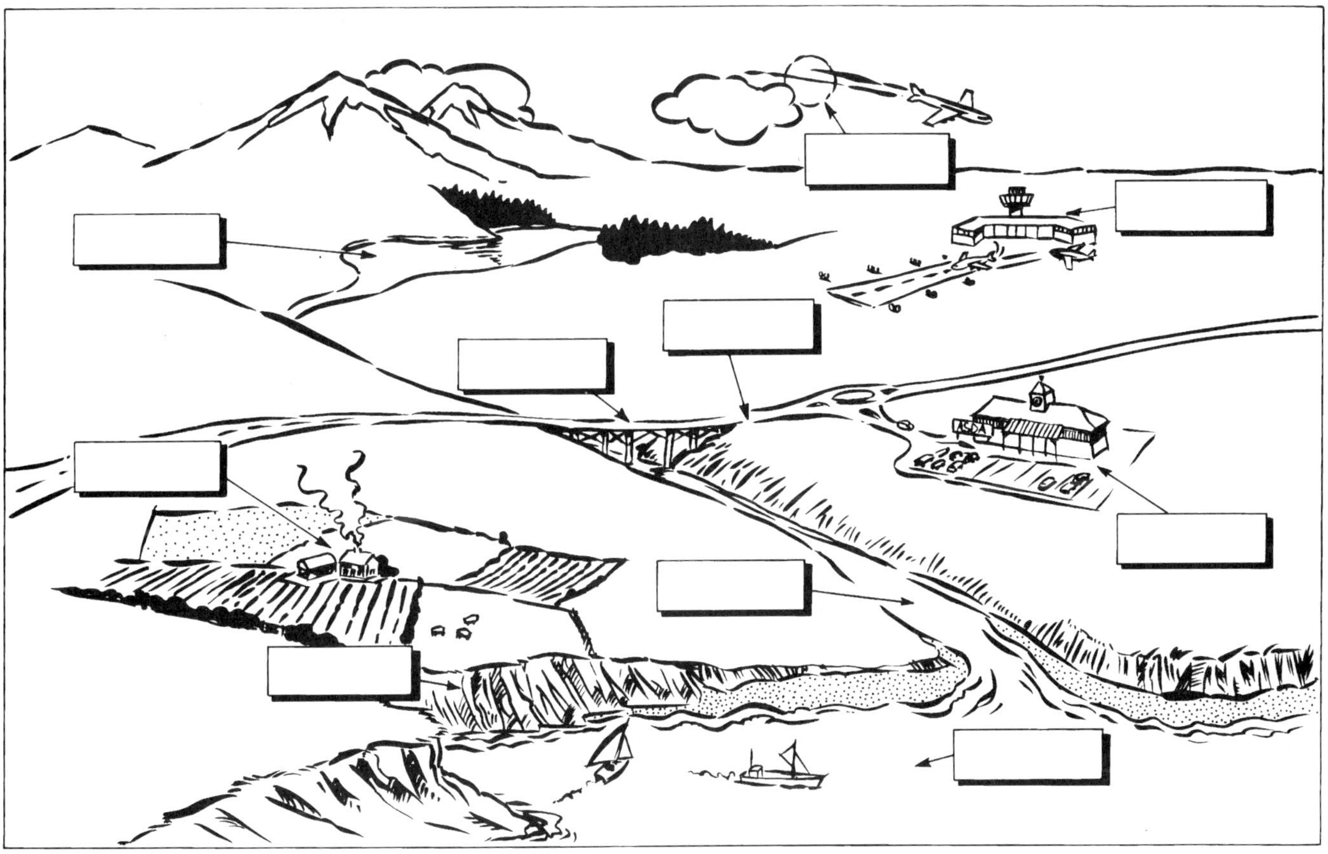

Recap *Human geography* is about ______________________________

____

Physical geography is about ______________________________

____

In this activity you will learn what geography is about

Geography is about the world around us.

- **Human geography** is about things which have been made by people, such as roads and towns.
- **Physical geography** is about natural things such as rivers and the weather. These things were **not** made by people.

Activities

1 Use the words in the Word box to label the picture below.

Word box

sea • lake • shop • river • farm • beach • airport
bridge • cliff • road • railway • factory • village • forest
motorway • clouds • church • volcano • mountain • sun

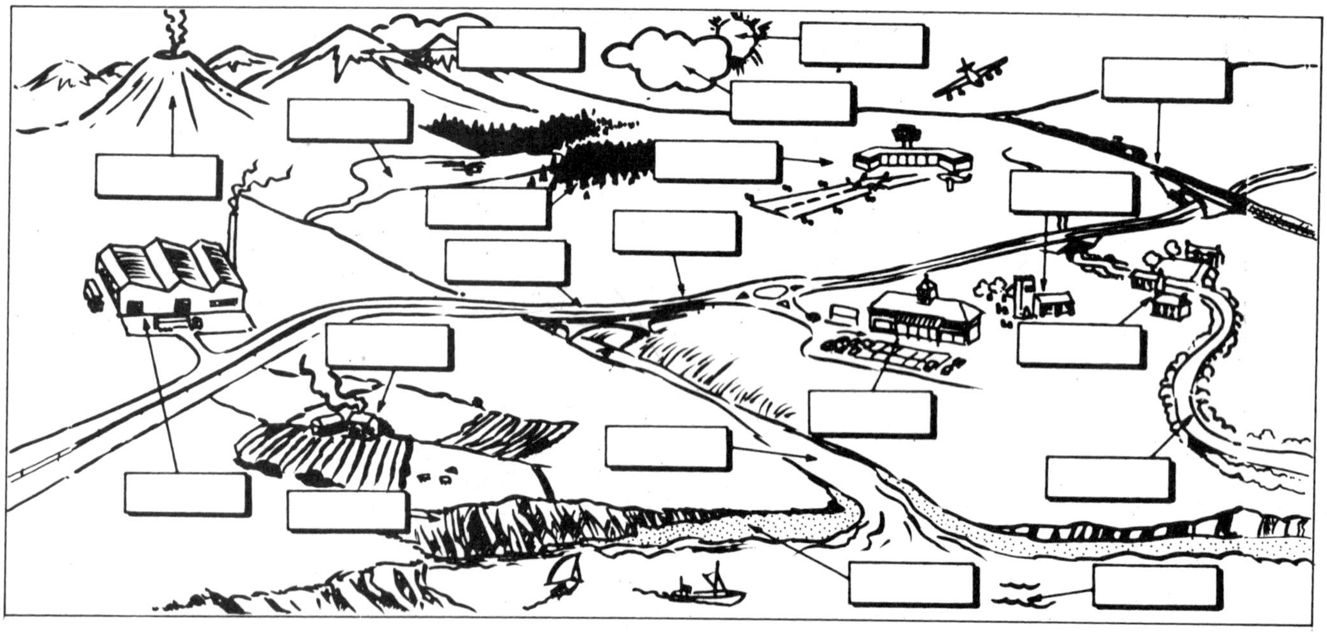

2 Colour the labels to do with **human geography** in **red**.

3 Colour the labels to do with **physical geography** in **blue**.

4 Think about your trip to school in the morning. Name **five human** features, and **five physical** features which you pass.

Recap Human geography *is about* ______________________________

____

Physical geography *is about* ______________________________

____

In this activity you will learn about the environment

The **environment** is everything around where we live.

- The **human environment** includes towns, roads and factories.
- The **physical environment** includes land, weather and soil.

Activities

1 Draw lines to join up the 'heads' on the left, and 'tails' on the right below.

Smoke from factories	by cars and lorries
Fumes given off	can kill fish
New houses	spoils the air
Dirty rivers	are built on farmland
Litter is dropped	spoils the peace and quiet
Traffic noise	on streets and beaches

2 Complete the following sentence by filling in the gap with **improve** or **spoil**

All these things ______________________ the environment.

3 Now draw lines to join up these 'heads' on the left, and 'tails' on the right.

Planting trees	helps fish
Nature reserves	are homes for animals
Cleaning up rivers	stops oil being used up
Saving energy	factories making pollution
Laws stop	improves the view

4 Complete the following sentence by filling in the gap with **improve** or **spoil**.

All these things ______________________ the environment.

Recap *The* ***environment*** *is* ____.

It can be ***sp*** ____________ *or* ***im*** ____________________.

In this activity you will learn about the environment

The **environment** is everything surrounding where we live.

- The **human environment** includes towns, roads and factories.
- The **physical environment** includes land, rivers, weather and soil.

Activities

1 Complete the crossword by filling the gaps in the sentences below.

_ _ E _	Planting trees improves the **v**______.
_ _ _ N _ _ _ _	**P**__________ trees improves the view.
_ _ V _ _ _	Dirty **r**______ can kill fish.
_ _ I _ _	New houses are **b**______ on farmland.
_ R _ _ _	**T**_____ are cut down.
_ _ _ _ O _	Using lead-free **p**_________ is better.
N _ _ _ _	Traffic **n**________ spoils the peace.
_ M _ _ _	Pass laws to ban **s**_____ from factories.
_ _ _ _ E _	People drop **l**__________ on the streets.
N _ _ _ _ _	**N**_________ reserves protect wildlife.
_ _ _ _ _ T _ _ _	Smoke and waste are **p**____________.

2 Colour the wordboxes in the crossword which **spoil** the environment in **red**, and the wordboxes which **improve** the environment in **green**.

Recap

The ***environment*** *is* __________________________________ .

People can ***s***___________ *it or* ***i***______________ *it.*

In this activity you will learn about the environment

The **environment** is everything surrounding where people, plants and animals live.

- The **human environment** includes towns, roads and factories.
- The **physical environment** includes land, rivers, weather and soil.
- The environment includes **resources**. These are things which people **use** such as coal, forests and water.

Activities

1 Fill in the gaps in the paragraph below:

People can harm the environment in many ways. They **cut** down t______ which lets the rain wash away the **soil**. **Smoke** from factories pollutes the a______, and factory waste in rivers **kills** f_______. **Oil** in the s_______, and **litter** can spoil beaches. We build new **roads** which destroy farmland and sp_______ the **view** of the **landscape**. People may drain a **pond** where fish live. **Car** fumes pollute the air in tow____. We are destroying the **ozone** layer. We can improve the en____________ by using lead-free **petrol**, cleaning up **rivers**, making **nature** reserves, and being sure to **plant** more trees than we c_______ down.

2 Colour the words shown in **bold** in the paragraph above in the wordsearch below.

L	O	R	T	E	P	P	R	R
A	O	Z	T	L	S	O	O	A
N	E	W	O	L	I	A	N	C
D	C	E	L	N	D	O	T	D
S	O	I	I	S	E	I	S	E
C	K	V	T	N	A	L	P	K
A	N	A	T	U	R	E	U	O
P	R	P	E	L	C	A	N	M
E	E	T	R	I	V	E	R	S

Things where the environment is **destroyed** go **diagonally**.

Things where the environment is **spoiled** go **up** or **down**.

Things where the environment is **improved** go **across**.

3 Write the letters which you have **not** coloured in the wordsearch in the spaces below. (Go from left to right from the top line of the square.)

_ _ _ _ _ _ _ _   _ _ _   _ _ _ _ _ _ _ .

Do you agree?

Recap *The* ***environment*** *is* ______________________________________.

People can ***s***____________ *it or* ***i***________________ *it.*

In this activity you will learn how to describe places

In geography we study **places**. We can show what a place is like by using a simple **drawing** and adding **labels**.

Activities

1 Here is a drawing of Niagara Falls in Canada. Complete the passage below by using the words from the drawing to fill in the gaps.

There is a very **w**______ **r**_________ which goes over two big **w**________________. The waterfalls make a **c**_________ **o**_________ **s**________. There is an **i**_________ with **t**_________on it between the waterfalls. A tourist **b**_________ is sailing in the river. In the background there is a large **t**_________ on the banks of the river. There is a **r**_________ with **c**_________ near a small **p**_________at the front of the picture.

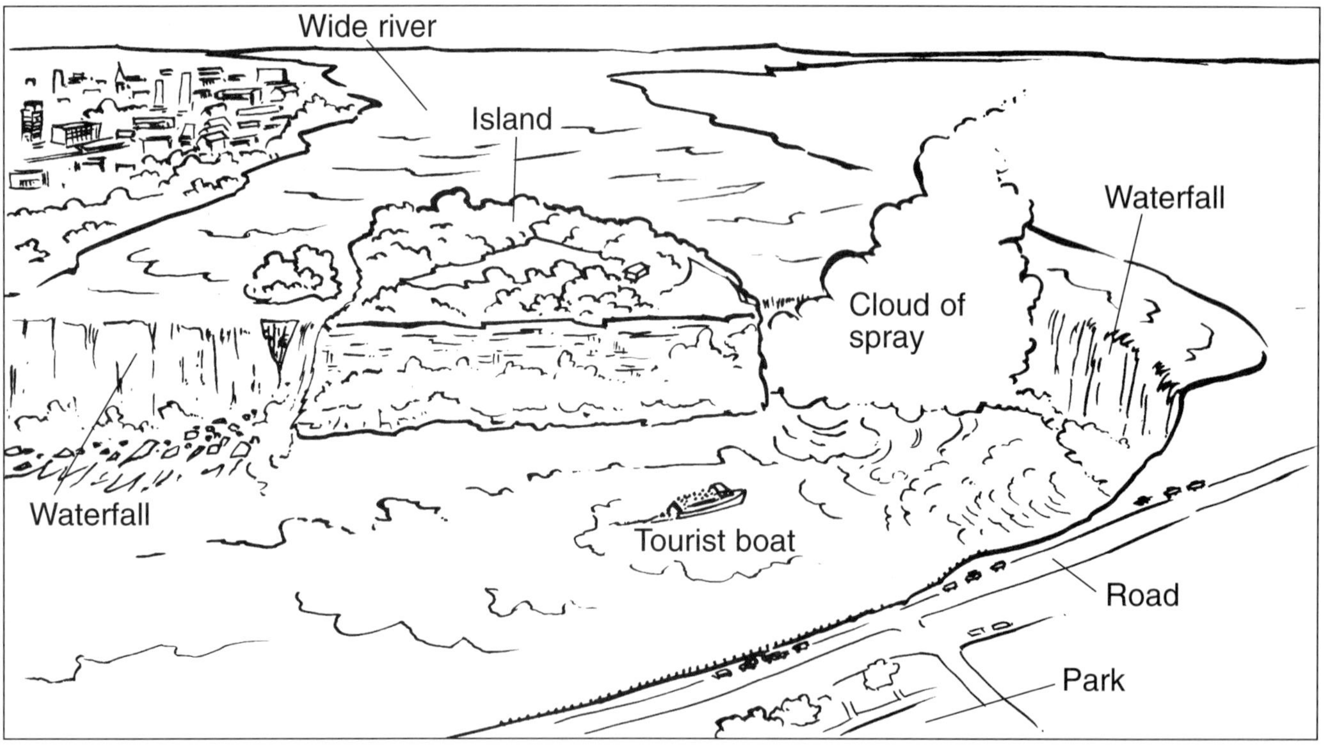

2 Colour the drawing to make it clearer.

Recap *We can show what a place is like by* ______________________________

____

In this activity you will learn how to describe places

In geography we study **places**. We can show what a place is like by using a simple **drawing** and adding **labels**. This is called a **fieldsketch**.

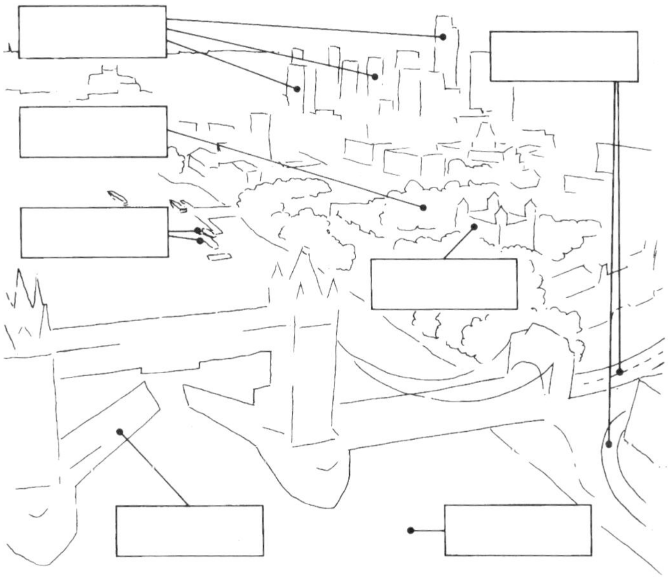

Activities

1 Here is a photograph of part of London. Complete the fieldsketch by going over the faint lines.

2 Use the words in the Word box to label your fieldsketch.

> **Word box**
>
> grass and trees • wide river • castle • bridge
> tall office blocks • boats • roads

3 Complete the gaps in the paragraph below to describe the photograph. Use the words from the labels on the fieldsketch.

This is a big city. There are many **t**_______ **o**_______ **b**_______ and a **w**_______ _______ with a **b**_______ across it. Near the bridge is a **c**_______ with **g**_______ and _______ around it. There are many **r**_______ with traffic, and **b**_______ on the river.

4 Colour the fieldsketch to make it clearer.

Recap *We can show what a place is like by ______________________________*

____.

This is called a ______________________________.

In this activity you will learn how to describe places

In geography we study **places**. We can show what a place is like by drawing a **fieldsketch**. This is a simple drawing which shows important features by **labels**. A fieldsketch is used to **describe** places.

Activities

1 Here is a photograph of a flooded village.

Complete the fieldsketch next to it. It has been started for you.

2 Use the words in the Word box to label your fieldsketch. One has been done for you:

Word box

metal roof • palm trees • people on the roof
flooded garden • floodwater • metal walls

3 Complete these three sentences to describe the photograph.

In the distance there are ______________________________

____

The land in the photograph has been ______________________________

____

The people are on the roof because ______________________________

____

4 Colour the fieldsketch to make it clearer.

Recap A **fieldsketch** is ______________________________

____

A fieldsketch is used to ***des***______________________________

In this activity you will learn about plans and maps

A **plan** is a picture of something seen from above. Plans show things smaller than in real life.

Maps show **places** seen from above, and also show things smaller than in real life.

Activities

1 Here are some pictures with plans next to them. Tick any which you think is a true plan of the picture.

Picture	**Plan**	✓	✗

2 Draw lines to match up each picture below with the correct plan.

Recap

A ***plan*** *is* ______________________________

A ***map*** *shows* ______________________________

In this activity you will learn about plans and maps

A **plan** is a picture of something seen from above. Plans show things smaller than in real life.

Maps show **places** seen from above, and also show things smaller than in real life.

Activities

1 The plan below shows a haunted house.

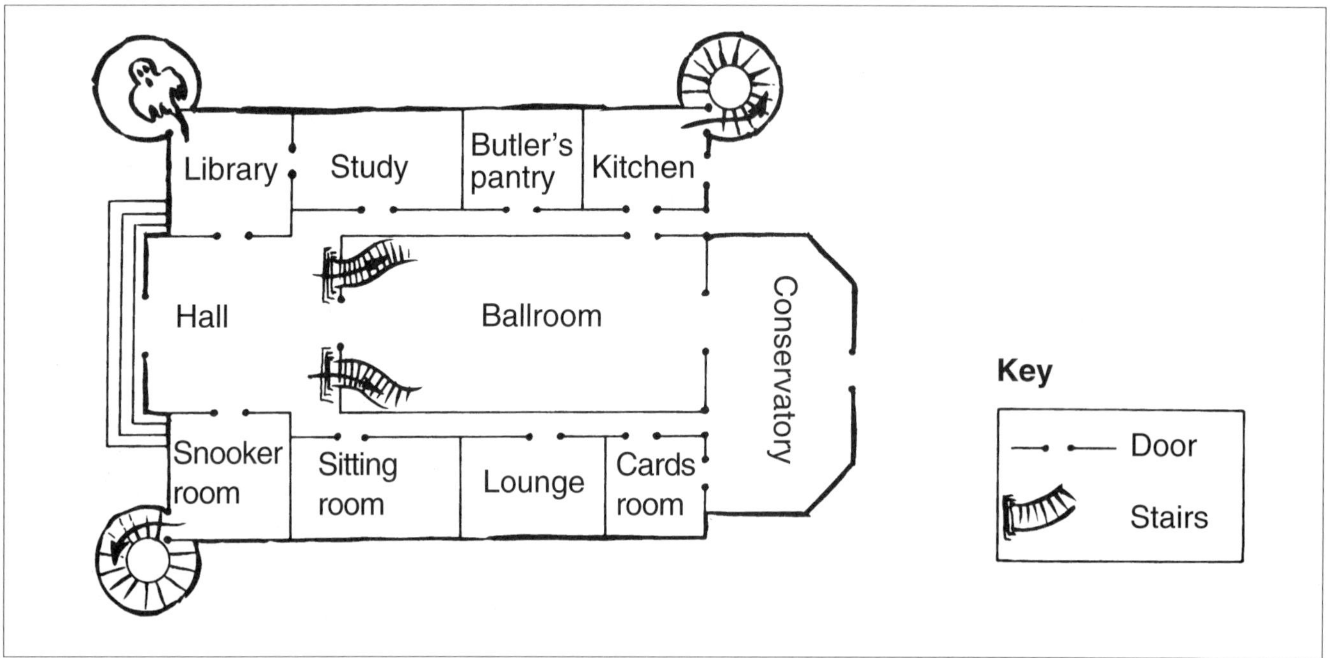

Underline the correct word in brackets in the following sentences.

- The biggest room is the (**Ballroom/Snooker Room**).
- The Hall leads to the (**Library/Sitting Room**).
- The servants' rooms are off the (**Butler's Pantry/Kitchen**).
- There are (**three/four**) doors into the Conservatory.
- The Study is between the Butler's Pantry and the (**Hall/Library**).
- The stairs go up from the (**Ballroom/Hall**).
- There are (**two/four**) staircases.
- The ghost is in the (**Cards Room/Library**).
- Going from the Hall to the Kitchen the Study is on the (**left/right**).

2 Colour the **smallest** room in **red**.
Colour the rooms with only **one** door in **yellow**.
Colour the **square** rooms in **blue**.

Recap A **plan** is ______________________________

A **map** shows ______________________________

In this activity you will learn about maps

Maps show **places** seen from above, and show things smaller than in real life.

Activities

1 Look at the picture and map below. They show the **same** place.
Match the names on the picture with correct places on the map. Label the map using the letters in the key.

2 Colour the map using the colours given in the key.

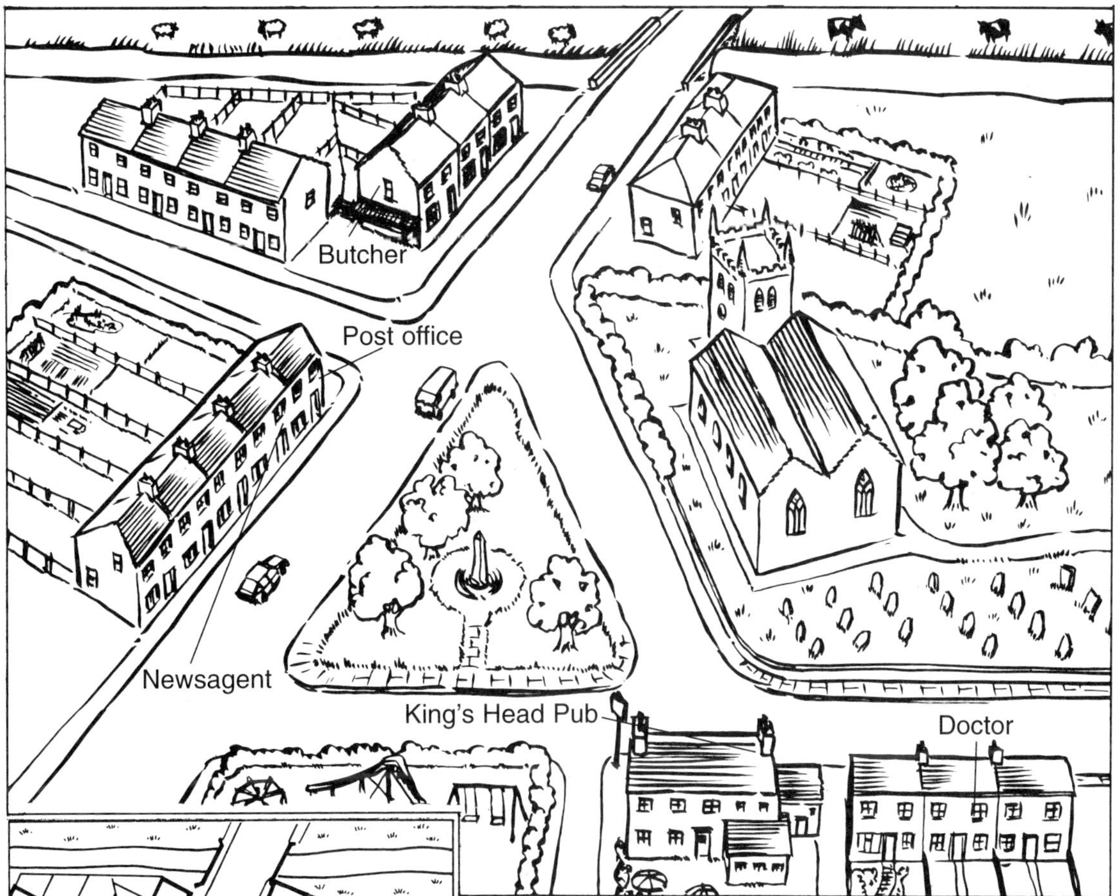

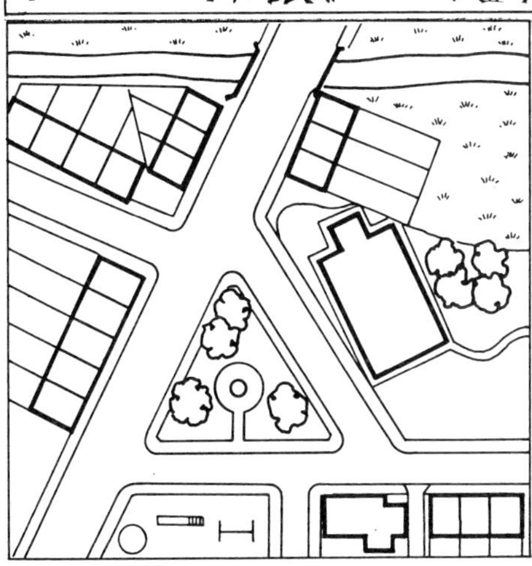

Key for map		**Colours for map**	
Kings Head Pub	**P**	Grass	**light green**
Butcher	**B**	Trees	**dark green**
Post Office	**PO**	Buildings	**red**
Doctor	**D**	Roads	**grey**
Newsagent	**N**	River	**blue**
Church	**CH**	Playground	**orange**
		Gardens	**yellow**

Recap A **map** shows ____

____

In this activity you will learn about latitude and longitude

The world is shaped like a **ball**. A **globe** is a map of the world. We can find out where places are in the world by using lines of **latitude** and **longitude**.

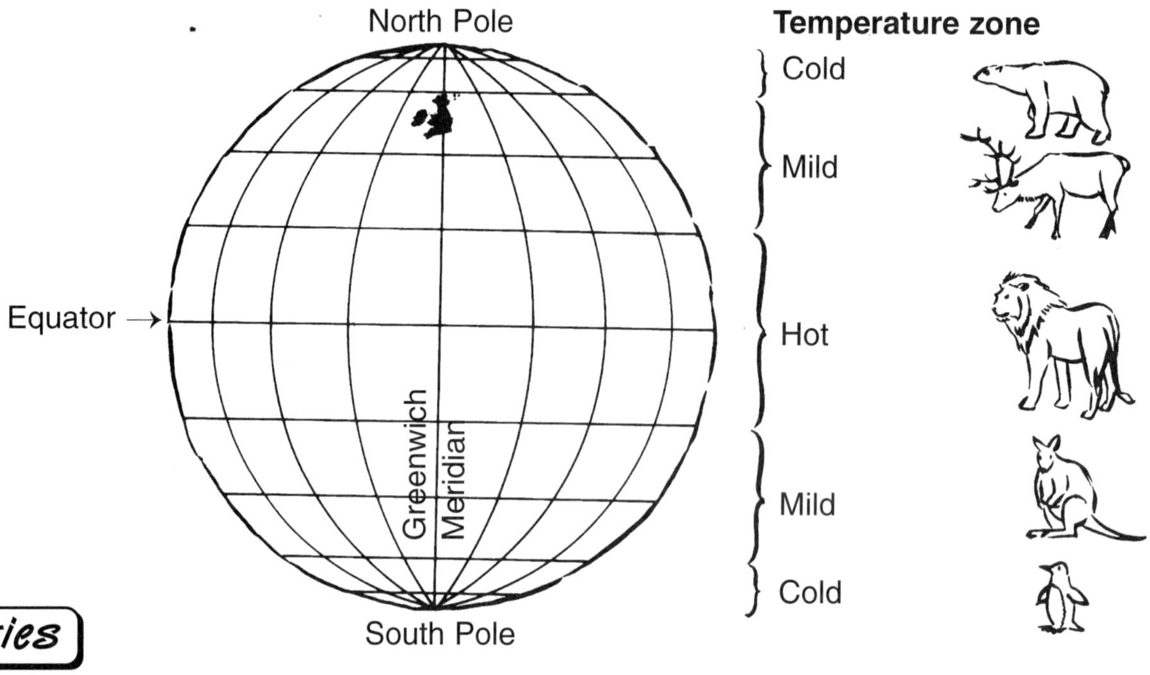

Activities

1 Look at the diagram above.

- Go over the **Equator** line in **purple**.
- Go over the other lines of **latitude** in **dark blue**.
- Go over the lines of **longitude** in **green**.
- Put a cross like this: ✗ where the **Equator** crosses the **Greenwich Meridian**.
- Shade the **hot** part of the world in **red.**
- Shade the **cold** parts of the world in **blue**.
- Shade the **mild** parts of the world in **yellow**.
- Underline which part of the world we live in, **hot**, **cold** or **mild**.
- Mark **London** on the diagram.

2 Fill in the gaps in the sentences below.

Lines of **latitude** go from side to **s**________. They tell us if a place is **n**________ or **s**________ of the **E**________________. Lines of **longitude** go up and **d**________. They tell us if a place is **e**________ or **w**________ of **London**.

Recap *Lines of* ***l***________________ *and* ***l***________________ *tell us where places are in the world.*

In this activity you will learn about latitude and longitude

We can find out where places are in the world by using lines of **latitude** and **longitude**.

Activities

1 Look at the world map below. Add the following labels in the correct places.

London **Latitude** **Longitude**

2 Go over the **Equator** line in **red** and the **Greenwich Meridian** line in **blue**.

- An **earthquake** is happening at **40° North, 40° East**. Mark this on the map with ✳.
- A **ship** is sinking at **20° South, 180° East**. Mark this on the map with ▼.
- An **alien rocket** has crashed at **60° North, 100° West**. Mark this on the map with ☆.

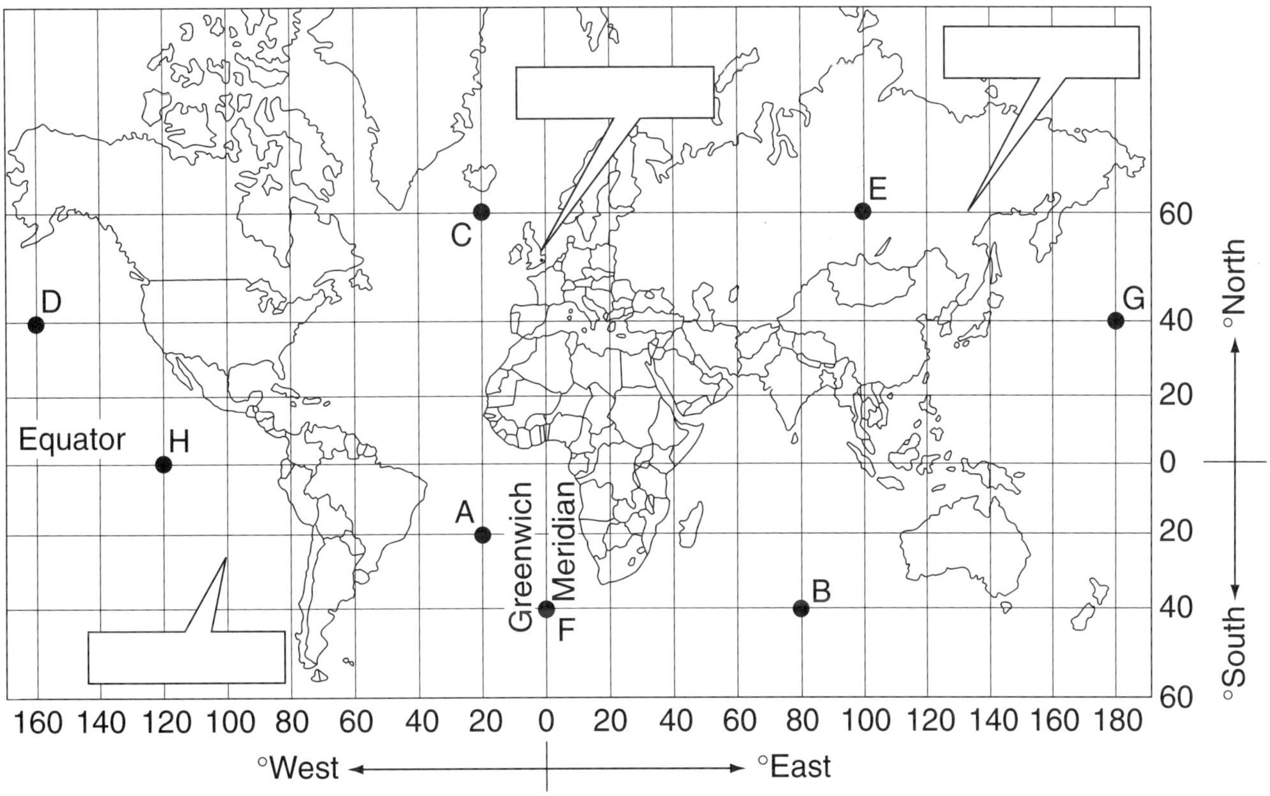

3 Complete the table below using the map to help you. The first one has been done for you.

Latitude	20°S	60°N	40°N	40°S			40°N	
Longitude	20°W	20°W	160°W	80°E	100°E	0°		120°W
Letter	**A**				**E**	**F**	**G**	**H**

Recap *Lines of* **l**_________ *and* **l**_________ *tell us where places are in the world. An important line of latitude is the* **E**_________.

In this activity you will learn about latitude and longitude

We can find out where places are in the world by using lines of **latitude** and **longitude**. Lines of **latitude** go across the world from **east** to **west**. Lines of **longitude** go from **north** to **south**.

A **map** of the world can be shown **flat** like the ones in an atlas, or like the one on the accompanying sheet.

We can make this into a **globe**. A globe is an accurate map of the world, shaped like a ball.

Activities

1 On the map on the accompanying sheet:

- Go over the **Equator** in **red**.
- Go over the **Greenwich Meridian** in **purple**.
- Go over the **Tropic of Cancer**, and the **Tropic of Capricorn**, in **orange**.
- Go over the **International Dateline** in **brown**.

2 Label the following continents in the correct boxes.

EUROPE ASIA AFRICA NORTH AMERICA SOUTH AMERICA AUSTRALASIA

3 Label the following oceans in the correct boxes.

ATLANTIC OCEAN PACIFIC OCEAN INDIAN OCEAN

4 Colour the **land** in **green**, and the **sea** in **blue**.

5 Instructions for making your globe:

- **Cut out** the 'globe' around the thick **cutting line**.
- **Fold down** all the **flaps**.
- **Stick Flap A** under **Side A**, **Flap B** under **Side B** and so on to complete the northern half of the world.
- Now you can **pad** the inside with **tissues** to make it more solid.
- Finally, **stick** the flaps around the **South Pole**.

Recap *Lines of l__________________ and l__________________ tell us where places are in the world. An important line of latitude is the E______________.*

In this activity you will learn about latitude and longitude

In this activity you will learn about graphs

In geography we **measure** things in order to **describe** them.

We can show these measurements on **graphs**.

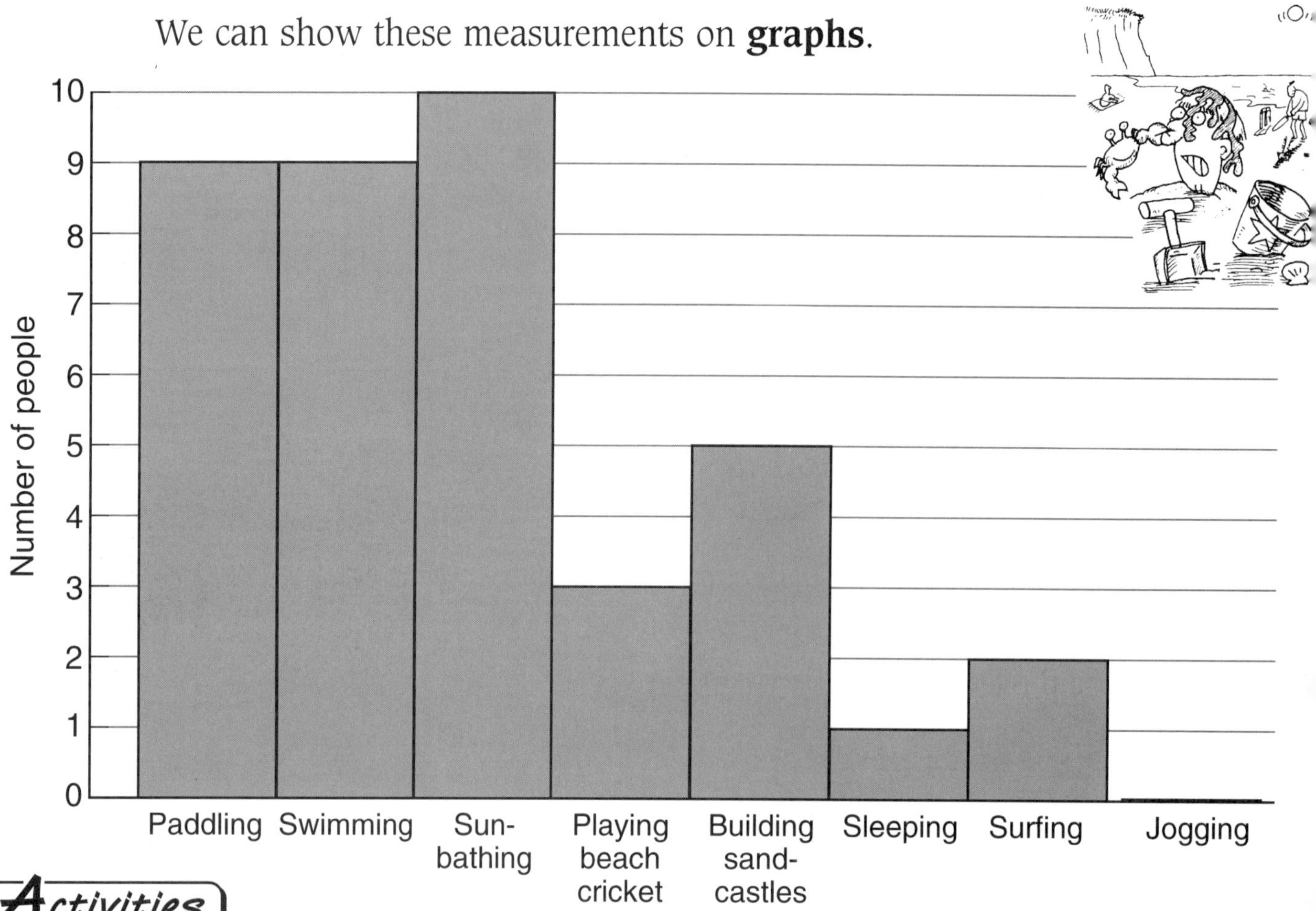

Activities

1 Look at the graph above which shows what people are doing on Seaweed Beach.

Circle the correct answer to the following questions.

- How many people are sunbathing? **12 11 10 9**
- How many people are surfing? **10 8 6 4 2**
- Two people are **surfing paddling sleeping swimming**.
- The most popular activity is **beach cricket sunbathing paddling building sand-castles swimming**.
- How many people are in (or on!) the water? **20 22 24**

2 Four people are **jogging**. Add the bar to the graph to show them.

Recap *Graphs are used in geography to* ***sh*** ________ *things which we* ***m*** ________.

In this activity you will learn how to describe the weather

To describe the weather we can talk about **temperature**, **rainfall**, **wind**, **cloud** and **sunshine**, and **visibility**.

Activities

1 Draw a line from each word in the circle below to the correct picture.

2 Draw a circle round each word below that describes today's weather.

Wind

Temperature

Rainfall

Raining
Calm
Mild
Dry
Misty
Sunny
Gales
Cloudy
Drizzling
Wet
Windy
Foggy
Hot
Cold

Visibility

Cloud and sun

Recap *When we describe the weather we can talk about* ***visibility, cloud*** *and* ***sunshine, r***____________, ***w***____________ *and* ***t***____________________.

In this activity you will learn how to describe the weather

To describe the weather we can talk about **temperature**, **rainfall**, **wind**, **cloud** and **sunshine**, and **visibility**.

Activities

1 Write **three** words from the Word box against the correct picture and title on the star diagram to describe the weather. One has been done for you.

Wind

1
2
3

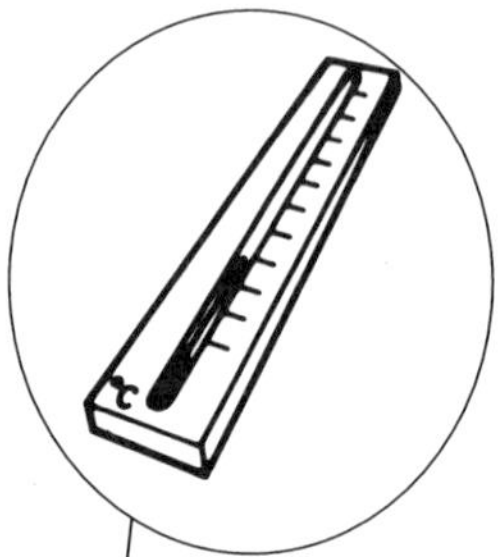

Temperature

1
2
3

Cloud and sun

1
2
3

What is the weather like?

Rainfall

1 Wet
2
3

Visibility

1
2
3

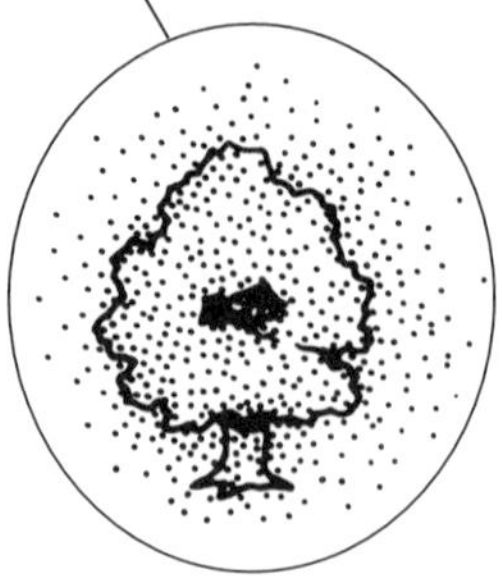

2 Look at the weather today. Look at the words on your star diagram. Colour the boxes of the ones which describe the weather today.

3 Write a description of the weather today. Say something about each of the things in the star diagram.

Word box

Calm •	Cool •	Hot
Sunny •	Clear •	Dry
Misty •	~~Wet~~ •	Cloudy
Foggy •	Snow •	Windy
Cold •	Gale •	Some

Recap *To describe the weather we can talk about* **t**________________,
cloud *and* **sun, w**__________, **v**__________ *and* **r**____________.

In this activity you will learn how to describe the weather

To describe the weather we can talk about **temperature**, **rainfall**, **wind**, **cloud** and **sunshine**, and **visibility**.

Activities

1 Do the word game below. This is how to do it.

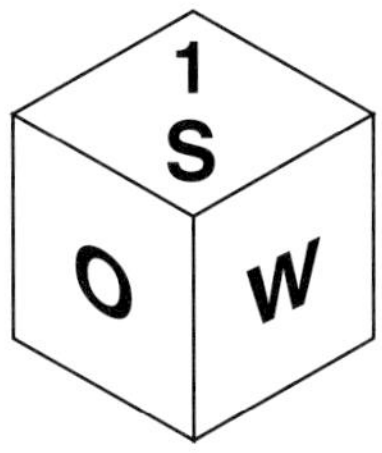

Clue: Cold material falling from the sky (4) **Answer: Snow**

Top letter starts the word **Right hand** letter ends the word
Left hand letter is another letter in the word
Fill in the answers at the bottom of the page.

2 Shade the boxes that are about **rainfall** in **blue.**

3 Shade the boxes that are about **temperature** in **red.**

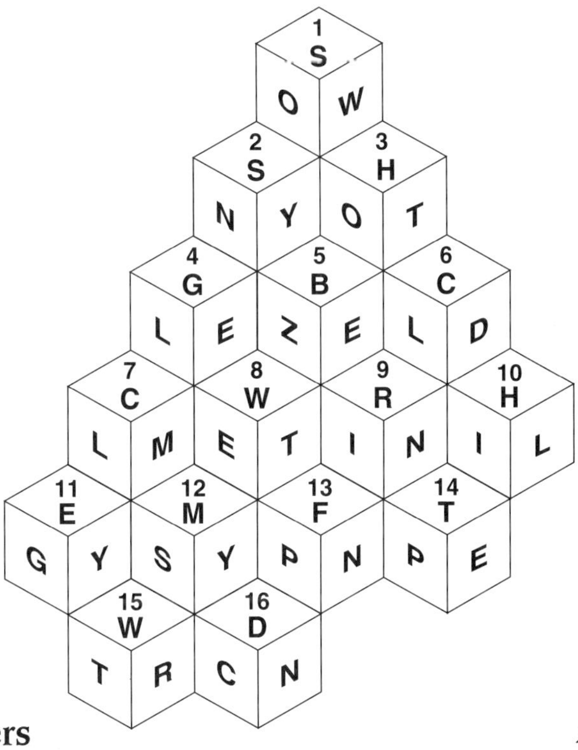

Clues

1 Cold material falling from the sky (4)
2 Could get a sun tan (5)
3 High temperature (3)
4 Strong wind (4)
5 Weak wind (6)
6 Low temperature (4)
7 No wind (4)
8 A lot of rain (3)
9 Wet material falling from the sky (4)
10 Hard material falling from the sky (4)
11 Thick pea soup. Low cloud (5)
12 Cannot see far, but not foggy (5)
13 Rain, snow, hail, sleet, dew (13)
14 How hot or cold a place is (11)
15 _____ forecast. On the News (7)
16 Wind _____ where the wind comes from (9)

Answers

1 *snow* ______
2 ______
3 ______
4 ______
5 ______
6 ______
7 ______
8 ______

Answers

9 ______
10 ______
11 ______
12 ______
13 ______
14 ______
15 ______
16 ______

Recap *To describe the weather we can talk about* ***rainfall, t**______,* ***visibility, sunshine*** *and* ***cl**______ and* ***w**______.*

You can keep a weather diary on this sheet by ticking a box in each section

Weather diary

Tick the right boxes to describe the weather today.

Date ______

Temperature		**Rainfall**		**Cloud/sun**		**Wind**		**Visibility**	
Hot	☐	Wet	☐	Cloudy	☐	Calm	☐	Clear	☐
Cool	☐	Dry	☐	Some cloud	☐	Windy	☐	Misty	☐
Cold	☐	Snow	☐	Sunny	☐	Gale	☐	Foggy	☐

What is the weather like today? ______

Draw a smiling face or a frowning face

Weather diary

Tick the right boxes to describe the weather today.

Date ______

Temperature		**Rainfall**		**Cloud/sun**		**Wind**		**Visibility**	
Hot	☐	Wet	☐	Cloudy	☐	Calm	☐	Clear	☐
Cool	☐	Dry	☐	Some cloud	☐	Windy	☐	Misty	☐
Cold	☐	Snow	☐	Sunny	☐	Gale	☐	Foggy	☐

What is the weather like today? ______

Draw a smiling face or a frowning face

Weather diary

Tick the right boxes to describe the weather today.

Date ______

Temperature		**Rainfall**		**Cloud/sun**		**Wind**		**Visibility**	
Hot	☐	Wet	☐	Cloudy	☐	Calm	☐	Clear	☐
Cool	☐	Dry	☐	Some cloud	☐	Windy	☐	Misty	☐
Cold	☐	Snow	☐	Sunny	☐	Gale	☐	Foggy	☐

What is the weather like today? ______

Draw a smiling face or a frowning face

Weather diary

Tick the right boxes to describe the weather today.

Date ______

Temperature		**Rainfall**		**Cloud/sun**		**Wind**		**Visibility**	
Hot	☐	Wet	☐	Cloudy	☐	Calm	☐	Clear	☐
Cool	☐	Dry	☐	Some cloud	☐	Windy	☐	Misty	☐
Cold	☐	Snow	☐	Sunny	☐	Gale	☐	Foggy	☐

What is the weather like today? ______

Draw a smiling face or a frowning face

Weather diary

Tick the right boxes to describe the weather today.

Date ______

Temperature		**Rainfall**		**Cloud/sun**		**Wind**		**Visibility**	
Hot	☐	Wet	☐	Cloudy	☐	Calm	☐	Clear	☐
Cool	☐	Dry	☐	Some cloud	☐	Windy	☐	Misty	☐
Cold	☐	Snow	☐	Sunny	☐	Gale	☐	Foggy	☐

What is the weather like today? ______

Draw a smiling face or a frowning face

Weather diary

Tick the right boxes to describe the weather today.

Date ______

Temperature		**Rainfall**		**Cloud/sun**		**Wind**		**Visibility**	
Hot	☐	Wet	☐	Cloudy	☐	Calm	☐	Clear	☐
Cool	☐	Dry	☐	Some cloud	☐	Windy	☐	Misty	☐
Cold	☐	Snow	☐	Sunny	☐	Gale	☐	Foggy	☐

What is the weather like today? ______

Draw a smiling face or a frowning face

In this activity you will learn about the climate of Britain

Britain is a small place but the weather here varies a lot from place to place. The west is wet, the north is cool and the south is warm.

Activity

Match each picture to a description by drawing a line between them. One has been done for you.

The west side of Britain has most mountains

The south of Britain is warmest

The west of Britain is wet

The east side of Britain is mostly flat

The east of Britain is not very wet

The north of Britain is coldest

Recap

The west side of Britain is mountainous and **w**____________. The east side of Britain is **f**____________ and dry. The north is **c**__________ and the south is **w**____________.

In this activity you will learn about the climate of Britain

Britain is a small place but the weather here varies a lot from place to place. The west is wet, the north is cool and the south is warm.

Activities

1 On **Map 1** shade the **warm** part of Britain in **red**.

2 On **Map 2** shade the **wet** part of Britain in **blue**.

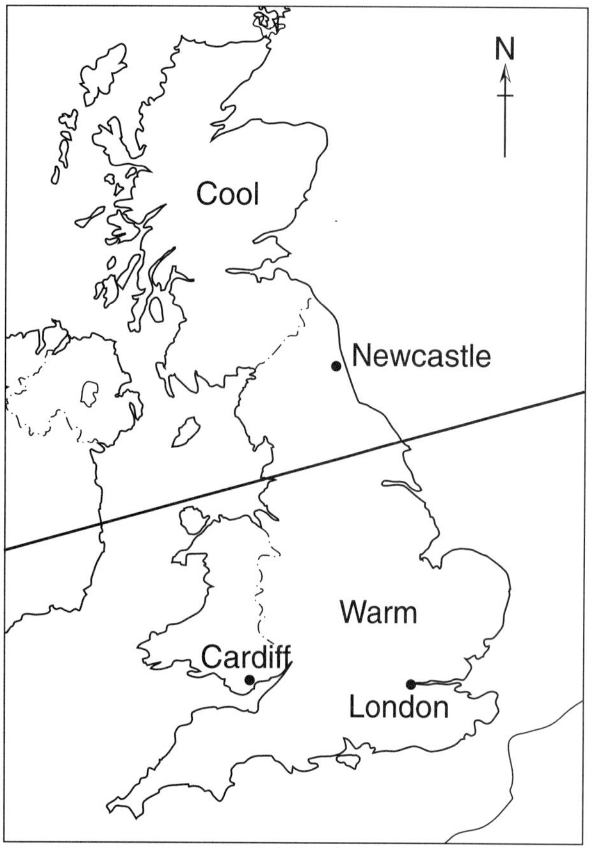

Map 1 Britain's temperature

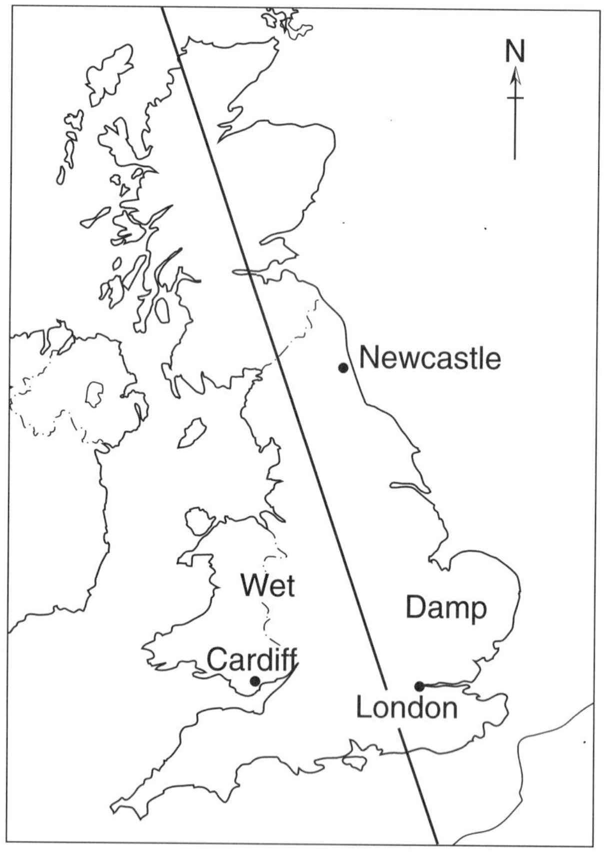

Map 2 Britain's rainfall

3 Draw lines to join up the 'heads' on the left and the 'tails' on the right below. One has been done for you.

The north is cooler	wetter than the east
The west is	than Cardiff
Cardiff is	than the south
London is drier	warmer than Newcastle

Recap *In Britain the north is cooler than the* ***s***__________*, and the west is wetter than the* ***e***__________*. This tells us about the climate of Britain.*

In this activity you will learn about the climate of Britain

Britain is a small place but the weather here varies a lot from place to place. The west is wet, the north is cool and the south is warm.

Activities

1 Choose **three** different colours and shade the **three** parts of Britain on **Map 1**.

2 Choose **two** colours and shade the **two** parts of Britain on **Map 2**.

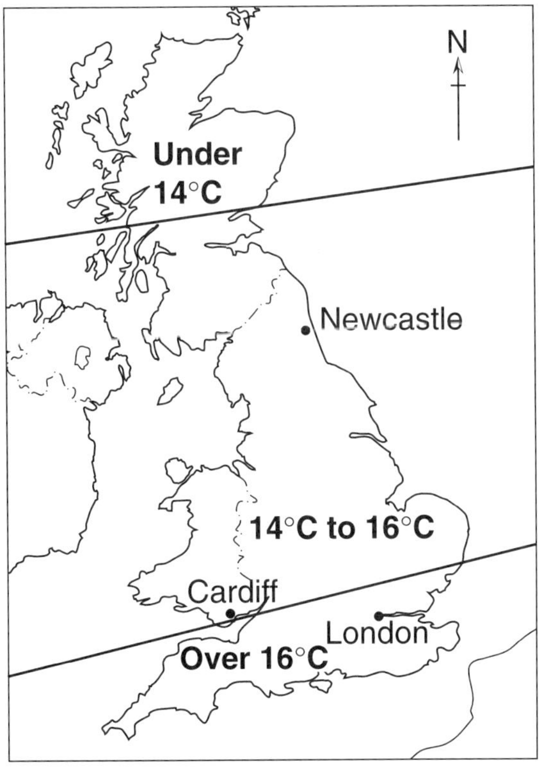

Map 1 Britain's summer temperature

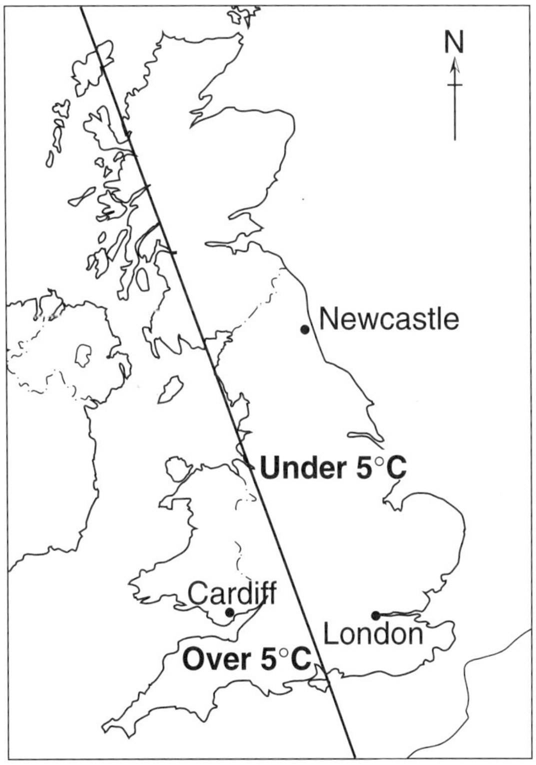

Map 2 Britain's winter temperature

3 Tick **true**, **false** or **not enough evidence** next to each statement in the table below.

	True	False	Not enough evidence
In summer the north is warmer than the south			
London is colder than Cardiff in winter			
Newcastle gets more sunshine than Cardiff			
In winter the west is warmer than the east			
Cardiff is warmer than Newcastle in winter and summer			
London's temperature is more than 16°C in summer			
Cardiff's temperature is less than 5°C in winter			
Christmas Day is very cold in London			

Recap *In Britain the north is* **c**________________ *than the South in summer.*

In winter the west is **w**______________ *than the east.*

In this activity you will learn about the climate of Britain

Britain is a small place but the weather here varies a lot from place to place. The west is wet, the north is cool and the south is warm.

Activities

1 On **Map 1** shade the high land in **brown**.

2 On **Map 2** shade the wet part of Britain in **blue**.

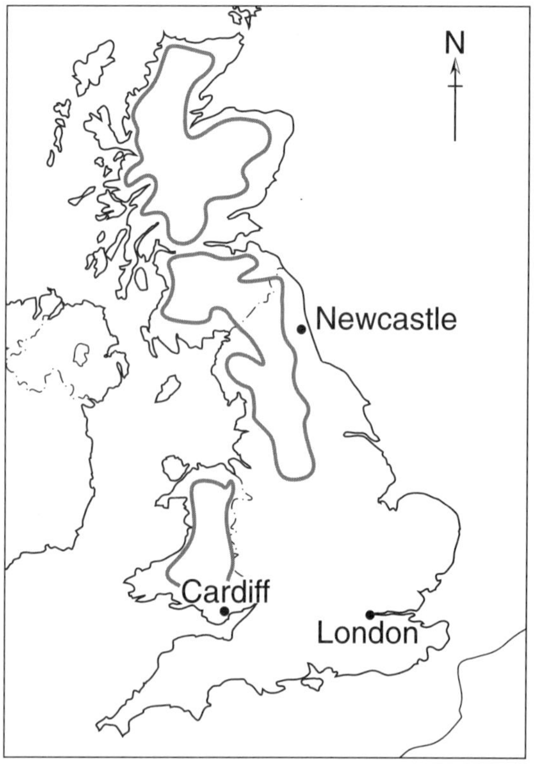

Map 1 Britain's high land

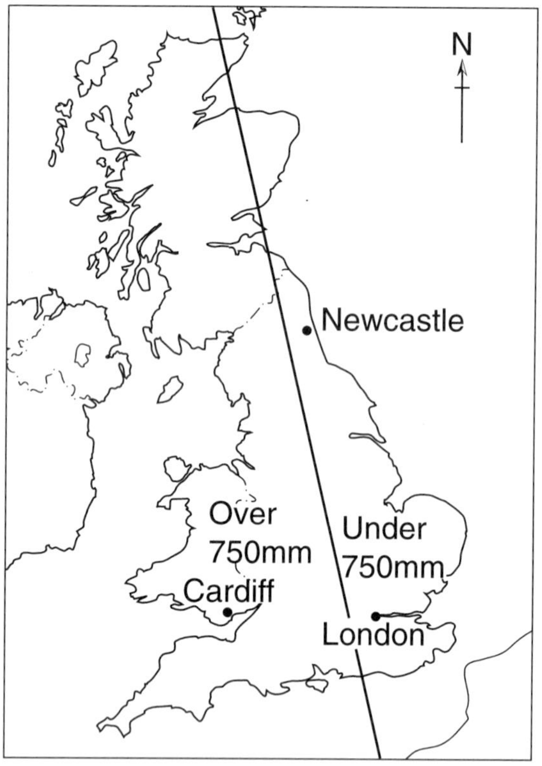

Map 2 Britain's yearly rainfall

3 Tick **true**, **false** or **not enough evidence** next to each statement in the table below.

	True	False	Not enough evidence
The west is wetter than the east			
The east is wetter than the west			
It rains every day in Cardiff			
London gets less than 750mm of rainfall per year			
The west side of Britain has a lot of high land			
Newcastle has a lot of rain in summer			
The north is wetter than the south			
Highland areas have most rainfall			

Recap *The west is* ***w***__________ *than the* ***e***__________ *because there is more high land in the west.*

In this activity you will learn about how it rains

It rains when water falls from the sky onto the land. This happens because:

A Warm air rises.
B Air cools as it rises. Water vapour turns into water.
C Clouds form in the sky.
D Rain falls from the clouds.

Remember that snow, sleet and hail are all types of water, and form in the same way as rain.

Activities

1 Finish the diagram below by joining the dots.

2 Using the information in the introduction fill in the four boxes **A**, **B**, **C** and **D** on the diagram.

3 Colour your diagram.

How it rains in mountain areas

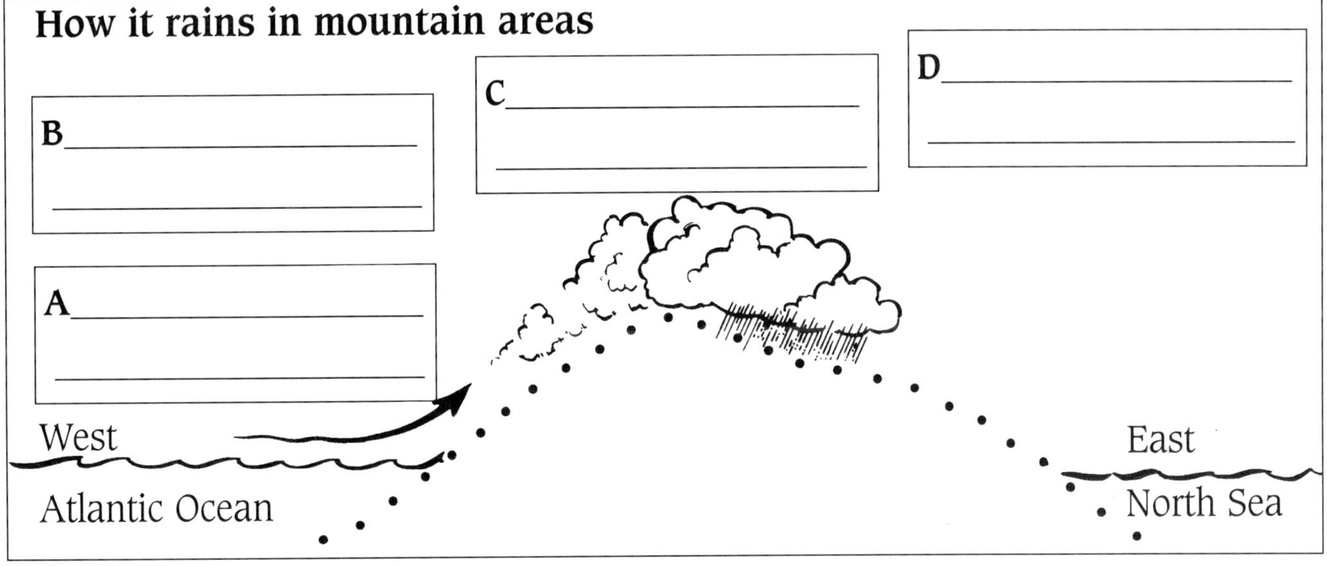

4 Fill in the gaps in the two sentences below.

- Mountains have **a lot of/not much** ______________ rainfall.
- Lowland areas have **a lot of/not much** ______________ rainfall.

Recap *Rain happens because air* ***ri***_________ *and then cools.* *Cl*_________ *form and then rain falls. This happens most in* *mo*______________ *areas.*

In this activity you will learn about how it rains

Rain falls because air rises into the sky carrying water vapour.

Activities

1 There are 10 sentences below which explain why it rains in mountain areas. They have been mixed up. **Cut them out** and then put them in the **right order** or **sequence**.
You can then either stick them onto a piece of paper, or write them out.

W As the air falls it warms and the rain stops.

I The moist air rises up the mountain side.

D The rain falls on the mountains.

R Moist air comes from the Atlantic Ocean.

N The air cools higher up.

H The water droplets make clouds.

A The clouds make rain (or snow in the winter).

S As the air cools the water vapour turns into water droplets.

A The moist air meets the mountains of the Lake District.

O The air passes over the mountains and starts to fall down the other side.

2 On the diagram below write the **letters** from the sentences in the correct boxes in the right order. One has been done for you.

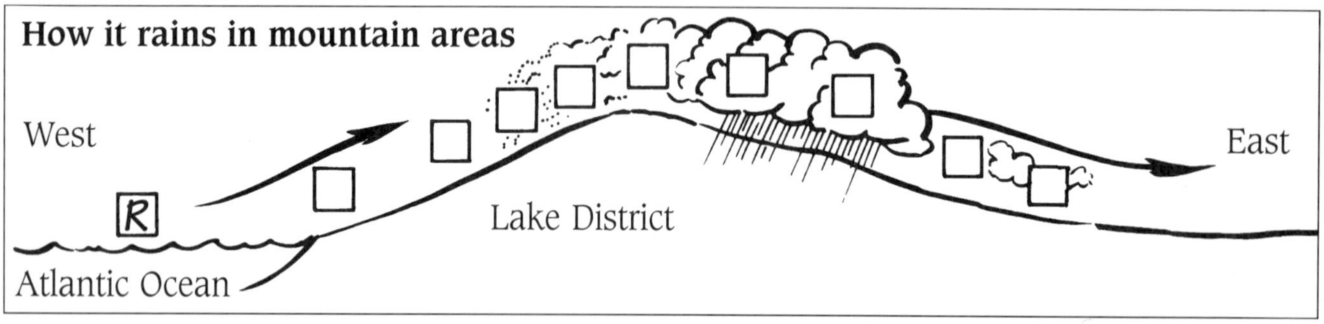

Recap *Rain happens because air* **r**__________ *and then cools.* **C**_________ *form and then rain falls. This happens most in* **m**________________ *areas.*

In this activity you will learn about how it rains

Rain falls because air rises into the sky carrying water vapour. In Britain most rain is caused in two ways.

- **Relief rainfall** which happens in hills and mountains.
- **Frontal rainfall** which happens when warm air rises over cold air.

Activities

1 Add the following labels to **Diagram 1**.
- **Air rises**
- **Clouds form**
- **Air cools**
- **Rain falls**

Shade the hills **brown**, and the sky **blue**.

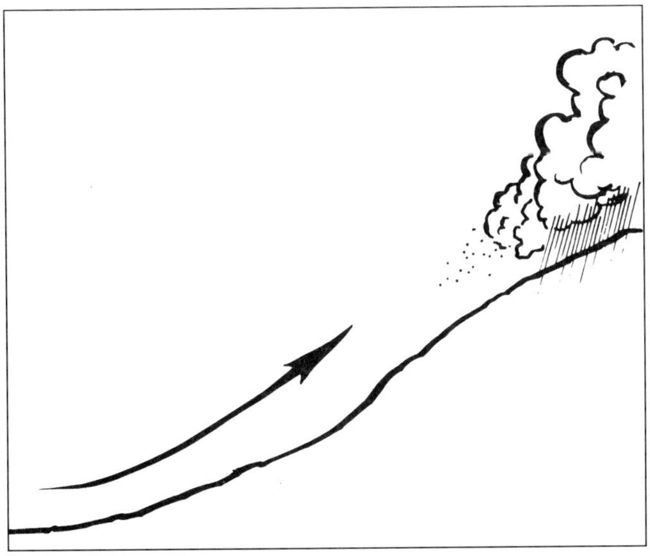

Diagram 1 Relief rainfall

2 Add the following labels to **Diagram 2**.
- **Air rises**
- **Clouds form**
- **Air cools**
- **Rain falls**

Shade the cold air **blue**, and the warm air **red**.

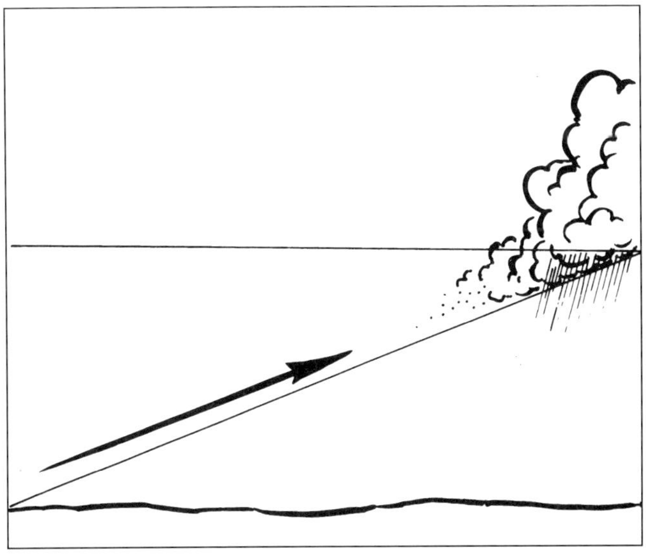

Diagram 2 Frontal rainfall

3 Use the words from the Word box to fill in the gaps in the passage below.

Word box

District	clouds
rainfall	snow
warm	lighter
cools	sky
vapour	west

Rainfall is water falling down to the earth from the ________. For this to happen water must be carried up into the sky. As the wind blows from the ________ it meets the hills of the Lake ________. The air goes up over the hills. As it rises the air ________ and the water vapour it holds turns into water. This water makes ________. The cloud droplets will make ________ on the hills. When ________ air meets cold air the warm air rises over the cold air because it is ________. As it gets higher the warm air cools down and the water ________ turns into water. This makes cloud and then rainfall. When it is colder we can have ________ instead of rain, but they are both made of water.

Recap *Rain and snow happen because air ________ in the sky. It then ________ and makes clouds. Rain falls from the clouds.*

In this activity you will learn about anticyclones

Some of the weather in Britain is made by **anticyclones**. These are **weather systems** that pass over the country and may last **many days**. Anticyclones give us very settled weather.

Activity

Study the picture of a playground during an anticyclone then tick **true**, **false** or **not enough evidence** next to each statement in the table below.

Picture of a playground at 12.15 pm on 14 June 1994.
The weather is made by an anticyclone.

	True	False	Not enough evidence
a It is winter			
b The weather is nice			
c It is windy			
d It is Saturday			
e It is a hot day			
f It is a sunny day			
g The weather will probably change tomorrow			
h The girl is on her way home from school			
i The girl is sunbathing			
j It is raining			
k The weather was the same yesterday			
l There was an anticyclone over Britain			

Recap *When we have an anticyclone in summer the weather is usually*

***sunny, h**__________ and **d**__________.*

In this activity you will learn about anticyclones

An **anticyclone** is an area of **high pressure** that gives us very settled weather. In summer it gives us lots of sunshine and hot days. In winter it gives us cold weather, sometimes with fog and mist, and sometimes with clear and sunny days.

Activities

1 Label the star diagram for an **anticyclone in summer** with the words in the Word box.

Word box

Clear skies
Hot days
Sunny days
Cool nights
Light winds
No rain
Settled weather for days

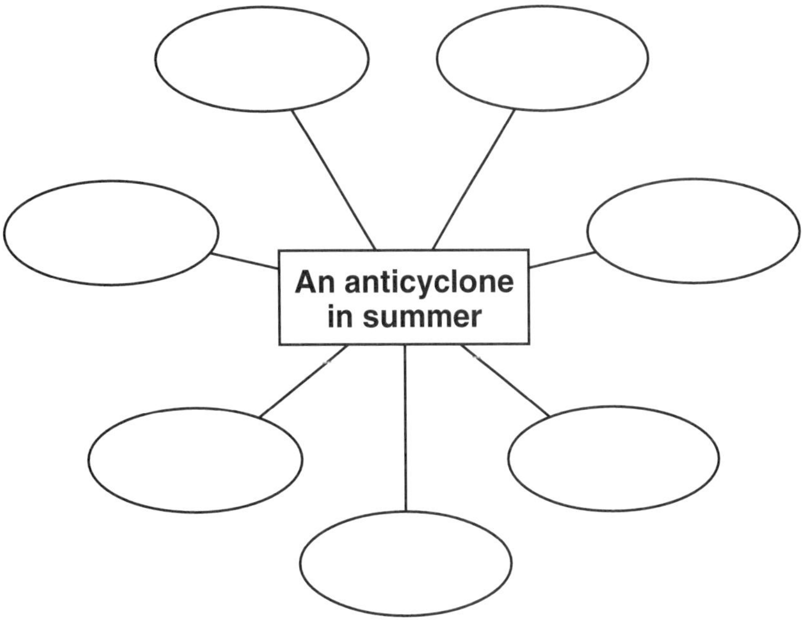

2 Label the star diagram for an **anticyclone in winter** with the words in the Word box.

Word box

Clear skies
Cold days
Sunny days
Very cold nights
Light winds
Fog and mist
No rain or snow
Settled weather for days

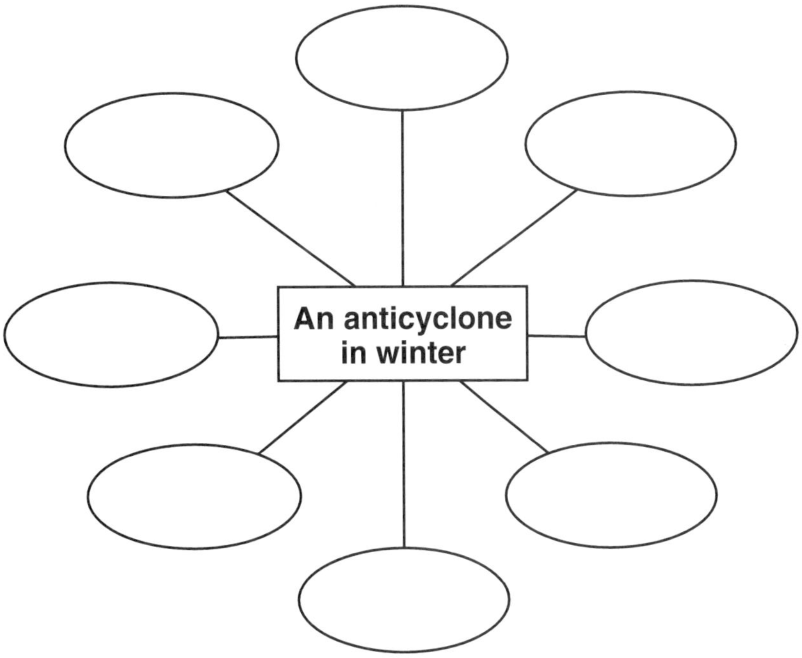

3 Look at the two star diagrams.
Use **red** and shade any boxes that are **the same** in summer and winter.
Use **blue** and shade any boxes that are **different** in winter and summer.

Recap *An anticyclone gives us sunny and settled weather. In summer it is very* ***h***________ *and in winter it is very* ***c***________.

In this activity you will learn about anticyclones

An **anticyclone** is an area of **high pressure** that gives us very settled weather. In summer it gives us lots of sunshine and hot days. In winter it gives us cold weather, sometimes with fog and mist, and sometimes with clear and sunny days.

Activities

1 Fit the words below into the correct place on the crossword. They will only fit one way. Start with the longest word and find out where it goes first. Most of the words describe the type of weather which you get with an anticyclone.

11 letter words
Anticyclone

10 letter words
Clear Skies
Light Winds

8 letter words
Forecast
Pressure
Thick Fog

7 letter words
Settled

6 letter words
Frosty
No Wind

5 letter words
Sunny

4 letter words
Calm
Cold
Mist

3 letter words
Dry
Fog
Hot

2 Answer the questions below by ticking the right answer.

In summer when we have an anticyclone we have
- **a hot days** ☐
- **b cold days** ☐

In winter anticyclones can give us
- **a snow** ☐
- **b fog and mist** ☐

Clear skies with an anticyclone give us
- **a a lot of sunshine** ☐
- **b not much sunshine** ☐

An anticyclone gives us
- **a settled weather** ☐
- **b unsettled weather** ☐

Recap *Anticyclones give us very* ***se*****________** *weather with clear* ________ *and lots of* ***s*****________***.*

In this activity you will find out about anticyclones

An **anticyclone** is an area of **high pressure** that gives us very settled weather. In summer it gives us lots of sunshine and hot days. In winter it gives us cold weather, sometimes with fog and mist, and sometimes with clear and sunny days.

Activities

1 Fill the gaps in the sentences below using the words from the Word box. They describe an anticyclone in **summer**.

Anticyclones give us clear skies so it is usually ____________.

Because it is sunny it is very ____________.

There is no **w**____________.

There is no cloud so there is no ____________.

This weather lasts for many ____________.

Word box

days
hot
sunny
wind
rain

2 Fill the gaps in the sentences below using the words from the Word box. They describe an anticyclone in **winter**.

Anticyclones give us clear skies so it is usually ____________.

Clear skies at night make it very ____________.

There is no **w**____________.

There is no cloud so there is no ____________ or **s**____________.

This weather lasts for many ____________.

Clear skies at night can give us ____________.

Word box

days
cold
sunny
wind
rain
snow
fog

3 Tick **yes** or **no** after each sentence in the table below.

	Yes	No
a When we have an anticyclone in summer it is a good time to go for a picnic		
b When we have an anticyclone in winter it is a good time to fly a kite		
c When we have an anticyclone in summer you can get a sun tan		
d When we have an anticyclone in winter it might snow on the way to school		
e An anticyclone is an area of high pressure		
f An anticyclone gives us days of unsettled weather		

Recap *Anticyclones give us days of* ***se***____________ *weather with clear* ***s***____________ *and lots of* ***s***____________*. It is* ***h***____________ *in summer and* ***c***____________ *in* ***w***____________*.*

In this activity you will learn about depressions

A lot of the weather in Britain is made by **depressions**. These are **weather systems** that pass from **west** to **east** over the country, and may last a **few days**.

Activity

Study the picture of a playground during a depression then tick **true**, **false** or **not enough evidence** next to each statement in the table below.

Picture of a playground at 8.30 am on 7 June 1994.
The weather is made by a depression.

	True	False	Not enough evidence
a It is winter			
b The weather is nice			
c It is windy			
d It is Monday			
e It is a warm day			
f It is a sunny day			
g The weather was like this yesterday			
h The girl is on her way home from school			
i The girl is called Alice			
j It is raining			
k The weather will be the same the next day			
l There was a depression over Britain on 7 June 1994			

Recap *When we have a depression the weather is usually* ***windy,***

c*___________ and* ***w****___________.*

In this activity you will learn about depressions

A lot of the weather in Britain is made by **depressions**. These are **weather systems** which pass from **west** to **east** over the country and may last a **few days**. They give us our changing weather.

Activities

1 Use the words from the Word box to label the diagram of a depression. The first letter has been done for you.

2 On the diagram shade the **cold air** and the **triangles** on the cold front in **blue**, and the **warm air** and the **half circles** on the warm front in **red**.

Word box

Cold front	Warm front
Cold air	Rain
West	East
Warm air	Cloud

Diagram of a depression

3 Find the words in the Word box in the wordsearch.

W	A	R	M	A	I	R	P	B	D	I	A	C
A	R	A	E	A	S	T	S	A	H	E	C	C
R	D	I	A	O	T	A	M	U	R	N	H	O
M	E	N	W	O	O	E	O	N	V	R	A	L
F	O	D	E	P	R	E	S	S	I	O	N	D
R	H	A	S	A	M	L	R	E	U	N	G	F
O	B	G	T	E	S	A	L	T	I	D	E	R
N	P	S	C	M	A	H	D	T	R	I	A	O
T	M	C	L	O	U	D	A	L	N	A	B	N
M	R	T	I	N	T	L	G	E	V	R	L	T
C	O	L	D	A	I	R	N	D	R	M	E	X

Word box

Cold front
Warm front
Warm air
Cold air
Rain
Cloud
West
East
Depression
Changeable
Storms
Unsettled

Recap *Britain has changing weather because we get **d**____________.*

In this activity you will learn about depressions

A lot of the weather in Britain is made by **depressions**. These are **weather systems** which pass from **west** to **east** over the country and may last a **few days**. They give us our changing weather.

Activities

1 On the diagram below shade the **warm air** in **red**, and the **cold air** in **blue**.

2 Use the diagram to find out which team each of the people below is supporting. Draw a line from their picture to the football ground on the diagram.

Diagram showing a depression on Saturday 11March at 3.00 pm, the same time as kick-off for the football matches at the five grounds.

It started raining just before kick off and I am now wet and cold.
I support ______________

It is cold but at least it has stopped raining. I got wet walking here from the bus stop.
I support ______________

It is cold and wet now, but it was warm and cloudy when I got here.
I support ______________

It is quite cold but very sunny. I can just see a few small clouds high in the sky.
I support ______________

It is quite warm and dry now with just a few clouds about. It was cloudy when I got here.
I support ______________

Recap Britain has changing weather because we get **d**__________ moving from **w**________ to **e**________.

In this activity you will learn about how the weather works

Activity

- Look at the words in the boxes below. Draw a line between any boxes which you think are linked. Write why they are linked on the line. One has been done for you.
- Draw as many links as you can between all the words. The more links you can do the better you understand the weather.

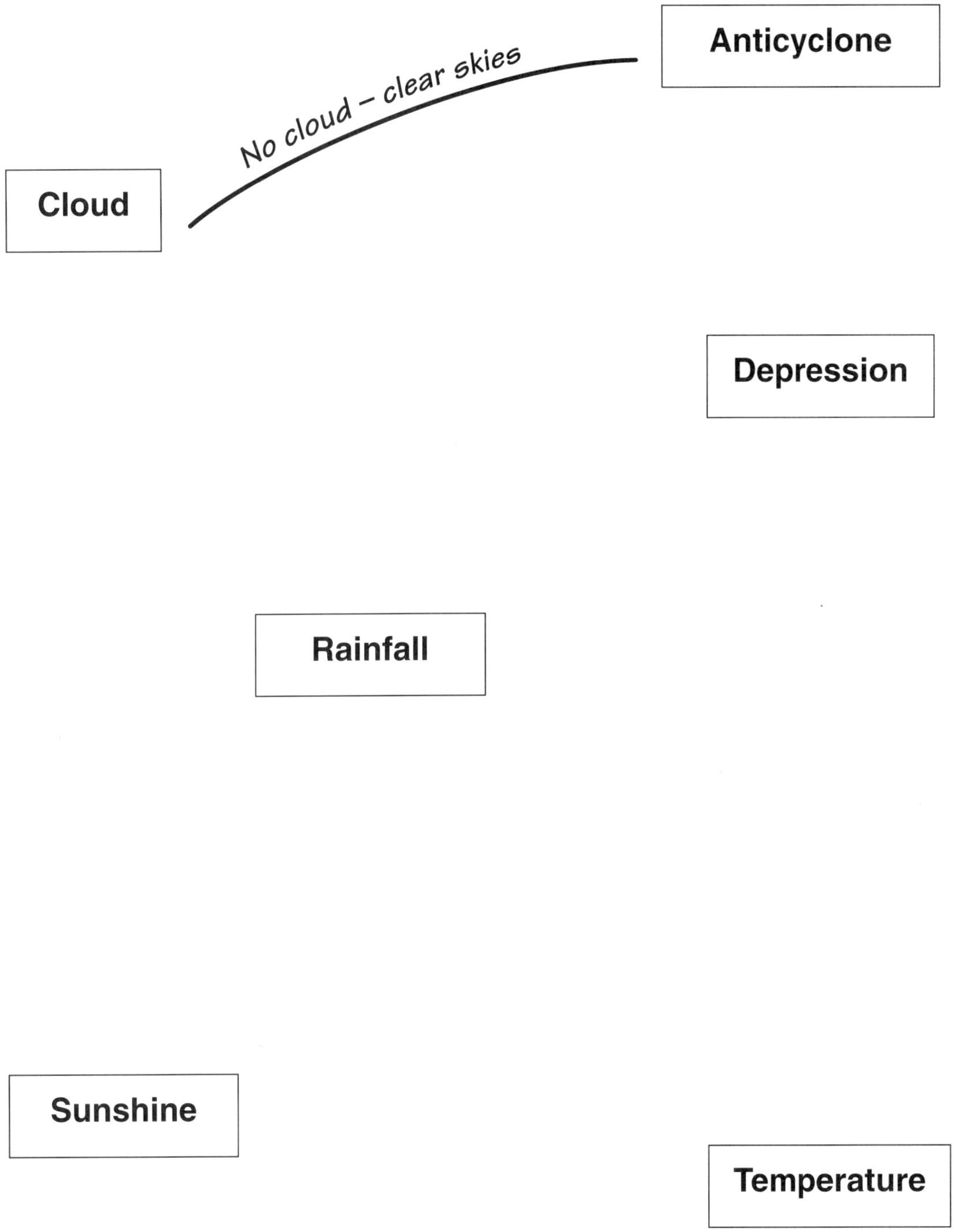

In this activity you will learn what happens when rain falls onto the land

When rain falls onto the land it either sinks into the ground, flows downhill into rivers, or stands in puddles and pools on the surface.

Activities

1 On the diagram showing children pouring water onto different surfaces, draw lines from each watering can to the descriptions below of what happens to the water.

2 Label the diagram using the words in the Word box.

Word box
Tarmac
Sandpit
Long jumper
Grass

Water stays on the surface in puddles.	Water slowly sinks into the ground.	Water quickly sinks into the ground.

3 Tick **true** or **false** next to each statement in the table below.

	True	False
Water sinks into tarmac		
Sand soaks up water quickly		
Grass soaks up water slowly		

Recap *When rain falls onto tarmac it stands in puddles. When rain falls onto sand it sinks into the ground* **q**____________. *When rain falls onto grass it sinks into the ground* **s**____________.

In this activity you will learn what happens when rain falls onto the land

When rain falls onto the land it either sinks into the ground, flows downhill into rivers, or stands in puddles and pools on the surface. Steep slopes let water run off quickly, and gentle slopes let water run off slowly. Plants let water sink into the ground.

Activities

Word box

puddles • quickly • tarmac
ground • slowly • quickly
forest

1 Look at the diagrams below. Fill in the gaps on each diagram using the words from the Word box, to show how water will flow into the river.

On steep slopes water runs off **q**________.

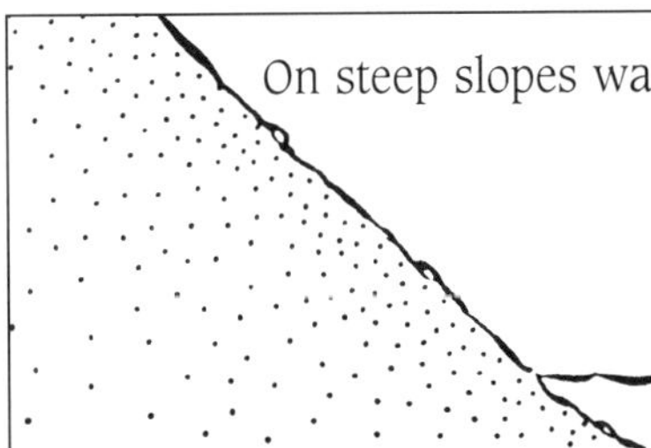

In **f**____________ water sinks into the ground.

On gentle slopes water runs off **s**________.

In cleared forest water runs off **q**________.

On flat land water lies in **p**____________ then sinks into the **g**________.

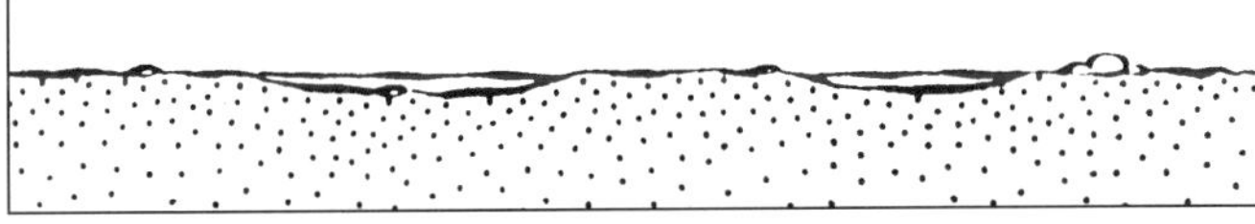

In towns water runs off very quickly because there is a lot of **t**_________ and concrete.

2 Fill in the gaps in the paragraph below using the words in the Word box.

Word box

slowly • forest
steep • quickly
gentle

Water runs off fastest down **s**____________ slopes and slowest down **g**__________ slopes. Water lies as puddles on **f**___________ land. Water runs off **q**____________ from tarmac and **s**____________ from forests. Cutting down forests (deforestation) also makes water run off quickly.

Recap *Water runs off quickly from* **s**___________ *slopes, and stands in pools on* **f**_______ *land. Forests have slow run off. Towns and cities have lots of concrete and* **t**___________ *and water runs off very* **q**__________.

In this activity you will learn about river basins

A **river basin** is an area of land where the rain collects and flows into a river and its tributaries. Rivers flow downhill into the sea.

Activities

1 Draw lines to join up the 'heads' on the left, with the 'tails' on the right below.

Source	is the area drained by a river
Tributary	is where the river starts
Mouth	is the edge of a river basin
River basin	is a small river that flows into a larger river
Watershed	is where the river ends, usually in the sea

2 Fill in the spaces on the diagram of a river basin below with the 'heads' from activity 1.

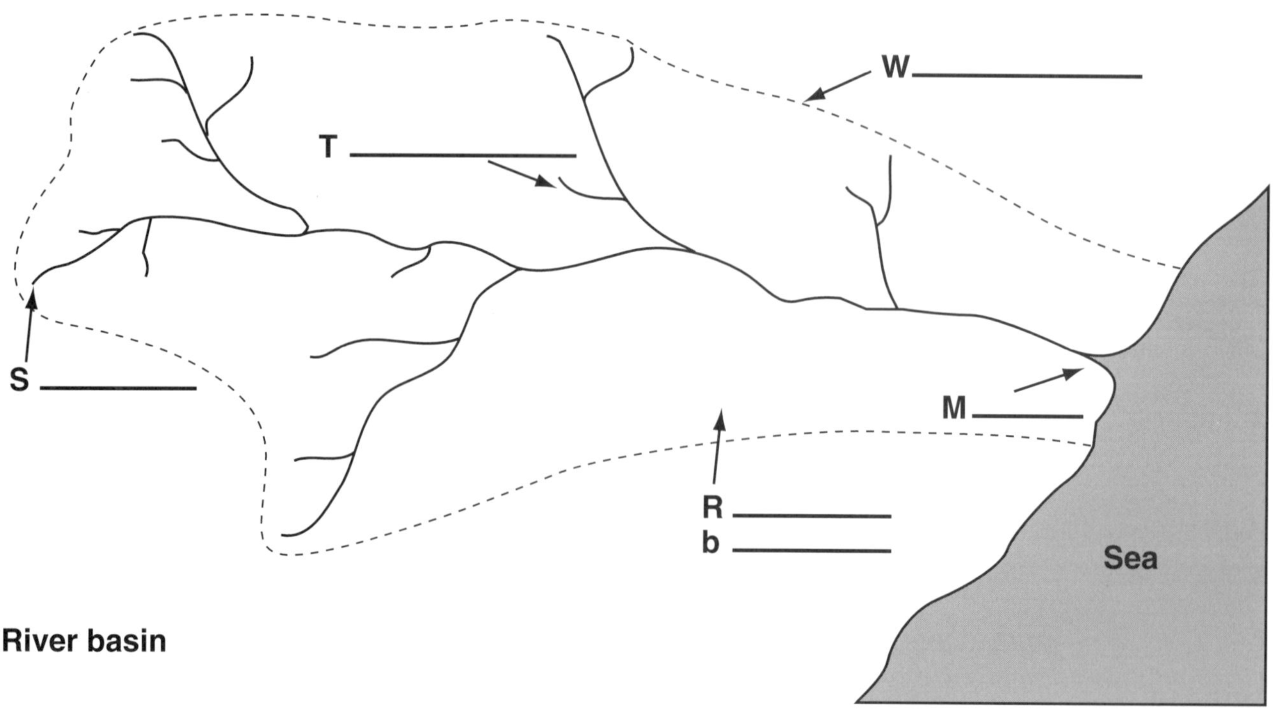

River basin

Recap A **river basin** is an area of land where the rain collects and flows into a ______________ and its ______________.

Rivers flow downhill into the ______________.

In this activity you will learn about river basins

A **river basin** is an area of land where the rain collects and flows into a river and its tributaries. A river starts at the **source** and flows downstream into the sea. The end of the river is the **mouth**. A smaller river flowing into a bigger river is called a **tribuary**.

Activity

Do the word game below. This is how to do it.

Clue: Small river flowing into a bigger river (9) **Answer:** Tributary

Top letter starts the word
Right hand letter ends the word
Left hand letter is another letter in the word

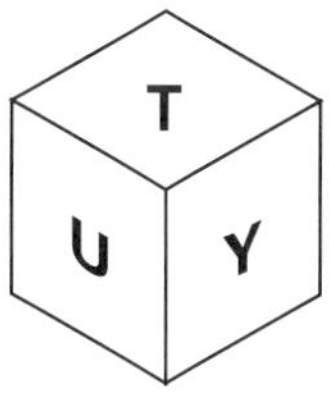

Fill in the answers to the clues in the spaces below.

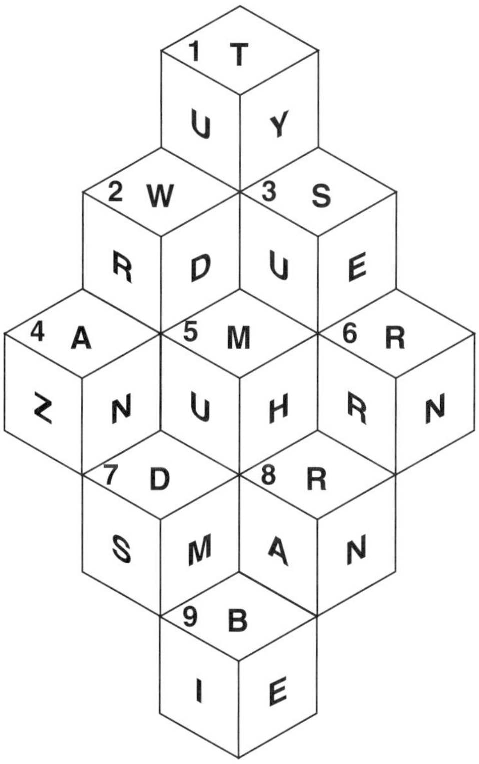

Clues

1 Small river flowing into a bigger river (9)
2 Hills at the edge of a river basin (9)
3 The start of a river (6)
4 Longest river in South America (6)
5 The end of a river (5)
6 The area drained by a river and its tributaries (Two words 5, 5)
7 The direction that a river flows (10)
8 Water falling from the sky (4)
9 One way to get over a river (6)

Answers

1 TributarY ______
2 ______
3 ______
4 ______
5 ______
6 ______
7 ______
8 ______
9 ______

Recap *The start of a river is the s______ and the end of a river is the m______.*

In this activity you will learn about river basins

A **river basin** is an area of land where the rain collects and flows into a river and its tributaries. A river starts at the **source** and flows downstream into the sea. The end of the river is the **mouth**. A smaller river flowing into a bigger river is called a **tributary**.

Activities

The River Tyne river basin

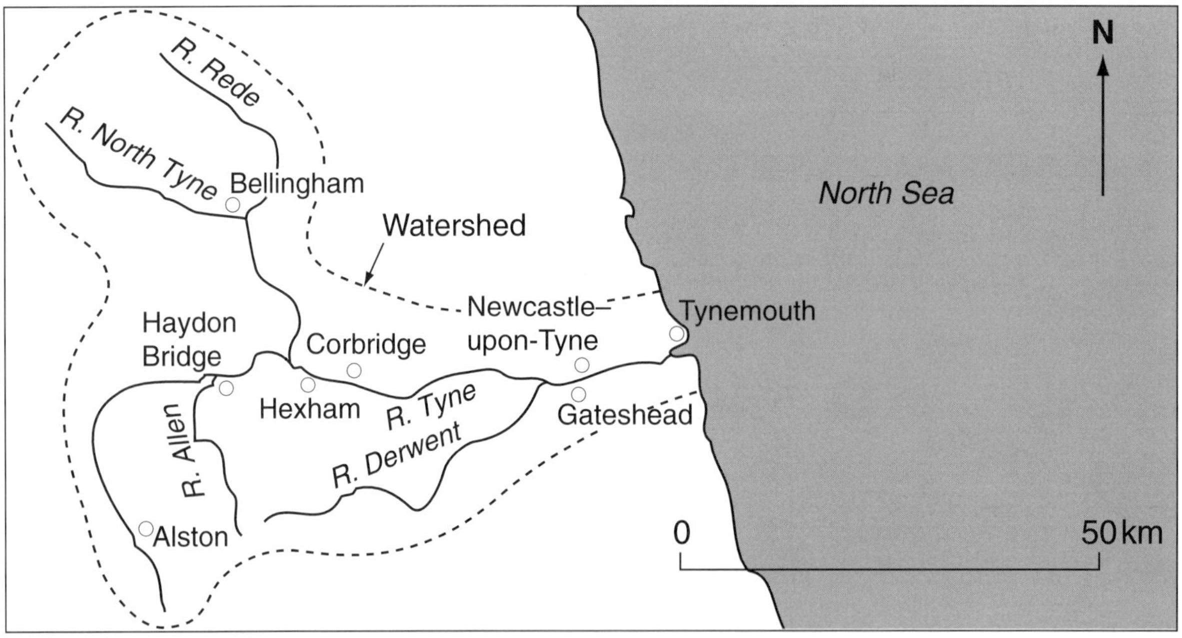

1 On the map above use **blue** to go over all the rivers.
Shade the sea in **blue** .
Colour the dots for the towns in **red**.
Shade the river basin in another colour. (The area inside the watershed.)

2 Answer the questions below. Use the map to help you.

- Name a tributary of the River Tyne. ____________________
- Name a town on the River North Tyne. ____________________
- Name the town at the mouth of the River Tyne. ____________________
- Which town is nearest to the source of the River Tyne? ____________________
- If you went down the River Tyne in a canoe which town would you pass through after Haydon Bridge? ____________________
- The River Tyne has three main tributaries. Name two of them.

____

Recap *The* ***River T*** ____________ *is an important river in North-east England. The main city on the river is* ***N*** ____________________ ***-Upon-Tyne.***

In this activity you will learn about some important rivers

There are many important rivers in Great Britain. Some rivers are longer than others.

Activities

1 Fill in the crossword below with the names of the rivers on the maps. Some letters have been filled in to help you.

This shows the title of the map

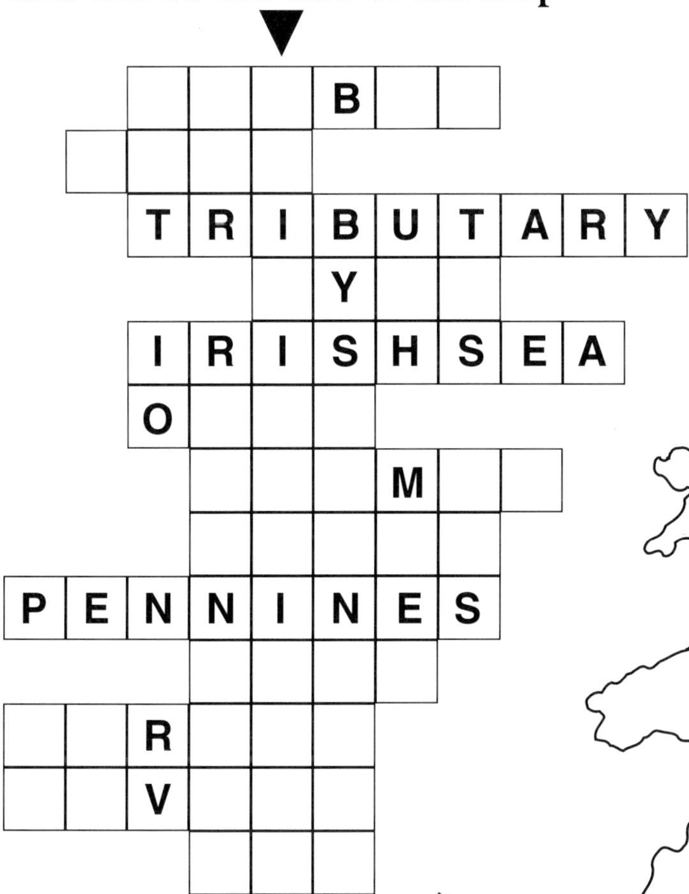

Map title ______________________________

2 The title of the map is shown on the crossword reading down from the arrow. Add the title to the map in the space provided.

Recap *Three examples of rivers in Great Britain are*

____________________, ____________________ *and* ____________________.

In this activity you will learn about some important rivers

There are many important rivers in the world. The longest river in the world is the **River Nile** in Africa. The **River Amazon** is the longest river in South America.

Some of the most famous rivers in the world are shown on the map below.

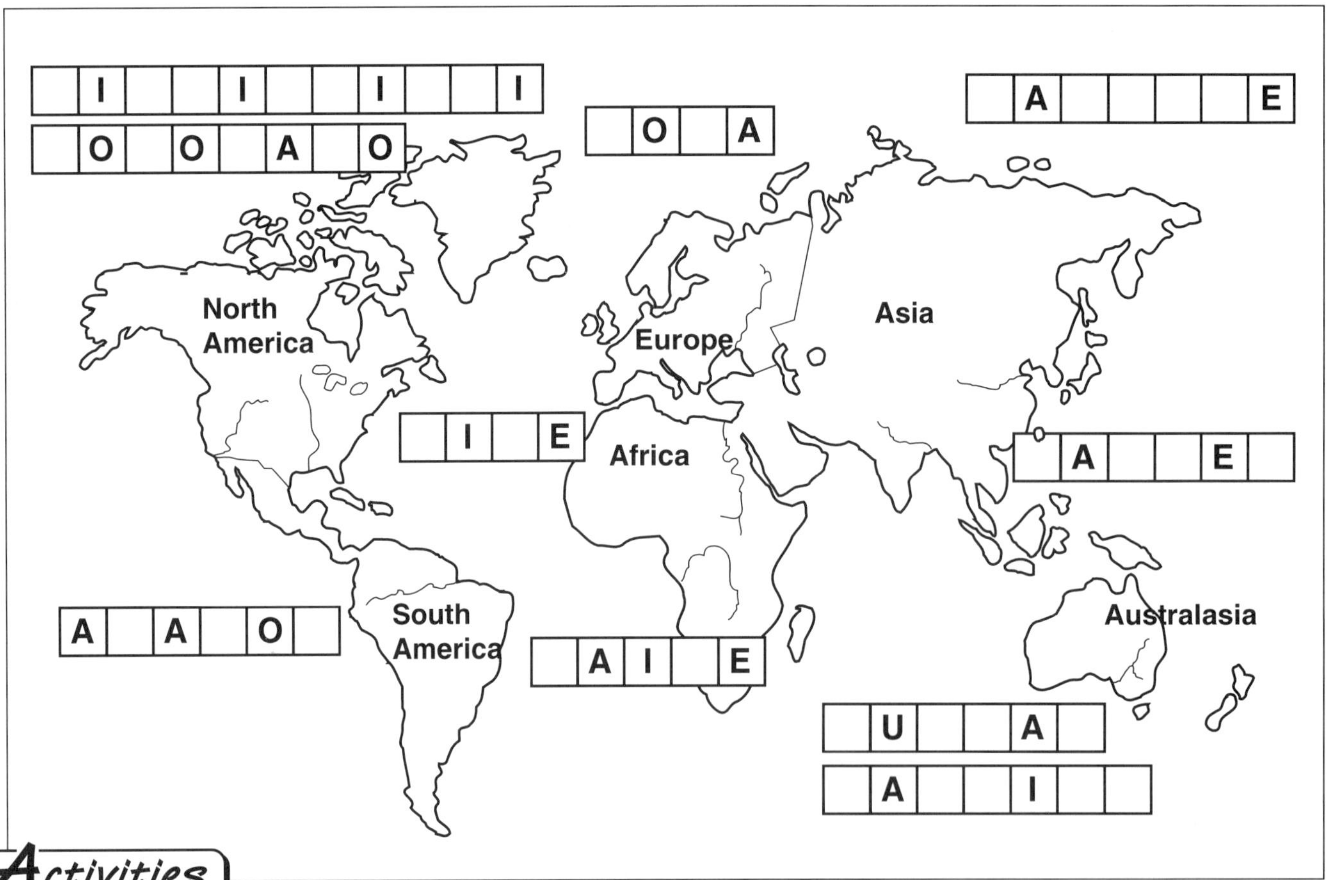

Activities

1 Fill in the names of each river marked on the map in the boxes. The vowels have been written in already to help you.

2 Complete the following statements by filling in the gaps. Use the map to help you.

The **River Amazon** is in the continent of **S**_____________ **A**____________________.

The **River Mississippi** is in the continent of **N**____________ **A**____________________.

The **River Ganges** is in the continent of **A**_________________.

The **River Murray Darling** is in the continent of **A**____________________.

The **River Volga** is in the continent of **E**_________________.

Recap *The longest river in the world is the* ***Nile*** *which is in the continent of A*_______________. *The longest river in* ***South America*** *is the River A*____________________.

In this activity you will learn about some important rivers

There are some very long rivers in the world. Rivers in Great Britain are very short compared to some rivers in other countries.

Activities 1 Read the passage below about rivers of the world.

The longest river in South America is the River Amazon which is 6518 km long. This is a bit longer than the Mississippi/Missouri in North America which is 6051 km. The River Nile in Africa is 6695 km long and is the longest river in the world. It is almost as twice as long as the River Volga (3690 km) in Europe! Asia has many long rivers but the longest is the Yangtze in China with a length of 5472 km.

Australia is mostly desert, but its longest river is the Murray Darling at 3718 km. The longest river in Great Britain is the Severn and measures just

2 Choose three colours. In the passage above underline **continents** with one colour. Underline **rivers** with another colour, and underline the **lengths** with the third colour.

3 Using the things you underlined in the passage above complete the fact files below. The first one has been done for you. Draw the rivers the correct length using the scale bar.

Fact File

Continent: North America **Longest river:** Mississippi/Missouri **Length:** 6051km

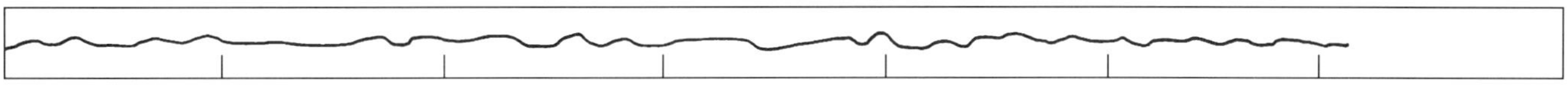

1000 km 2000 km 3000 km 4000 km 5000 km 6000 km 7000 km

Continent: ____________ **Longest river:** ____________ **Length:** ________

1000 km 2000 km 3000 km 4000 km 5000 km 6000 km 7000 km

Continent: ____________ **Longest river:** ____________ **Length:** ________

1000 km 2000 km 3000 km 4000 km 5000 km 6000 km 7000 km

Continent: ____________ **Longest river:** ____________ **Length:** ________

1000 km 2000 km 3000 km 4000 km 5000 km 6000 km 7000 km

Continent: ____________ **Longest river:** ____________ **Length:** ________

1000 km 2000 km 3000 km 4000 km 5000 km 6000 km 7000 km

Continent: ____________ **Longest river:** ____________ **Length:** ________

1000 km 2000 km 3000 km 4000 km 5000 km 6000 km 7000 km

Recap *Rivers in Great Britain are quite short. The longest river in the world is the **River** ____________ which is in **A**____________.*

In this activity you will learn about floods in Bangladesh

Bangladesh is a very poor country in **Asia** which has floods nearly every year.

Activities

1 Draw lines to join up the 'heads' on the left, and the 'tails' on the right below, to explain why Bangladesh has floods.

Bangladesh has heavy rains	is very flat.
The country	called monsoons.
The country is very	This is called deforestation.
Trees have been cut down.	low-lying.

2 Draw lines to join up the 'heads' on the left, and the 'tails' on the right below, to help explain how floods affect people in Bangladesh.

Many people near the river	are under water.
The rice crop was ruined	get help into Bangladesh.
They now drink dirty water	and catch diseases like cholera.
Roads and railways	so the people might starve.
It is hard to	are drowned.

3 What help do the people of Bangladesh need when they have been flooded? Look at the things being said by the woman in Bangladesh. Colour in the things that you think she **really needs**.

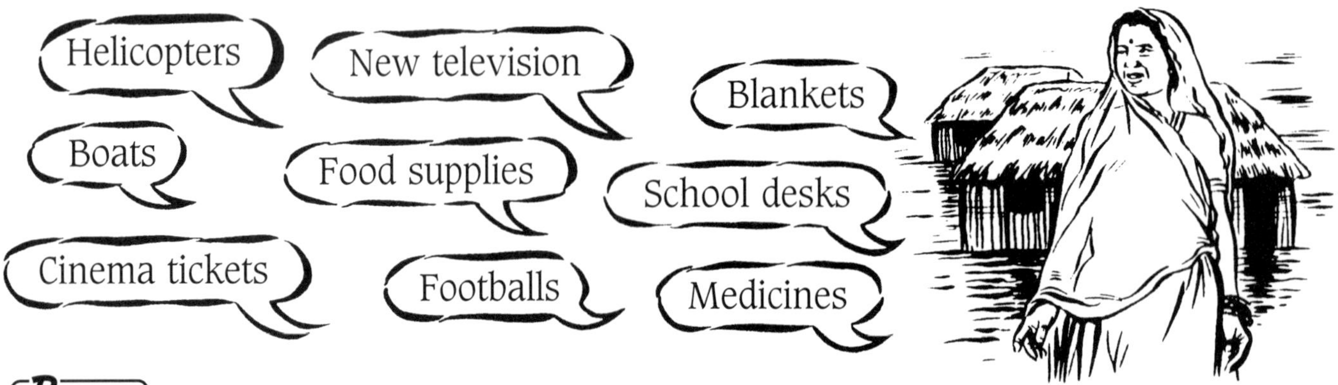

Recap *Bangladesh has* **f**____________ *most years because it is* **flat, low-lying** *and has heavy rains called* **m**________________.

In this activity you will learn about floods in Bangladesh

Bangladesh is a very poor country in **Asia**. It has floods nearly every year because the **River Ganges** overflows its banks.

Causes are reasons **why** floods happen. **Effects** are problems the floods make for people and the land.

Activities

1 Read the ten statements in the boxes below. Some are the causes of floods and some are the effects of floods.

Shade the causes in **red** and the effects in **blue**.

- **Many people are drowned**
- **Heavy monsoon rains fall**
- People are dying from diseases because they are drinking dirty water
- Crops are ruined by the flood water so people will starve
- *Bangladesh is very low-lying*
- ***Many people are left homeless***
- **The River Ganges is getting silted up**
- Deforestation in the Himalayas
- *Roads and railways have been swept away*
- **Bangladesh is very flat**

2 Choose any **four** causes of flooding and write them in the table below.

3 Choose any **four** effects of flooding and write them in the table below.

Four causes of flooding in Bangladesh

Four effects of flooding in Bangladesh

Recap *Bangladesh has floods most years. Problems like floods in Bangladesh have* ***c***__________ *(these are the reasons why floods happen) and* ***e***__________ *(these are the problems the floods create).*

In this activity you will learn about floods in Bangladesh

Bangladesh is a very poor country in **Asia**. It has floods nearly every year because the **River Ganges** overflows its banks.

The newspaper report below describes the floods in **September 1988**.

Floods cause major problems in Bangladesh

The heaviest monsoon rains to hit Bangladesh have left over 1000 people dead, and 25 million homeless. The rice crop has been lost and over 35 million people face starvation over the next few months.

The sugar cane and jute crops have also been destroyed. These would have been sold by farmers to make some money.

Many people have climbed onto their roofs to escape the water, but many poisonous snakes are also on the roofs and many people have been bitten.

The water supply has been ruined and now people are having to drink dirty water. This is making them very poorly with dysentry and cholera.

Trying to get help is very difficult because most of the roads and railways are under water. Many bridges over the River Ganges have been washed away. The airport is under water making it difficult to get help from rich countries like Britain and the USA. Bangladesh badly needs things like helicopters, food, medical supplies, blankets and water purification tablets.

Activities

1 Read the newspaper article above.

Using **red**, underline anything about **deaths**, **diseases** and **homelessness**.
Using **green**, underline anything about **crops**, **food** and **water**.
Using **blue**, underline anything about **transport problems**.
Using **black**, underline anything about **help needed**.

2 Fill in the boxes below using the information that you have underlined in the newspaper article.

Deaths, diseases and homelessness	Crops, food and water ______
______	______
______	______
______	______

Transport problems ______	Help needed ______
______	______
______	______
______	______

Recap Bangladesh has floods most years. The floods create problems such as **deaths, d**__________ and **homelessness**. Crops are damaged causing **st**__________. Help is needed from **r**__________ countries like Britain.

In this activity you will learn why floods happen

When a **river** breaks its banks and flows over dry land, this is called a **flood**. There are different reasons why rivers flood.

Activities

1 Follow the winding rivers below to find out what each person has said about their flood.

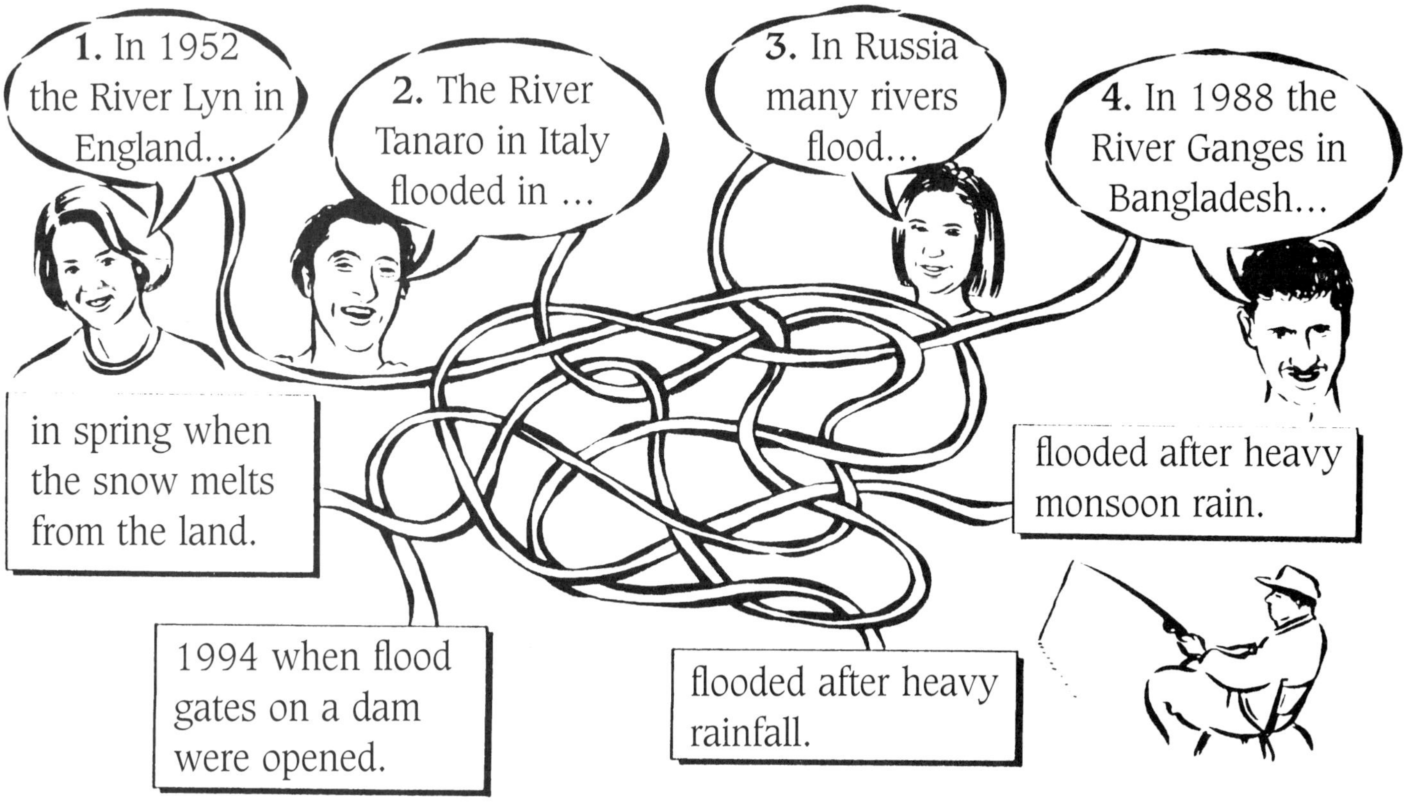

2 Use the information above to complete the following sentences.

- In 1952 the **River Lyn** in England ______________________________

  ____
- The **River Tanaro** in Italy flooded in______________________________

  ____
- In **Russia** many rivers flood ______________________________

  ____
- In 1988 the **River Ganges** in Bangladesh ______________________

  ____

Recap *Rivers can* ***flood*** *because of heavy* ***r****________,* ***snow melting*** *or* ***flood gates*** *being opened on a* ***d****________.*

In this activity you will learn why floods happen

When a **river** breaks its banks and flows over dry land, this is called a **flood**. Some floods happen because of **nature**, and some happen because of the things **people** do.

Activities

1 Look at the table below. Decide if the things listed make floods happen or stop floods from happening. Tick the correct answer.

2 On the table shade the **natural** things in green, and the **human** things in red.

	Make floods happen	Stop floods happening
Planting trees		
Building cities		
Building dams on rivers		
Cutting down trees		
Heavy rainfall		
Snow melting in spring		
Building higher river banks		
A dam collapsing		

3 Find the words in the Word box below in the wordsearch. They are all words to do with flooding. Words can either go across or down. One has been done for you.

Word box

- Bangladesh
- Banks
- China
- Cities
- Dam
- Ganges
- Italy
- ~~Melt~~
- Monsoon
- Rain
- Spring
- Tarmac
- Trees
- Deforestation

C	H	I	N	A	D	A	U	C	I	S	L	F
A	L	T	L	N	B	N	C	(M	E	L	T)	C
O	T	A	R	M	A	C	E	B	I	R	R	B
S	P	L	E	R	N	A	D	E	A	N	E	O
X	A	Y	M	E	G	A	N	G	E	S	E	S
W	O	N	O	D	L	U	R	R	Y	C	S	P
R	I	E	N	B	A	N	K	S	V	I	R	R
T	A	P	S	I	D	K	M	R	L	T	A	I
D	E	F	O	R	E	S	T	A	T	I	O	N
A	S	L	O	T	S	B	N	I	V	E	S	G
M	N	W	N	S	H	Y	A	N	C	S	D	Z

Recap Floods happen because of **n**________________ and **h**________________ things.

In this activity you will learn why floods happen

When a **river** breaks its banks and flows over dry land, this is called a **flood**. **Coastal areas** flood when the **sea** covers the land.

Activities

1 Look at what the three people are saying.

Use **green** to colour in the things that make river floods happen.

Use **blue** to colour in the things that make coastal floods happen.

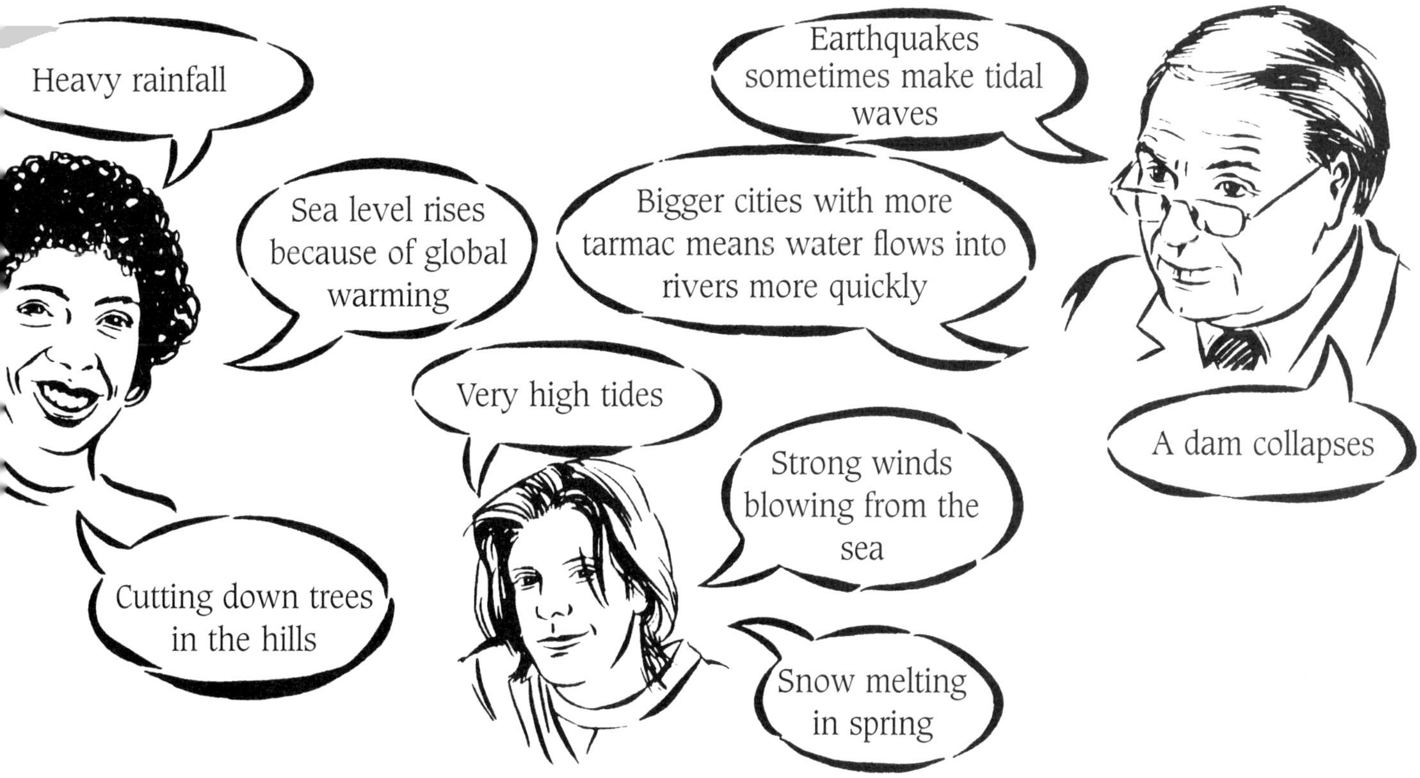

2 Write any **two** reasons why rivers flood, and any **two** reasons why coasts flood in the table below.

Rivers flood because	**Coasts flood because**
1 ______________________________	1 ______________________________
2 ______________________________	2 ______________________________

Recap *Floods can happen on* ***r***__________ *or at the* ***c***__________.

In this activity you will learn about the water cycle

The **water cycle** is the never ending movement of water from the sea, into the sky, onto the land and back into the sea.

Activities

1 Find the words in the Word box below in the wordsearch. They are all words to do with the water cycle. Words can go either across or down. One has been done for you.

Word box

Air
Cloud
Condensation
Dew
Evaporate
Groundwater
Hail
Lake
Rain
River
Run off
Sea
Snow
Stores
Stream
Surface water
~~Transfer~~
Transpiration
Water cycle

L	D	T	A	E	M	V	R	N	E	Y	H	T	C
P	S	X	W	R	N	U	A	O	T	S	A	A	O
M	T	R	A	N	S	P	I	R	A	T	I	O	N
A	O	N	T	H	T	I	N	H	S	X	L	J	D
H	R	M	E	A	T	R	G	L	E	N	E	T	E
A	E	G	R	O	U	N	D	W	A	T	E	R	N
S	S	R	C	A	P	D	E	R	Z	M	I	A	S
O	L	A	Y	N	I	E	W	B	R	S	D	N	A
P	L	L	C	E	W	A	Q	C	U	N	I	S	T
O	R	C	L	O	U	D	R	U	N	O	F	F	I
G	W	I	E	C	A	F	U	H	S	W	O	E	O
S	U	R	F	A	C	E	W	A	T	E	R	R	N
K	S	I	V	U	D	N	G	O	R	A	A	S	Y
A	E	V	A	P	O	R	A	T	E	N	I	C	E
B	A	E	R	R	H	J	G	L	A	K	E	N	J
A	I	R	E	A	M	V	U	O	M	N	A	O	R

2 Fill in the table below using words from the wordsearch. One has been done for you.

	Words to do with precipitation	Words to do with water on the land
1	*Rain*	*River*
2		
3		
4		
5		

Recap *The **water cycle** is the never ending movement of water from the ________ into the sky, onto the ________ and back into the sea.*

In this activity you will learn about the water cycle

The **water cycle** is the never ending movement of water from the sea, into the sky, onto the land and back into the sea.

Activities

1 Do the word game below. This is how to do it.

Clue: Two examples are the Irish and the North (3)
Answer: Sea

Top letter starts the word
Right hand letter ends the word
Left hand letter is another letter in the word

Fill in the answers to the clues in the spaces below.

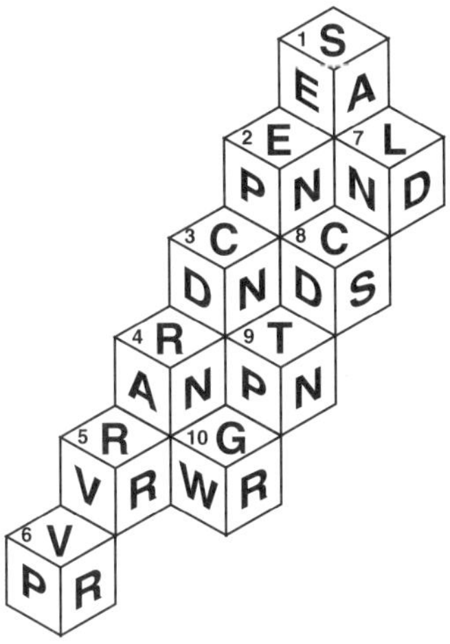

Clues

1 Two examples are the Irish and North (3)
2 Water turning into water vapour (11)
3 Water vapour turning into water (12)
4 Water falling from the sky (4)
5 Water flowing downhill (5)
6 Water __________, a gas (6)
7 Rain falls onto the _____________ (4)
8 White and grey things in the sky (13)
9 Trees let water vapour into the sky (13)
10 Water that sinks into the ground (11)

Answers

1 ________________________
2 ________________________
3 ________________________
4 ________________________
5 ________________________
6 ________________________
7 ________________________
8 ________________________
9 ________________________
10 ________________________

2 Fill in the answers to clues 1–5 in the boxes below to show how the water cycle works.

The Water Cycle

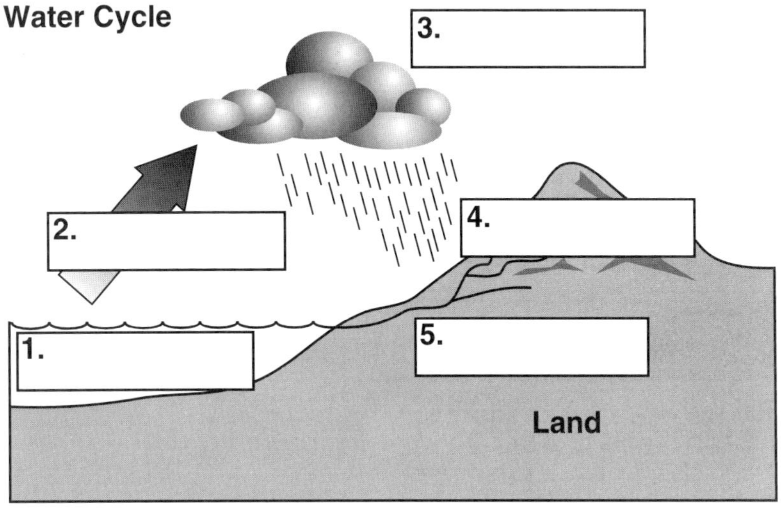

Recap *Water vapour turning into water is called **c**________________. This forms **r**_________, and is part of the water **c**____________.*

In this activity you will learn about the water cycle

The **water cycle** is the never ending movement of water from the sea, into the sky, onto the land and back into the sea.

Activities

1 Complete the diagram of the water cycle below by filling in the gaps using the words in the Word box. Colour in the diagram.

Word box

Ground water • Precipitation • Condensation
Transpiration • Surface water • Evaporation

2 Complete the passage below by filling in the gaps using the words in the Word box.

Word box

Transpiration
Ground water
Rivers
Precipitation
Clouds
Cycle
Evaporation
Vapour

The water ____________ is the never ending movement of water from the sea to the sky, onto the land, and back into the sea.

The sun heats the water which turns it into gas called water **v**____________. This process is called **ev**__________________. The water vapour cools in the sky and turns back into water. this makes **c**_______________. **Pr**_______________________ (usually rainfall) then takes water back onto land.

Most water flows downhill in **r**____________. Some sinks into the rocks and is called **g**____________ ____________. The water flows back into the sea. Some water is used by plants and they send water vapour back into the sky from their leaves. This is called **tr**_______________.

Recap *Water* ***e***__________________________ *into the sky. It falls on the land as* ***p***________________________. *Rivers take water back to the* ***s***_________. *This is known as the* ***w***_________________ ***c***___________________.

In this activity you will learn about water supply

We use a lot of **water** in the home every day. We need to have a good supply of water so that we can turn on the tap when we need water for **washing**, **cooking** and **drinking**.

Activity

Using the figures below draw a cartoon in each of the boxes to show how we use water in the home. Give each one a title and write how much water is used. One has been done for you.

Washing up	**14 litres**	**Flushing toilet**	**50 litres**
Cleaning car	**9 litres**	**Washing and bathing**	**50 litres**
Drinking and cooking	**4 litres**	**Washing clothes**	**14 litres**

Use *Washing up*

14 **litres**

Use ____________

____ **litres**

Use ____________

____ **litres**

Use ____________

____ **litres**

Use ____________

____ **litres**

Use ____________

____ **litres**

Recap We use a lot of water in the home each day for

w____________, **cooking** and **d**____________.

In this activity you will learn about water supply

Cities need lots of water for people and industry. In Britain, the west has most water (**supply**), and fewest people (**demand**). The East has most people (**demand**), and the least water (**supply**).

Activities

1 Colour the map below. Use **blue** for the area with **most water** and **fewest people**, and **green** for the area with **most people** and **least water**.

2 Shade each bubble above in the same colours as the map. Colour the ones that are to do with the **west** in **blue**, and the ones that are to do with the **east** in **green**.

Recap *Not all parts of Britain have the same water* ***supply*** *and the same* ***demand*** *for water. The west has* ***m***__________ *water than it needs, and the east has* ***l***__________ *water.*

In this activity you will learn about water supply

In Britain our water supply comes from **wells**, **springs**, **lakes** and **reservoirs**. The water is carried to our homes through pipes. It is usually clean and safe to drink.

Activities

1 Complete the crossword by answering the clues below.

Clues

1 A hole dug into the ground to reach water. (4)

2 A wall built across a river to make a reservoir. (3)

3 Oceans and seas are made of this type of water. (4, 5)

4 A man made lake. (9)

5 Water flowing down hill e.g. Tyne, Usk, Thames. (5)

6 Large areas of fresh water. (5)

7 U________________ water. Water in the rocks below the ground. (11)

8 Tubes to carry water to your home. (5)

9 Turn these on to get water in the bath. (4)

10 The largest man made lake in Britain. (On the River North Tyne.) (7)

11 A place where clean, fresh water comes out of the ground. (6)

12 Water forms this on a cold day. (3)

13 White stuff falling in winter. (4)

2 On the crossword colour the words that are to do with **water storage**, e.g. lakes, in **blue**.

Recap *In Britain our water supply comes from **wells, springs, lakes** and r__________________.*

In this activity you will learn about using water from the River Nile

In places where there is not enough rainfall, people need to water their crops. This is called **irrigation**. In **Egypt** the water for irrigation comes from the **River Nile**. Farmers need to **lift** the water from the river onto the land. Most farmers use a **shaduf** to do this.

Activities

1 Complete the diagram below of a shaduf by joining the dots.

2 Draw lines to join the 'heads' on the left, and the 'tails' on the right below.

Egyptian farmers can only grow crops	very close to the River Nile.
A shaduf is used	watering the crops.
Irrigation is	to lift water from the river onto the fields.
Egypt gets	if they irrigate the land.
Most people in Egypt live	very little rainfall.

Recap *Water from the River* **N**_______ *is used to* **i**____________________ *crops in Egypt. Most farmers use a* **s**_______________ *to lift water from the river.*

In this activity you will learn about using water from the River Nile

The **River Nile** is the longest river in the world. It is 6690 km long. It flows north from the equator and passes through the **Sahara Desert**, which is the largest desert in the world. The River Nile is very important to the people of **Egypt** because it gives them water to grow crops.

To save water, a dam was built across the River Nile at a town called **Aswan**. The **Aswan Dam** created a big lake called **Lake Nasser** which is 500 km long.

Activities

3 letter words
Dam
Hot

4 letter words
Crop
Lake
Nile
Rain
Salt
~~Silt~~
Year

5 letter words
Aswan
Cairo
Egypt
Sudan

6 letter words
Africa
Desert
Floods
Nasser
Sahara
Shaduf
Uganda

8 letter words
Khartoum
Lake Tana

10 letter words
Irrigation

13 letter words
Mediterranean

1 Complete the crossword using the words listed above. Start with the longest words first. One word has been done for you.

2 On the crossword colour the names of countries or cities in **red**.

Recap *The longest river in the world is the* ***River N*****__________***. It is 6690 km long and passes through the* ***S*****____________** ***Desert.*** *It is used to irrigate crops in* ***E*****____________***.*

In this activity you will learn about using water from the River Nile

To save water in **Egypt**, a dam was built across the **River Nile** at a town called **Aswan**. The **Aswan Dam** created a big lake called **Lake Nasser** which is 500 km long. The lake has had some **good effects** on Egypt, and it has also had some **bad effects**.

Activities

Read each comment below made by Mr Hassan.

1 Colour the comments that are talking about the **good effects** of the Aswan Dam in **red**.

2 Colour the comments that are talking about the **bad effects** of the Aswan Dam in **green**.

3 Write **two advantages** and **two disadvantages** of the Aswan Dam in the spaces below. Use the diagram above to help you.

Advantages of the Aswan Dam

1 ____

____

2 ____

____

Disadvantages of the Aswan Dam

1 ____

____

2 ____

____

Recap *Lake Nasser was created when the A_______________ D____________ was built. The lake has* ***advantages*** *and* ***d****________________________.*

In this activity you will learn about the function of a settlement

The **function** of a settlement is the reason why it was built. Different types of settlement have different functions. Some examples are:

- A **resort** – a place where people go for a holiday.
- A **port** – a place where ships bring things into, and take things out of, the country.
- A **market town** – a place where people, especially farmers, used to come to buy and sell things.

Activities

1 Complete the speech bubbles below. Use the words in bold in the sentences above.

I live in a______________ town. People come here to buy and sell things.

I live in a______________. It is where ships bring things into, and take things out of, the country.

I live in a______________. People come here for a holiday.

2 Some buildings are only found in settlements with a certain function. Complete the sentences below using the words in the Word box.

Word box

Funfair and amusement arcades
Docks and warehouses
Market place

A ________________________ are likely to be found in a **resort**.

A ________________________ is likely to be found in a **market town**.

________________________ are likely to be found in a **port**.

Recap

*The **function** of a settlement is* ________________________

In this activity you will learn about the function of a settlement

The **function** of a settlement is the reason why it was built. Different types of settlement have different functions.

I live in an **industrial town**. Many people work in factories.

I live in a **resort**. People come here for a holiday.

I live in a **market town**. People come here to buy and sell things.

I live in a **port**. It is where ships bring things into, and take things out of, the country.

Activities

Some types of buildings are found in all settlements. Others may only be found in settlements with a certain function.

1 Complete the table below by ticking the boxes to show the buildings found in each type of settlement. The first one has been done for you.

	Resort	Industrial Town	Market Town	Port	
Factory		✓			
Funfair					
Houses					
Market place					
Shops					
Docks					
Coal mine					

2 In the end column, add ticks to show the type of buildings found in your town or city. What function do they have?

____

Recap The **function** of a settlement is ______________________

____

In this activity you will learn about the function of a settlement

The **function** of a settlement is the reason why it was built. Different types of settlement have different functions. Larger settlements may have more than one function. The function of a settlement may change over time.

- A **resort** is a place where people go for a holiday.
- A **port** is a place where ships bring things into, and take things out of, the country.
- A **market town** is a place where people, especially farmers, used to come to buy and sell things.
- An **industrial town** is a place which has factories, or maybe a coal mine.

Activities

1 Look at the map, and then complete the sentences below. Use the information above to help you.

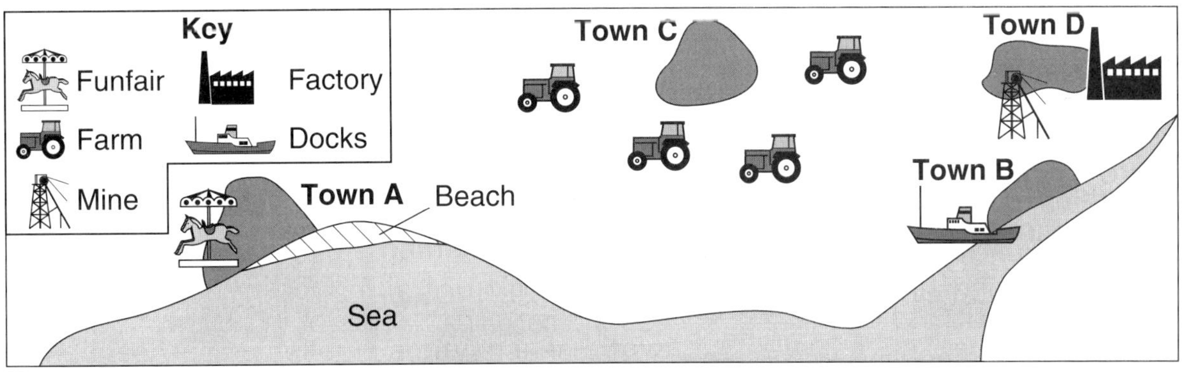

Town A is a __________ because ______________________________

____.

Town B is a __________ because ______________________________

____.

Town C is a __________ town because ______________________________

____.

Town D is an __________ town because ______________________________

____.

2 What is the function of your town or city? ______________________________

3 In your exercise book or folder, describe how the function of the town or city in which you live has changed over time.

Recap *The* ***function*** *of a settlement is* ______________________________

____.

A settlement may be a ***r***__________, *a* ***p***__________, *a* ***m***__________ *town, or an* ***in***__________ *town.*

In this activity you will learn about the site of a settlement

The **site** of a settlement is the place where it is built. A good site needs many things. The diagram below shows the thoughts of villagers long ago.

Activity

Use the words in the Word box to complete the sentences below.

Word box

crops • bad weather • enemies • fuel • grass
cooking • building • animals • soil • washing

Wood is needed for **f**________ and **b**_________ houses.

Water is needed for **c**_________ and **w**_________ clothes and people.

A **good view** is needed to see **e**_________ coming.

Shelter is needed to protect the village from **b**_____ **w**_________.

To get **food** the villagers would need good **s**_________ to grow **c**_______, and good **g**_________ for the **a**_________ to eat.

Recap *The **site** of a settlement is*______________________________.

In this activity you will learn about the site of a settlement

The **site** of a settlement is the place where it is built. Long ago people lived in small groups. They had to think about many things when choosing a good place to live.

Activities

1 Match up the 'heads' and 'tails' below of the things people needed, and the reason why they needed them. One has been done for you.

Wood	for their animals to eat
Water	to see their enemies coming
Good soil	for building homes
Good grass	from bad weather
Shelter	to cook with and to drink
Good view	for fuel
More wood	to grow crops

(Wood → for building homes)

2 A perfect site was almost impossible to find. Most had good points and bad points. Look at the drawing below which shows four possible sites for a settlement: **A**, **B**, **C** and **D**. Use the information on the drawing to complete the table below.

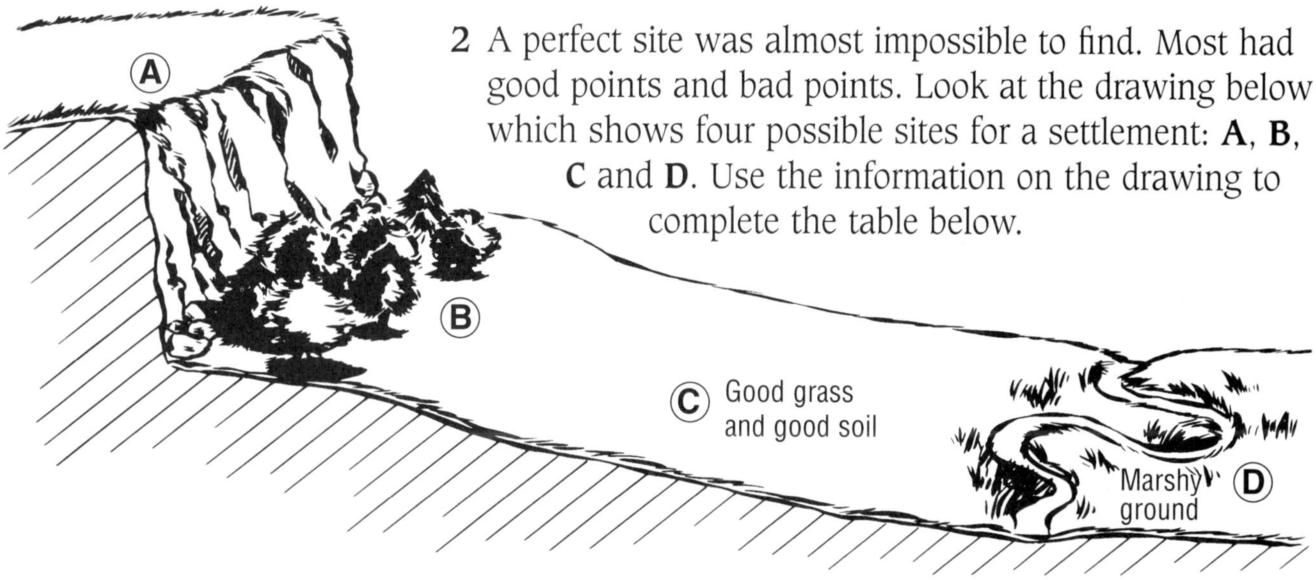

Site	One good point	One bad point
A		*A long way from the water*
B	*Plenty of wood for fuel*	
C		*Open ground, so not easy to defend*
D		

Recap *The* ***site*** *of a settlement is* ____________________________.

In this activity you will learn about the site of a settlement

The **site** of a settlement is the place where it is built. Long ago when people were looking for a good place to live they had to think about many things. A good site would need to be:

- Near a stream or river for **water**.
- Near a **wood** for fuel.
- Near **wood or stone** for buildings.
- Near good **grass** for their animals.
- Near good **soil** to grow food.
- Away from **marshy ground**.
- **Sheltered** from bad weather.
- Easy to **defend** against an attack.

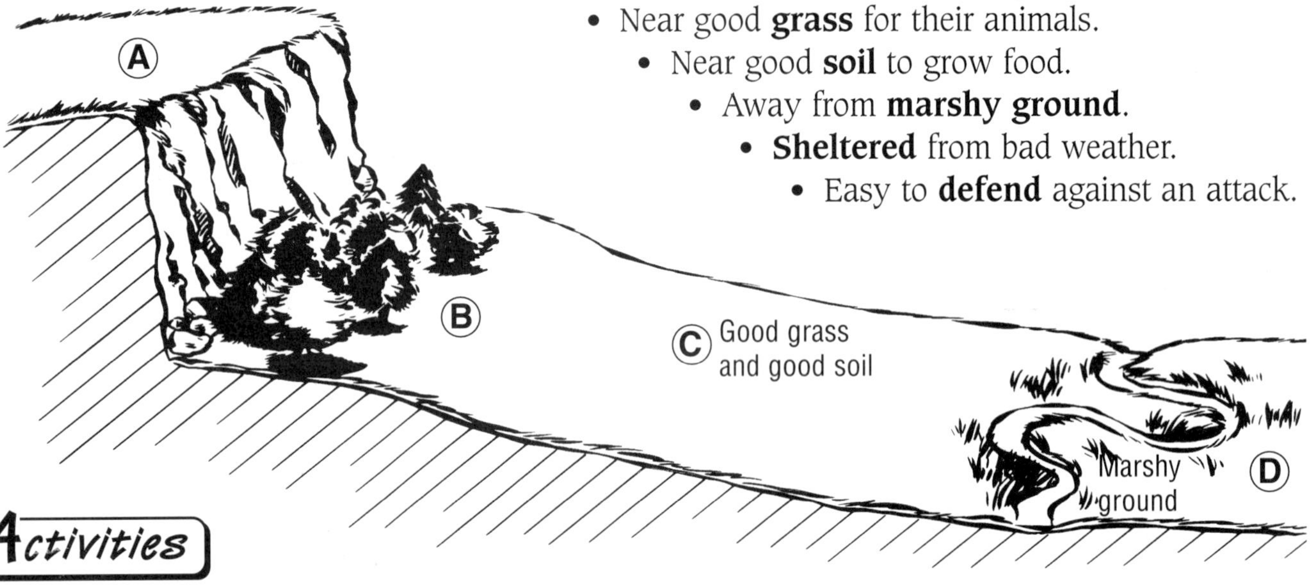

Activities

1 Look at the sketch below which shows four possible sites for a settlement, and then fill in the table. Part of it has been done for you.

Site	One **good point** about this site	One **bad point** about this site
Ⓐ		*A long way from the water*
Ⓑ	*Plenty of wood for fuel*	
Ⓒ		
Ⓓ		

2 Which site do you think would be the best? ______________________

3 In your exercise book or folder say why have you chosen this site. The list of eight things at the top of the page will help you.

Recap

*The **site** of a settlement is ______________________.*

Some things a good site would need to be near are: ____________,

____________, ____________, and ____________.

In this activity you will learn about settlement patterns

A settlement pattern is the **shape** of the settlement.

- A **dispersed** settlement pattern means that all the buildings are **spread out**.
- A **nucleated** settlement pattern means that all the buildings are grouped **together**.
- A **linear** settlement pattern means the buildings are found in a **long line**.

Activities

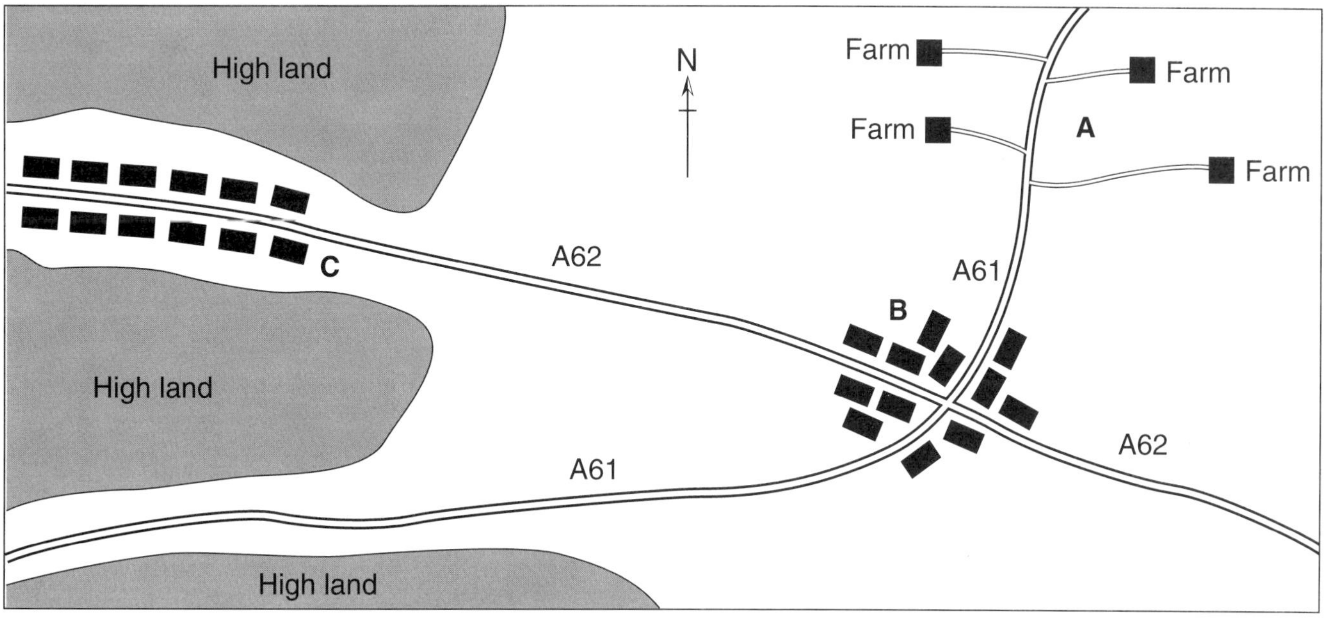

1 Look at the map above. Complete the sentences below by underlining the correct answer in brackets.

- Settlement A is a (**dispersed/nucleated/linear**) settlement.
- Settlement B is a (**dispersed/nucleated/linear**) settlement.
- Settlement C is a (**dispersed/nucleated/linear**) settlement.

2 Complete the following sentences by underlining the correct ending in brackets.

- The occupation of the people who live in Settlement A is likely to be (**fishing/farming/mining**).
- Settlement B is centred around a (**crossroads/hill/lake**).
- Settlement C is a linear settlement because it is (**spread out/too far north/in a narrow valley**).

Recap By **settlement pattern** we mean ______________________________

____.

In this activity you will learn about the good and bad points of living in a town

Most people in Britain live in a town or city. There are many **good points** and **bad points** about living in a town.

Activities

1 Find the words in the Word box in the wordsearch below. Words can go forwards, backwards, up, down or diagonally. All the words are things you might find in towns.

H	J	A	S	R	A	C	H	S
P	O	L	L	U	T	I	O	N
L	B	S	N	C	J	N	U	T
Y	S	B	P	R	D	E	S	C
S	W	T	U	I	S	M	E	R
H	F	A	S	M	T	A	S	O
O	P	C	S	E	L	A	I	W
P	O	R	E	T	T	I	L	D
S	C	O	N	C	E	R	T	S

Word box

hospitals	pollution
litter	cinema
houses	jobs
waste	discos
crowds	cars
concerts	crime
shops	

2 Fill in the table below using the words from the Word box. One has been done for you.

Good points about living in a town	Bad points about living in a town
	Pollution

Recap There are many ________ points and many ________ points about living in towns.

In this activity you will learn about the good points and bad points of living in a town

Most people in Britain live in a town or city. This is because they believe that there are many **benefits** or good points about living, and working, in large settlements.

People like living in towns because:

There are bigger and better **shops**.

There are more **jobs**.

There are more **houses** and **flats** to buy or rent.

There's more **entertainment** and special **events**.

Getting about is easier because **transport** is better.

There are more services such as **hospitals**.

Activities

1 Complete the crossword below. Use the words in **bold** in the speech bubbles. These show some of the **benefits** of living in towns.

2 People living in towns also face many **problems** or bad points. Use the clues to complete the crossword below.

Clues

1 No jobs
2 Lots of cars, lorries and buses
3 Spoiling the environment
4 Waste
5 Deliberately destroying something
6 Sweet papers and crisp packets thrown in the street
7 Breaking the law
8 Can damage your hearing

Recap *Living in a town or city brings many **b** ______________________*
*but it also brings many **p**______________________.*

In this activity you will learn about the good points and bad points of living in a town

Most people in Britain live in a town or city. This is because they believe that living in a large settlement has many **benefits**. Towns and cities also have many **problems**.

Activities

1 Use the words listed below to complete the crossword. All the words are things you find in towns or cities. Tip – begin with the longest words first.

9 letter words
Hospital
Pollution

7 letter words
Cinemas
Traffic
Schools

6 letter words
Houses
Crowds
Events

5 letter words
Crime
Noise
Shops

4 letter words
Jobs
Cars

2 Fill in the table below using the words from the crossword.

Benefits of living in a town	Problems found in towns

3 In your exercise book or folder, write a paragraph describing what could be done to reduce the problems of litter, crime or traffic in towns or cities.

Recap *Living in towns has many ________________. It also has many ________________.*

This activity you will learn how settlements change over time

No settlement remains the same for ever. Settlements **change** over time.

The map below shows how Cardiff has grown.

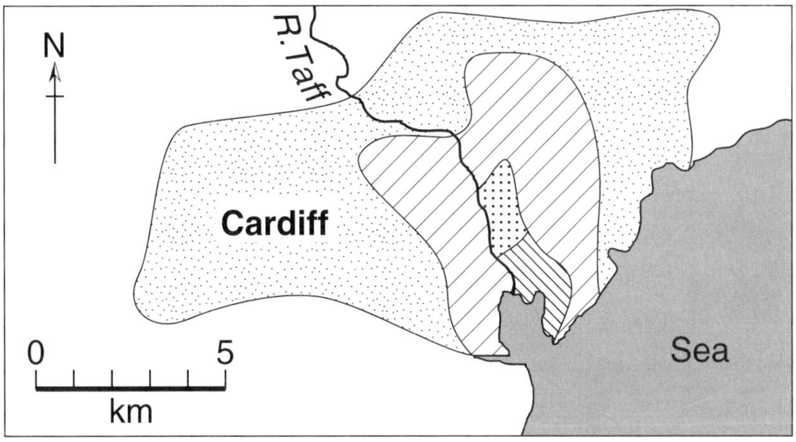

Key

Size of Cardiff in 1695

Size of Cardiff in 1795

Size of Cardiff in 1895

Size of Cardiff in 1995

Population

1695 = 1,000
1795 = 5,000
1895 = 100,000
1995 = 300,000

Activities

1 Colour the map using the following colours:

- **light blue** for the **sea**
- **black** for the **size of Cardiff in 1695**
- **dark blue** for the **size of Cardiff in 1795**
- **red** for the **size of Cardiff in 1895**
- **yellow** for the **size of Cardiff in 1995**.

2 Complete the **line graph** below to show how the population of Cardiff has grown.

3 Complete the sentences by underlining the correct answer in brackets.

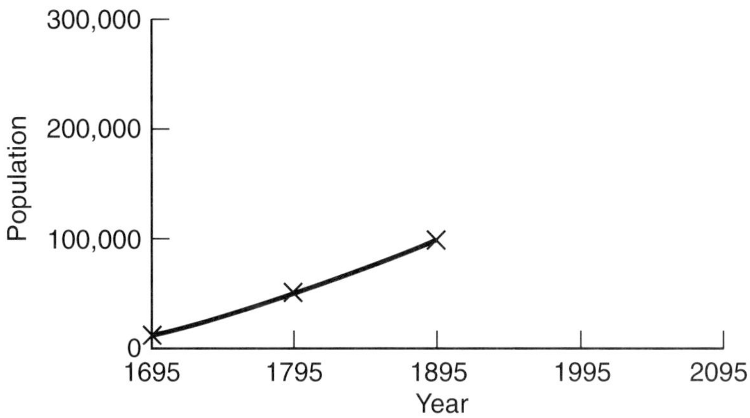

Since 1695 the population of Cardiff has (**increased/decreased**.)

The most rapid (**increase/ decrease**) was between (**1695–1795/1895–1995**).

Recap

Settlements never remain ______________________.

They ______________ over time.

In this activity you will learn how settlements change over time

No settlement remains the same for ever. Settlements **change** over time. The diagrams below show the same village in 1890 and in 1990.

Diagram A Village in 1890

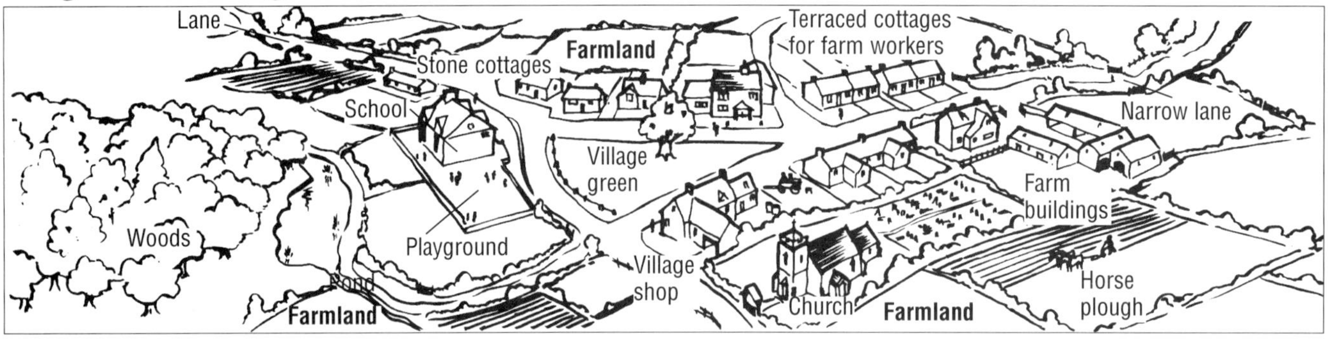

Diagram B Village in 1990

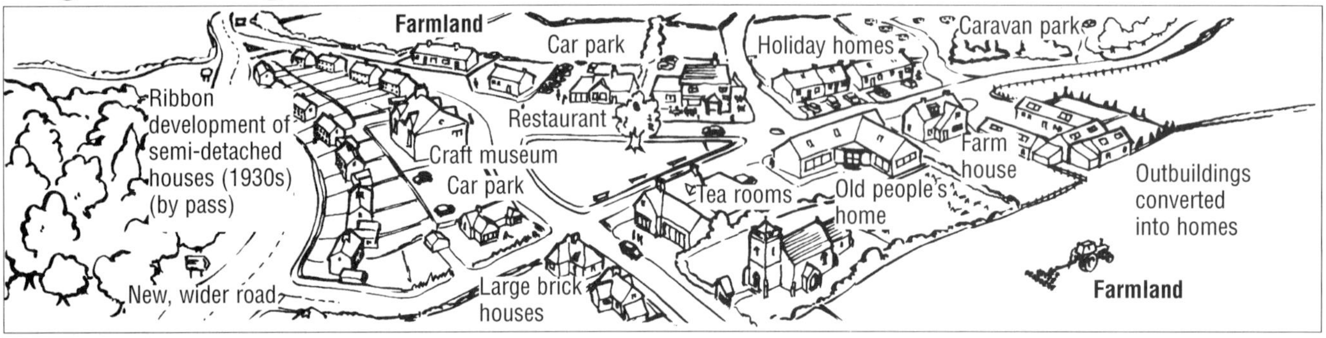

Activities

1 Look at **Diagrams A** and **B** above. Complete the table showing how the use of the buildings has changed.

Village in 1890	**Village in 1990**
School and playground	
	Holiday homes
	Restaurant
	Tea rooms
Farm buildings	

2 What has happened to the pond? ____________________

3 Is the settlement where you live changing? ____________________

If so, how? ____________________

Recap *Settlements never remain ______________. They ______________ overtime.*

In this activity you will learn how settlements change over time

No settlement remains the same for ever. Settlements **change** over time. New **shops** open, old **buildings** are knocked down, new **houses** are built and new **roads** may open.

1965

Baker	Grocer	Fishmonger	Butcher	Ladies' Clothes	Hardware (DIY)	Greengrocer	Men's Clothes	Bank

HIGH STREET

1995

Supermarket	Fish and Chip shop	Empty	Empty	Knocked down	Video Hire shop	Chinese Take-Away	Bank

HIGH STREET

Activities

1 The plan above shows the High Street in a small town in 1965, and 1995.

Complete the paragraph below using the words in the Word box.

Word box

video hire • four • supermarket • two • grocer
clothes • bank • hardware • eight • butcher

In 1965 there were a total of __________ shops and a bank. In 1995 there were only ____________ shops left open. The ______________ shop has been knocked down and there are _________________ empty shops. Now people buy their food from the _____________________. In 1965 they had to go to more than one shop such as the ________________ and ________________to buy food. Only one building has remained the same, and that is the ___________. People who want to buy________________________ now have to look elsewhere. The ______________ shop now means people do not have to go to the cinema to see a film.

Recap

2 In your exercise book or folder describe how the settlement where you live is changing.

Settlements never remain __________. They ________________ over time.

Some examples of how they change are: ________________________________

____.

In this activity you will learn about land use patterns in towns

Land use describes what the land is used for. In most towns the land use changes as you move outwards from the town centre. The way the land is used makes up a land use **pattern**.

Central Business District (CBD)

Shops, offices, banks, entertainment

Inner City

Old terraced housing

Suburbs

Newer houses

Countryside

Open space farmland.

Activities

1 Use the words in the Word box to complete the sentences below.

The centre of the town is called the ______________.

In the inner city you will find **o**__________ houses built in **t**_____________.

In the suburbs you will find **n**___________ houses with more **s**_____________ around them.

The edge of the town is where the **c**__________________ begins.

Word box

countryside	older
newer	CBD
terraces	space

2 In which part of the town are each of the following land uses most likely to be found? Complete the table by placing each land use under the correct heading.

Large shops farmland open space small houses larger houses old factories offices new houses cinemas small villages banks

CBD	Inner City	Suburbs	Countryside

Recap *Land use describes* ____________________________________

In this activity you will learn about land use patterns in towns

Land use describes what the land is used for, e.g. shops, farming, roads, factories or parks. The way the land is used makes up a land use **pattern**.

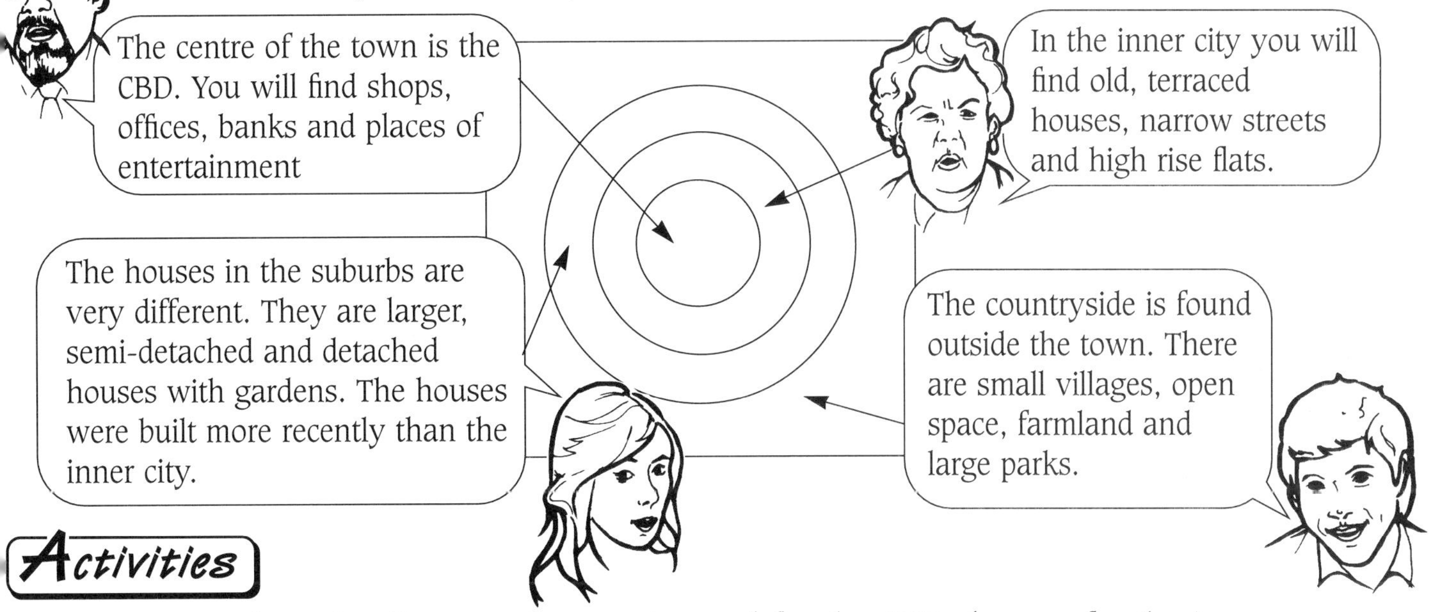

Activities

1 Colour the diagram above using **red** for the **CBD**, **brown** for the **inner city**, **yellow** for the **suburbs** and **green** for the **countryside**.

2 Imagine you are travelling from the town centre outwards. Which order would the following zones come in? Mark them on the line below.

Inner city • countryside • CBD • suburbs

Town centre ————————————————→

3 Complete the table below by ticking **true** or **false** for each statement.

	True	False
Farmland and open space is found in the **countryside**		
The centre of the town is called the **BBC**		
There are no houses in the **centre** of the town		
Modern houses are found in the **suburbs**		
Old factories are found in the **inner city**		

4 If you live in a town or city, which part do you live in? ____________

Recap *Land use describes ______________________________.*

The way the land is used makes up the land use ___________.

In this activity you will learn about land use patterns in towns

Land use describes what the land is used for, e.g. shops, farming, roads, factories or parks. The way the land is used makes up a land use **pattern**. Although no two towns will be the same, most have similar land use patterns which make up zones.

Activities

1 Complete the sentences below by underlining the correct answer in brackets. Use the diagram of **land use zones** to help you.

Farmland and open space is found in the (**Countryside/CBD/Inner city**).

The centre of the town is called the (**BBC/ABC/CBD**).

There are no houses in the (**Inner city/Outer suburbs/CBD**).

Modern houses would be found in the (**Inner suburbs/Outer suburbs/CBD**).

Old factories would be found in the (**Inner city/Countryside/Outer suburbs**).

Land use zones

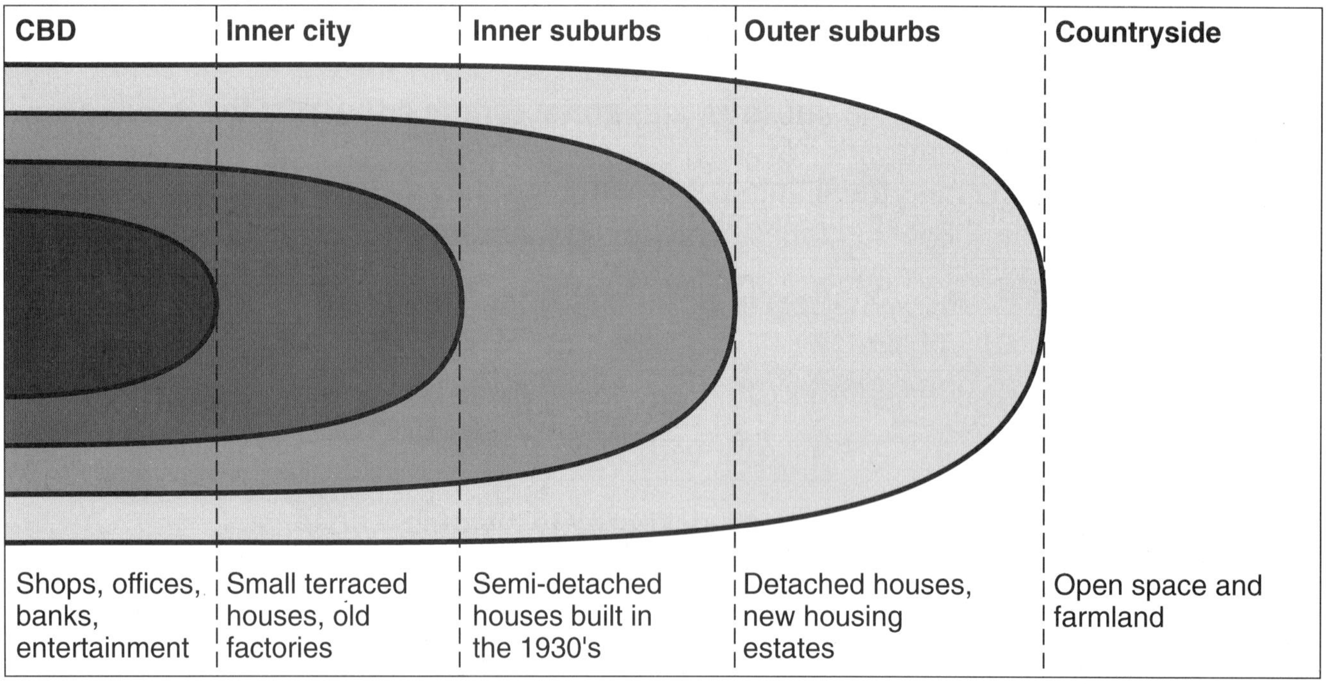

2 If you live in a town or city which part do you live in? ____________________

3 In your exercise book or folder, describe the CBD in either the town you live in, or the nearest town or city. How is it different from other zones in the town?

Recap

Land use describes ______________________________.

*There are five **zones** found in a town. They are:* ____________________

____

____

In this activity you will learn about the size of settlements

All settlements vary in **size**. Some are quite small, while others are very large. The type of settlement is named according to how many people live there.

Activities

1 Study the table of settlement types. Then complete the sentences below by filling in the gaps.

Settlement type	**Approximate number of people living in each settlement**
Hamlet	10 to 200
Village	more than 200
Town	more than 10 000
City	more than 100 000

The smallest settlement is called a ____________.

The largest settlement is called a ____________.

If more than 200 people lived in a settlement it would be called a ____________.

If more than 20 000 people lived in a settlement it would be called a __________.

2 There are always more smaller settlements than larger ones.

Look at the map below. Count the number of each type of settlement.

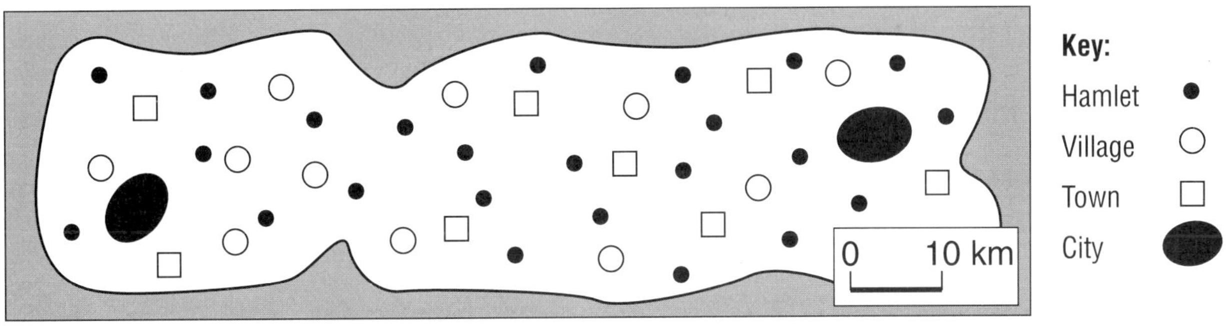

Number of **hamlets** ________ Number of **villages** ________

Number of **towns** ________ Number of **cities** ________

Recap *The four types of settlement are* ______________________________

____

In this activity you will learn about the size of settlements

All settlements vary in **size**. Some are quite small, while others are very large. The type of settlement is named according to how many people live there. Larger settlements offer more **services** (such as shops, banks, doctors, frequent buses) than smaller settlements.

Settlement type	**Examples of services**	**Approximate number of people living in each settlement**
Hamlet	Telephone box	10 to 200
Village	Church, Post Office, shop, junior school	more than 200
Town	Many shops, superstore, many churches, at least one senior school, doctors, dentists, optician, banks, small hospital, railway station	more than 10 000
City	Large railway station, large shopping complex, many other shops, several large schools, cathedral, university, football team, museum	more than 100 000

Activities

1 Complete the sentences below by underlining the correct word in bold. Use the table above to help you.

The smallest settlement is called a **town/hamlet**.

The largest settlement is called a **village/city**.

There are **many/few** services on offer in a city.

There are **more/fewer** services found in a village than in a town.

Churches are found in **all/some** settlements.

If a settlement has 20 000 people living there then it would be called a **town/city**.

2 The drawings below show different services. Which is the **smallest** settlement each would be found in? Write your answer below each drawing.

1

2

3

4

__________ __________ __________ __________

Recap *The four types of settlement are* ____________________

____

In this activity you will learn about the size of settlements

All settlements vary in **size**. Larger settlements offer more **services**.

Settlement type	**Examples of services**	**Approximate number of people living in each settlement**
Hamlet	Telephone box	10 to 200
Village	Church, Post Office, shop, junior school	more than 200
Town	Many shops, superstore, many churches, at least one senior school, doctors, dentists, optician, banks, small hospital, railway station	more than 10 000
City	Large railway station, large shopping complex, many other shops, several large schools, cathedral, university, football team, museum	more than 100 000

Activities

1 Complete the table below by ticking **true** or **false** for each statement.

	True	**False**
The smallest settlement is called a **hamlet**		
The largest settlement is called a **town**		
There are more services on offer in a **city** than in a **town**		
If a settlement has 20 000 people living there then it is called a **city**		

2 There are always more smaller settlements than larger ones. Usually, larger settlements are a long way from other large settlements. Smaller settlements are closer to each other.

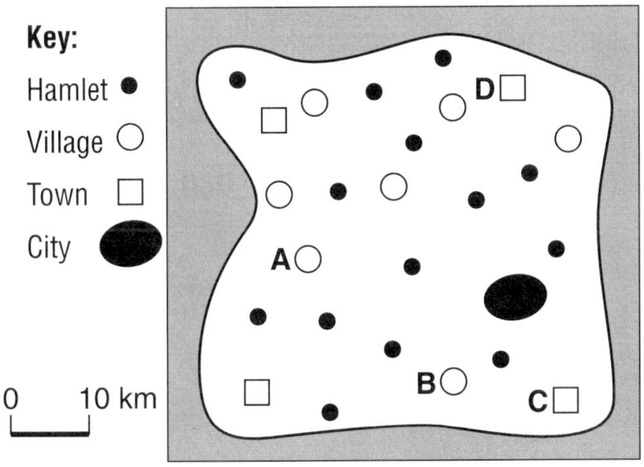

Look at the map.
Count the number of each type of settlement.

Hamlets ______ Villages ______

Towns ______ Cities ______

Use the scale to measure the distance from:

Village **A** to Village **B** ______________

Town **C** to Town **D** ______________

Remember to give your answer in kilometres.

Recap *The four types of settlement are ________________________________*

____.

Larger settlements offer more ________________________________.

In this activity you will learn about shopping

Most of us visit shops a lot. There are some things we need to buy very often. These items are called **low order goods**, such as food, newspapers and magazines. Other things we don't need to buy so often. These items are called **high order goods**, such as furniture and clothes.

Activities

1 Find the **low order goods** in the Word box in the wordsearch. Words can go across, down, backwards or diagonally.

N	M	I	L	C	V	A	M	M
T	E	S	B	R	E	T	A	I
O	A	W	I	I	G	O	G	L
I	T	E	S	S	E	O	A	K
L	K	E	C	P	T	T	Z	S
E	C	T	U	S	A	H	I	U
T	H	S	I	F	B	P	N	G
R	E	J	T	A	L	A	E	A
O	E	L	S	W	E	S	S	R
L	S	P	A	O	S	T	Z	C
L	E	A	Y	B	R	E	A	D

Word box

newspaper • vegetables • toothpaste toilet roll • bread • sweets • soap biscuits • sugar • magazines • milk • crisps • meat • fish • cheese

2 Use the clues to complete the crossword below. These are all **high order goods**.

1									**H**						
2									**I**						
3									**G**						
4									**H**						
5									**O**						
6									**R**						
7									**D**						
8									**E**						
9									**R**						
10									**G**						
11									**O**						
12									**O**						
13									**D**						
14									**S**						

Clues

1. Wear these on your feet
2. Chairs, tables, etc.
3. Presents
4. Dresses, trousers, etc.
5. Watch your favourite programmes on this
6. Cover the floor with these
7. Listen to CDs on this
8. Gold and precious stones
9. Makes you smell nice
10. Cover your eyes with these in summer
11. A multi-media machine
12. Read these
13. Rent one of these when you want to watch a film
14. CDs, tapes, records etc.

Recap ***Low order goods*** *are bought __________. __________* ***order goods*** *are bought occasionally.*

In this activity you will learn about shopping

There are four main types of **shopping centres**.

A **shopping street** has several shops together found close to a housing estate or a main road. Shoppers may call more than once a week. There may be a specialist shop such as a chemist and a take-away.

The corner shop is small and found close to where people live. It sells items that people buy every day, e.g. bread, milk and newspapers.

An **out-of-town shopping centre** is found on the edge of town, close to main roads. Large supermarkets are found here. People visit weekly and buy all their shopping in one visit.

In the **town centre** there are large shops which sell more expensive items. Most people travel to get to these shops, so they visit them less than once a week. There may be covered shopping areas.

Activities

1 Where are people **most likely** to buy the items listed in the table? Tick the correct boxes. You may tick more than one box for each item. Use the information in the diagram to help you.

Item	Corner shop	Shopping street	Town centre	Out-of-town shopping centre
Expensive gifts				
Milk				
Medicines				
Weekly shopping				
Sweets				
Video film hire				
Jewellery				
Cheap petrol				

2 Which type of **shopping centre** does each of the following sentences describe? Match the 'heads' with the correct 'tails'.

Heads	Tails
Many large shops, streets closed to traffic, covered shopping areas	Corner shop
People walk here daily to buy items they may have forgotten	Out-of-town shopping centre
A line of shops found close to a main road or housing estate	Town centre
Large shops where you can buy all you need, with free parking, and cheap petrol	Shopping street

Recap Some things we need to buy **o**________________.
We usually travel **f**______________ to buy special things.

In this activity you will learn about shopping

A class of pupils asked twenty people in their local **town centre** about the way they did their shopping. The questions and answers are shown below.

	Answers	**Number of people**
1 How often do you shop here?	Everyday	2
	Once a week	6
	Once a month	12
2 How far have you travelled?	0-2 miles	4
	2-5 miles	10
	over 5 miles	6
3 How did you get here?	Bus	2
	Car	15
	Walk	3
4 What did you buy?	Food	______
	Clothes, shoes	______
	Special present	______

Activities

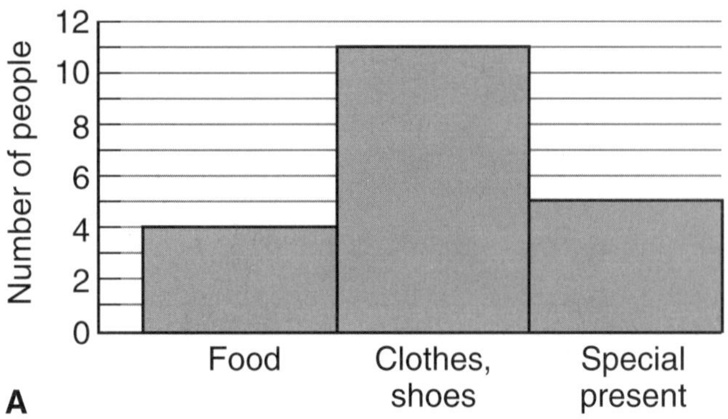

A

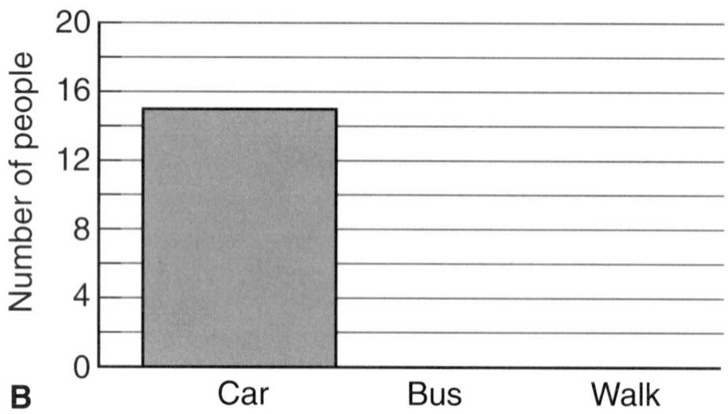

B

1 **a)** Use Graph **A** to fill in the answers to question 4 of the survey.
  b) Complete Graph **B** using the answers from question 3 of the survey.

2 Complete the sentences below by underlining the correct answer in brackets.
  Most people get to town by (**car/walking/bus**).
  Most people come to town to buy (**food/clothes, shoes/special present**).
  Most people visit the town centre (**daily/weekly/monthly**).
  Most people live less than (**2 miles/2-5 miles/over 5 miles away**).

3 **a)** How often do you visit your local town centre? ______________________

  b) What sort of things do you buy when you get there? ______________________

  ____

Recap *People visit their town centre about ______________________.*

Most people travel ______________________ to get there.

In this activity you will learn about town centre and out-of-town shopping

You can play **the 'Let's Go Shopping' game** on your own, or with a friend. You will need two counters and a dice. One counter will head for the **town centre** and the other will head for the **out-of-town superstore**. The object of the game is to see which counter gets **home** first. Count the number of throws it takes each counter to get **HOME**.

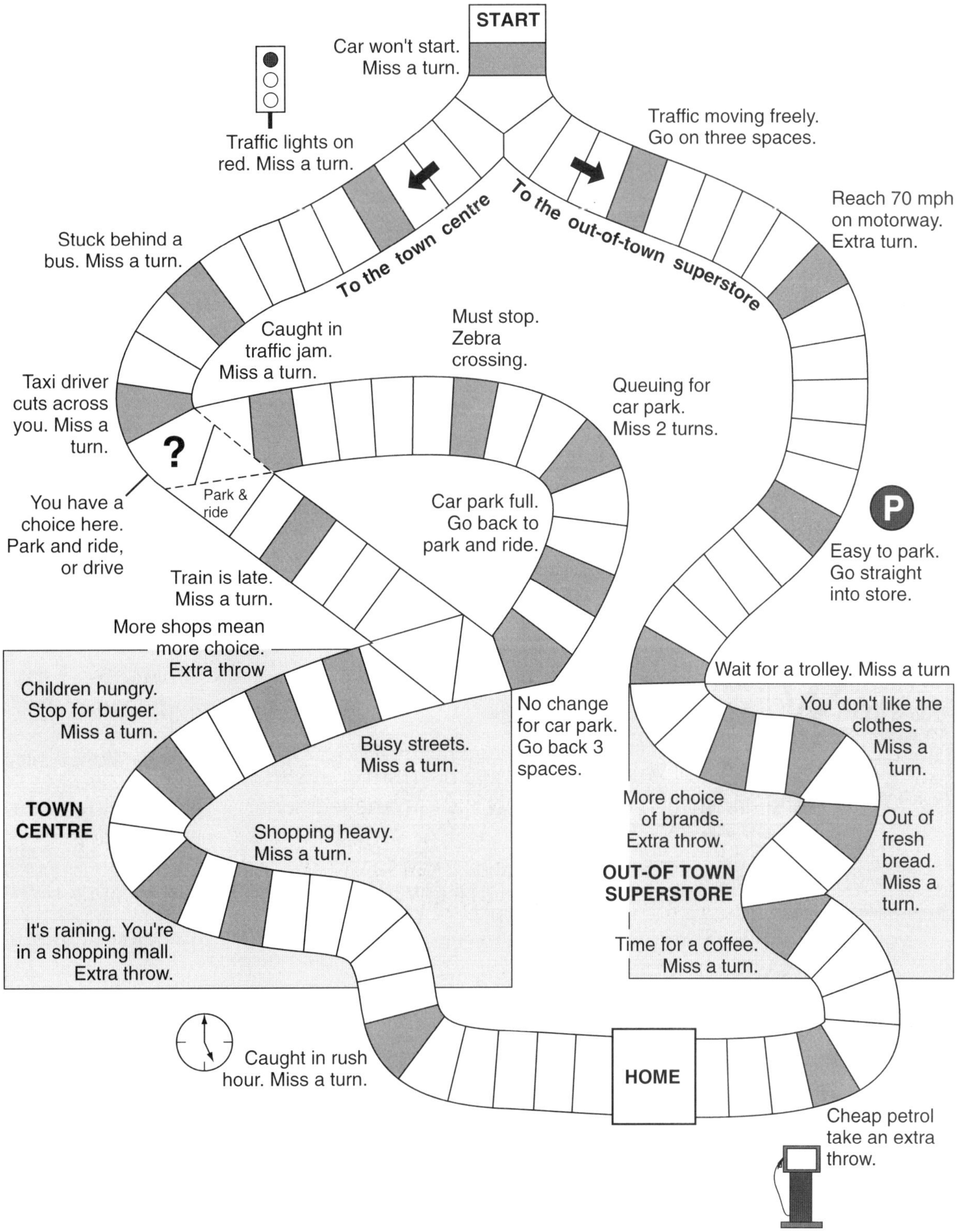

In this activity you will learn about out-of-town shopping

There are many **advantages** in building a superstore close to the edge of town.

Activities

1 Use the words in the Word box to complete the sentences below.

The land is **c**__________.

There is a lot of **s**________.

P__________ can be bought cheaply.

Lorries can deliver goods **e**__________.

People can get here **q**__________.

Near to the town means many **c**____________.

Word box
- cheap
- quickly
- space
- easily
- petrol
- customers

2 Look at the plan of a superstore. Use the information in the plan to match the 'heads' and 'tails' below.

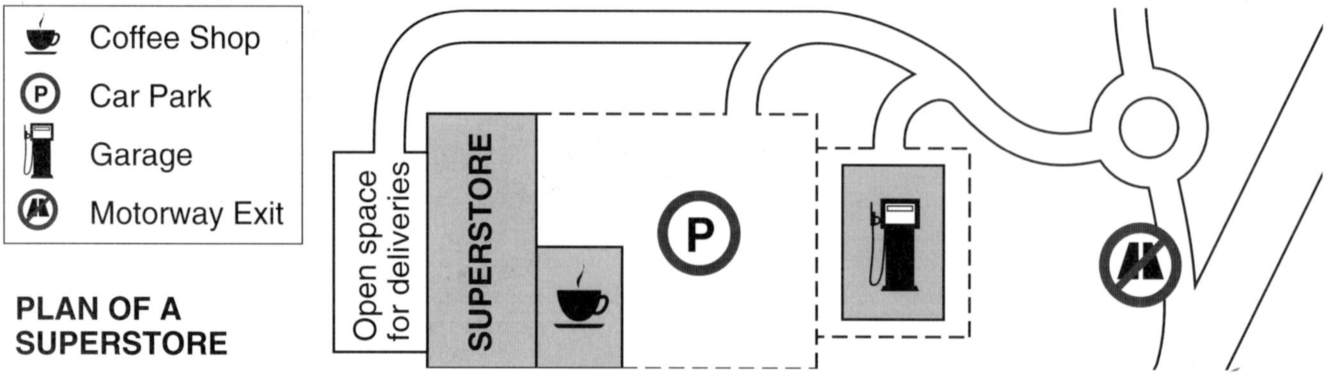

PLAN OF A SUPERSTORE

After shopping people can rest	is needed for deliveries
A good thing for drivers is	there is a large car park
Near a motorway exit saves lorry drivers	in the coffee shop
Parking is easy because	time and money
Open space at the back of the store	cheap petrol

Recap *Two **advantages** of building a superstore close to the edge of a town are:*

1 ______________________________

2 ______________________________

In this activity you will learn how land use in towns changes

Land use in towns **changes over time**. The Isle of Dogs is part of London's Docklands. Between 1960 and 1981 it became rundown. In 1981 the London Docklands Development Corporation was set up to improve the area. The sketch below shows some of the things they did.

Activities

Word box
new jobs
open space
transport
leisure
housing

1 Complete the speech bubbles above using the words in the Word box.

2 The two bar graphs below show the types of jobs in London's Docklands in 1978 and 1996.
Use the figures below to complete the graph for 1996.

Percentage of jobs

	1978	1996
Factories	43	20
Services	51	75
Building	6	5

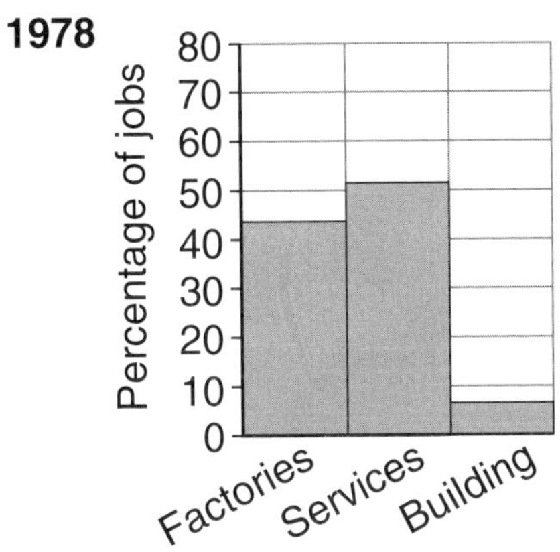

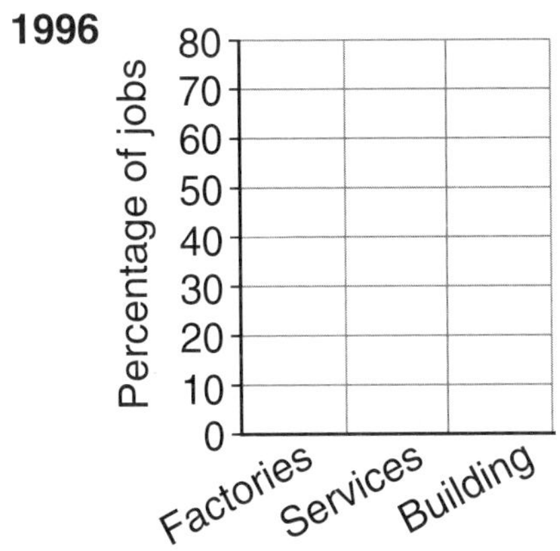

3 How have the types of jobs changed from 1978 to 1996? ______________________________

____

Recap *Land use in towns* ***c***_________ *over time. One such change is in the types of* ***j***_________ *available.*

In this activity you will learn how land use in towns changes

Land use in towns **changes over time**. This is particularly true of inner city areas. One such area is London's Docklands.

Activities

1 The statements below describe land use in London's Docklands in 1960 and 1996.

Complete the table by writing each statement in the correct place. Two have been done for you.

Poor, narrow streets

Modern houses and flats

Hi-tech offices

New light railway

Small and cramped

Nowhere to relax

Plenty of open space

Dirty and polluted

Old smoky factories

Waterfront bars and restaurants

	1960	1996
Housing		
Industry		
Transport	*poor, narrow streets*	
Environment		
Leisure		*waterfront bars and restaurants*

2 Some people who live in the area think the changes that have happened are good. They are the **winners**. Other people who live in the area think the changes are **not** so good. They are the **losers**. The table below shows four comments made by people who now live in the area.

Complete the table by writing the group of people shown next to the comment you think each made.

young couple **company director** **school leavers** **old dock workers**

The new houses cost a lot of money. We cannot afford to buy them.	
The new jobs are no use to us. We do not have the right skills.	
We moved here because the land is cheap. We are making a good profit.	
There are plenty of jobs for us. We have been trained in the new technology.	

3 In the table above shade the **winners** in **red**, and **losers** in **blue**.

4 Choose one **winner** and one **loser** and describe how they will benefit or lose out as a result of the changes that have occurred. Write your answer in your exercise book or folder.

Recap *Land use in towns* ***c***__________ *over time. Whenever changes occur there are always* ***w***__________ *and* ***l***__________.

In this activity you will learn about different types of transport

Transport is very important. It is used to carry **people** and **goods** from place to place. There are many different types of transport. The type of transport used depends on many things.

Activities

1 Imagine you have to deliver an important parcel from London to Paris. You have a choice of using **road**, **rail** or **air** transport. You have to consider several things.

Complete the table below by writing the following things in the correct place. Two have been done for you.

The Channel Tunnel means I can go straight to Paris.

The station is a long way from where I have to go.

I'd have to get to the airport first.

The ferry charges will add to my costs.

I can go directly from door to door.

It only takes just over an hour flying time.

Good points		Bad points
	Road	
The Channel Tunnel means I can go straight to Paris	**Rail**	
	Air	*I'd have to get to the airport first*

2 You also have to consider the **time** it takes, and the **cost**.

Complete the table below by working out the **total cost** for rail and air transport.

	Time	Approx. Distance	Cost per km	Total cost
Road	6 hours	400 km	30p	£120
Rail	5 hours	400 km	40p	
Air	3 hours	350 km	£1	

3 Which type of transport is quickest? ______________________

4 Which type of transport is cheapest? ______________________

5 Which type of transport would **you** choose? ______________________

Give **two** reasons for your choice

a ______________________

b ______________________

Recap *Many things have to be considered when deciding which type of transport to use. Two things are 1 ______________ 2 ______________.*

In this activity you will learn about different routes

A **route** is the path taken on a journey. The shortest route between two places is a **straight line**. It is not always possible to follow a straight line.

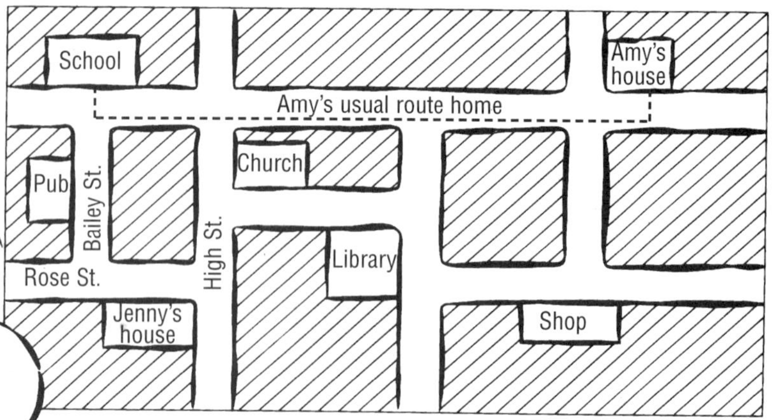

Activities

1 Jenny and Amy plan a **three** stage journey. The map shows the route they will take. Follow part **A** of their journey on the map.

A From **School to Jenny's house**. Jenny and Amy leave school. They cross the road and walk down **Bailey Street**. They pass the Rovers Return pub on their **right**. They turn **left** into **Rose Street** and go into Jenny's house.

2 Complete the routes below. Use the map to help you.

B **Jenny's house to the library**. They leave Jenny's house and go up

____________ **Street**. At the **church** they turn ____________ into

____________ **Street**. The **library** is on their ____________.

C Draw on the map the route they should take from the **library to Amy's house**. They want to visit the shop on the way.

3 Amy has taken a different route home today. Underline the words below which describe Amy's **usual** route home. Use the map to help you.

straight line/many turns **shorter/longer** **quicker/slower**

4 Complete this sentence. Amy and Jenny have not travelled in a straight line because

____

Recap *The shortest route between places is usually a*

*s*________________ *l*____________.

In this activity you will learn about different routes

A **route** is the path taken on a journey. Different types of transport take different routes.

Planners have to think about many things when deciding where to build a new road.

Activities

Word box

• motorways • steep • railways • roads

1 Add the words in the Word box to the labels on the map below.

__________ slopes have winding roads

__________ take the shortest routes where they can

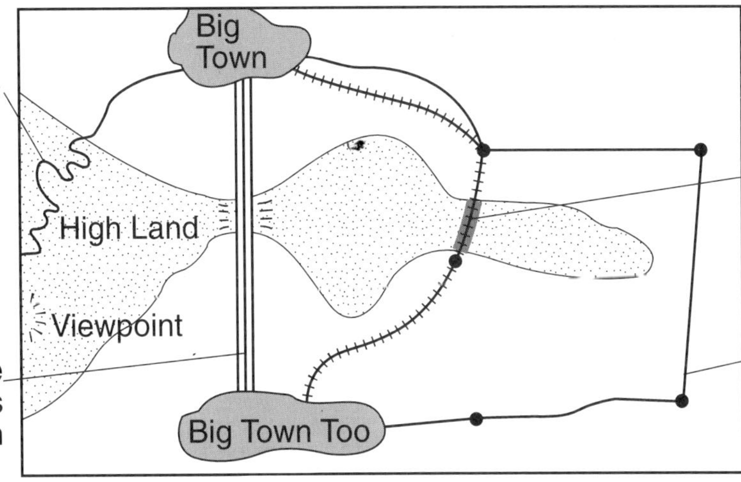

__________ follow flatter land and tunnels are built through high land

__________ visit all the towns and villages

2 Planners have to consider physical (**natural**) factors, **human** factors and the **environment** when deciding where to build a new road. Place the words in bold below under the correct heading in the table.

Building costs | Farmland destroyed? | Wildlife | Marshy ground? | Steep slopes | Is it the quickest route? | towns to be by-passed | Is it the shortest route? | Woodland | Rivers to be crossed | Parkland destroyed?

Physical (natural)	Human	Environment

3 Building roads across rivers is expensive because ______________________________
____.

Recap *Planners have to think about* ***m***________ *things when deciding on a route for a new road. They have to consider* ***p***______________ *factors,* ***h***______________ *factors and the* ***e***______________________.

In this activity you will learn about different routes

A **route** is the path taken on a journey. The shortest route between two places is a **straight line**. It is usually the quickest and cheapest route to take. It is not always possible to follow a straight line.

1 Your task is to plan a route for a road between Emmerdale and Brookside. The straight line route between the two towns – shown on the diagram – will cost **£68 million**. It is **not** the cheapest route. Each square with a number in it shows the cost of building in that square. Before you start colour your map using the following colours to make it clearer.

10s show where a river has to be crossed. Colour these squares in **blue**.
6s show high land. Colour these squares in **brown**.
5s show where a bridge has already been built. Colour these squares in **yellow**.
4s show marshy ground. Colour these squares in **light blue**.
Ts are where trees are growing. Colour these squares in **green**. **You cannot build in these squares.**
Ps are protected areas. Colour these in **red**. **You cannot build in these squares.**

Now plan your route. Remember it must be cheaper than the straight line.

Emmerdale

		2	2	2	2	2	2	2	2	2	2	2	6	6	6	6	6
		2	2	2	2	2	2	2	2	2	2	2	2	6	6	6	6
2	2	6	6	6	2	2	2	T	T	T	T	2	2	2	6	6	6
6	6	6	6	6	6	T	T	T	T	T	T	2	2	2	2	6	6
2	2	2	6	6	6	2	2	2	2	2	2	2	2	2	2	2	6
2	2	2	2	6	6	2	2	2	2	2	2	2	2	2	2	2	10
2	2	2	T	T	2	2	P	P	P	2	2	2	2	2	2	10	2
2	2	2	2	2	2	2	2	P	P	2	2	2	2	2	10	2	2
6	2	2	2	2	2	2	2	6	6	2	2	2	2	4	5	2	2
6	2	2	2	T	T	T	2	6	6	2	2	2	4	4	10	4	2
6	2	2	2	T	T	T	2	2	2	2	2	2	4	10	4	2	2
6	6	6	2	2	2	2	2	2	2	10	10	4	10	4	4	2	2
2	6	2	2	2	2	2	2	2	10	2	2	10	2	2	2	2	2
2	2	6	2	2	2	2	2	10	2	10	2	4	2	2	2	2	2
2	2	2	2	2	2	2	10	2	2	2	2	2	2	2	2	2	2
10	2	2	2	2	2	10	2	2	2	2	2	2	2	2	2	2	2
2	10	2	T	2	5	2	2	2	2	2	2	2	2	2	2		
2	2	10	2	10	2	2	2	2	2	T	T	2	2	2	2		

Brookside

2 The shortest route costs **£68 million**. How much does your route cost? __________

3 Complete this sentence. The straight line route was expensive because ____________________

____

4 You are now allowed to cut down trees. Plan another route to see if you can find an even cheaper one.

Recap *The shortest route between places is a* **s**__________ **l**______. *It is not always* **p**__________ *to follow a* **s**__________ **l**______ *because* ______________________________.

In this activity you will learn about transport networks

The roads and railways that join places together make up the **transport network**. Roads and railways **link** places together.

Activities

1 Join up the numbers on this diagram to complete the transport network for Wagon Wheel Island.

Wagon Wheel Island

2 Each dot on the island is a **place**, and the large dot in the centre of the island is a large place. Each line on the island is a **link** between places.

Underline the correct answers to the questions below.

How many **places** are there on Wagon Wheel Island? **6** **8** **9** **11**

How many **links** are there on Wagon Wheel Island. **10** **12** **14** **16**

Complete the following sentence by underlining the correct word in brackets.

The (**largest/smallest**) place is found in the centre of the island because it has (**few/many**) links.

3 Places that have many links have a **high density** network. Places that have few links have a **low density** network.

Complete the diagram showing a high density network by joining each dot with **all the other** dots. The first set of links have been done for you.

Complete the diagram showing a low density network by joining each dot with **only two other** dots. The first one has been done for you.

High Density Network (many links)

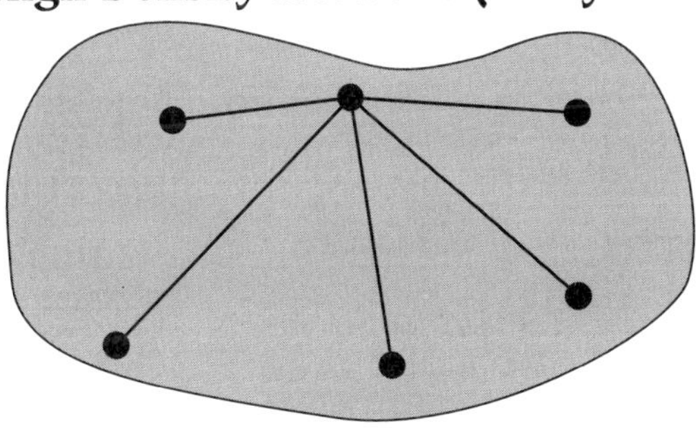

Low Density Network (few links)

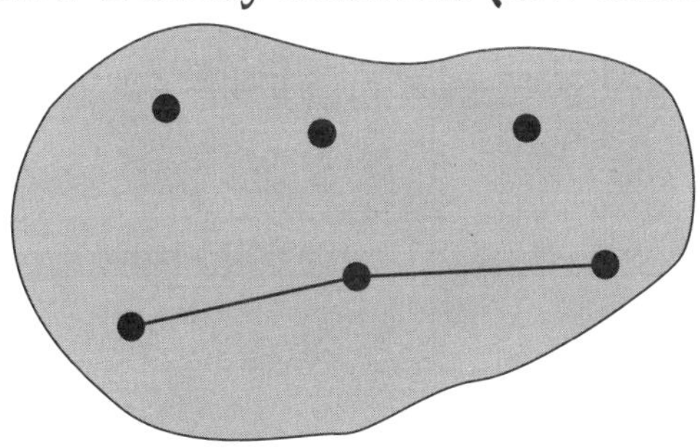

Recap *The roads and railways that join places together make up the*

*t*__________________ *n*__________________.

In this activity you will learn about transport networks

The roads and railways that join places together make up the **transport network**. Roads and railways **link** places together.

Activities

1 Build up a transport network on the diagram opposite by drawing a line between the following towns.

A to B	**C to D**
A to C	**E to C**
A to E	**C to F**
B to C	**E to F**

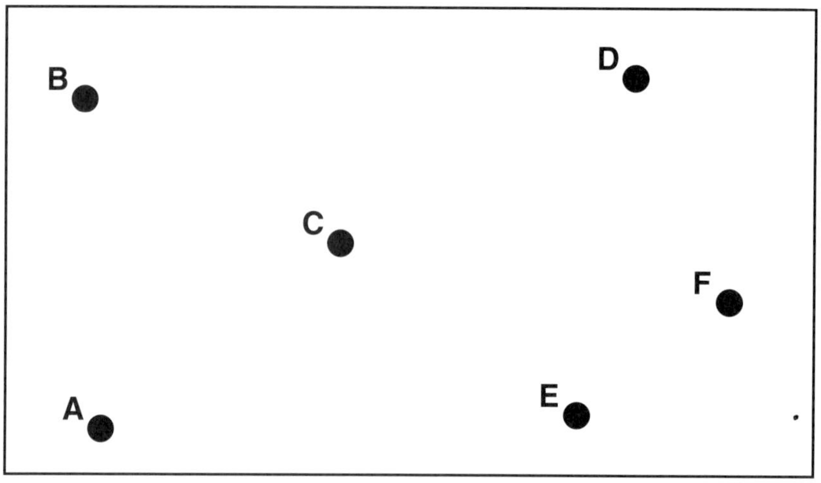

2 Lines that join places together are called **links**. The place with the most links is easiest to get to. Places with many links are likely to grow into large towns.

Complete the table by counting the number of links that each place has in the diagram above.

Place	Number of Links
A	3
B	
C	
D	
E	
F	

3 Complete the sentences below using the table and diagram to help you.

The **easiest** place to get to is place ______ because it has ______ links.

The **most difficult** place to get to is place _____ because it has only ______ link.

The **largest place** is likely to be place ____ because ______________________________

____.

The **smallest place** is likely to be place ____ because ______________________________

____.

Recap *The roads and railways that join places together make up the **t**__________________ **n**______________. Larger places usually have more **l**___________.*

In this activity you will learn about transport networks

The roads and railways that join places together make up the **transport network**. A **high density** network has **many** roads and railways. A **low density** network has **few** roads and railways. The connections between places are called **links**.

Activities

Compare the transport networks of South-east England and South Wales.

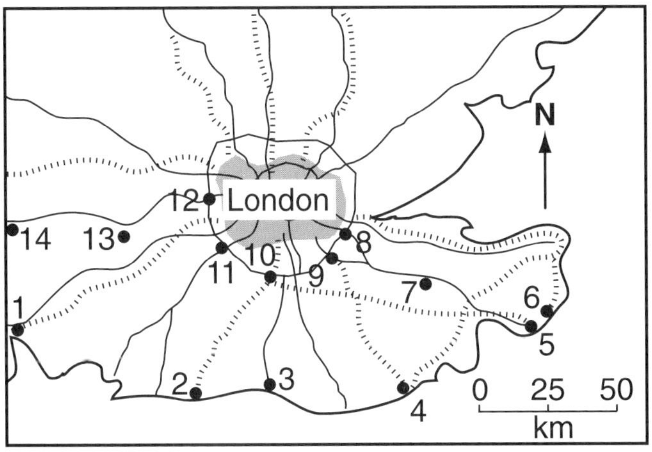

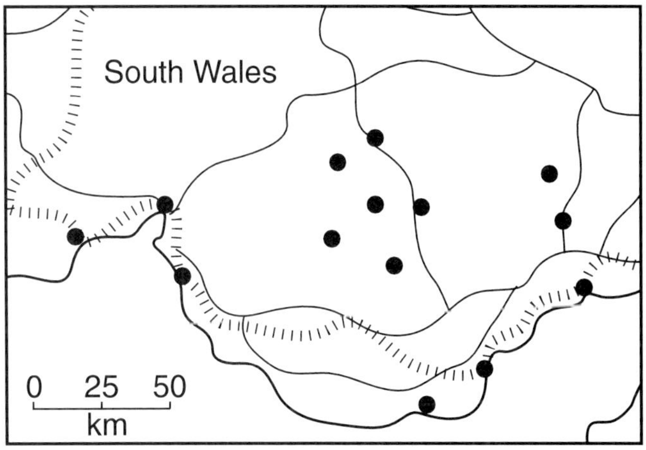

1 Complete the network for South-east England by joining the numbered dots on the map above.

2 The statements below describe, and give reasons for, the different networks shown above. Write the correct place, South-east England or South Wales, next to each statement. Use the maps above to help you. The first one has already been done for you.

High density road network with many links	*South-east England*
Low density road network with few links	
More settlements so more routes are needed	
Fewer settlements so not so many routes needed	

3 The maps below show two islands, each of which has six places. Draw in a high density network on **Busy Island** and a low density network on **Lazy Island**.

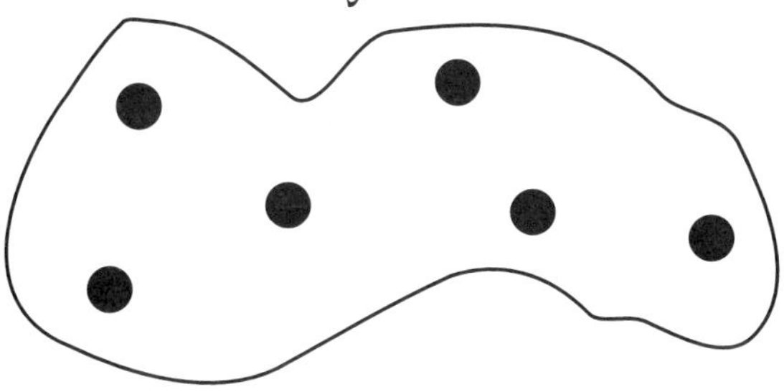

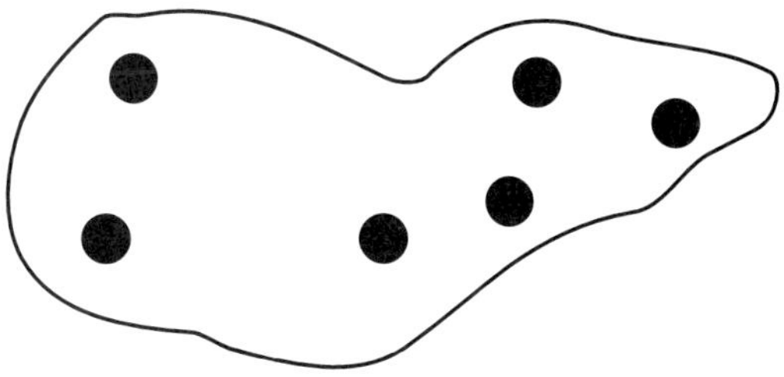

Recap *The roads and railways that join places together make up the*

t__________ n__________. A high density transport network has

m________ links. A l______ d____________ network has few links.

In this activity you will learn about transport developments

Recent changes in transport means that places are **easier** to get to. Places can now be reached more quickly.

Activities

1 Complete the graph below using the travelling speeds shown in the table. The first one has been done for you.

	Travelling speed
Luxury coach	70 mph
High speed train	168 mph
Jumbo jet	550 mph
Concorde	1450 mph

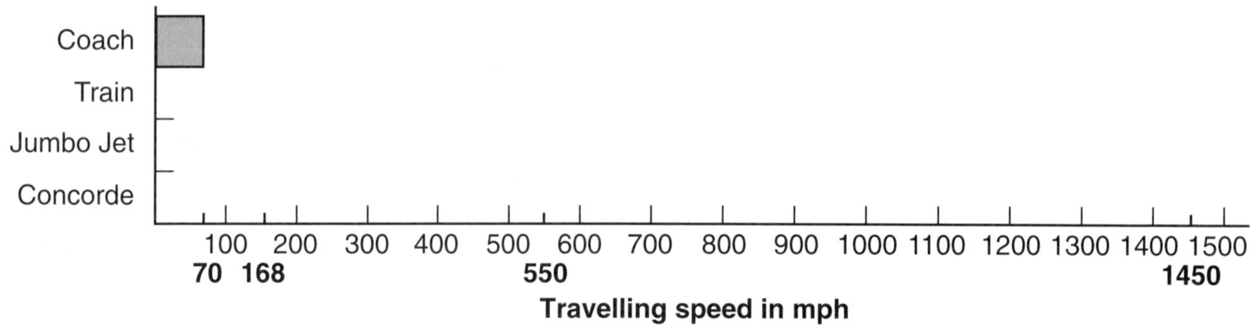

2 Is Florida getting closer to London?

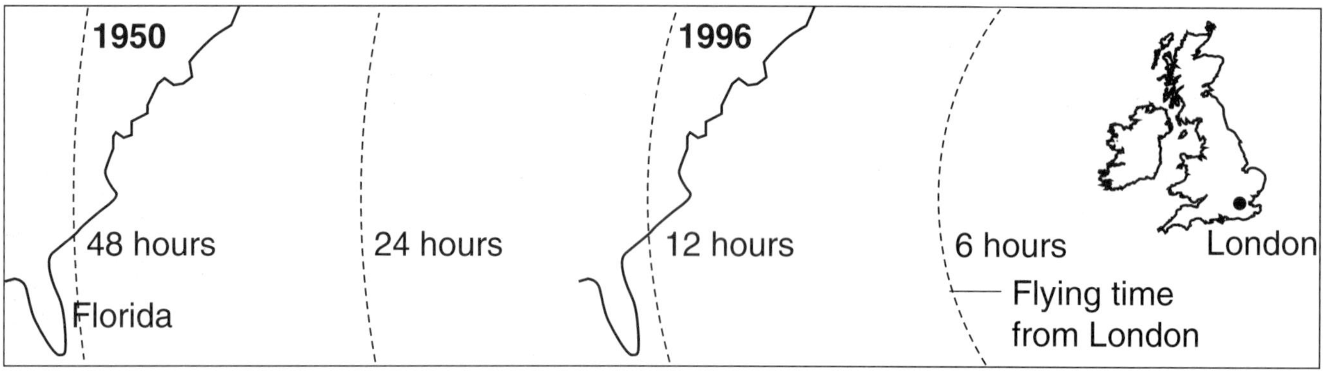

Tick **true** or **false** next to the statements in the table below. Use the map to help you.

	True	False
In 1950 it took 48 hours to fly from London to Florida		
In 1996 it took 12 hours to fly from London to Florida		
Florida is now much closer to London than it was in 1950		

Recap *Recent changes in transport have made places **e**__________ to get to.*

In this activity you will learn about transport developments

Recent changes in transport have meant that places can be reached more quickly now than they could forty years ago. A place that is easy to get to is said to be **accessible**.

Activities

Time to travel from London to Edinburgh

1950's			1990's		Reasons for change
	15 hours	**Road**		8 hours 30 minutes	*More tunnels and bridges*
	10 hours	**Rail**		4 hours 15 minutes	
	2 hours	**Air**		1 hour 15 minutes	

1 Complete the table below by putting the following statements in the **Reasons for change** column. The first one has been done for you.

more tunnels and bridges **electrifying lines** **motorways** **faster jets** **high speed trains**

2 Tick **true** or **false** for the statements below. Use the table above to help you.

	True	False
It now takes less time to get from London to Edinburgh		
The quickest way to travel from London to Edinburgh is by rail		
The biggest difference in time between 1950 and 1990 is by road		

3 **Accessibility** depends on four things. Complete the spider diagram below using the words in the Word box.

______________ – how long does it take?

______________ – how many different ways are there of getting there?

?

Word box
cost
distance
time
routes

Accessibility

______________ – how far is it?

______________ – how much is it to get there?

£

Recap *Recent changes in transport have meant that it is now much **q**____________ and **e**__________ to get to places. Places are now more **a**________________.*

In this activity you will learn about transport developments

Recent developments in transport have not always been good news. Transport can cause congestion and **environmental pollution**.

Activities

1 Look at the newspaper headlines below. Tick the box in the table to show the type of pollution caused by each headline. You may have more than one tick for each headline.

1. Oil slick wrecks beaches
2. Traffic noise increasing
3. Birds frightened by aircraft noise
4. Fractured pipeline causes river pollution
5. *Traffic fumes rot buildings*
6. 10 mile traffic jam hits M25
7. New road threatens Amazon Rainforest
8. Woods destroyed when by-pass built
9. Long delays expected at airports
10. *Famous view spoilt by new car park*

	Water	Air	Land	Noise
1				
2				
3				
4				
5				

	Water	Air	Land	Noise
6				
7				
8				
9				
10				

2 A motorway is to be built near to where you live. The **benefits** and **problems** that this will bring are listed below. Put each statement under the correct heading in the table.

Faster journeys   Easier to get to places   Noise   Fumes   Congestion
Trees cut down   Brings more jobs to area   More industry moves in
May bring more shops   Farmland destroyed   Houses have to be knocked down

Benefits	Problems

3 In your exercise book or folder write about a transport problem you have experienced.

Recap *Transport developments can cause* ***e***____________________

*p*________________.

In this activity you will learn about the problems of traffic in towns

Too much traffic in towns can cause many **problems**.

Activities

1 Complete the crossword below using the words in the Word box.
All the words are to do with traffic problems.

Word box

jams
slow traffic
lorries
pollution
wastes time
dirty fuel
parking
congestion
buses
danger
accidents
vibration
roadworks
delays
fumes

2 Draw lines to join up the 'heads' on the left and the 'tails' on the right below.

Traffic jams are dangerous because	buildings and roads
Pollution is high because of the	wastes a lot of time and money
Delays, because of roadworks and congestion,	they can lead to accidents
Heavy traffic can cause damage to	noise and fumes

Recap *Too much* ***t*** _______________ *in towns can cause many* ***problems.***

In this activity you will learn about the problems of traffic in towns

Too much traffic in towns can cause many **problems**.

Activities

1 Fit the words in the Word box into the correct boxes in the diagram opposite.

Businesses	The effects of traffic congestion	Health
Pollution		**Damage**

Word box

accidents • to buildings
potholes in road • noise
loss of money • wastes time
stress • fumes

2 People have different views on how to ease the growing problem of **traffic congestion**. Some possible solutions are shown in the table below.

Complete the table by ticking the correct box for each solution. The first one has been done for you.

Possible solution	1 Encourages public transport	2 Makes life easier for car drivers	3 Makes life more difficult for car drivers
Cheaper fares	✓		
Build more roads			
Park and ride schemes			
Raise the price of petrol to £3 per litre			
More car parks			
Fewer car parks			
Frequent bus services			
Make car parking expensive			
One way systems to help traffic to move			

3 Complete this sentence.

Building more roads would help to ease traffic jams by ______________________________

____

Recap *Too much* ***t***___________ *in towns can cause many* ***problems.***
One solution to the problem is ______________________________.

In this activity you will learn about the problems of traffic in towns

Too much traffic in towns can cause many **problems**. Traffic jams cause delays, cost money and can lead to pollution and accidents. The number of cars on the roads is increasing rapidly.

Activities

1 The graph below shows how the number of cars on the road in the UK has increased from **1950** to **1990**. Complete the line graph by adding in number of cars for 1980 and 1990. Join them up with a line.

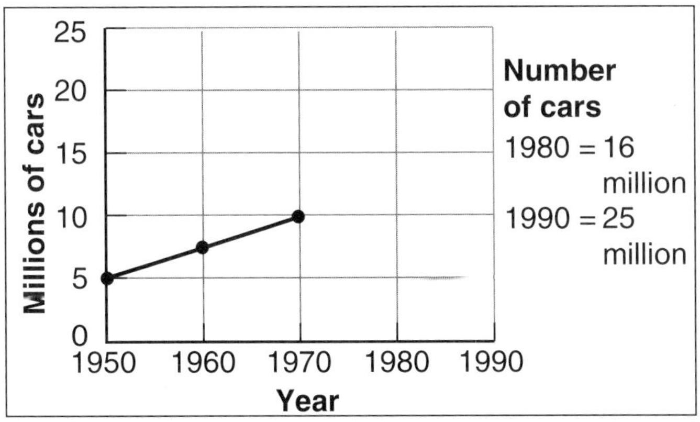

2 Complete the following sentences.

The number of cars on the road has ____________________ rapidly over the past 40 years.

At first the rate of increase was ____________________. But between 1980 and 1990 the rate of increase was much more ________________________.

3 The list below shows possible ways to reduce the problem of too much traffic in towns. Some would lead to more cars being used, while others would lead to fewer cars being used.

Write the words in bold from each statement under the correct heading in the table.

Give **buses and bicycles** priority in towns.
Better traffic flow with **one-way systems**.
Build a **by-pass** around the town.
Make **public transport** more reliable.
Offer **cheap bus fares**.
Pedestrians only in town centre.

Would lead to more cars being used	Would lead to fewer cars being used

4 Complete the sentences below.

Building more roads in towns would help because ____

____.

Making bus fares very cheap would help because ____

____.

Recap *Too much* ***t***_____________ *in towns can cause* ***problems****. Two problems caused by too many cars are* ***1*** ______________________________

2 ______________________________.

In this activity you will learn about building a by-pass

A **by-pass** is a new road that is built around a town. Deciding where to build a by-pass is never easy.

Activities

1 Decide if each point in the table below is a **good point**, or a **bad point**, and then tick the correct box.

Nice scenery may be destroyed		
Good farmland will be dug up		
Fewer heavy lorries will go through the village		
There will be less pollution in the village		

2 One advantage of building a by-pass is that it saves time.

a Look at the map and graph below and then complete the following sentences.

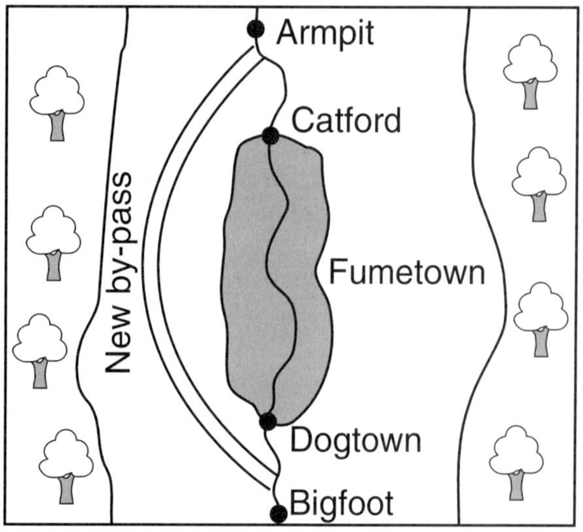

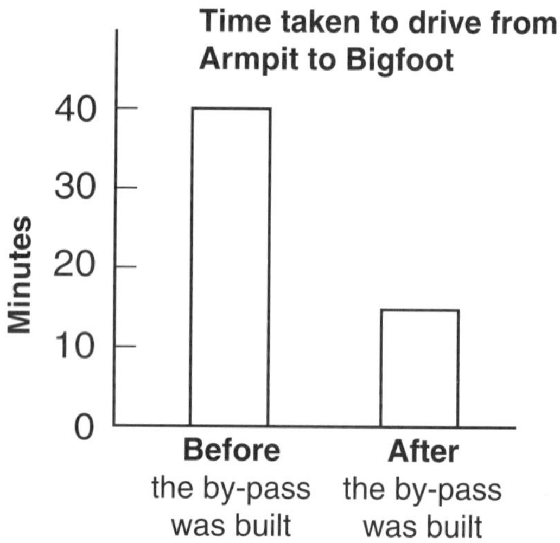

Before the by-pass was built around Fumetown it used to take ______ minutes to get from Armpit to Bigfoot. Since the by-pass has been built it now takes ______ minutes.

b Underline the correct answer in brackets in the sentences below. It now takes less time to get from Catford to Dogtown because there is (**more/less**) traffic going through Fumetown.

Recap *A b______________ is a new road that is built around a town.*

In this activity you will learn about building a by-pass

A **by-pass** is a new road that is built around a town. Deciding where to build a by-pass is never easy.

Activities

1 Some people will be **in favour** of building a by-pass. Match up the people with the speech bubbles below.

A lorry driver **A young mother** **A shop keeper** **local resident**

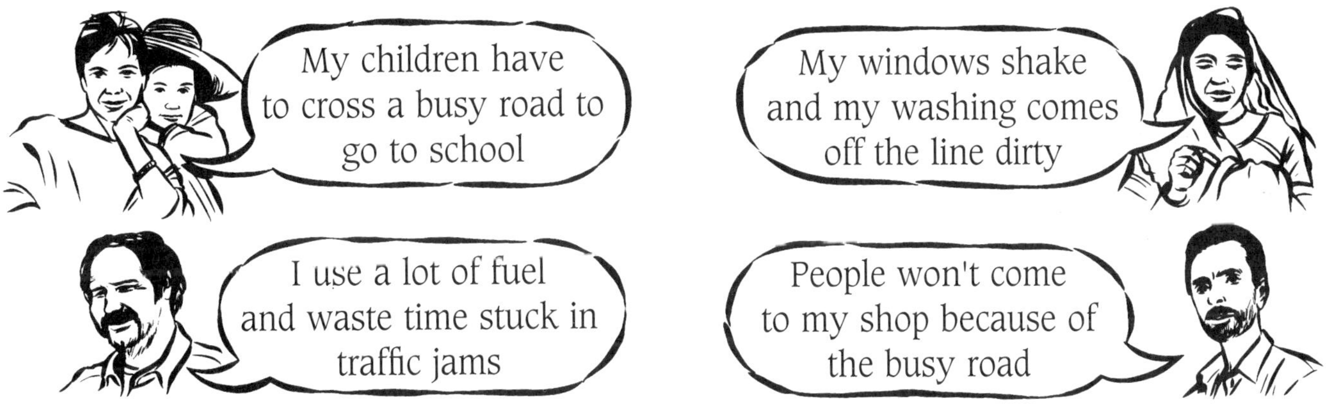

2 Some people are **against** the building of a by-pass. Draw lines to join up the 'heads' on the left with the 'tails' on the right below.

Historian	They want to dig up my best land
Farmer	Building the new road will only increase the amount of traffic
Conservationist	Many hundreds of trees will be cut down
Local resident	The local beauty spot and two picnic areas will be destroyed
Environmentalist	This is the places where an ancient battle took place

3 How do you think the following people would feel about the building of a new by-pass?

Walkers who enjoy the countryside ______________________________

____.

A local factory owner ____________________________________

____.

Recap *Deciding where to build a* ***by-pass*** *is never easy. Some people will be in* ***f***____________ *of the by-pass, while other people will be* ***a***____________ *it.*

In this activity you will learn about building a by-pass

A **by-pass** is a new road that is built around a town. Deciding where to build a by-pass is never easy. There will always be **good points** and **bad points** about any route chosen.

Activities

1 The map below shows the suggested route for a by-pass around Samtown.

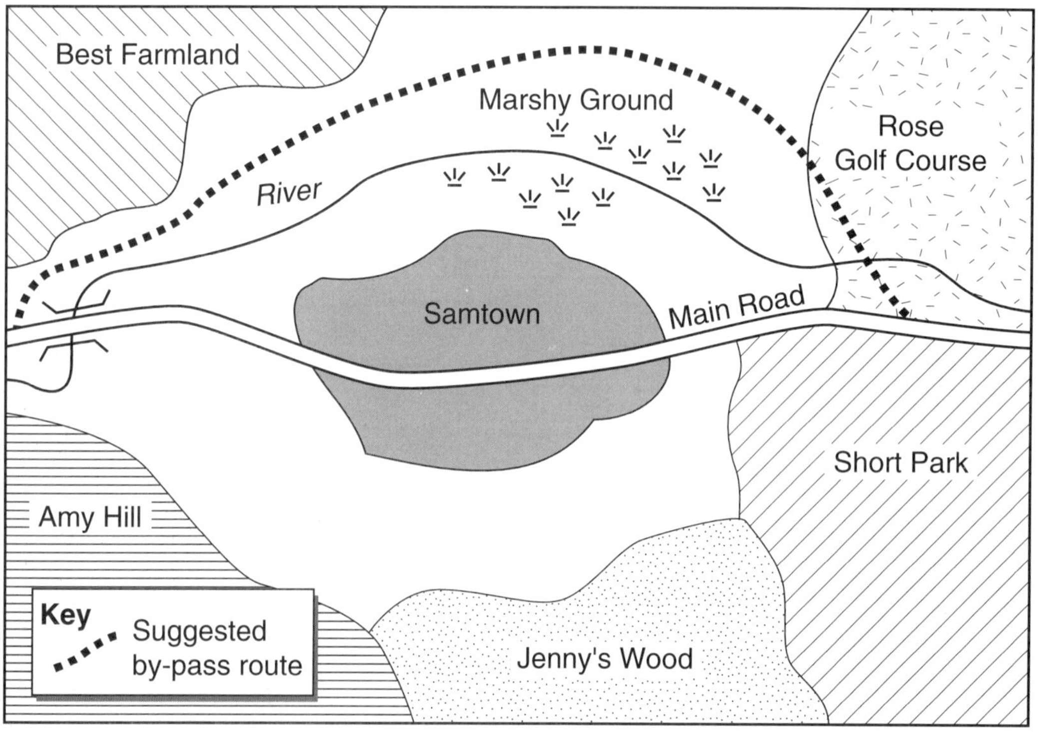

Complete the table below showing the good points and bad points about the suggested route of the by-pass. Use the map to help you. The first one has been done for you.

Suggested route	Good point	Bad point	Reason
Crosses the river		✓	*Costly bridges would have to be built*
Goes through farmland			
Avoids marshy ground			
Cuts through a golf course			
Avoids the hills			
Avoids Jenny's Woods			

2 The route shown above was not acceptable because there were too many objections from the farmer and the golfers. Draw an alternative route on the map.

3 I have chosen this route because ______________________________

____

Recap *Deciding where to build a by-pass is never **e**__________. All routes have **g**________ points and **b**_______ points.*

The Transport Game

This is a game for three players. In the game you have to get from **London** to **Paris**. Each player must choose a different type of transport to use. You will need a dice and three counters. Take it in turns to throw the dice. The object of the game is to get to Paris first. When you have finished the game answer the questions at the bottom of the page.

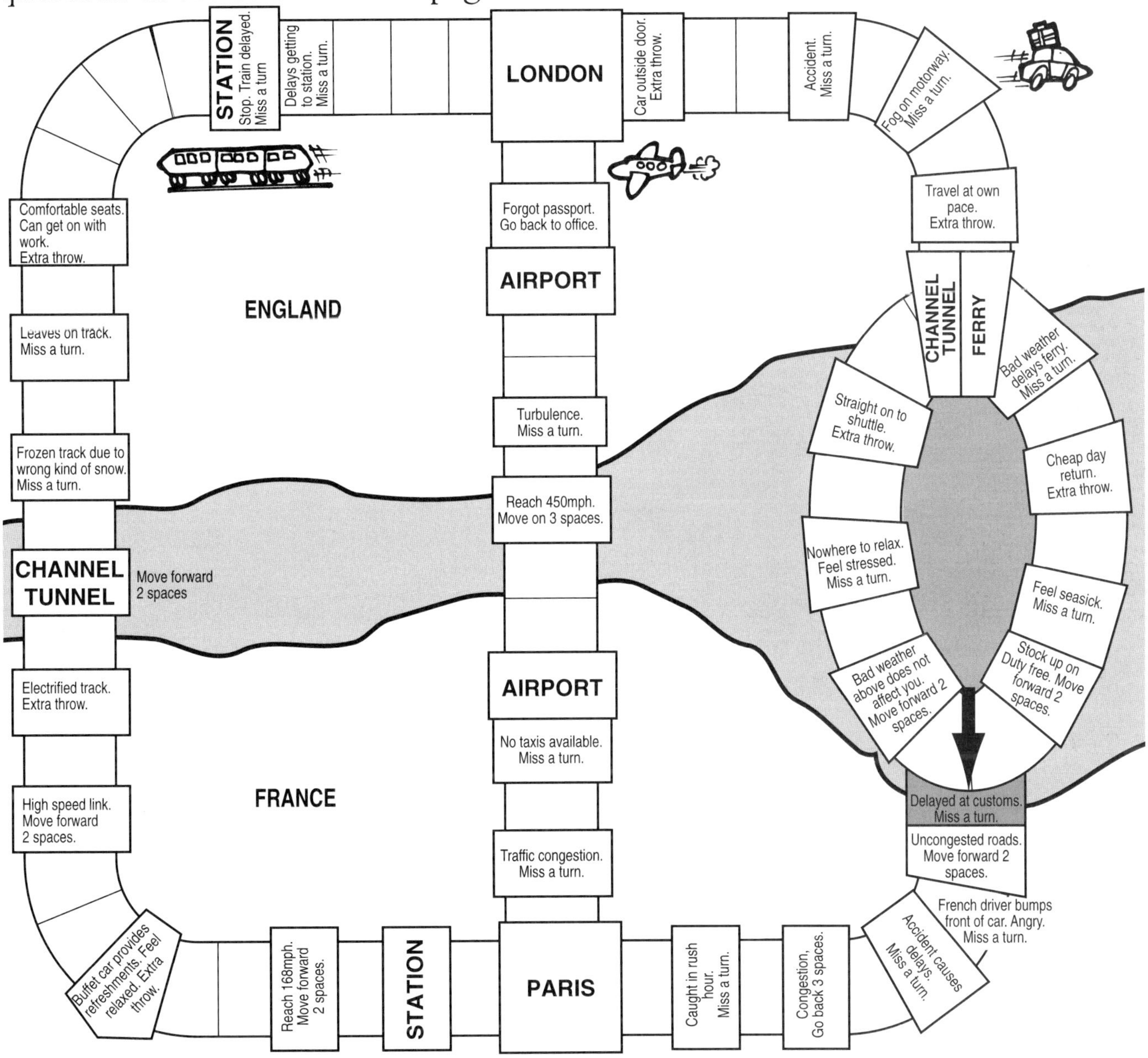

1 Which type of transport was the quickest? ______________________________

2 Why do you think this is? ______________________________

____.

Recap *There are many different types of* ***t***______________________.

Some are ***q***__________________ *than others.*

In this activity you will learn about the Channel Tunnel

If we want to visit Europe from the United Kingdom we have to cross the English Channel. There are now **three** ways of doing this since the **Channel Tunnel** was opened in May 1994. We can go by sea, by air, or by train, through the Channel Tunnel. The Channel Tunnel allows us to get to other countries and cities in Europe more quickly.

Activities

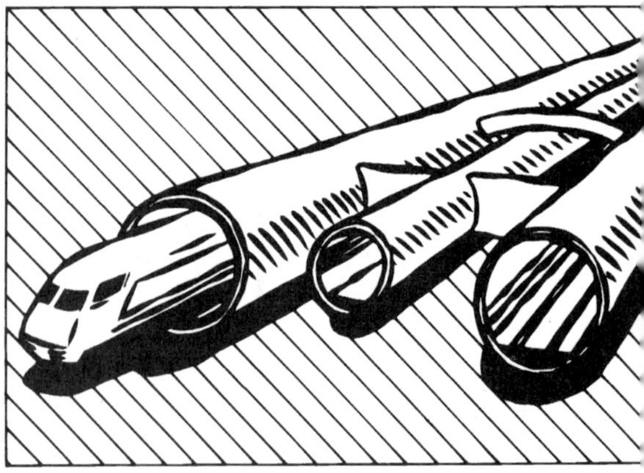

1 The Channel Tunnel

Complete the paragraph below adding the words in the Word box in the correct place.

Word box

Thirty five • two • May • one • trains

The Channel Tunnel was opened in _________ 1994. There are _________ main tunnels and _________ service tunnel. People travel through the tunnel on high speed ___________. The total crossing time is about ____________ minutes.

2 You will need an atlas for this activity.

On the map opposite colour:
- the English Channel in **blue**
- the land in **green**.

Label the following countries:
- France
- Belgium
- UK
- Germany
- Netherlands

Label the following cities:
- Paris
- London
- Brussels
- Amsterdam
- Berlin

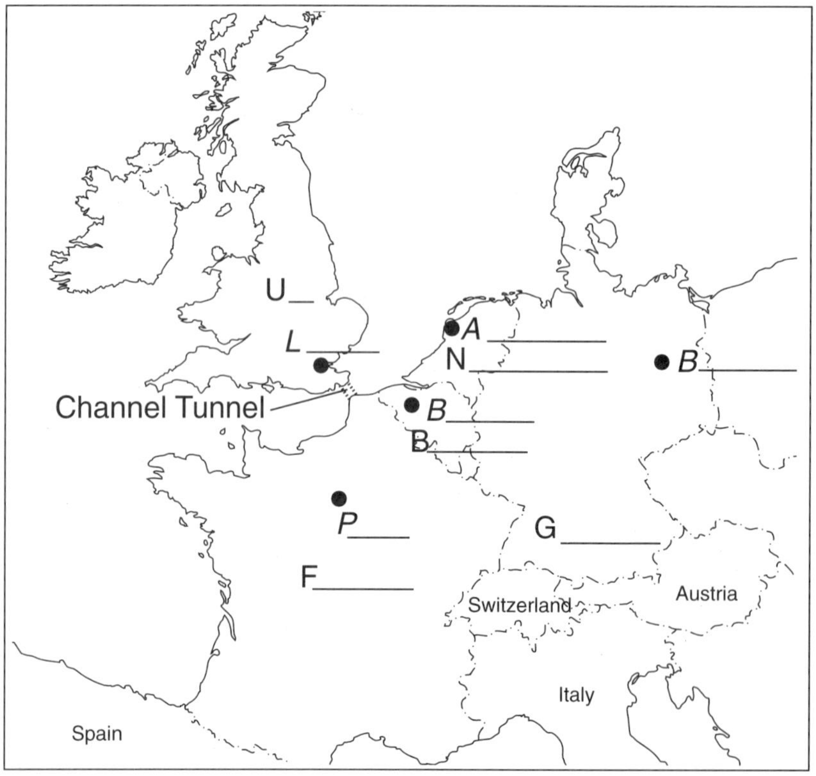

Recap *The **Channel Tunnel** was opened in ______________. It means that there are now **t**_________ ways to cross the **E**_____________ Channel.*

In this activity you will learn about Greater London

Greater London is an example of a large **urban region**. This means most of the land has been built upon. It is very crowded and has many famous buildings.

Activity

Look at the post card shown below. The top half shows the pictures on the front. The bottom half shows the back of the post card.

Complete the back of the post card by filling in the gaps using the information on the front to help you. (Address the post card to a friend or a relative.)

Dear__________
London is very busy! There are lots of famous buildings to see such as St. ________ ________
and the T________ of ________.
I've been to the W____ ____ for sh________ and seen the o________ blocks in The ____. I've tried all kinds of f________ in the restaurants.
The t________ j____ are awful and even the L________ U________ is crowded!
See you soon!
Love ____________

To:
(name)____________________
(street)____________________
(town))____________________
(country & post code)
____

Recap G____________ L____________ is an example of an u__________ **region**. It is very c____________.

In this activity you will learn about Greater London

Greater London is an example of a large **urban region**. This means most of the land has been built upon. Over **six million** people live in London and many other people travel there to work in banks, shops and offices. This makes the roads in London very **congested**. Many **tourists** visit London to see the famous **buildings**, and for **sporting events**. Heathrow and Gatwick are the main airports.

Activities

1 Fit the words below into the correct place on the crossword. Start with the longest word. These words are all things found in Greater London.

16 letter words
St. Paul's Cathedral

14 letter words
Administration

11 letter words
River Thames

10 letter words
Congestion

8 letter words
Heathrow

7 letter words
Mosques
Crowded
Gatwick
Offices
Wembley
West End

6 letter words
Museum

5 letter words
Banks
Music
Shops
Queen

4 letter words
City
Tube
Oval
Soho

3 letter words
bus

___ ___ ___ ___ ___ ___ ___   ___ ___ ___ ___ ___ ___
1 2 3 4 5 6 7   8 9 10 11 12 13

2 Some of the squares on the crossword are numbered. Fill the letters in the numbered squares into the numbered spaces above to make a title for the crossword.

3 Use some of the words in the crossword to write three sentences about Greater London. (You may write this in your exercise book or folder if you prefer.)

____

____

____

Recap G__________ L__________ is an example of an u__________ r__________. Over ______ __________ people live there.

In this activity you will learn about the climate and landscape of Greater London

- **Climate** describes what the weather is usually like.
- **Landscape** describes what an area looks like.
- Landscape can be made of **human** and **physical** features.

Activities

The spider diagram below describes the climate and landscape of Greater London.

1 Colour the boxes to do with **climate** in **blue**.

2 Colour the boxes to do with **landscape** in **red**.

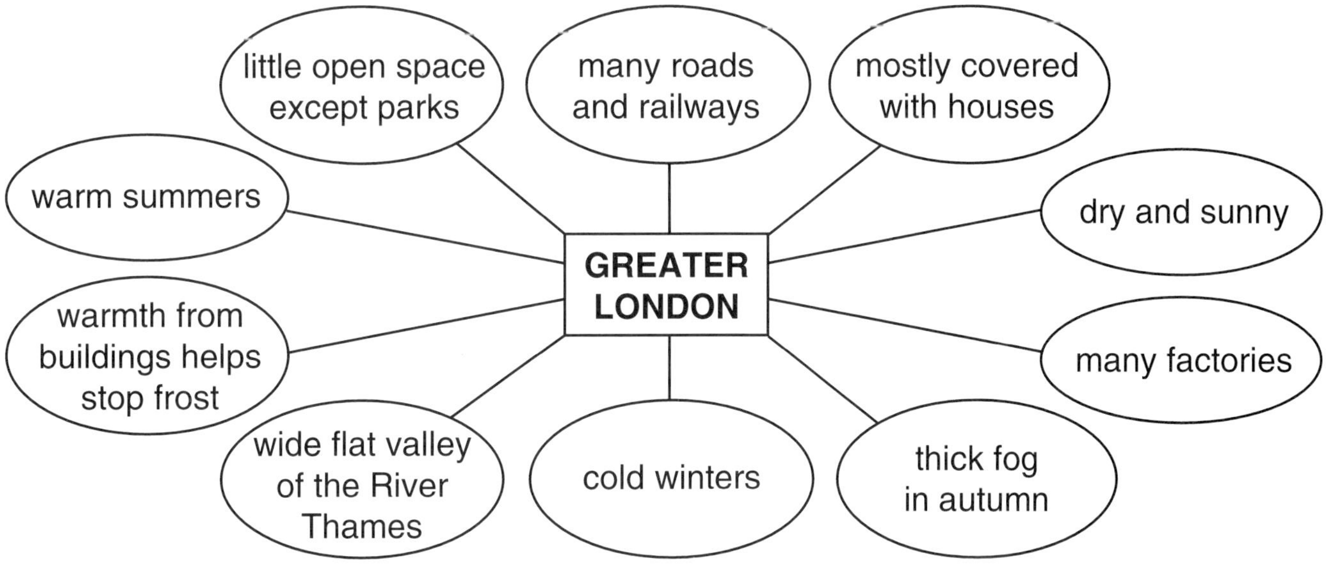

3 Write **three** features about the **climate** of Greater London which you think are the most important. ____________________ ____________________ ____________________ ____________________ ____________________	Write **three** features about the **landscape** of Greater London which you think are the most important. ____________________ ____________________ ____________________ ____________________ ____________________

Recap Many **h**__________ and **p**____________ features make up the climate and landscape of **G**____________ **L**__________.

In this activity you will learn about the climate and landscape of Greater London

- **Climate** describes what the weather is usually like.
- **Landscape** describes what an area looks like.
- Landscape can be made of **human** and **physical** features.

Activities

Look at the map below which shows Greater London.

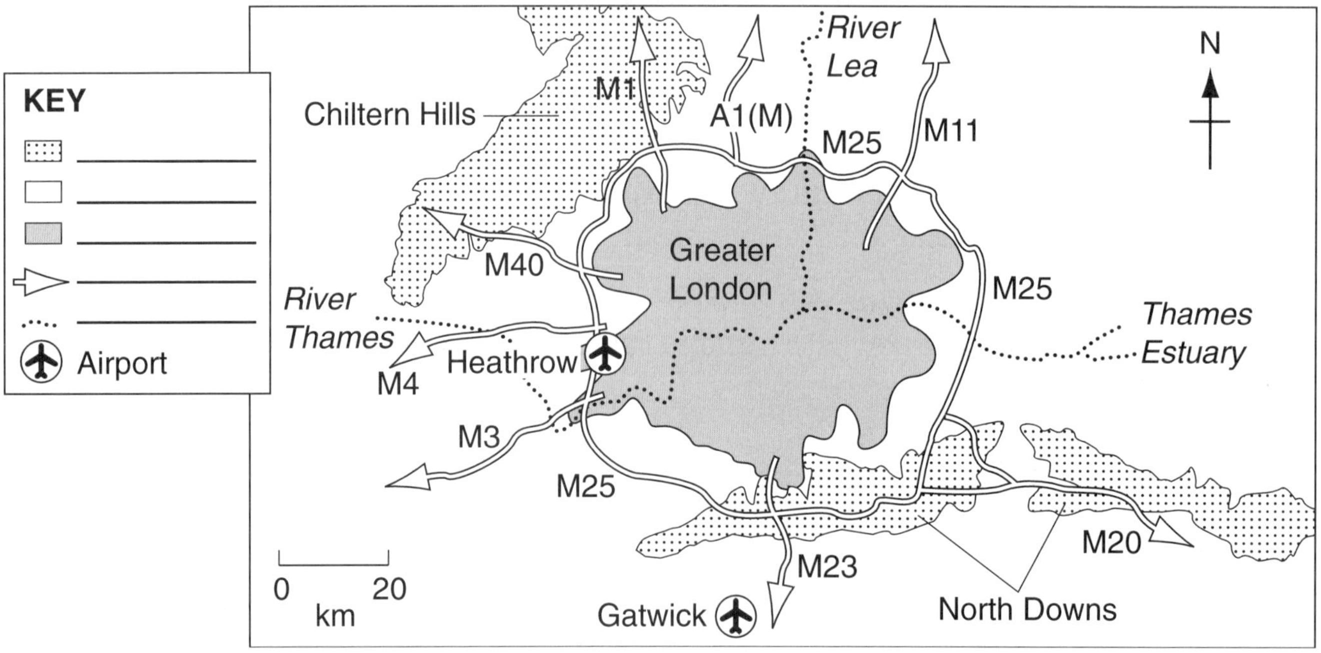

1 a) is **high land**. Colour this **brown** on the map.

b) is **low land**. Colour this **green** on the map.

c) is **Greater London**. Colour this **red** on the map.

d) is a **motorway**. Colour these **light blue** on the map.

e) is a **river**. Colour these **dark blue** on the map.

f) Complete the key next to the map.

Recap *H____________ and p______________ features make up the climate and landscape of G______________ L_____________.*

In this activity you will learn about the climate and landscape of Greater London

- **Climate** describes what the weather of a place is usually like.
- **Landscape** describes what an area looks like.
- **Landscape** can be made of **human** and **physical** features.

Activities

The box below contains ten statements about the climate and landscape of Greater London.

Thick fogs in autumn.	Little open space except parks.
Cold winters (below 5°C).	Wide, flat valley of the River Thames.
Mostly covered with houses.	Many large factories and shops.
Warm summers (above 16°C).	Many busy roads and railways.
Low rainfall (about 600 mm per year).	Warmth from buildings helps prevent frosts at night.

1 Copy these statements into the table below. You have to decide whether each one is about **climate** or **landscape**, and also whether each one is a **human** or **physical** feature. Four have been done for you.

	Climate	**Landscape**
Human features	Warmth from buildings helps prevent frosts at night __________ __________ __________ __________	Little open space except parks __________ __________ __________ __________
Physical features	Low rainfall (about 600 mm per year). __________ __________ __________ __________	Wide, flat valley of the River Thames. __________ __________ __________ __________

2 Using the table to help you, underline the correct word in brackets in the sentences below.

The **climate** of Greater London is mainly due to (**human/physical**) features.

The **landscape** of Greater London is mainly due to (**human/physical**) features.

Recap *H__________ and p__________ features make up the climate and landscape of G__________ L__________. The landscape is mainly made up of h__________ features.*

In this activity you will learn how Greater London developed

Greater London is the biggest city in Britain. It had a very good site. London **grew** in size because it had many **functions**.

Activities

1 Look at the map below:

- Colour the labels about the **site** of London in **yellow**.
- Colour the labels about the **functions** of London in **orange**.

2 a) Do the **yellow** boxes show mainly things that were important long ago? (**Yes/No**)

b) Do your **orange** boxes show the functions of **long ago** or **today**? Answer '**long ago**' or '**today**' here: ______________

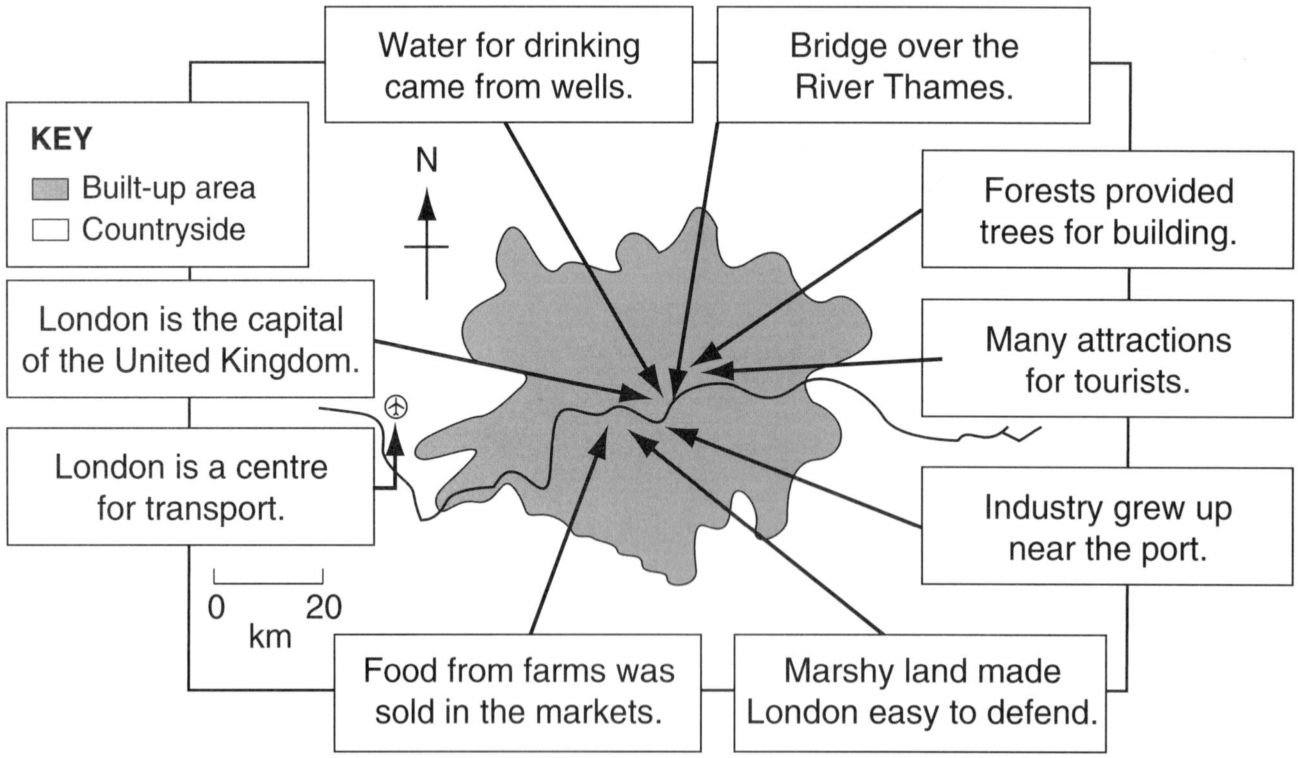

3 a) Complete the map by colouring the **built-up** area in **red** and the **countryside** in **green**. Use the **key** to help you.

b) Colour the **River Thames** in **blue** and label it on the map.

Recap *Greater London is Britain's biggest* ***c***_______. *It had a good* ***s***_____ *and has grown because of its important* ***f***___________.

In this activity you will learn how Greater London developed

People have lived in London for over two thousand years. **Greater London** has grown into Britain's largest city. It is the centre of the South-east region and the capital of the UK.

Activities

1 Look at the map of Greater London shown below:

- The **oldest** part of London is in the centre. Colour this **red**.
- The **newest** part is around the outside. Colour this **yellow**.
- Colour the part of London which is **between** the oldest and the newest parts in **orange**.
- Now colour in the **key** in the correct colours to complete the map.

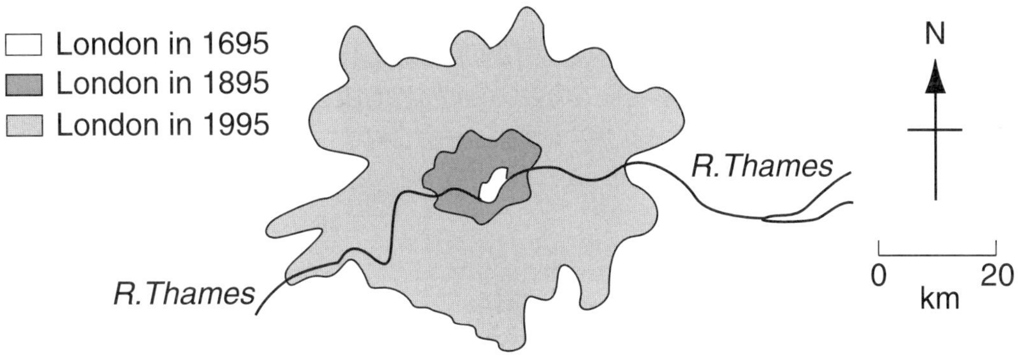

2 The table below shows the **population** of Greater London in different years. Use the figures below to complete the **line-graph** to show the changes in the number of people living in Greater London. It has been started for you.

Year	Population
1800	1.0 million
1850	2.5 million
1900	6.0 million
1950	8.5 million
1970	7.5 million
1980	6.7 million
1990	6.2 million

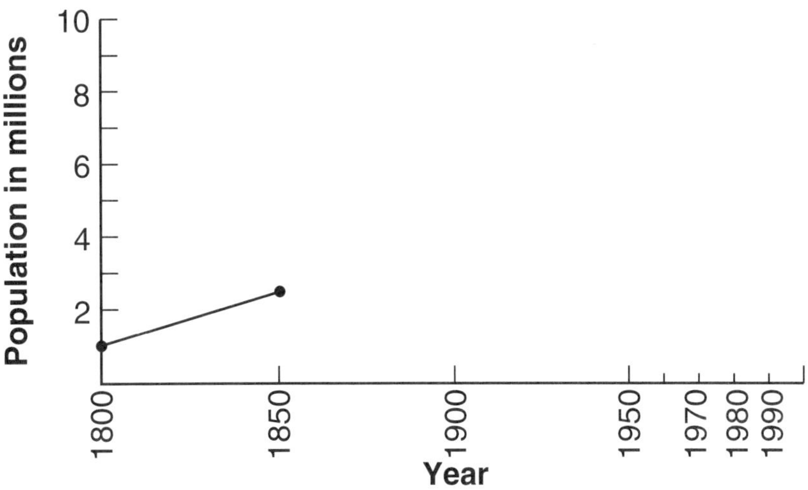

Recap *The map and graph show that Greater London has grown very quickly. Its biggest population was in ________. Over ________ million people live there now.*

In this activity you will learn how Greater London developed

People have lived in London for over two thousand years. Greater London has grown into Britain's largest city. This is part of an article about Greater London:

The Development of London

People have lived in the London area for many years. The Romans built a city there two thousand years ago. They chose a site which was an island surrounded by marsh next to a bridge over the River Thames. They got drinking water from wells and wood for building from nearby forests.

London became England's capital city. The kings and queens lived there. This helped London to become the centre of fashion and entertainment. The government was there which made London the most powerful city. Industries grew up near to the port on the River Thames. When railways and roads improved, more and more houses were built and the city expanded.

London is now an important city for banking, shopping, entertainment and tourism. Over six million people live there and many more travel there every day to work from the towns and villages in the South-east region. Now some parts of London are very run-down. There are terrible traffic jams and the air is polluted. Many people do not have jobs or proper houses.

Activities

1 Read the article above.

- Using **red** underline anything about the **original site** of London.
- Using **green** underline anything about **why London grew**.
- Using **blue** underline anything about London's **present-day functions**.
- Using **black** underline anything about London's **present-day problems**.

2 Use the information that you have underlined to write what you can in your folders under the following headings.

The original site	**Present-day functions**
Why London grew	**Problems**

Recap Greater London has over ________ _____________ people.

It grew because it had a good **s**_______ and many **f**______________. It now has some problems due to its size such as **t**______________ **j**________.

In this activity you will learn about transport in Greater London and the South-east

- Greater London and the South-east have many **transport routes**. This is because there are many people living there.
- Good transport routes help industry to grow but **roads**, **railways** and **airports** can cause **problems** for some people.

Activities

The cartoon below shows six people who live in the London area. What they think is shown in the bubbles below:

I can get to work in London quickly and I don't have to park the car.

____

There are no roundabouts or traffic lights on the motorway.

____

The planes taking off are very noisy.

____

I can get to Paris in three hours by train through the Channel Tunnel.

____

The fumes from the cars cause air pollution.

____

New roads destroy the countryside.

____

1 Write under the correct bubble the person who said each statement.

2 Colour the bubbles which show the **advantages** of transport in **red**. Colour the bubbles which show the **disadvantages** of transport in **blue**.

Recap *There are many* ***transport r***____________ *in Greater London and the South east. These have advantages and* ***dis***________________.

In this activity you will learn about transport in Greater London and the South-east

Greater London and the South-east have many **transport routes**. This is because there are many people living there who have to travel to get to work. People also travel to go shopping and to visit friends. People from other parts of Britain travel through the South-east to get to the Channel Tunnel.

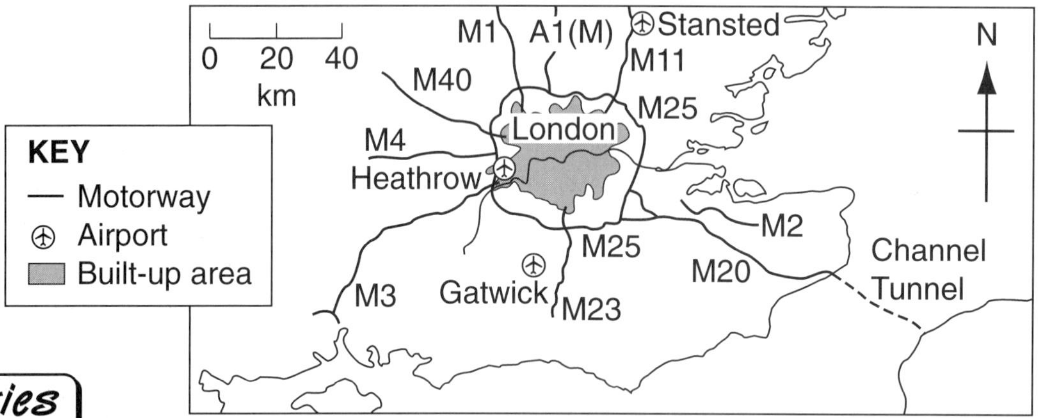

Activities

1 This map shows some transport routes in the South-east:

- Which motorway goes all around London? ____________________.
- Which motorway goes from the **M25** to the **Channel Tunnel**? ______________.
- Which three motorways would you use to get from **Stansted Airport** to **Gatwick Airport**? ____________, ____________ and ______________.
- Which airport is to the **north-east** of Greater London? __________________.

2 The Pie chart below shows how people travel to work in London:

- Nearly **half** the people go by **Tube**
- About the **same** number go by **car** as by **bus.**
- Over a **quarter** go by **train**.
- Only **1%** go by **bicycle** or **motorcycle**.

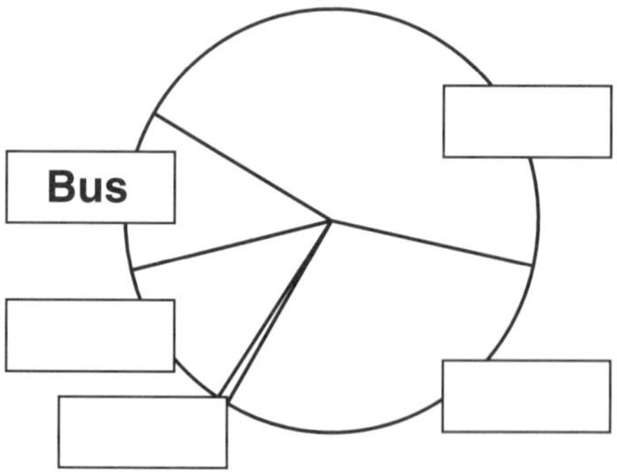

Complete the chart by writing **Tube**, **car**, **train** and **cycle** in the correct space on the chart.

3 Write **one** advantage of travelling in London by **Tube** rather than by **car**.

____

Recap *There are many* **t**____________ **r**________ *in Greater London and the South-east. People travel in London mainly by* **T**________, **t**__________, **c**__________ *and* **b**__________.

In this activity you will learn about transport in Greater London and the South-east

Greater London and the South-east have many **transport routes**. This is because there are so many people, towns and industries there. People from other parts of Britain travel through the South-east to reach the Channel Tunnel.

Activities

1 Read the passage below.

Mr Jones flew into Heathrow Airport from New York. He took a taxi to his hotel in Central London and unpacked his bags. He walked to the nearest Underground station and took the train to Tower Bridge. He got on the Docklands Light Railway and travelled to his meeting at Canary Wharf. Afterwards he walked through the foot-tunnel under the River Thames to Greenwich and visited the Cutty Sark, an old sailing ship. He travelled back to the centre of London by boat along the River Thames and took a sight-seeing bus trip around London before taking the Underground back to his hotel.

- Underline everything about travelling by **air** in **green**.
- Underline everything about travelling by **railway** in **black**.
- Underline everything about travelling by **road** in **red**.
- Underline everything about travelling by **water** in **blue**.

2 The table opposite shows the percentage of people who travel around London by five different kinds of transport. The total adds up to 100%. Complete the table by writing in the number of people who travelled by **bicycle/motorcycle**.

Underground	45%
Train	30%
Car	12%
Bus	12%
Bicycle/Motorcycle	___ %

3 Try to solve this '**M25 Puzzle**':

If **Clara** wants to go from **Oxford** to **Purley**, can you look at the map and work out who wants to go from: (Use the letters on the map to find their names.)

- Luton to Stansted ____________
- Luton to Hatfield ____________
- Thorpe Park to Hatfield________
- St Albans to Maidstone ________
- Heathrow to Gatwick __________
- Windsor to Purley ____________
- Redbridge to Hendon __________
- Windsor to Basingstoke ________
- Maidstone to Purley ___________

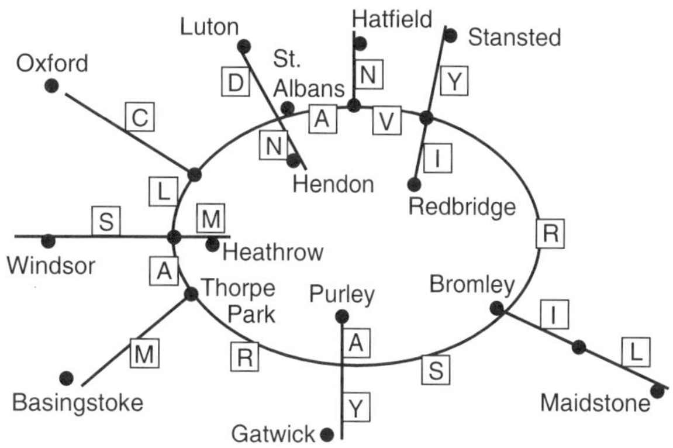

Recap *The South-east has many* ***t***_______________ ***r***____________.

*Four ways of travelling in London are*_______________________________

____.

In this activity you will learn about the pressures on the area around Greater London

Greater London has grown bigger and bigger in size.

- A **green belt** was set up to stop London from getting too big.
- A **green belt** is a ring of countryside around a city where building is not allowed. Now many people want to build on the green belt.

Activities

1 The pictures below show nine things which some people wish to build on the green belt. Write the titles of the drawings in the boxes. The first one has been done for you.

Houses

Airport

Hotels

Downword

S	H	O	P	P	I	N	G	M	A	L	L	S		
			M											
			T					P						
			H											
						I								
							B							
		O												
			H											
	A													

Theme parks

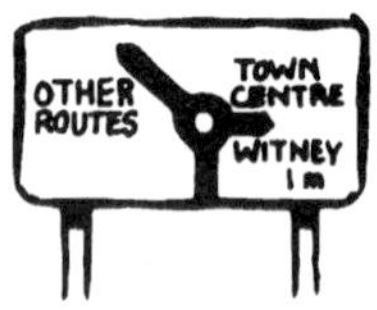

By-passes

Motorways

Offices

Shopping malls

Industry

2 Write the downword from the puzzle in the gap in the sentence below.

The _ _ _ _ _ _ _ _ _ is a ring of land around Greater London where building is restricted.

Recap *The g__________ b_______ was set up to stop Greater London from growing too big. Now some people wish to build h__________, r_________ and other things there.*

In this activity you will learn about the pressures on the area around Greater London

Greater London has grown bigger and bigger in size.

- A **green belt** was set up to stop London from getting too big.
- A **green belt** is a ring of countryside around a city where building is not allowed. Now many people want to build on the green belt.

Activities

1 The cartoons below show a **developer** (**A**) who wishes to build things in the green belt area and a **conservationist** (**B**)who wants to keep the green belt as open space.

Join the speech bubbles up to the person who would say them.

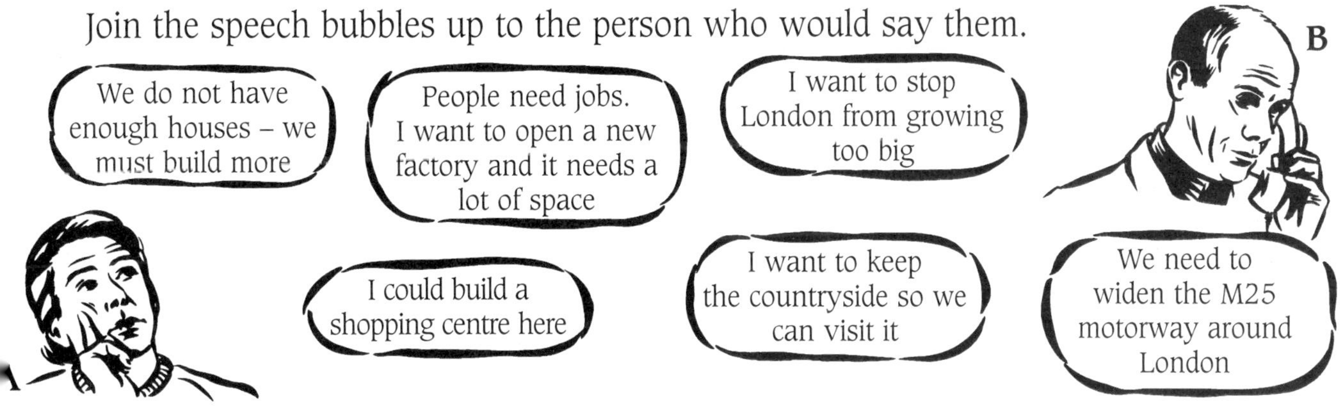

2 Which of the reasons do you think is the most important for:

The developer ______________________________

______________________________.

The conservationist ______________________________

______________________________.

3 Do you think we should protect the green belt from being built on?

Draw a picture of yourself in the box on the right saying 'Yes!' or 'No!'

Now give your reasons ______________________________

____

Recap *The **g**_________ **b**______ was set up to stop Greater London from growing too big. Now some people wish to build ___________, ___________, and ___________ there.*

In this activity you will learn about the pressures on the area around Greater London

Greater London has grown bigger and bigger in size.

- A **green belt** was set up to stop London from getting too big.
- A **green belt** is a ring of countryside around a city where building is not allowed. Now people want to build on the green belt.

Activities

1 Here is a list of **land uses**:

- **Motorway** • **Houses** • **Forest** • **Farm** • **Factory** • **Park**
- **By-pass** • **Reservoir** • **Golf** course • **Rubbish** dump • **Open** space

- Underline the land uses which are **allowed** in the green belt in **green**.
- Underline the land uses which are **not allowed** in the green belt in **red**.

2 All the words written in **bold** in the list above are in the wordsearch opposite. Colour them in carefully. Words can go across, down, forwards, backwards or diagonally.

H	E	R	T	H	Y	F	O	R
D	M	O	T	O	R	W	A	Y
S	G	K	H	U	O	I	R	H
F	O	R	E	S	T	E	E	S
S	L	A	O	E	C	F	S	I
E	F	P	S	S	A	P	Y	B
X	E	K	E	R	F	N	T	B
N	S	U	M	R	R	E	Y	U
R	I	O	V	R	E	S	E	R

3 Look at the letters which have **not** been coloured in on the wordsearch.

Start at the **top left-hand corner** and go along each row in turn.

Write the letters which are **not** coloured in into the gaps below in the order in which you read them.

They will spell out the names of **four counties** around Greater London which contain green belt land.

_ _ _ _ _ _ _ _ _ _ _ _ _

_ _ _ _ _   _ _ _ _   _ _ _ _ _ _

Recap *The **green belt** is* ____

____.

Now some developers wish to build ______________________ *there.*

In this activity you will learn about different views on changes in the South-east

- Many changes are happening in the South-east as people build new roads, shops and houses.
- Some people **like** these changes but other people **do not** like them.

Activities

1 Look at the diagram below and follow the lines to see which of the people would **like** the new theme park and which people would **not** like it.

NEW THEME PARK OPENS

Businessman
Teenager
Manager of a cinema nearby
Person who lives next to the new theme park
Person looking for a job
Driver who uses the roads near the new theme park

2 Put a ✔ next to the people who would **like** the theme park and a ✘ next to the people who would **not like** it, in the list below:

Businessman ____
Teenager ____
Manager of a cinema nearby ____
Person who lives next to the new theme park _____
Person looking for a job _____
Driver who uses the roads near the new theme park _____

3 Choose one of the people and explain **why** they would either **like** or **dislike** the new theme park.

Person ____

Reason ____

Recap *Many* ***ch***_________ *are happening in the South-east. Some people* ***l***____ *these changes, but other people do not.*

In this activity you will learn about different views on changes in the South-east

- Many changes are happening in the South-east as people build new roads, factories and shops.
- Many people **like** these changes but other people **do not** like them.

Activities

Look at the map below. It shows a small town in the South-east. A new road has been built to **by-pass** the town.

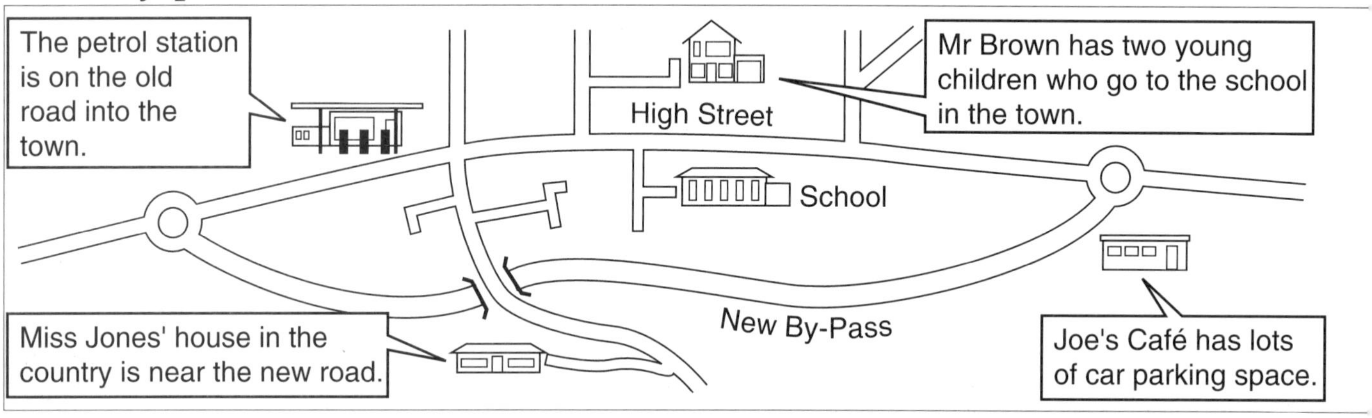

1 Draw lines to join up the '**heads**' on the left and the '**tails**' on the right below to show different people's views on the new by-pass road.

Write in the person who would say each sentence in the bubbles at the start.

Cafe Owner **Miss Jones** **Petrol Station Manager** **Mr Brown**

I want the new road because	I will sell less petrol
I want the new road because	it will be very noisy
I don't want the by-pass because	it will make the High Street safer
I don't want the by-pass because	it will bring me more business

2 In your exercise book or folder, draw a poster to show either:

- Why you might **like** the new by-pass road or
- Why you might **not like** the new by-pass road

Remember: Give information, use colour, make it interesting.

Recap *Many changes are happening in the South-east such as*

____.

Some people l______ these changes, but other people do not.

In this activity you will learn about different views on changes in the South-east

Many changes are happening in the South-east as people build new roads, factories and shops. Many new **shopping malls** have been built in the South-east in recent years. Some people like these new shopping malls but other people do not like them because different people have **different views**.

Activities

1 Put these five sentences into the correct order to show what happens when a new shopping mall opens. You may copy and cut them out to stick them in the correct order.
- There are fewer people shopping in the old High Street.
- Big shops move into the new mall when it opens.
- Shops left in the old High Street lose trade and close down.
- New shopping mall is planned.
- More people shop in the new mall to visit the big shops there.

2 Study these maps which show a town centre **before** and **after** a new shopping mall was built:

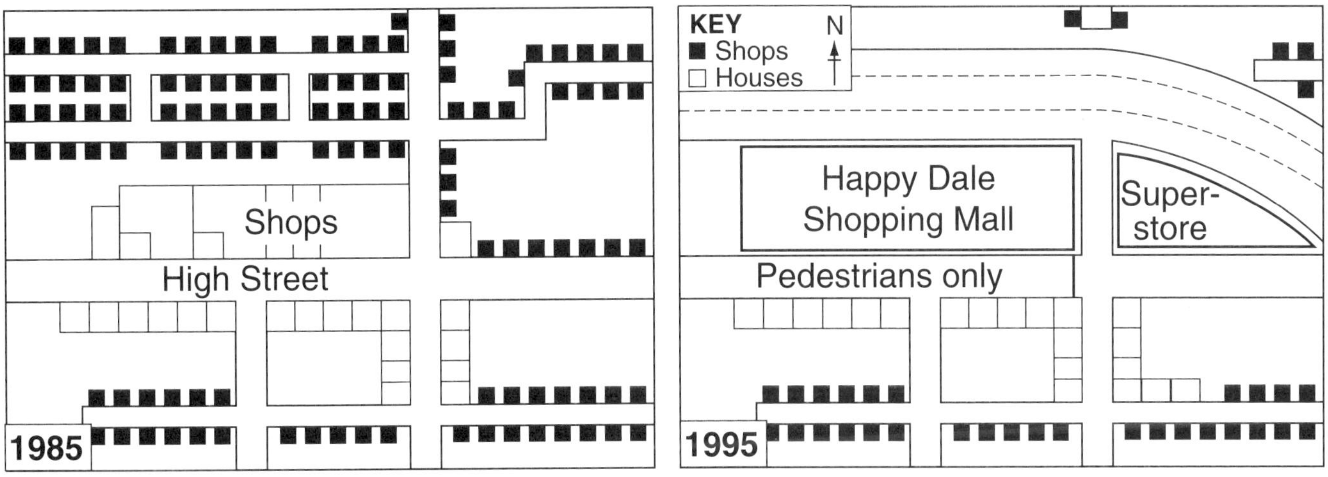

Write down **one** change between the two maps for each of these headings:

Shops ______________________

Houses ______________________

Roads ______________________

3 Write down **one** kind of person who might be:

In favour of the new mall ______________________

Against the new mall ______________________

Recap *Many changes are happening in the South-east such as* ______________________

____

*Some people l*________ *these changes but others do not because different people have different v*__________.

In this activity you will learn about places in north-east England

England is divided into counties. Cities and towns are urban areas where lots of people live. Most towns and cities are found near rivers.

Most towns are found near rivers. Newcastle upon Tyne is on the north bank of the River Tyne and is in the county of Tyne and Wear. Gateshead and Sunderland are also in Tyne and Wear with Gateshead on the south bank of the Tyne and Sunderland on the Wear.

The city of Durham is on the River Wear and in County Durham. Chester le Street is in the same county and on the same river as Durham.

Morpeth, in Northumberland, is found on the River Wansbeck. Alnwick on the River Aln and Rothbury on the River Coquet are both in Northumberland.

The River Tees flows through the county of Cleveland and the two towns of Middlesbrough and Stockton are found there.

Activities

1 Choose **three** colours. One for rivers, one for cities and towns and one for countries. In the passage above underline the three groups of things with the colours.

2 Complete the table below by matching up the towns with the correct rivers and countries. Use the things underlined in the passage above.

Alphabetical list of towns in northern England		
Town	**River**	**County**
Alnwick	*Aln*	*Northumberland*
Chester le Street		
Durham		
Gateshead		
Middlesbrough		
Morpeth		
Newcastle		
Rothbury		
Stockton		
Sunderland		

Recap *Most towns are found near* **r**______________. *Newcastle is found on the north bank of the River* **T**______________.

In this activity you will learn about places in north-east England

There are many towns in northern England. The largest is **Newcastle upon Tyne** which is the regional centre. Most people in north-east England will visit Newcastle occasionally.

Activities

1 Study the map showing ten towns and cities and their populations. (How many people live in each place?)

2 Complete the table below by putting the places in rank order from the largest to the smallest.

Map showing ten north-east towns and their populations

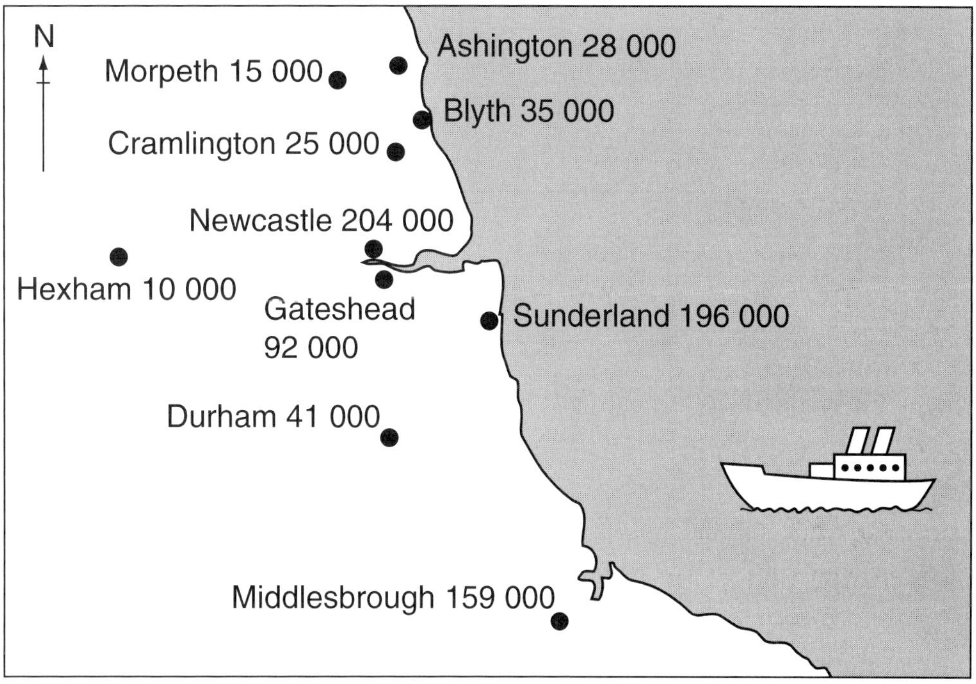

Rank	Name of town or city	Population
1		
2		
3		
4		
5		
6		
7		
8		
9		
10		

Recap *The largest city in northern England is N____________________ upon T_________.*

In this activity you will learn about places in north-east England

There are many towns in northern England. The largest is **Newcastle upon Tyne** which is the regional centre. Most people in north-east England will visit Newcastle occasionally.

Activities

1 Use the clues to complete the crossword below. The name of the region's largest city is written through the crossword.

2 Shade the names of towns and cities with a colour.

	Clues
n _ _ _ _ _	Japanese car company
_ e _ _	River which Sunderland is on
w _ _ _ _ _ _ _	End of the Roman Wall
_ _ _ _ _ c _	Castle town on the River Aln
_ _ _ _ a _	City and county D____
_ _ _ _ s _ _ _ _	Over the river from Newcastle
_ _ t _ _	Newcastle's underground railway
S _ _ _ _ _ l _ _ _	New city on the Wear
_ e _ _ _ _	Market town on the River Tyne. H_____
_ _ _ _ _ u _ _ _ _ _ _ _ _	Largest county in region
_ _ _ p _ _ _	County town of Northumberland. M_______
_ _ o _ _ _ _ _	Slang for Newcastle people. G_______
n _ _ _ _ _ _ _	Sea to the east of the region
t _ _ _	River of Middlesbrough
_ _ _ _ _ _ y _ _ _	Coastal resort near Newcastle
_ _ n _	River of Newcastle and Hexham
_ _ _ _ e _ _ _ _	County Middlesbrough is in

Recap

The largest city in the northern region is N_____________ *upon* T______.
Newcastle is located on the north bank of the River T______.

In this activity you will learn about north-east England

There are many images of north-east England. Some are historical and others are to do with the modern city of Newcastle upon Tyne. Newcastle is the regional centre of the north-east.

Activities

1 Tick **good**, **bad** or **neither** next to each statement about the north-east region in the table below.

	Good	Bad	Neither
All the coal mines in the region have closed leaving many people unemployed			
The Metro Centre attracts millions of visitors every year who spend a lot of money			
The climate is cool and damp			
Newcastle has lots of entertainment			
Newcastle United football team have a lot of fans. St James Park is full every game			
There are traffic jams in Newcastle every morning			
A million people live in Tyne and Wear			
A lot of Japanese companies are opening factories in the region. They give work to thousands of people			
The North Sea at Whitley Bay is cold			
Not many people live in Northumberland			
The Tyne Bridge crosses the River Tyne			
Newcastle people speak Geordie			
There are lots of castles in Northumberland			
There are three very large hospitals in Newcastle, the RVI, the General and the Freeman			
There are two Universities in Newcastle			

2 Are there more **good** points about the north-east region than **bad**? (**Yes/No**)

Recap *The regional centre of north-east England is*

N______________________. It has two Universities and three

h______________________ as well as entertainment.

In this activity you will learn about north-east England

There are many images of north-east England. Some are historical and others are to do with the modern city of Newcastle upon Tyne. Newcastle is the regional centre of the north-east.

Activity

Draw lines to join up the '**heads**' on the left and the '**tails**' on the right below.

Swan Hunters	Japanese car company in the north-east
Newcastle United play	make ships on the River Tyne
The Metro system	are north-east cities
Spanish City is	is a large indoor shopping centre
The Metro Centre	people born on Tyneside
The Tyne Bridge and the Swing Bridge	famous Geordie musicians
Nissan is a	football at St James Park
Geordies are	cross the River Tyne in Newcastle
Sting and Mark Knopfler are	in Whitley Bay
Newcastle and Sunderland	is a commuter railway on Tyneside

Recap *Newcastle is the* **r**__________________ *centre for north-east England. The city provides entertainment and* **w**______________ *for many people in the region.*

In this activity you will learn about north-east England

There are many images of north-east England. Some are historical and others are to do with the modern city of Newcastle upon Tyne. Newcastle is the regional centre of the north-east.

Activities

1 Match the descriptions with the pictures on the map of north-east England below.

2 Colour the **North Sea** in **blue** and the **land** in **green**.

3 Colour the pictures of any **three** places that you have visited, or would like to visit.

North-east England

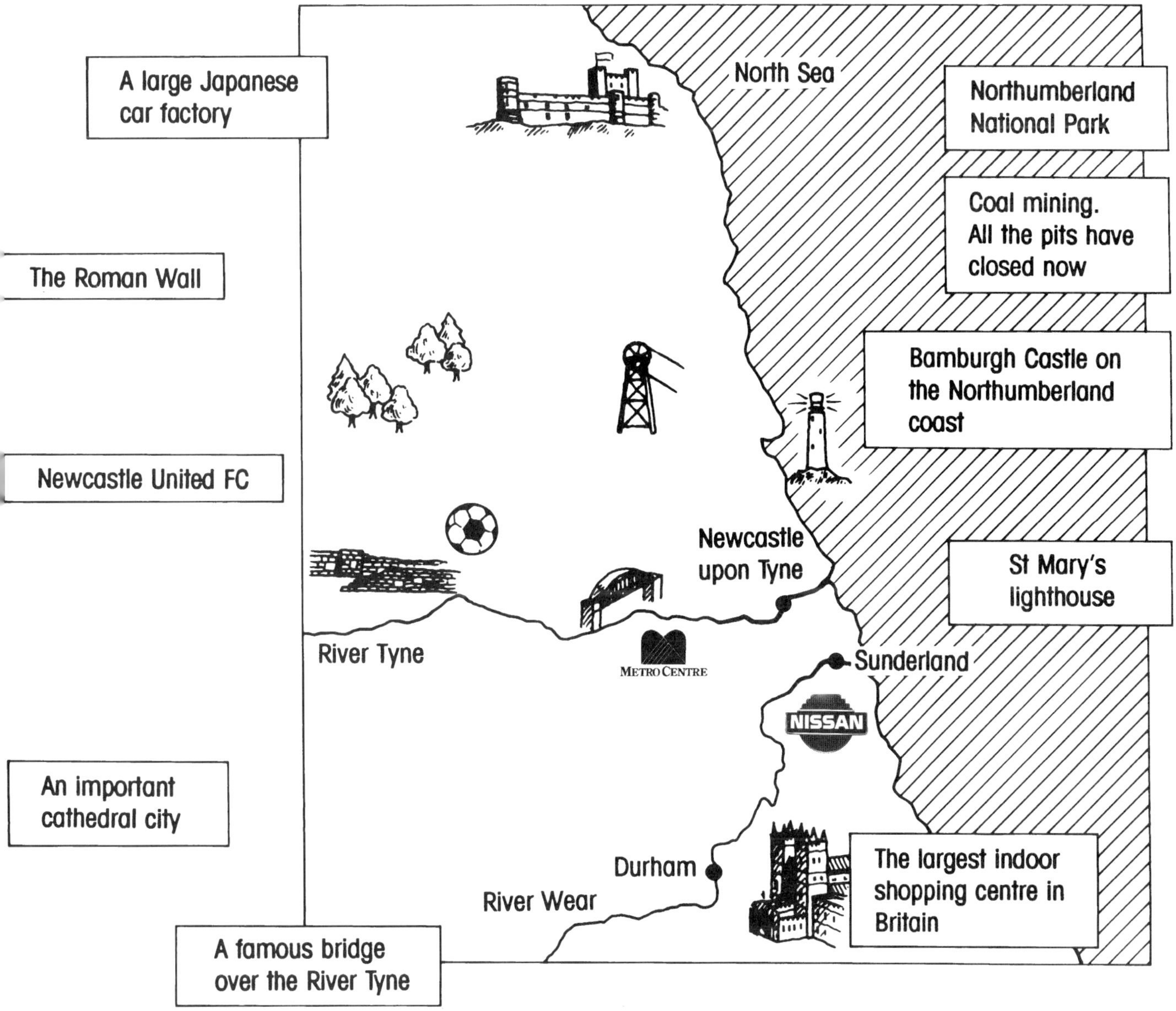

Recap *In north-east England there are many historic sites like B____________ castle and the Roman W________. The region once had lots of C________ mines but all the pits are closed now.*

In this activity you will learn about the climate of north-east England

The climate of north-east England is cool and damp. London is warmer than the north-east and Cardiff is wetter.

Activities

1 Study the table below showing the climate of Newcastle upon Tyne. Join the climate descriptions to the correct month.

2 Which two months are left when you have finished?

__________________________ ____________________________

3 On the table below use a coloured pencil to shade the months used in Activity 2.

Climate of Newcastle upon Tyne

Month number	1	2	3	4	5	6	7	8	9	10	11	12
Month	Jan	Feb	Mar	Apr	May	Jun	Jul	Aug	Sep	Oct	Nov	Dec
Temperature °C	5	5	6	8	10	12	15	14	13	10	9	6
Rainfall mm	55	45	43	45	50	46	74	75	53	61	60	58

The warmest month → July

61 mm of rainfall and 10 °C

A winter month with 5 °C and 55 mm rainfall

The wettest month

The same temperature as October but less rainfall

Temperature of 13 °C

Same temperature as January but drier

Summer month with 46 mm of rainfall

Month with least rainfall

6 °C and some of the 58 mm might fall as snow

January	**July**
February	**August**
March	**September**
April	**October**
May	**November**
June	**December**

Recap *Newcastle upon Tyne is cooler than* ***L***______________ *and drier than* ***C***______________. *North-east England is* ***c***______________ *and* ***d***______________.

In this activity you will learn about the climate of north-east England

The climate of north-east England is cool and damp. London is warmer than this region and Cardiff is wetter.

Activities

1 Use the figures in the table below to complete the temperature and rainfall graphs for Newcastle upon Tyne. These figures show the climate of north-east England. January and July have been done for you.

Climate of Newcastle upon Tyne

Month	Jan	Feb	Mar	Apr	May	Jun	Jul	Aug	Sep	Oct	Nov	Dec
Temperature °C	5	5	6	8	10	12	15	14	13	10	9	6
Rainfall mm	55	45	43	45	50	46	74	75	53	61	60	58

2 Join the dots with a smooth line then go over the line in **red**. Colour each bar carefully in **blue**.

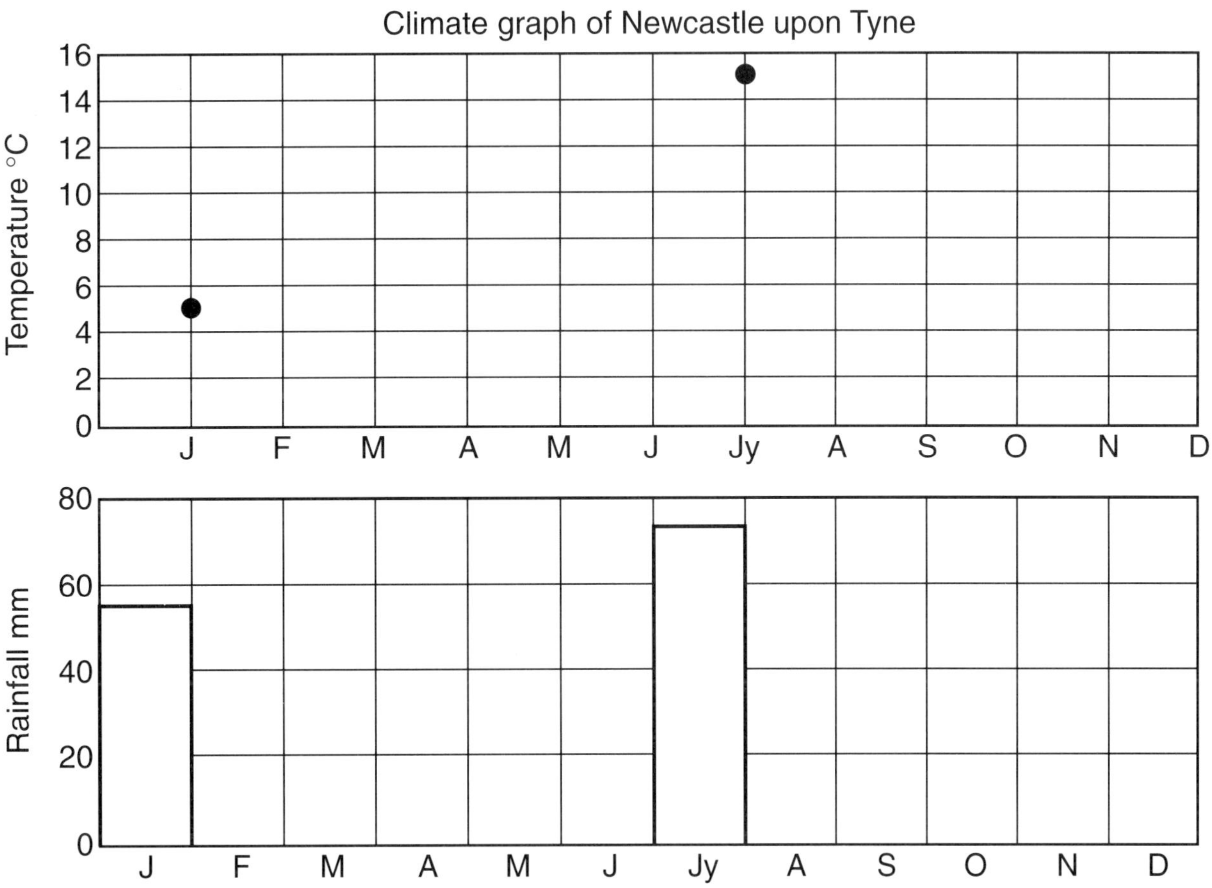

Recap Newcastle upon Tyne is cooler than **L**________________ and drier than **C**________________. North-east England is **c**______________ and **d**______________.

In this activity you will learn about the climate of north-east England

The climate of north-east England is cool and damp. There is often a breeze blowing from the North Sea which keeps summer temperatures lower on the coast than further inland. London is warmer than this region and Cardiff is wetter.

Activities

1 Complete the climate graphs below by joining the dots on the temperature graph with a **red** line, and colouring the bars on the rainfall graph in **blue**.

Climate graphs of Newcastle upon Tyne

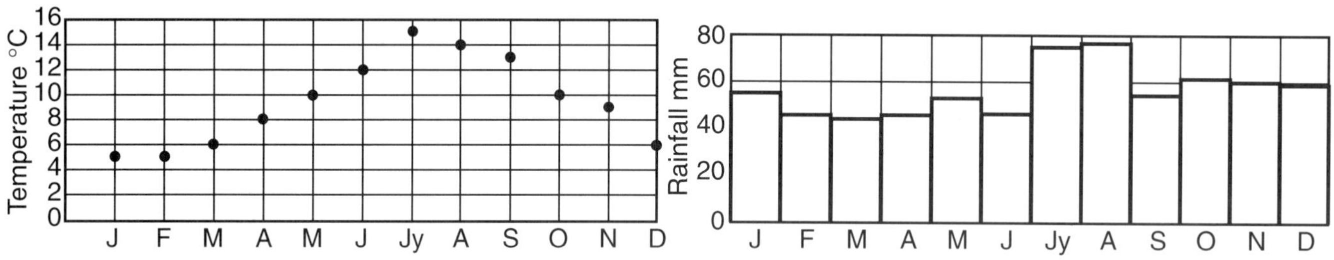

2 Tick **true**, **false** or **not enough evidence** next to each statement in the table. Use the climate graphs to help you.

	True	False	Not enough evidence
Summers are usually wetter than winters			
It snows a lot in January			
January temperature is 8 °C			
June is a sunny month			
July temperature is 15 °C			
November has 60 mm of rainfall			
From July to December the temperature falls			
From January to June the temperature falls			
It rains every day in August			
Winters are warmer that summers			
October is a windy month			
February is colder than November			
Hailstones are a problem in June			
The River Tyne freezes over in winter			

Recap *The climate of Newcastle upon Tyne is* **c**_________ *and* **d**_________. *There is often a cold breeze blowing from the* **N**___________ *Sea which keeps summer temperatures on the coast lower than further inland.*

In this activity you will learn about how north-east England developed

There used to be a lot of coal mining in north-east England. The Northumberland and Durham coalfield covers most of the region. Mining provided work for thousands of people. By the 1990s there were no coal mines or mining jobs left.

Activities

1 Put the sentences below in the correct order to explain what happened to coal mining in the north-east. You can copy and cut them out to stick them in the correct order.

By 1996, there were no pits left and no work. All the pits had closed.
Ten years later most of the pits had closed and only 50 were left employing 48 000 people.
In 1981 32 000 people were working in 25 pits; most of them, were near the coast.
Many pits closed when the coal ran out, and by 1961 147 pits employed 116 000 people.
In 1947 there were 188 pits employing 149 000 people. These were spread over the whole of Northumberland and Durham.

2 Write the number of pits and the number of workers onto the time line below.

Time line showing the number of pits and workers in the Northumberland and Durham coalfield. 1947 to 1996.

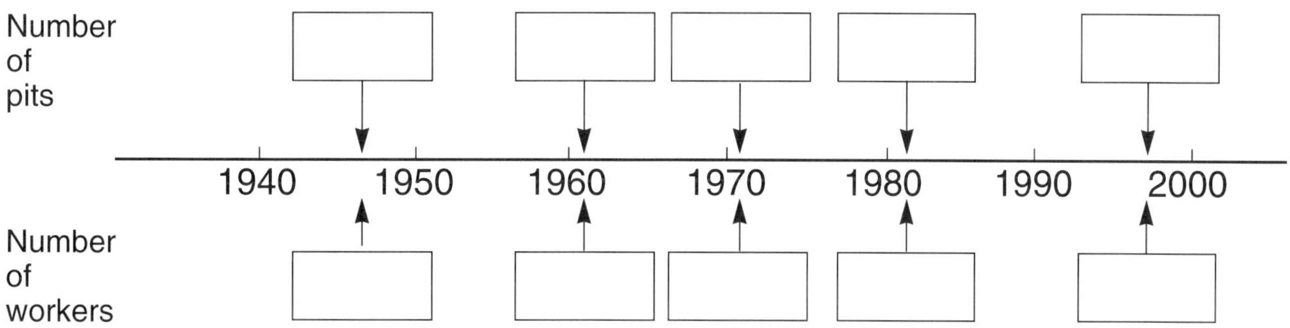

Recap *Coal mining was very important in north-east England. Pits were found on the* **N**________________________ *and* **D**____________________ *coalfield.*

In this activity you will learn about how north-east England developed

As coal mines have closed many people have been made unemployed in the north-east. The region now has a lot of Japanese factories which provide many jobs. The main Japanese company is Nissan which makes cars in a large factory near the city of Sunderland.

Activities

1 Read the conversation between Mr Newburn and Mr Yokama.

Underline all the reasons why Mr Yokama chose Sunderland for the car factory. You could underline as many as nine different reasons.

Mr Yokama, why did you build the factory near Sunderland?

I had been told by other Japanese people that the north-east was a good place to come. We would get money from the government to give jobs and we could sell more cars in Britain and Europe.

What was good about north-east England Mr Yokama?

There were a lot of workers on Tyne and Wear and I knew they could be trained for work in the factory. We could use Tyneside as a port to send cars to Europe and to bring parts in from Japan.

What was good about the site?

The site was very good. It was a large area of flat land (it was once an airport). Two big roads are nearby; the A1(M) and the A19 which can be used by delivery lorries. The people work very hard and do not go on strike.

2 Which do you think are the **two main reasons** why Nissan was built near Sunderland?

1 ____

____

2 ____

____

Recap *Nissan makes **c**________. The factory is located near the city of **S**________________. Nissan is a **J**________________ company.*

In this activity you will learn about transport in north-east England

The north-east region is linked to other places by transport routes. You can get to other places by sea, air, road or rail.

Diagram to show various transport links with Newcastle and travelling times

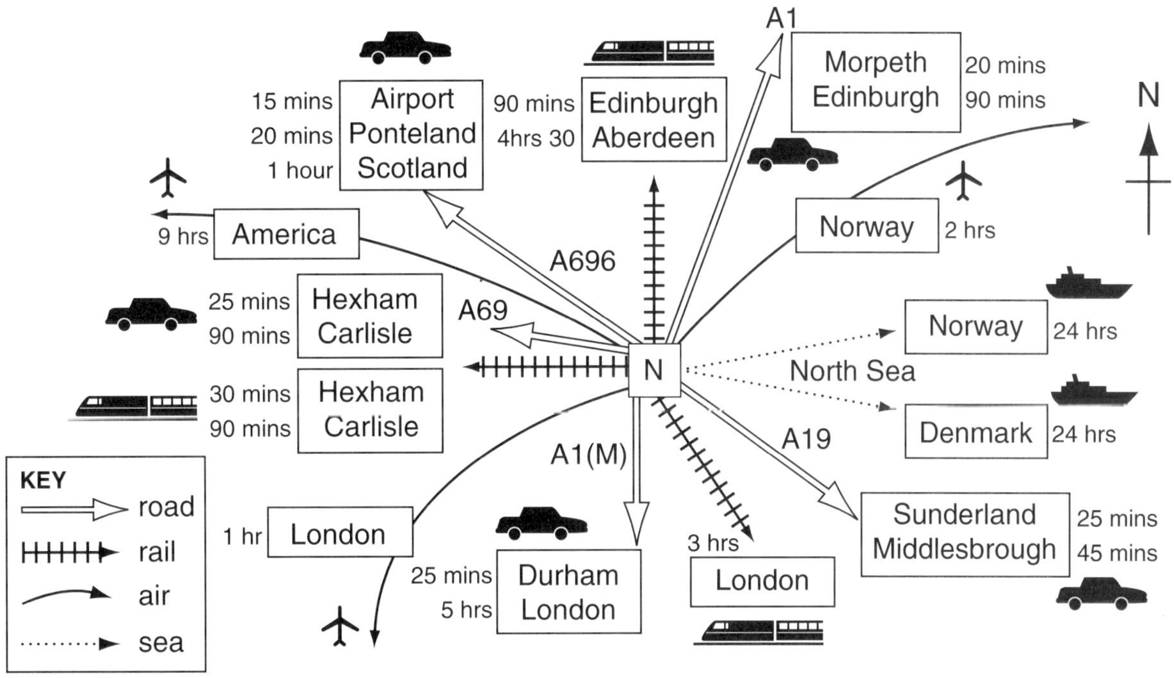

Activities

1 Using the diagram above tick **true** or **false** next to each statement in the table below.

2 Use a colour for each symbol in the key. Shade the key and then shade the transport types on the diagram.

	True	False
The A1(M) leads to Carlisle		
You can get to Norway by ferry		
You can get to Hexham by train or by road		
The A190 leads to Sunderland		
It takes 3 hours to fly to London		
You can go to Edinburgh by ferry		
Aberdeen is south of Newcastle		
Trains are slower than planes		
America is a long way away		
The A1(M) leads to Durham and London		

Recap *From Newcastle you can get to places by road, rail, **a**_______ and **f**__________.*

In this activity you will learn how Newcastle is linked to other places

Newcastle is a major city so it is linked with other places by transport. Many roads meet in the city of Newcastle.

Diagram to show which roads lead to Newcastle upon Tyne

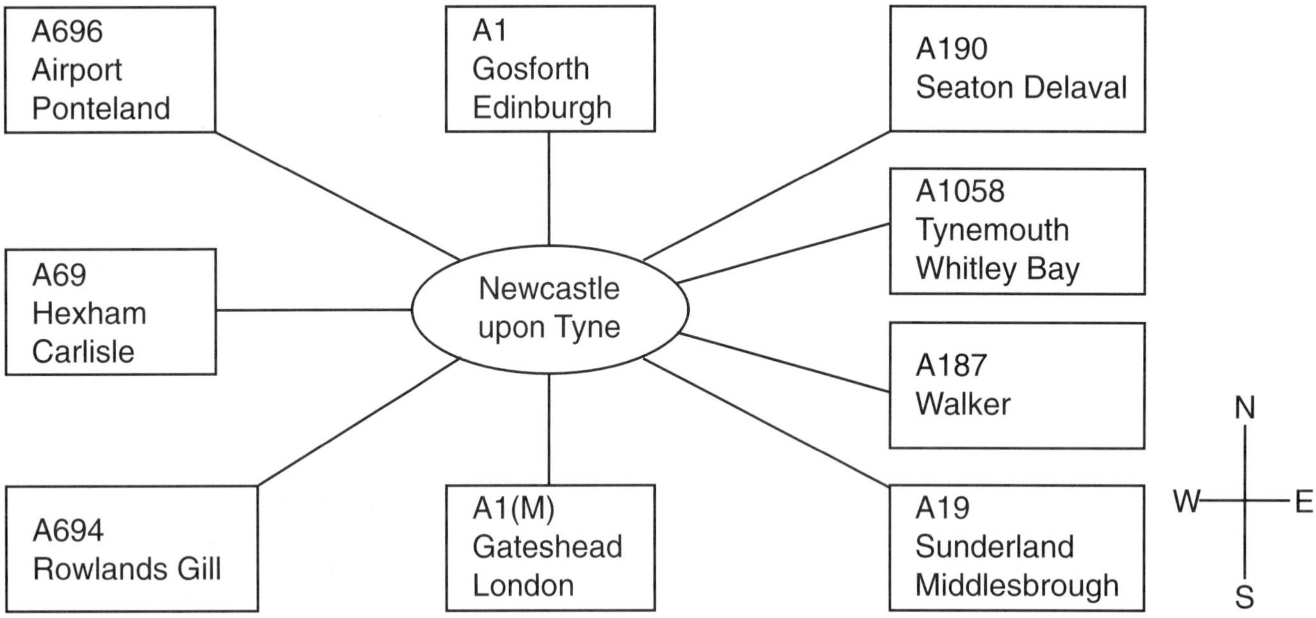

Activities

1 Study the diagram and fill in the gaps in the sentences below.

- Which road leads to Walker? ________________
- To get to the airport I would use the ____________
- Hexham and Carlisle are on the ________________
- I live in Seaton Delaval and drive along the ________ to get to Newcastle.
- To get from Ponteland to Sunderland I would go along the _______ and the ______
- Whitley Bay is on the coast. The A_______ is called the Coast Road.
- To get from London to Edinburgh I would use the ___________
- To get from Rowlands Gill to Tynemouth I would use the ______ and the ________
- The __________ is known as the West Road because it leads to the west.
- The A__________ leads to the north.

2 Use a colour to underline all the places named in the questions in Activity 1.

Recap N__________________ *is a major city and is linked to other towns and cities by* **r**__________. *Many roads meet in the city.*

In this activity you will learn about Wales

Wales is one of four countries that make up the **United Kingdom**. It is much smaller than England. It has a population of about 3 million people.

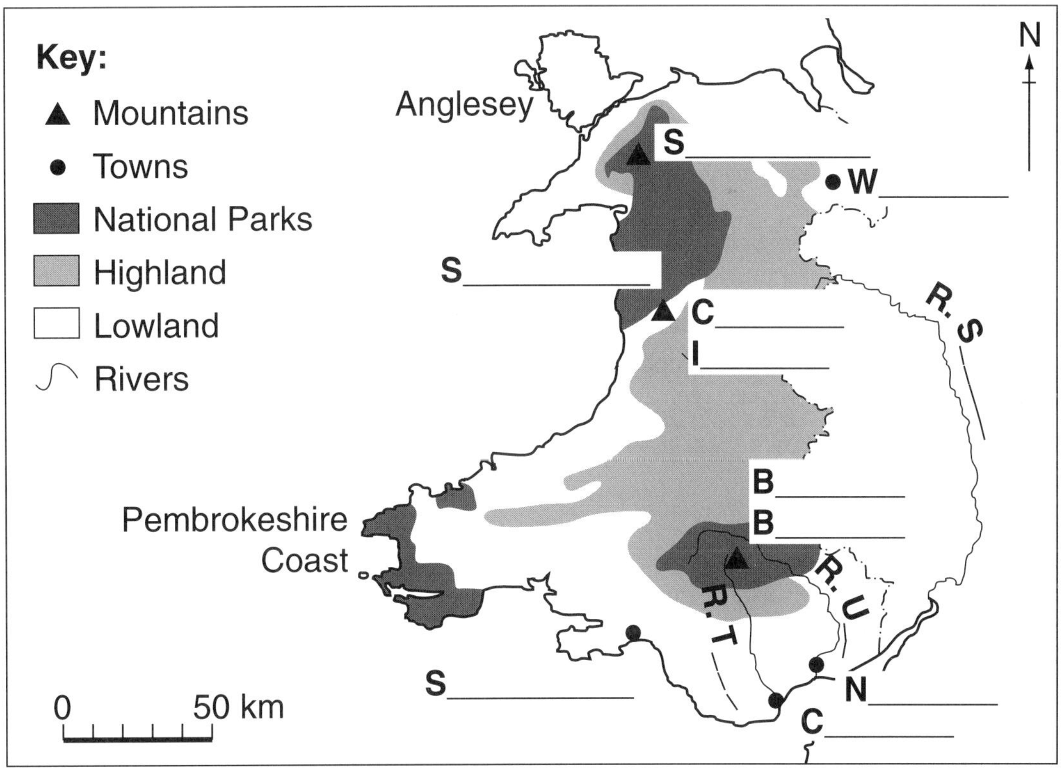

Activities

1 On the map above colour: the highland in **brown**,
the lowland in **light green**,
the National Parks in **dark green**,
the sea in **light blue**.

2 Complete the map by marking on the places listed in the table below. Use an atlas to help you.

Rivers	Mountains	Towns	National Parks
Taff	Snowdon	Cardiff	Brecon Beacons
Usk	Cader Idris	Swansea	Snowdonia
Severn		Newport	
		Wrexham	

Recap *Wales is one of* f__________ *countries that make up the*

U_______________ K_______________.

In this activity you will learn about Wales

Wales is one of four countries that make up the **United Kingdom**. It is much smaller than England. It is a hilly country with many mountains.

Activities

1 All the places listed below can be found in Wales. Find them in the wordsearch. Words can go up, down, backwards and diagonally.

Rivers	**Towns**
Taff	Aberystwyth
Wye	Cardiff
Severn	Swansea
Usk	Merthyr Tydfil
Tawe	Wrexham
Mountains	**Others**
Snowdon	Snowdonia
Pen-y-Fan	Brecon Beacons

A	B	R	E	C	O	N	F	S	W	T
S	B	E	A	C	O	N	S	N	R	T
N	P	E	N	Y	F	A	N	O	E	A
O	X	H	R	B	R	T	A	W	X	F
W	N	S	W	Y	U	E	M	D	H	F
D	R	G	E	E	S	L	E	O	A	I
O	E	T	U	N	K	T	Y	N	M	D
N	V	A	A	F	F	I	W	D	R	R
I	E	W	M	E	R	T	H	Y	R	A
A	S	E	T	D	Y	F	I	L	T	C
F	A	T	R	O	P	W	E	N	L	H

2 Underline the correct answers in the sentences below. Use the map opposite to help you.

Wales is a **flat/hilly** country.

Most large towns are found in **north/south** Wales.

Wales has **three/four** National Parks.

The river **Taff/Severn** flows through Cardiff.

Cardiff/Swansea is the capital of Wales.

Wales is **larger/smaller** than England.

Map of Wales

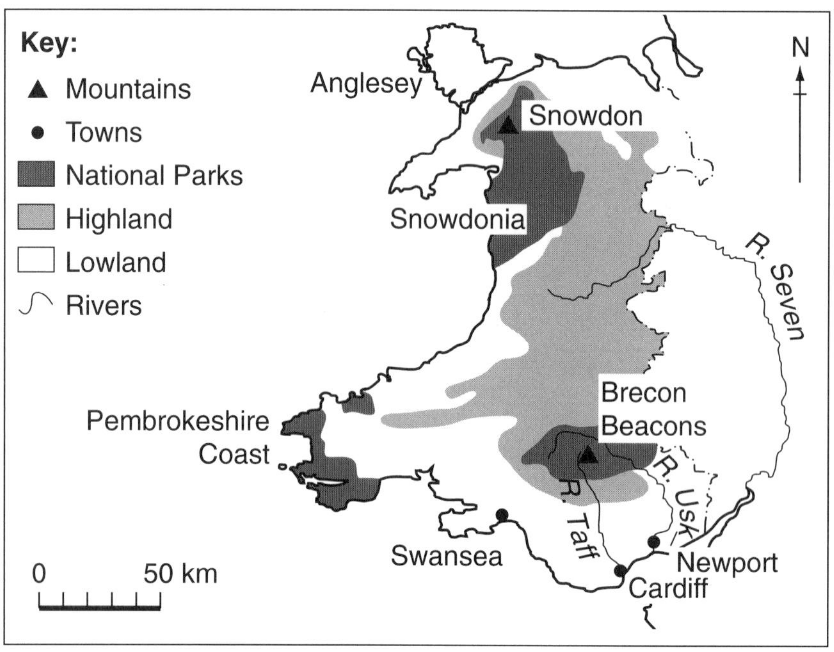

Recap *Wales is one of f__________ countries that make up the United Kingdom. It is much s______________ than England.*

In this activity you will learn about Wales

Wales is one of four countries that make up the United Kingdom. It is much smaller than England. It is a hilly country. Cardiff is the most important city in Wales. It has a population of 300,000 which means one in ten people living in Wales lives in Cardiff.

Activities

1 Listed below are some words associated with Wales. Fit them into the crossword beginning with the longest words.

12 letter words
Severn Bridge

10 letter words
Eisteddfod

9 letter words
Snowdonia
Daffodills
Mountains

8 letter words
coalmine

7 letter words
valleys
singing
Cardiff
St David
tourism

6 letter words
dragon
chapel

5 letter words
Welsh
rugby
leeps
sheep
music

4 letter words
Taff
rain

2 Cardiff is an important city for many reasons. Write the words in the Word box into the statements below.

- A centre for the ________ with theatres, cinemas and is the home of the Welsh National Opera.
- A centre for __________, the 1999 rugby world cup final will be played there.
- A ______________ centre with main stations for national express and inter city rail.
- A ____________ centre with museums and a castle.
- A ____________ centre, the Welsh Office is found here.
- A major ______________ centre with covered arcades and pedestrianised streets.
- A ____________ centre with the head offices of many companies.
- A major ___________ centre with hotels and many places to visit.
- A centre for ____________ with universities and a teaching hospital.

Word box
arts
historical
transport
sport
shopping
business
political
education
tourist

Recap *C______________ is the most important place in W__________.*

In this activity you will learn about the climate of Wales

The **climate** of Wales varies from place to place. The weather in the mountains can be very different from the climate of Cardiff shown below.

Activities

Climate graphs for Cardiff

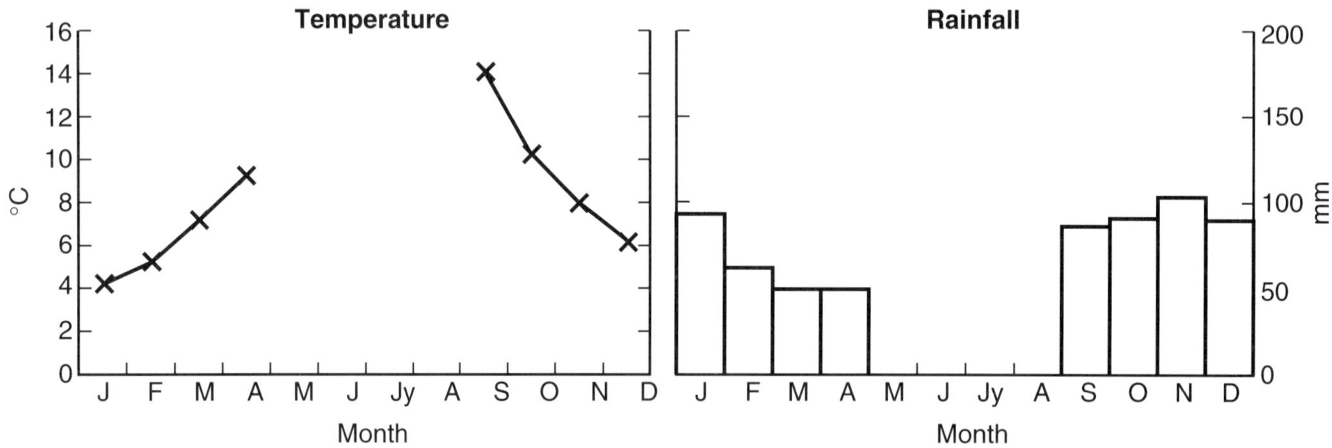

1 Use the figures on the right to complete the climate graphs for Cardiff. Draw a **red** line to show the temperature and **blue** bars to show the rainfall.

	Temperature	Rainfall
May	11°c	70 mm
June	13°c	60 mm
July	16°c	80 mm
August	15°c	100 mm

2 Complete the following sentences by underlining the correct month in brackets.

In Cardiff the **wettest** month is (**January/March/November**)

In Cardiff the **warmest** month is (**April/July/August**)

In Cardiff the **driest** month is (**December/September/March**)

In Cardiff the **coolest** month is (**January/November/October**)

3 Complete the following paragraph by **underlining** the correct word in the brackets.

The temperature in the mountains of Wales will be (**cooler/warmer**) than Cardiff because temperature (**falls/rises**) as you go higher. The mountains of Wales will be much (**drier/wetter**) than Cardiff because higher ground usually gets (**more/less**) rain than lower ground.

Recap *The c____________ of Wales v____________ from place to place.*

In this activity you will learn about the climate of Wales

The three maps below show what the climate is like in Wales. As you can see the climate of Wales varies from place to place.

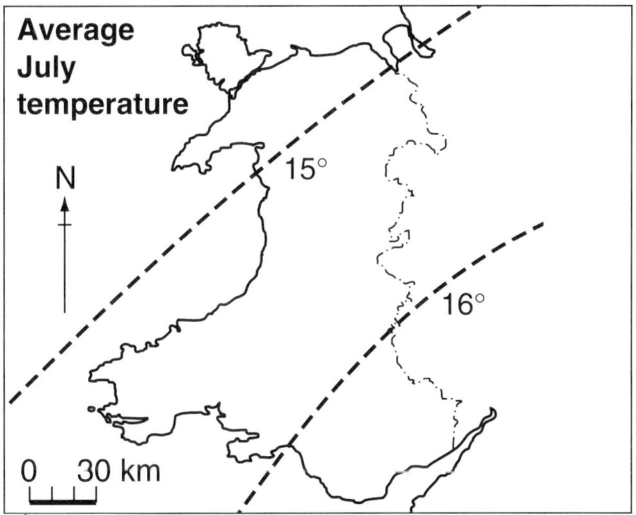

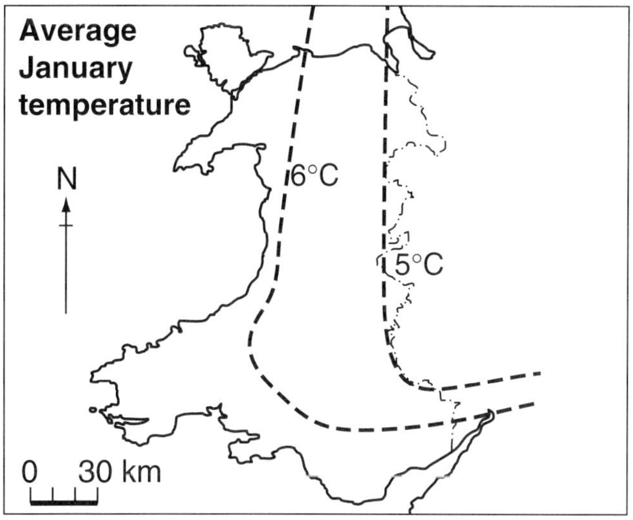

Activities

1 Are the following statements **true** or **false**. **Tick** the correct box. The maps above will help you.

	True	False
In July average temperatures in Wales decrease from south east to north west		
In January temperatures in Wales decrease from east to west		

2 Colour in **red** on the map the part of Wales where average July temperatures are **above** 16°C.

3 Colour in **blue** on the map the part of Wales where average January temperatures are **between** 5°C and 6°C.

4 Use the two maps above and the rainfall map opposite to complete the table below.

	Average July temperature	Average Jan. temperature	Average rainfall
Barry			
Pwllheli			
Builth Wells			
Rhyl			

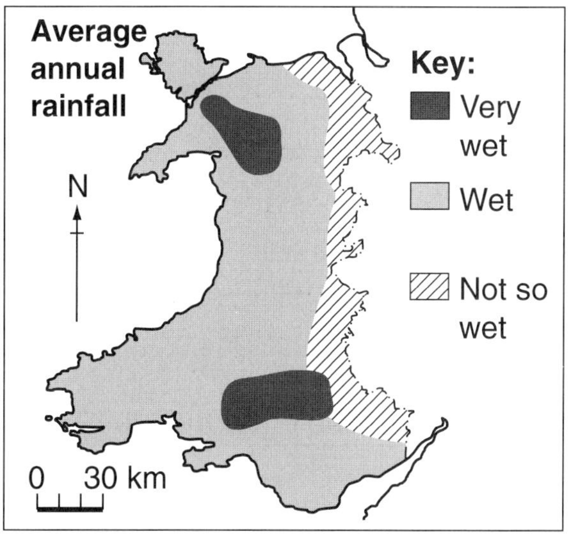

Recap *The* ***c***________________ *of Wales varies from* ***p***____________ *to* ***p***____________.

In this activity you will learn about how the climate of Wales varies from place to place

The climate of Wales varies from place to place. The reasons are outlined below.

Activities

1 Draw lines to join the **'heads'** and **'tails'** below.

It is cooler in the mountains because	it rains more on higher ground
It it wetter in the mountains because	the sea keeps temperatures up
It is cooler on the coast in summer because	temperatures fall with height
It is warmer on the coast in winter because	the sea keeps temperatures down

2 Look at the table below and compare the climate of Snowdon with the climate of Llandudno.

	January Temp.	July Temp.	Annual Rainfall	Average amount of daily sunshine
Llandudno	5°C	15°C	750 mm	4.5 hours
Snowdon	-3°C	8°C	3300 mm	2.5 hours

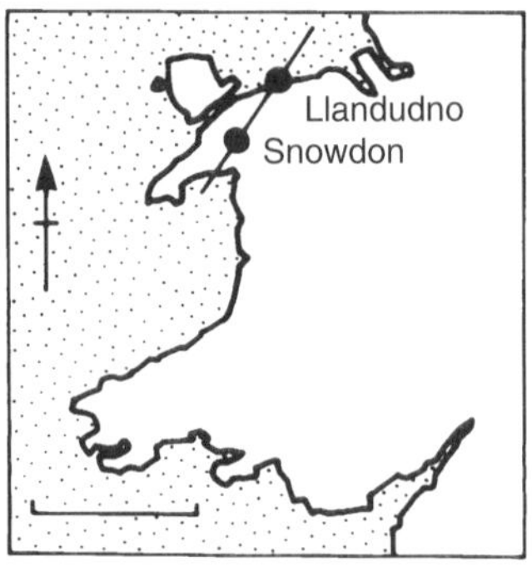

Cross section from Snowdon to Llandudno

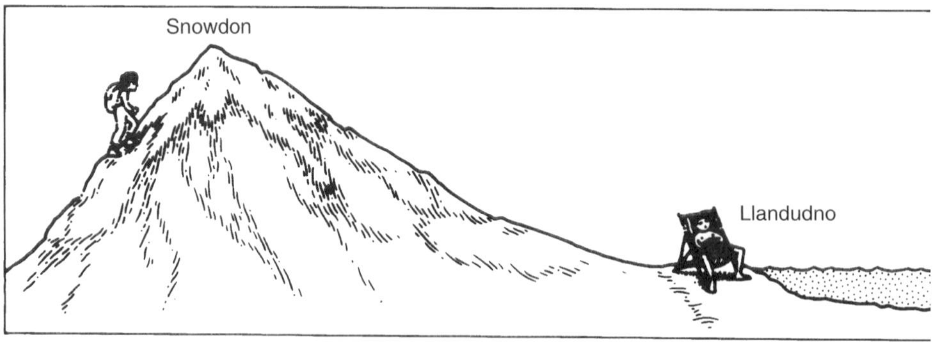

Complete the sentences below. The **'heads'** and **'tails'** above will help you.

L____________ is warmer than **S**____________ because __________________

S____________ is wetter than **L**____________ because __________________

Llandudno receives more sunshine than Snowdon because

____

____

3 Explain why Llandudno would be warmer in **winter** than Newtown which is further inland.

____

____

Recap *The **c**____________ of Wales **v**____________ from place to place. The climate in the **m**________________ is different from that found on the coast.*

In this activity you will learn about industrial developments in South Wales

South Wales has been a major industrial centre for 150 years. However, the type of industry found there has changed over the past 30 years.

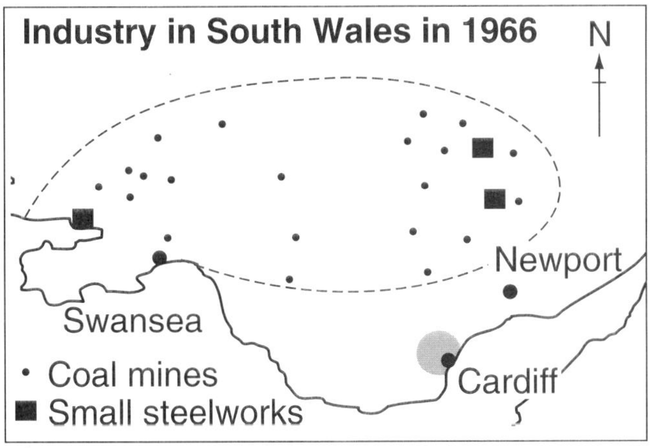

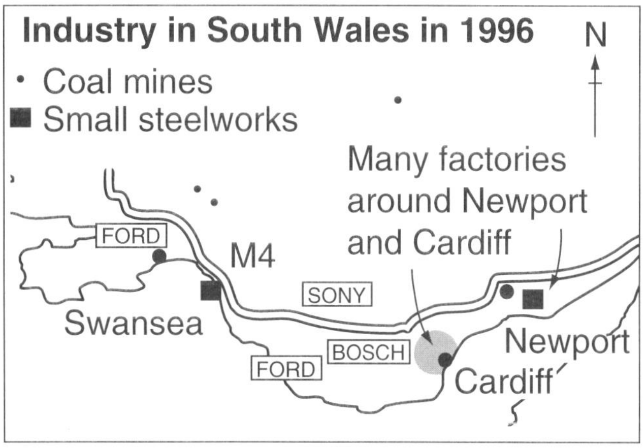

Activities

1 The statements below refer to industry in South Wales in 1966 and 1996. **Tick** the correct box for each statement. The maps above will help you.

	1966	1996
Many coal mines		
Few coal mines		
Many factories		
Few factories		
Most industry found on the coalfield		
Most industry found close to the M4 motorway		

2 Complete the following paragraph below by adding the words found in the Word box.

Word box
M4
transport
coalfield
power

In 1966 most industry in South Wales was found on the ___________. This is because coal was the main source of ________. In 1996 most industry is found along the _____ motorway. The most important thing now is for factories is to be near good ___________ links.

Recap *The type of industry found in South Wales has* ***c***__________ *over the past 30 years.*

In this activity you will learn about industrial developments in South Wales

Sony, a large Japanese company, recently opened a new factory near Bridgend in South Wales. They make televisions there. The diagram below shows some of the reasons why Sony chose to build their factory in South Wales.

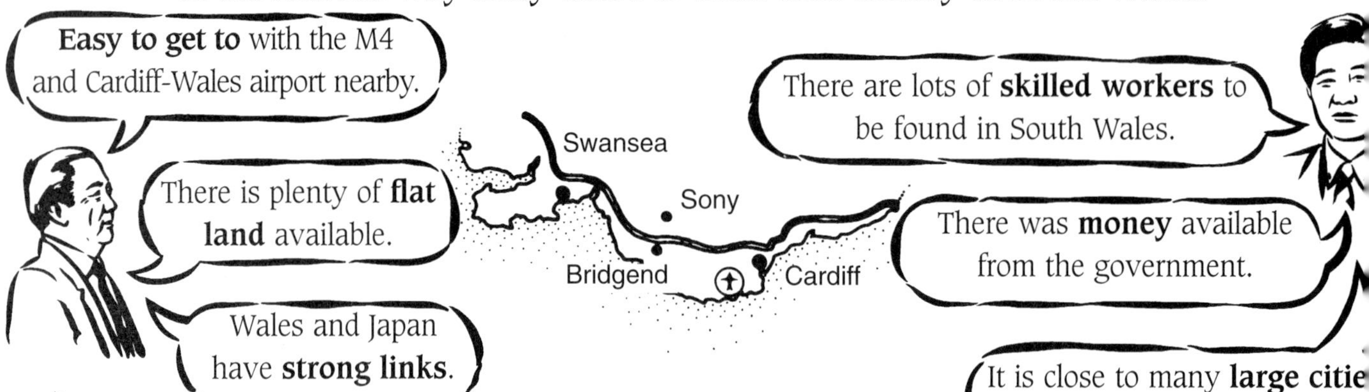

Activities

1 The table below shows what Sony had to consider when deciding where to build a new factory. Complete the table by adding the words found in the Word box. Use the diagram above to help you. The first one has been done for you.

Word box

reputation	site
transport	grants
markets	labour

Reputation	other Japanese companies have been successful in Wales
	to bring raw materials in and take finished goods out
	a large area of flat land close to a motorway is essential
	making televisions is a highly skilled job
	many people live in the UK and Europe
	government money is always important

2 Complete the following sentences using your own words.

Good **transport** links are important to Sony because ______________________

____

Being close to a large **market** is important because______________________

____

Recap *Four reasons why Sony decided to build their factory in South Wales are ____________, ____________, ____________ and ____________.*

In this activity you will learn about developments in the Welsh countryside

Much of Wales is rural where farming is the most important activity. Gwyn Jones has worked on Bontfaen farm for the past 30 years. In recent years he has been forced to change the way he uses his land.

Part of Bontfaen Farm in 1966

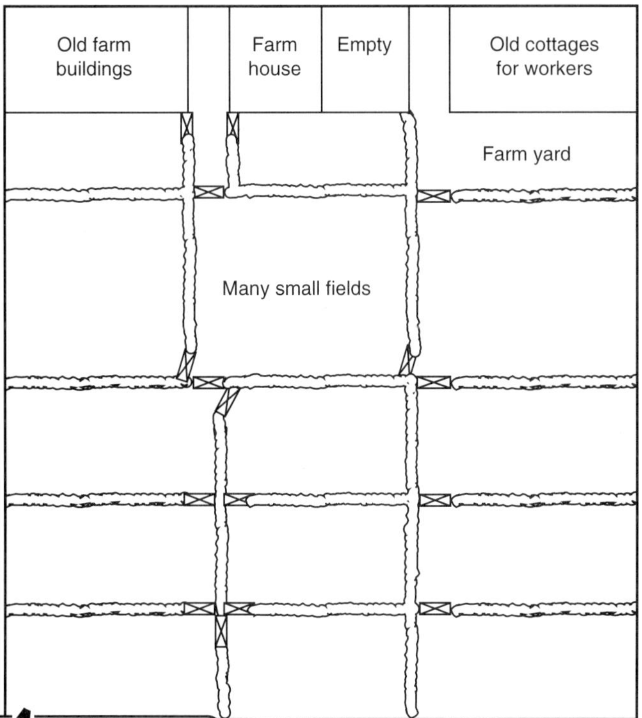

Part of Bontfaen Farm in 1996

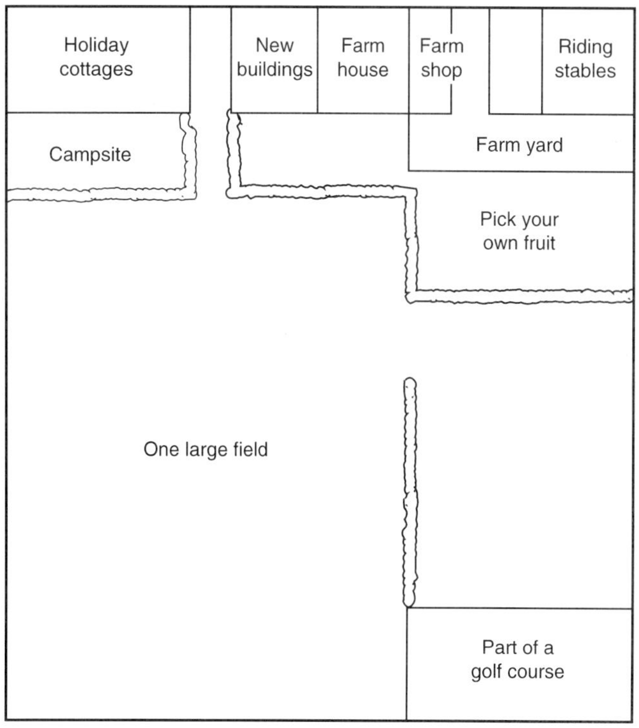

Activities

1 Look at the maps above. List four changes that have occurred in the way this farmer uses his land.

1 ______________________ **2** ______________________

3 ______________________ **4** ______________________

2 One of the reasons why farmers have been forced to change the way they use their land is because they have found it difficult to make a living from farming only. **Describe** how Gwyn Jones is trying to make extra money from:

Day trippers ______________________________

____

Holiday makers ______________________________

____

In recent years farmers in Wales have been forced to c______________ the way they use their l__________.

In this activity you will learn about transport in Wales

The main transport routes in Wales run from east to west. It is very difficult to travel quickly from south to north.

Activities

Three friends travelled from Cardiff in South Wales to Bangor in North Wales. Each took a different type of transport. Jaymesh travelled by car. Rosie travelled by train. Sam travelled by coach. Their journeys are described below. The map shows the routes taken. They all set off at 9.00 a.m.

There were no motorways. The roads were quite narrow in places. We got stuck behind tractors and lorries many times. We finally arrived in Bangor at 4.00 p.m.

I was surprised we travelled through England for much of the route. I had to get out at Crewe to change trains. I arrived at 2.00 p.m.

At first we headed west not north. We travelled through many towns, stopping each time. It was very slow. I arrived in Bangor at 5.30 p.m.

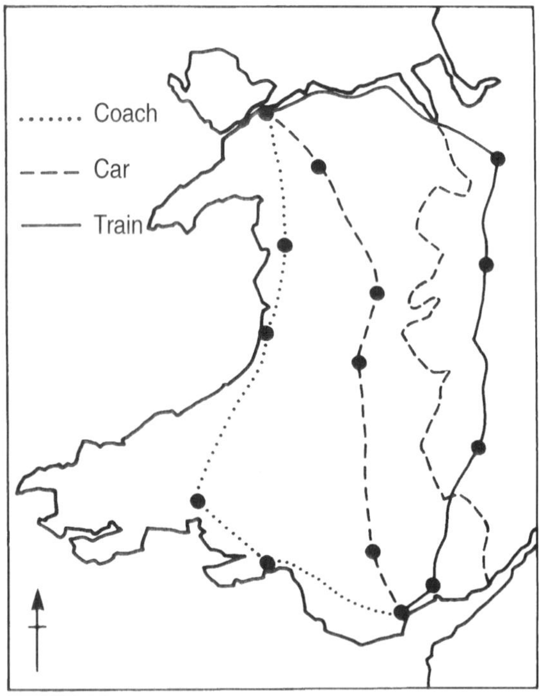

1 Use the information above to complete the table.

		Start time	Arrival time	Journey time
Jaymesh	Car	9.00 a.m.		
Rosie	Train	9.00 a.m.		
Sam	Coach	9.00 a.m.		

2 What special problems did each traveller face on the way?

Jaymesh ____________________

Rosie ____________________

Sam ____________________

Recap *The main transport routes in Wales run from **e**________ to **w**________.*

In this activity you will learn about transport in Wales

The two main transport routes in Wales run from east to west. In North Wales it is easier to travel to Liverpool and Manchester than it is to travel to South Wales. In South Wales it is easier to travel to Bristol and London than it is to travel to North Wales.

Activities

Map to show transport routes in Wales

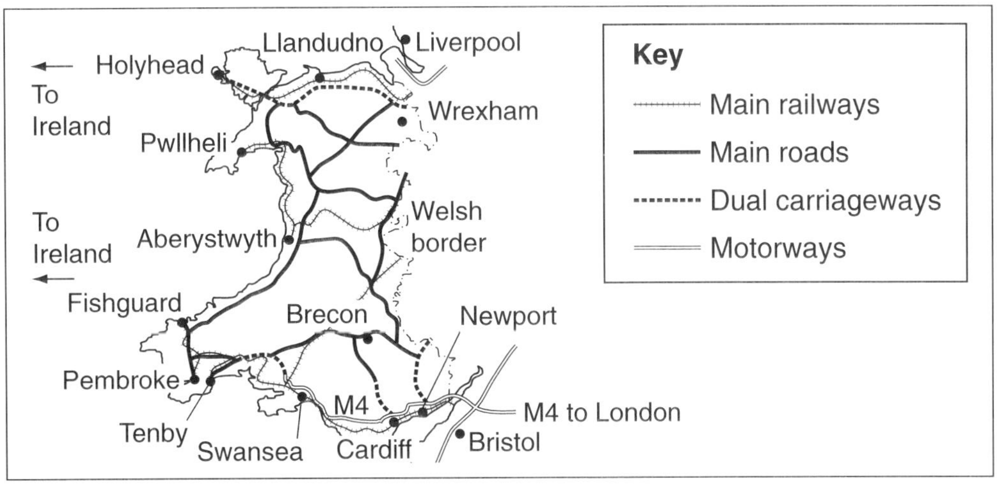

1 Complete the graph below by drawing in the travelling times to London. *Note: 1 cm=1 hour*

Travelling times from North Wales to South Wales

Car ______ 7 hours

Train ______ 5 hours

Coach ______ 8 hours

Travelling times from South Wales to London

Car ______ 3 hours

Train ______ 1¾ hours

Coach ______ 3½ hours

2 The reasons why it takes so long to travel from north to south in Wales are shown in the table below. Draw lines to join up the **'heads'** and **'tails'** below. The map above will help you.

Central Wales is hilly	so fewer routes are needed
Hills mean that	is with Merseyside and NW England
There are fewer settlements in mid Wales	so it is difficult to build roads
Much of North Wales's trade	is with SW England and London
Much of South Wales's trade	lots of detours have to be taken

Recap *The two main transport routes in Wales run from* ***e****______ to* ***w****______.*

In this activity you will learn about direction

This diagram shows the **four** main directions. These are **north**, **south**, **east** and **west**.

North is usually at the **top** of a map.

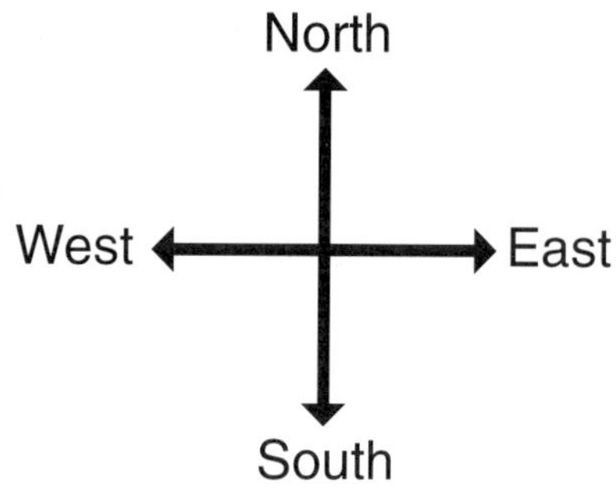

Activities

1 Solve these puzzles to work out the directions. The first one has been done for you.

B ← A ① **A** to **B** = <u>WEST</u>	C → D ② **C** to **D** = ____		
B ← A ③ **A** to **B** = ____	C → D ④ **C** to **D** = ____	F ↑ E ⑤ **E** to **F** = ____	
A ↓ B ⑥ **A** to **B** = ____	C → D ⑦ **C** to **D** = ____	E → F ⑧ **E** to **F** = ____	
A → B ⑨ **A** to **B** = ____	C → D ⑩ **C** to **D** = ____	E → F ⑪ **E** to **F** = ____	H ↑ G ⑫ **G** to **H** = ____
B ↑ A ⑬ **A** to **B** = ____	D ← C ⑭ **C** to **D** = ____	E → F ⑮ **E** to **F** = ____	
B ↑ A ⑯ **A** to **B** = ____	C → D ⑰ **C** to **D** = ____	E ↓ F ⑱ **E** to **F** = ____	

2 Fill in the first letter from each puzzle above, into the spaces in the grid below, to spell out a message.

W (1) __ (2)   __ (3) __ (4) __ (5) **T TO** __ (6) __ (7) __ (8)   **TH** __ (9)

QU __ (10) __ (11) __ (12)   **O** __ (13)   __ (14) __ (15)   **D** __ (16) __ (17) __ (18)   **DAY.**

Recap

*The main **directions** are **n**________, **s**________, **e**________ and **w**________.*

In this activity you will learn about direction

There are **four** main directions. These are **north**, **south**, **east** and **west**. Between these there are four other directions: **north-east**, **north-west**, **south-east**, and **south-west**.

These directions are shown on this diagram.

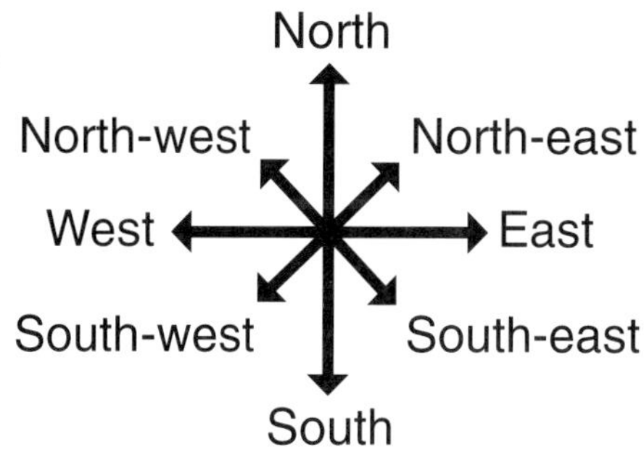

Activity

Start at the large dot on the spotty grid on the right. Follow the directions to go from dot to dot to draw an animal. Cross out the directions as you go.

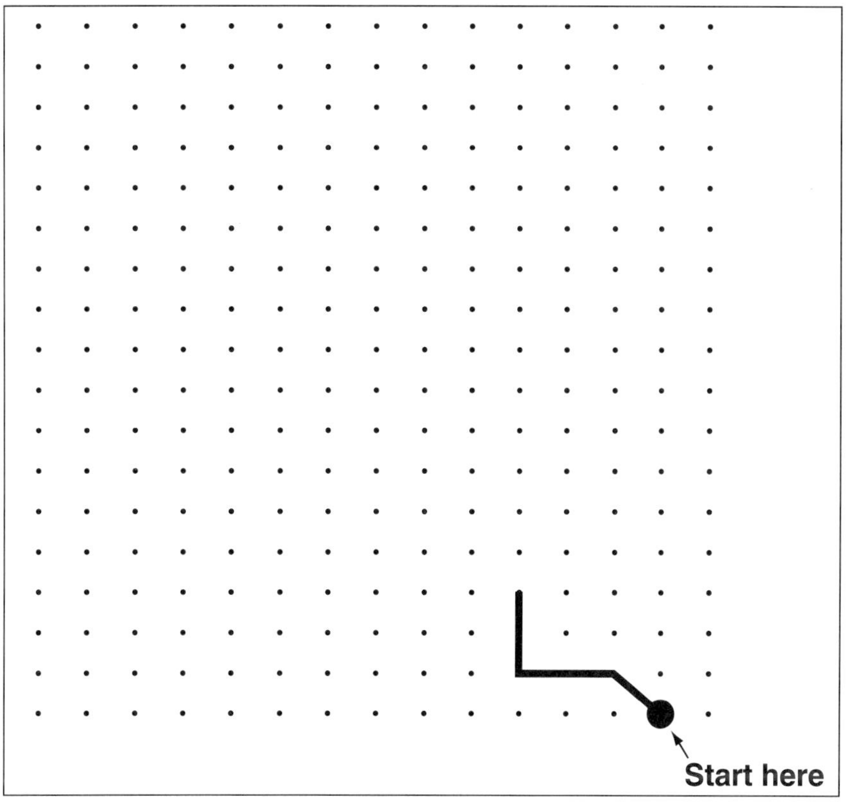

Directions

Go **North-west**, then **West**, then **West**, then **North**, then **North** ... **(this far has been done for you)**.

North North North North-east North-east East South-east North North West West North North North North East East North West North-west West North-west North-west South South-east South South South South-west West West South-west South-west South South South South South South-west South South-west West North-west North North-west South South South South-east East East East North-east North-east North-east East South-east South South East East East East.

I have drawn a ________________.

Recap *The main directions are* ***n***_________, ***s***__________, ***e***__________ *and* ***w***__________.

In this activity you will learn about direction

There are four main directions. These are **north**, **south**, **east** and **west**. Between these there are four other directions: **north-east**, **north-west**, **south-east**, and **south-west**.

These directions are shown on this diagram.

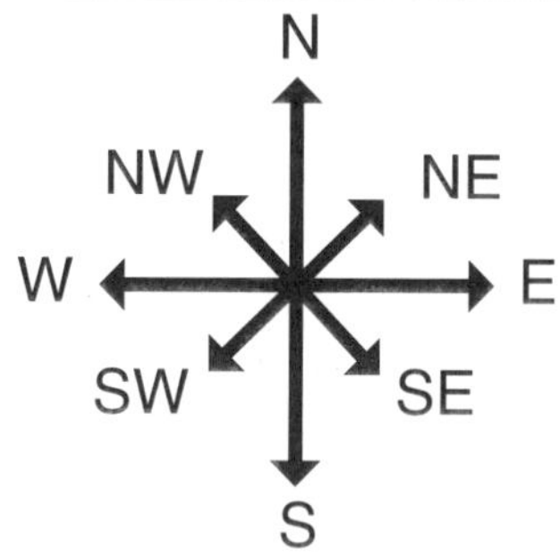

Activity

You can practice directions by playing the game below in pairs. You will need two dice and two counters to play.

- One player choses the blue 'start' and one the red 'start'. The winner is the first one to get to the same coloured 'end' square.
- Throw the two dice, add up the scores and move your counter one space in the direction shown on this table below.
- If your move takes you off the board you have to go back to your 'start'.

Total of dice	Direction
2	any direction
3	South-east
4	North-east
5	West
6	South
7	stay where you are
8	East
9	North
10	South-west
11	North-west
12	any direction

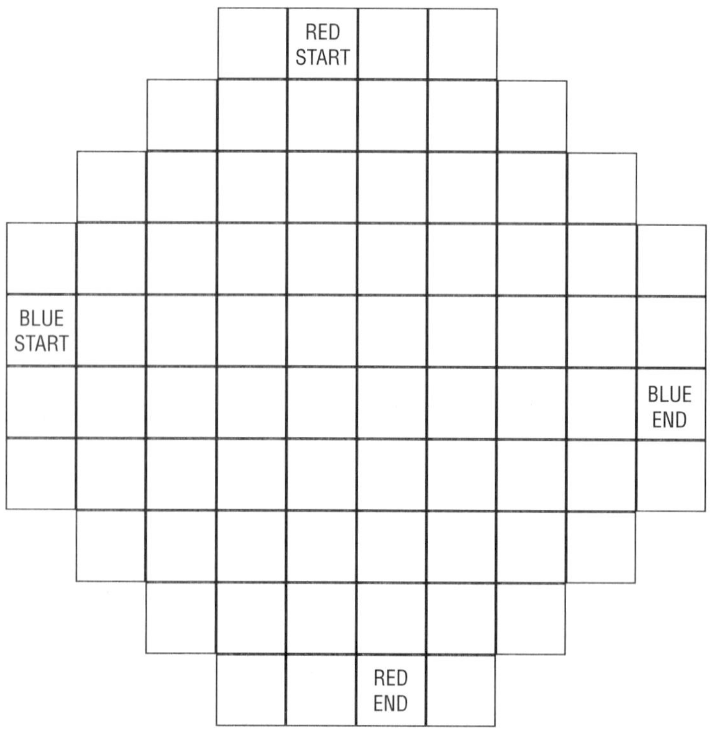

Recap

The main directions are ______________________________

In between these are ______________________________

In this activity you will learn about scale

Maps show places **smaller** than they are in real life.

The **scale** on a map lets us measure real distances.

Activities

1 Map **A** shows a simple map of Britain. Copy it, square-by-square, on to Map **B**. It has been started for you.

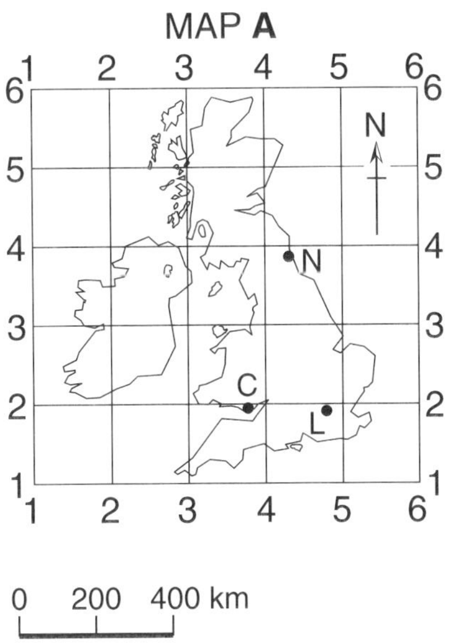

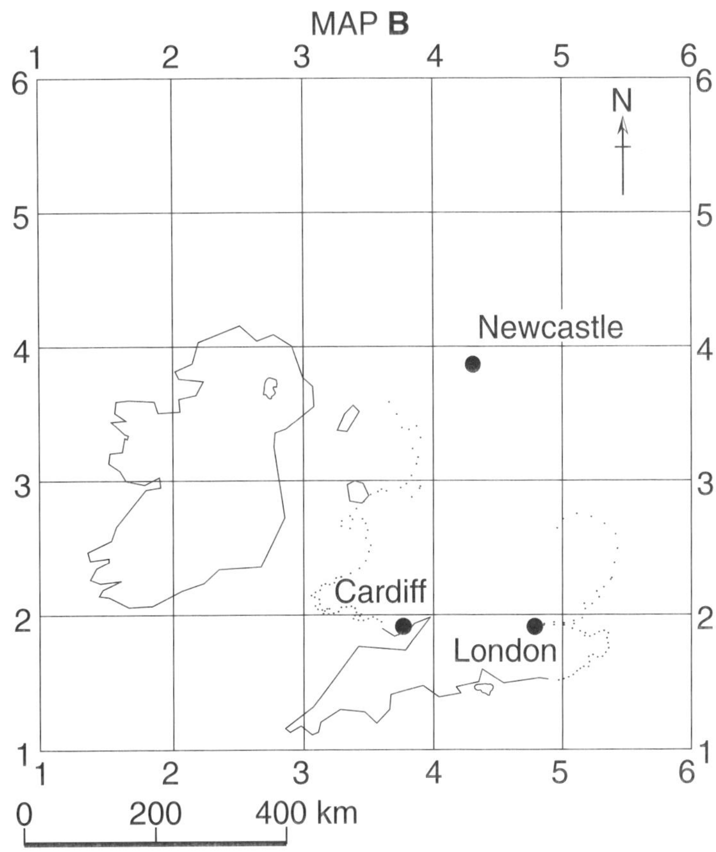

Well done! You have drawn your copy to a larger **scale**.

2 Look at your map, and join up the following 'heads' and 'tails'.

On Map A each square equals	400 km
On Map B each square equals	200 km
The distance from London to Newcastle is	200 km across
The distance from Newcastle to Cardiff is	200 km across
The distance from Cardiff to London is	400 km

3 Colour the **sea** on Map **B** in **blue**, and the **land** in **green**.

Recap *We measure distances on a map using the s__________.*

In this activity you will learn about scale

Maps show places **smaller** than they are in real life.

The **scale** on a map lets us measure real distances.

Activity

Here is a map of a desert island where you want to bury some treasure. Start at the **ship** and follow the instructions below, using the scale to help you. Each square is one square kilometre.
Mark your path on the map as you go.

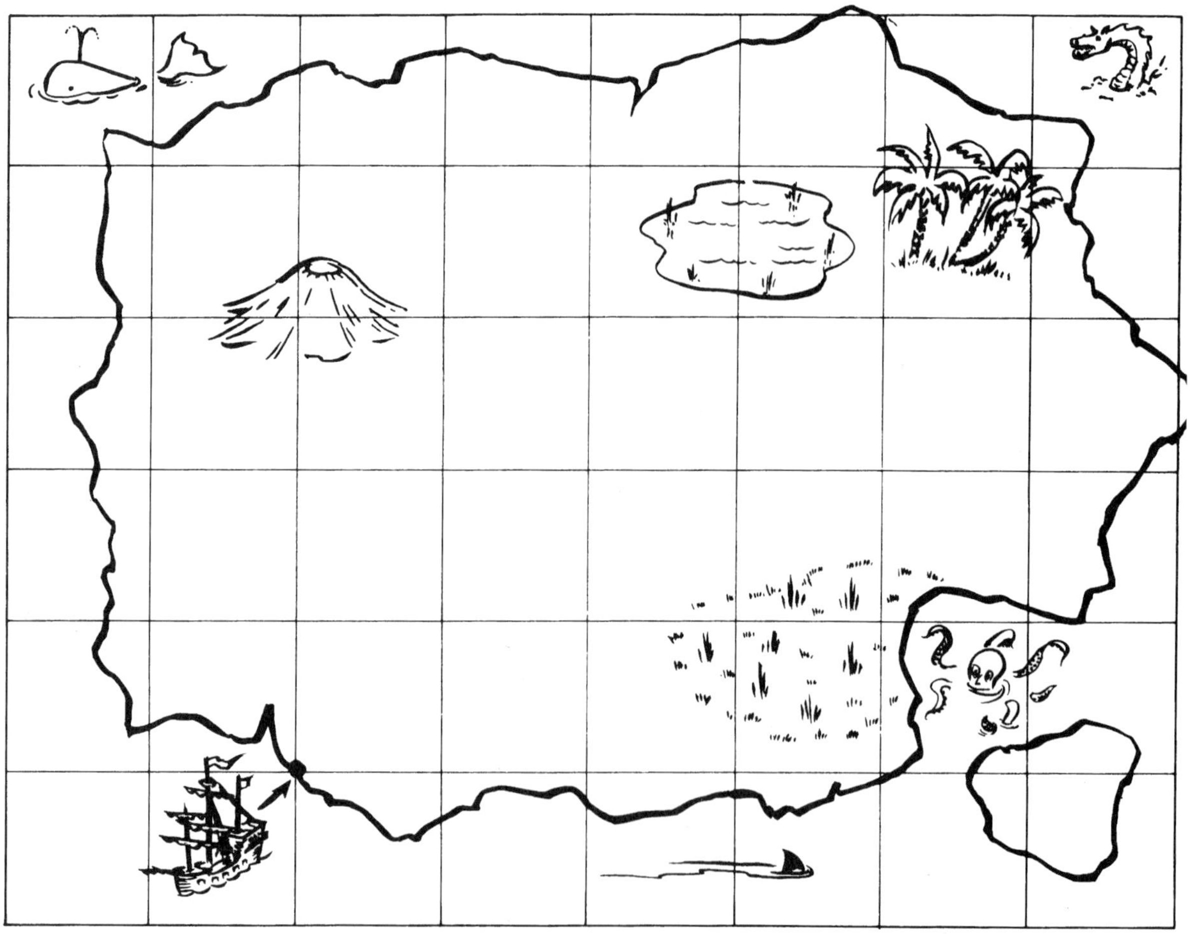

0 1 2 km

1 Go **north** for **2** km.
2 Go **east** for **4** km.
3 Go **north** for **3** km.
4 Go **west** for **1** km.
5 Go **south** for **1** km.
6 Go **west** for **4** km.
7 Go **south** for **3** km.
8 Go **east** for **2** km.
9 Go **north** for **2** km.
10 Go **east** for **1** km.
11 Go **south** for **3** km.
12 Put ✗ and bury the treasure.

To get straight back to the ship you have to go ________ for ________ km.

Recap *We measure distances on a map using the* **s**________.

In this activity you will learn about scale

Maps show places **smaller** than they are in real life.

The **scale** lets us measure real distances on a map or diagram.

Activities

1 Fill in the gaps below.

A scale of **1 cm : 1 km** means that every **2 cm** represents **2 km**. **5 cm** represents ______.
________ represents **10 km**. ________ represents **15 km**.

2 Here is a picture of Arabella the 'Angular Cat'.

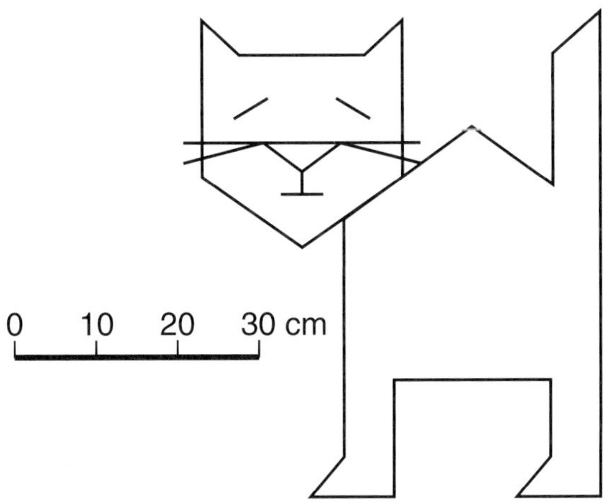

- On the scale-line every **1 cm** represents ______ in real life. This is a scale of **1:10**.
- Use the **scale-line** next to her to measure her.
- What is the length of her back paw? ________.
- How high is the tip of her tail above the ground? ________.
- How long is one of her whiskers? ________.
- How long is her eye? ________.
- If Fred Flea hops from the tip of one ear to the tip of the other how far does he go? ______.

3 Draw Arabella's 'cat-kennel' to scale in the space next to her.

The 'cat-kennel' is this shape.

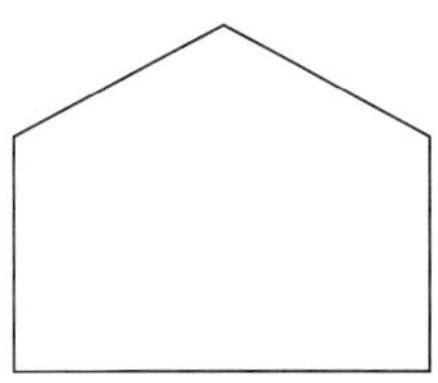

The kennel is: **70 cm across**,
60 cm high in the **middle**,
45 cm high on **each side**.

4 In your excercise book or folder draw a diagram of your book, or your pencil-case, using the same scale (1 : 10).

5 Now choose something else and try and draw it to scale (1:10).

Recap ***Scale** is used* ____.

In this activity you will learn about map symbols.

A **symbol** is a simple **picture** or a letter on a map.

The meaning of the symbols is shown in a list called a **key**.

Activity

Here is a map of 'Water-world'.

Use the map and the key to answer these questions.

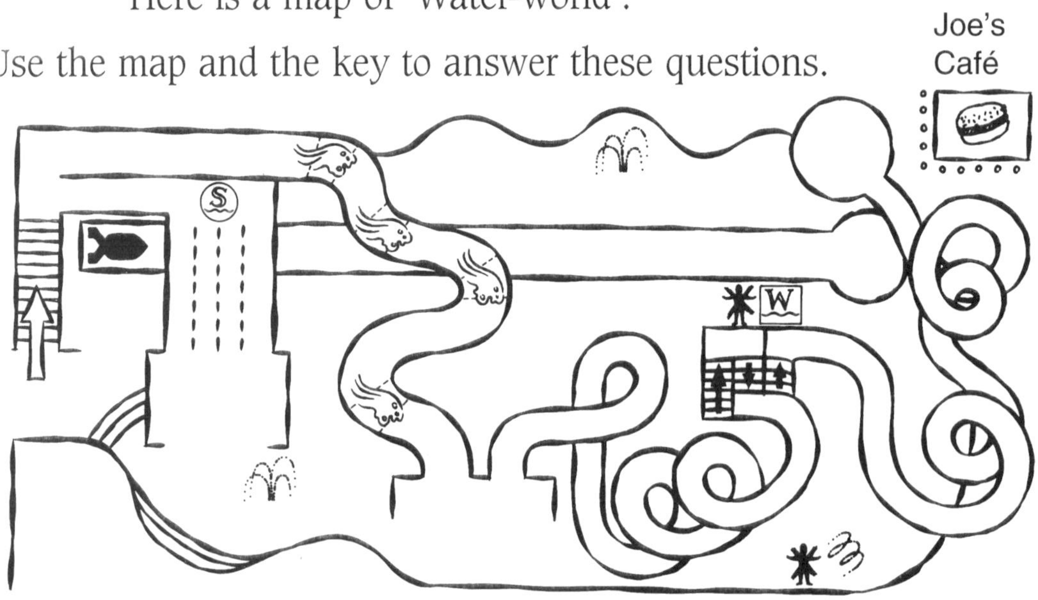

Key:

- Fountain
- Burger bar
- Rapids
- Water torpedo
- Corkscrew
- Whirlpool flume
- Water slide
- No children
- Ice cream
- First aid

- How many fountains are there? ______________________________
- Where can you buy a hamburger? ______________________________
- Which two rides go over the top of the **Water Torpedo**? ______________________________

  ____
- Which **two** rides are dangerous for young children? ______________________________

  ____
- Colour the **Rapids Ride** in **blue**.
- Colour the **Corkscrew** in **red**.
- Make up a symbol for an **ice-cream stall**. Draw it in the space in the key. Use it to show where you would put an ice-cream stall on the map.
- Make up a symbol for **first-aid**. Add a first-aid post to the map.
- Which ride do you think you would like best? ______________________________

Recap A **map symbol** is ______________________________

In this activity you will learn about map symbols

A **symbol** stands for something on a map. It may be a simple **picture** or a **letter**.

The meaning of the symbols is shown in a list called the **key**.

Activities

Here is a map of **School Island**. This map shows **physical features**.

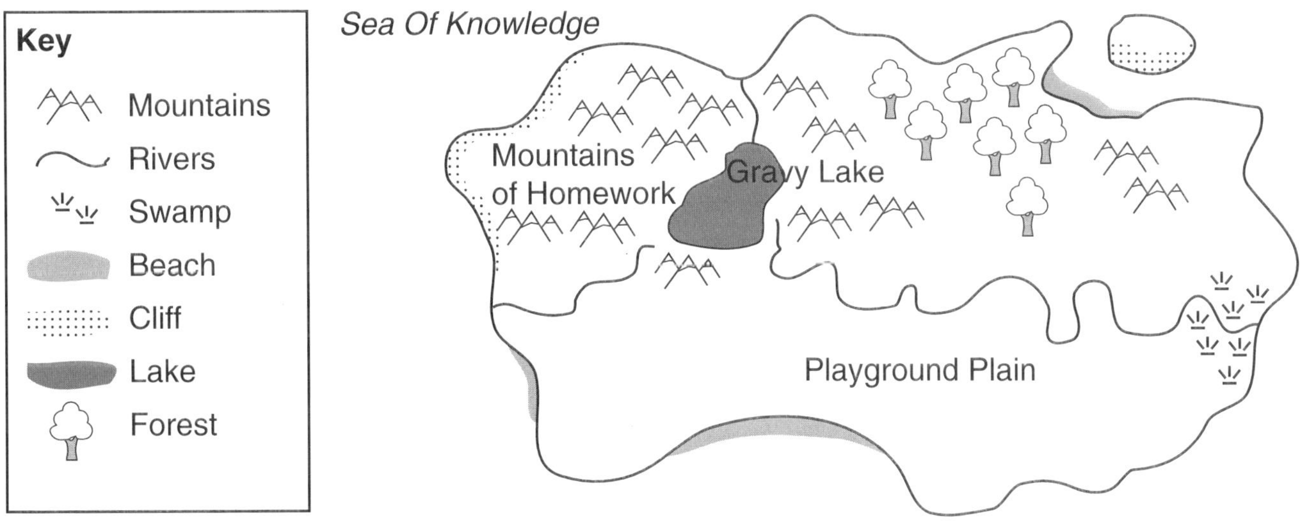

1 Add the **human features** of School Island to the map below. Use the symbols given in the key to mark on the **towns**, **roads**, and **airport**. Remember to use the map showing the physical features to work out the best places to put the human features.

2 Give the towns and counties any names you like. (Try to make them interesting!)

3 Make up some symbols for other human features, such as a **railway line**, **church**, or **hotel**. Show them in the key and add them to the map.

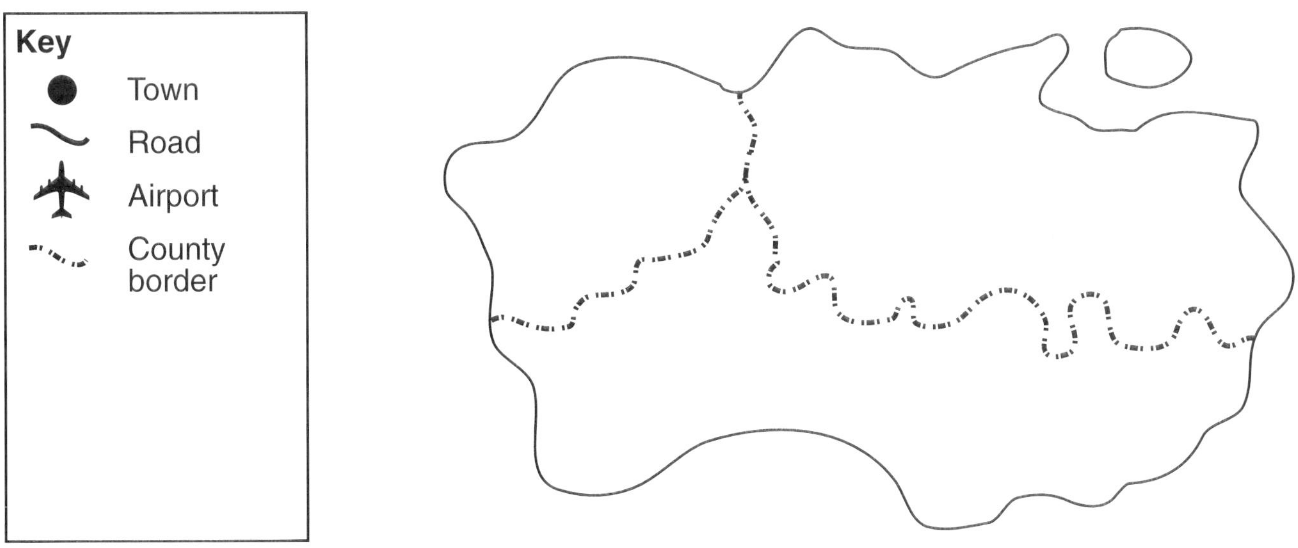

Recap A **map symbol** is ________________________________

In this activity you will learn about map symbols

A **symbol** stands for something on a map. It may be a simple **picture**, a **coloured line**, a **letter** or an **abbreviation** of a longer word.

The meaning of the symbols is shown in a list called the **key**.

Activities

The map below shows **Skull Island**.

Use the symbols in the key and the instructions below to complete the map.

- Add **cliffs** along the southern shore of **Jaw Island**.
- Add a row of **houses** in a line along the northern shore of **Jaw Channel**.
- Add a **river** flowing north from **Nose Lake** to the sea at the northern tip of the island.
- Add a **lighthouse** on the coast to the **north-east** of **Eye Volcano**.
- Add a **village** of five houses on the coast to the **north-west** of **Socket Volcano**.
- Add a **road** from the line of houses on the northern shore of Jaw Channel, along the **western edge** of the island, to the **village** with five houses.
- Add a **road** from the **village** to the **lighthouse**.
- Add a **church** between **Nose Lake** and **Eye Volcano**.
- Add a **path** from the **lake** to the **church**, and on to the **lighthouse**.
- Add a **swamp** where the **river** meets the **sea**.
- Add a **beach** along the **southern shore** of **Jaw Channel.**

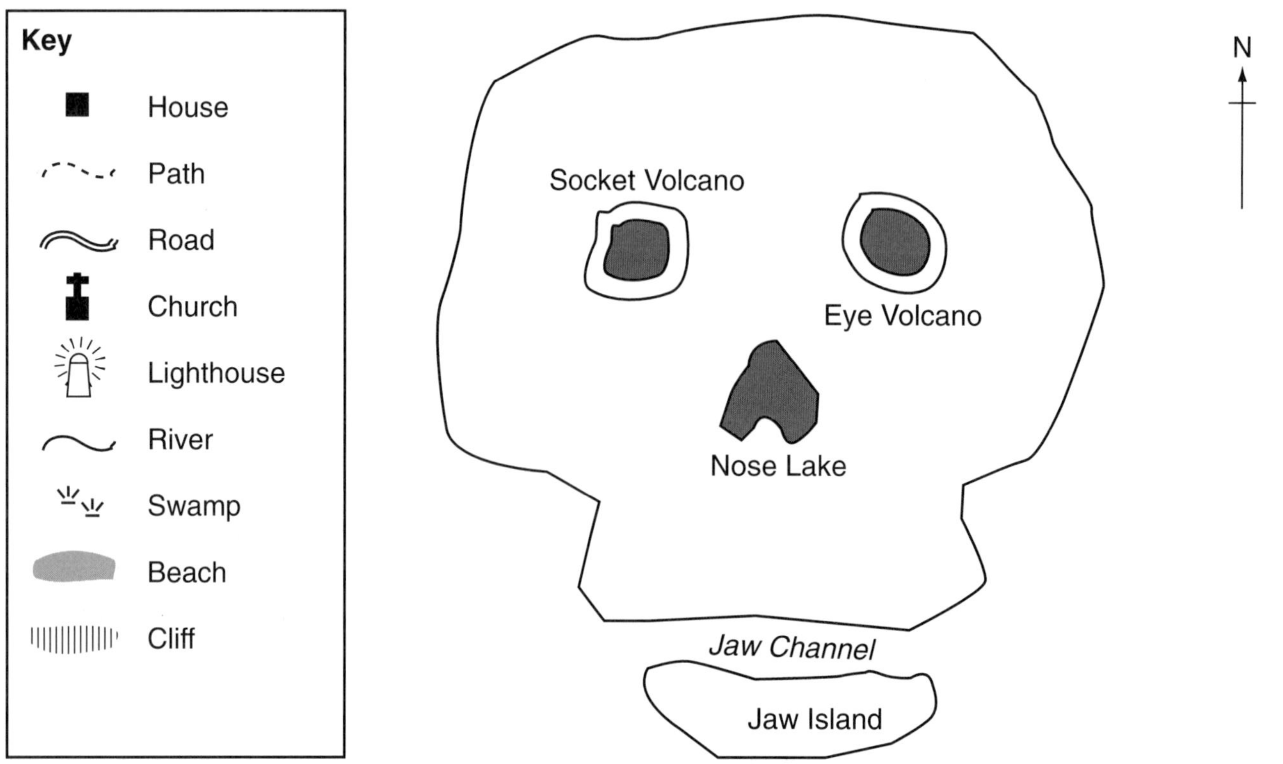

Recap *A map symbol is* ______________________________

In this activity you will learn about four figure grid references

Many maps have a **grid** of squares drawn on the map to make it easy to find things.

Grid References are the numbers which name a grid square. Grid squares need **four** numbers or **figures** to name them.

Activities

1 Look at the diagram below and complete the grid references. The first one has been done for you.

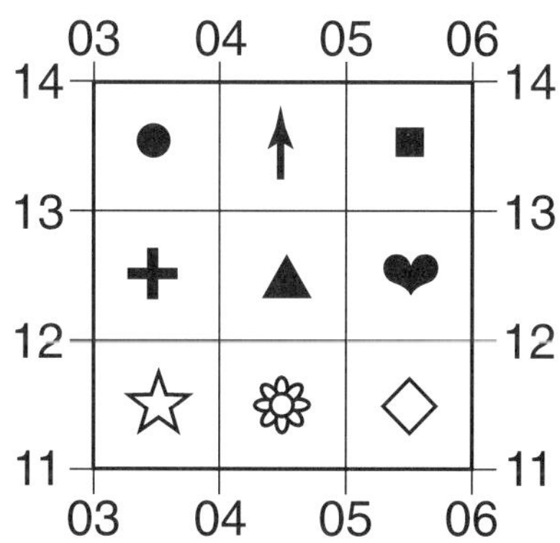

The ● is in square 0313.
The ✿ is in square 04_ _.
The ❤ is in square 05_ _.
The ◇ is in square _ _ _ _.
The ☆ is in square 0311.
The ✚ is in square _ _ _ _.
The ↑ is in square 0413.

2 Follow the lines below to find the **grid references** at the end. Look them up in the diagram underneath to see what prize each person has won at the fair.

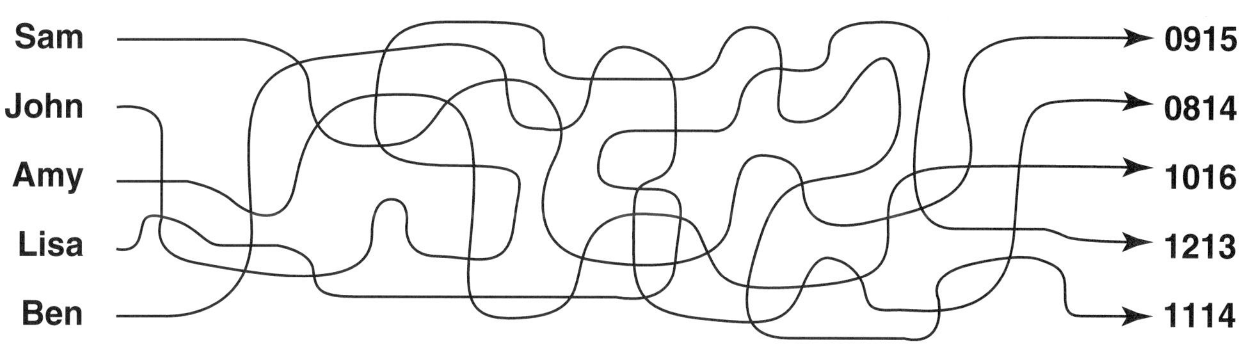

Sam has won ______________________________

John has won ______________________________

Amy has won ______________________________

Lisa has won ______________________________

Ben has won ______________________________

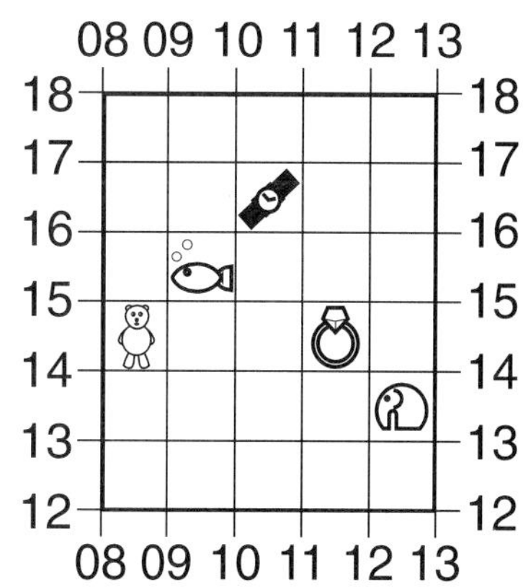

Recap ***Four figure grid references*** *are the numbers which help us to find* ***g****_______* ***s****_____________ on maps.*

In this activity you will learn about four figure grid references

Many maps have a **grid** of squares drawn on the map to make it easy to find things. **Four figure grid references** are the numbers which help us to find a particular square.

- The **first two** numbers of a grid reference are found along the **bottom** or **top** of a map.
- The **last two** numbers of a grid reference are found up the **sides** of a map.

Activity

Use the following grid references to work out the coded message in the diagram below. Write the letter which appears in each square in the correct space. (If the square is empty, it is the space between words.)
Cross out the references as you go.

1	0423	**6**	0624	**11**	0226	**16**	0429
2	0029	**7**	0822	**12**	1025	**17**	0224
3	0723	**8**	0329	**13**	0023	**18**	0620
4	1022	**9**	0621	**14**	0828	**19**	0427
5	0728	**10**	0926	**15**	1021	**20**	1029

Coded message

__ __ __ __ __ __ __ __ __ __ __ __ __ __ __ __ __ __ __ __
1 2 3 4 5 6 7 8 9 10 11 12 13 14 15 16 17 18 19 20

	00	01	02	03	04	05	06	07	08	09	10
29	A	B	C	D	E	F	G	H	I	J	!
28	K	L	M	N	O	P	Q	R	S	T	?
27	U	V	W	X	Y	Z	A	B	C	D	,
26	E	F	G	H	I	J	K	L	M	N	“
25	O	P	Q	R	S	T	U	V	W	X	
24	Y	Z	A	B	C	D	E	F	G	H	“
23	I	J	K	L	M	N	O	P	Q	R	-
22	S	T	U	V	W	X	Y	Z	A	B	
21	C	D	E	F	G	H	I	J	K	L	
20	M	N	O	P	Q	R	S	T	U	V	.

Recap

Four figure grid references help us to find ***g***_________ ***s*** _________ *on a map. The first two numbers are found along the* ***b*** __________, *the last two are found up the* ***s*** ________.

In this activity you will learn about four figure grid references

Many maps have a **grid** of squares drawn on the map to make it easy to find, or **locate**, things. **Four figure grid references** are the numbers which help us to locate a particular square.

- The **first two** numbers tell us how far to go along the **bottom** or **top** of the map.
- The **last two** numbers tell us how far to go up the **sides** of the map.

Activity

The grid below contains a mystery picture. Some of the squares have been coloured in black. Complete the rest of the picture by colouring in the grid squares as follows.

Orange	0805								
Brown	0706	0906	0802	0800					
Yellow	1310	1409	1508	1307	1509	1410	1408	1407	
Red	0003	1302	0608	1008	1108	0909	0709	0311	1203
	0508	0708	0908	0203	0809	0808			
Green	1100	1303	1405	1505	1001	0100	0411	0410	0109
	0306	0002	0101	1403	1000	0111	0110	0009	0105
	0305	0204	1404	1201	0210	1304	1101	0200	0211
	1102	1504	0509	0206	0205	0104	0102	0201	0510
	1202	0001	0609	0610	0010	0511			

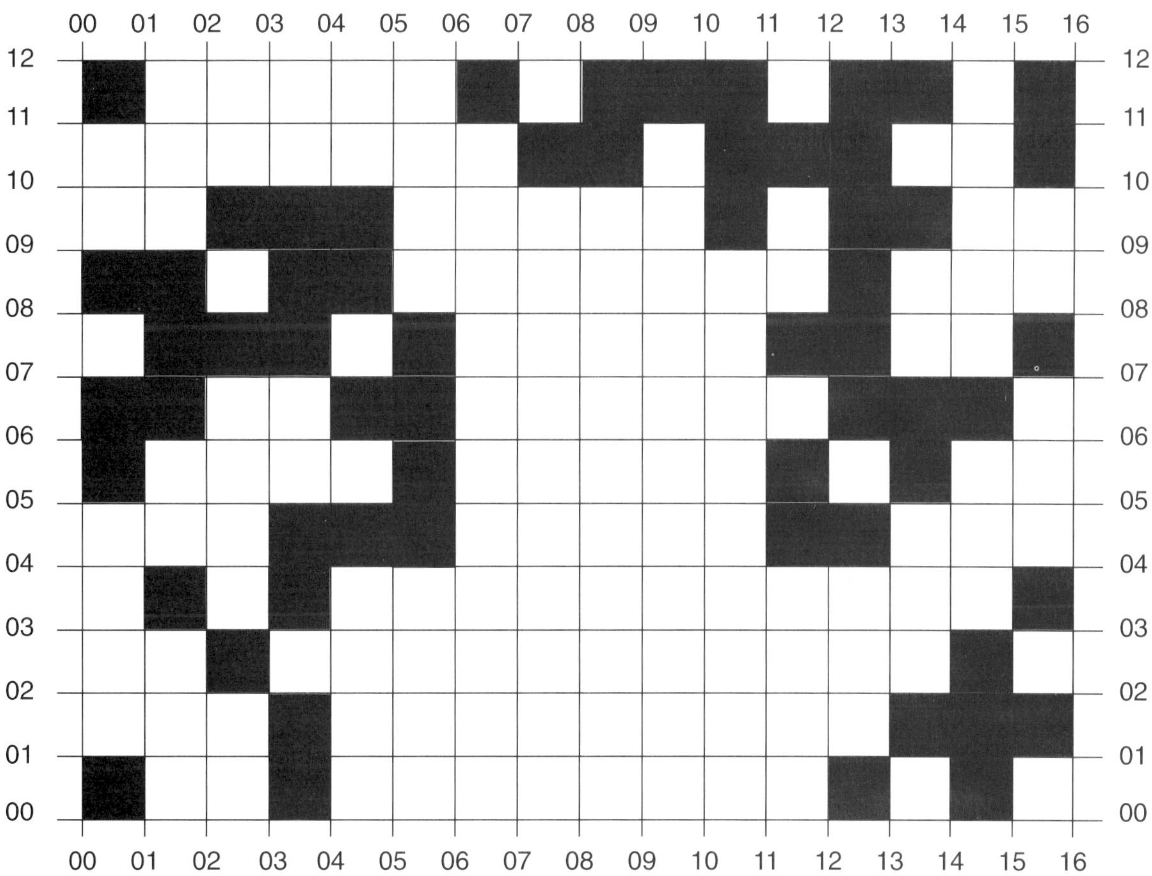

Recap *Four figure grid references are used to l__________ a particular g_____ s__________ on a map. The first two numbers ____________________ __________. The last two numbers ________________________.*

In this activity you will learn about six figure grid references

We can find **exact points** on a map by using **six** numbers or **figures**.

- The **first three** numbers tell us how far to go along the bottom or top of the map. The **third** number tells us the number of **tenths** of a grid square.
- The **last three** numbers tell us how far to go up the side of the map. The **sixth** number tells us the number of **tenths** of a grid square.

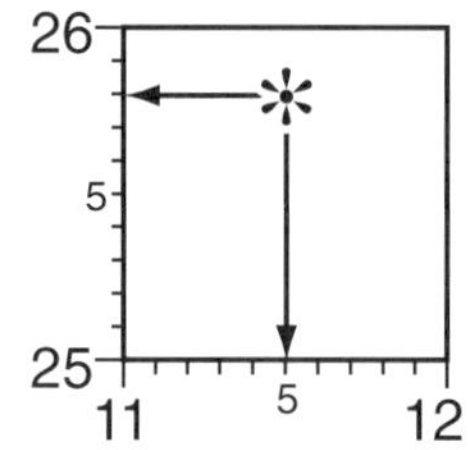

The ⁕ in this diagram is at **115 258**

Activities

1 Look at the map below. It shows **Danger Island**

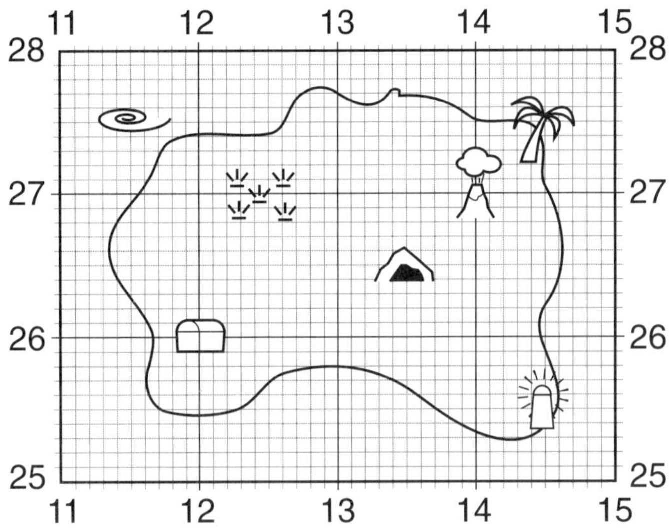

Using the map and the key, **underline** the correct answer for each of the following statements.

There is a **lighthouse** at	255 145	145 255	140 155.
There is a **cave** at	135 265	135 275	265 145.
There is **treasure** at	125 265	265 130	120 260.
There is a **palm tree** at	145 272	142 275	273 145.
At **113 276** there is a	whirlpool	swamp	cave.
At **124 270** there is a	wreck	swamp	whirlpool.
At **140 270** there is a	swamp	whirlpool	volcano.

2 Now mark ● at **135 255**, ✱ at **130 270** and ✗ at **111 259.**

Recap S______ **figure grid references** help us to find **exact** p__________ on maps.

In this activity you will learn about six figure grid references

We can find **exact points** on a map by using **six** numbers or **figures**.

- The **first three** numbers tell us how far to go along the bottom or top of the map. The **third** number tells us the number of **tenths** of a grid square.
- The **last three figures** tell us how far to go up the side of the map. The **sixth** number tells us the number of **tenths** of a grid square.

On a map you will have to estimate the tenths of each grid square.
Remember that five tenths is half a grid square.

Activity

Use the following **six figure grid references** to plot points **1** to **25** on the grid below. The tenths have been marked on for you.
Then join them up in order to see who's hiding!
Numbers **1** to **4** have been done for you. Cross out the references as you go.

1	020 530	**6**	050 530	**11**	060 510	**16**	054 510	**21**	027 505
2	025 529	**7**	060 518	**12**	060 502	**17**	045 510	**22**	030 505
3	030 524	**8**	075 508	**13**	054 502	**18**	037 511	**23**	024 522
4	034 524	**9**	090 502	**14**	054 505	**19**	033 502	**24**	020 521
5	045 531	**10**	075 505	**15**	055 505	**20**	027 502	**25**	016 519

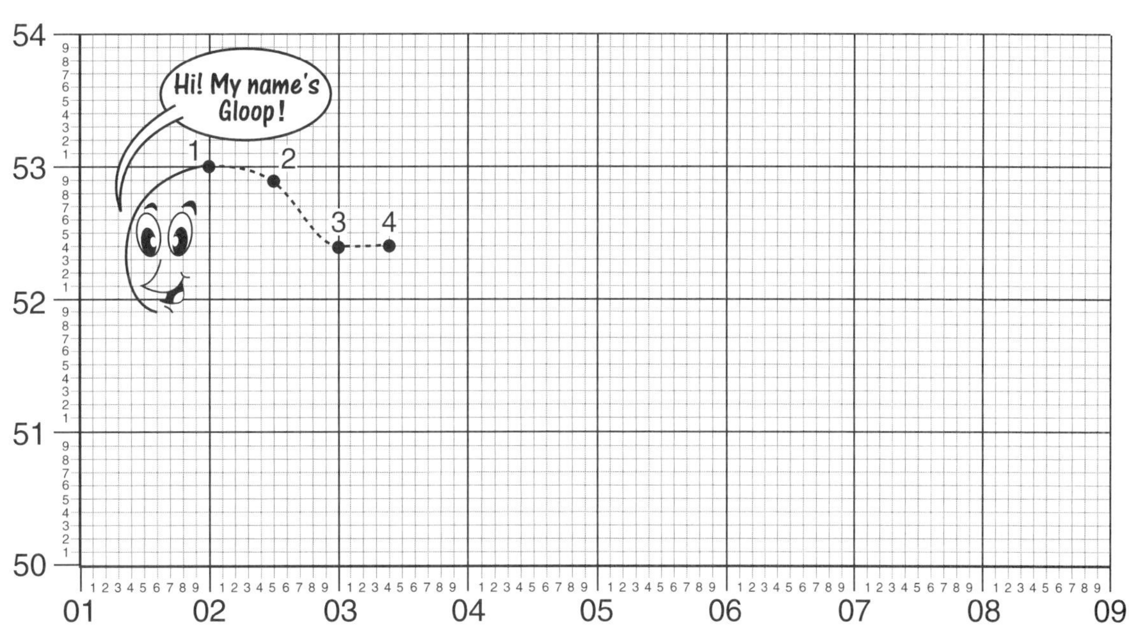

Recap *Six figure grid references help us find **exact points** on a map.*

*The **first three** numbers* ______________________________

____

*The **last three** numbers* ______________________________

____

In this activity you will learn about six figure grid references

We can find or **locate exact points** on a map by using **six** numbers or **figures**.

- The **first three** numbers tell us how far to go along the bottom or top of the map. The **third** number tells us the number of **tenths** of a grid square.
- The **last three** numbers tell us how far to go up the sides of the map. The **sixth** number tells us the number of **tenths** of a grid square.

On a map you will have to **estimate** the tenths of each grid square.

In this activity the tenths have been marked on for you.

Activities

1 Use the following **six figure grid references** to plot points **1** to **37** on the grid below. Join them up as you go to show a mystery creature.

1	030 513
2	022 518
3	020 510
4	009 510
5	014 516
6	014 541
7	003 542
8	000 545
9	010 562
10	008 567
11	010 584
12	014 576
13	015 564
14	020 573
15	028 580
16	026 569
17	021 561
18	028 555
19	037 553
20	045 550
21	056 538
22	060 528
23	061 530
24	063 527
25	065 528
26	065 524
27	067 524
28	063 517
29	057 512
30	060 508
31	028 508
32	028 511
33	032 514
34	041 514
35	033 523
36	033 527
37	041 531

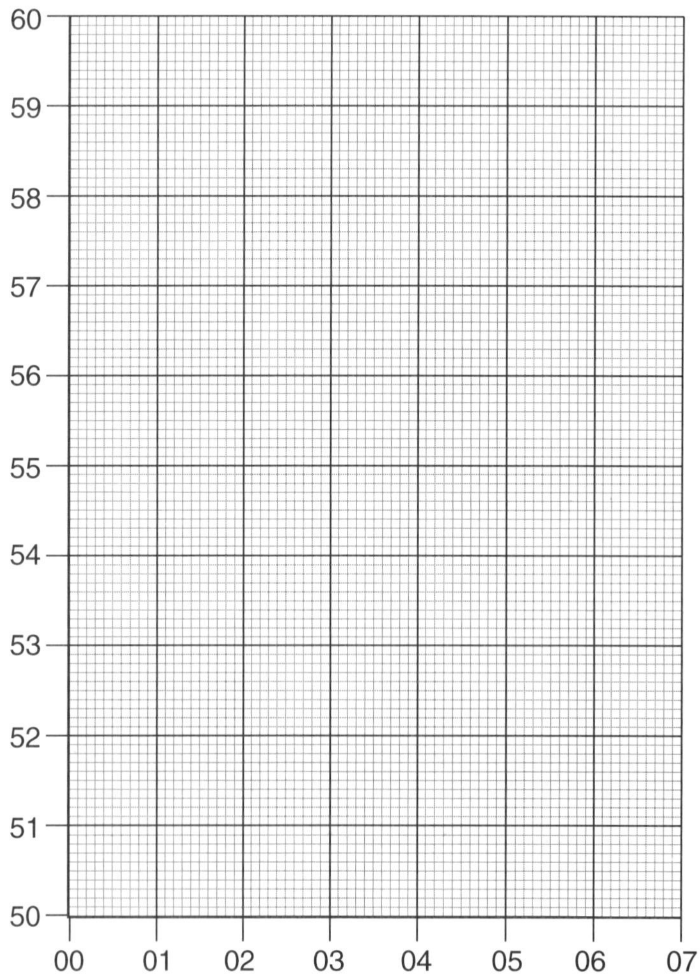

2 Give the creature a triangular-shaped eye. Write down the six figure grid references of the three corners of the eye.

1 _ _ _ _ _ _ **2** _ _ _ _ _ _ **3** _ _ _ _ _ _

Recap **Six figure grid references** help us to find **exact p**______________ on a map.

In this activity you will learn how height is shown on a map

Height can be shown on a map by using:

- **spot heights**. These show the exact height of a place.
- **layer colouring.** Here different heights are shown in different colours.

Activities

Study the map of the island below.

Word box

Between 10 and 20
Between 20 and 30
Over 30
Under 10

1 Boxes **A**, **B**, **C** and **D** point to **spot heights**. Fill in the height in each box.

2 Fill the heights in the Word box into the correct boxes **E**, **F**, **G** and **H** below.

3 Mark with a ✗ the highest point on the map.

4 Colour in the island with the colours shown on the map. Colour in the key with the same colours.

5 Go over the **0 metres** line in **blue**. This is the **coastline** because 0 metres is **sea level**.

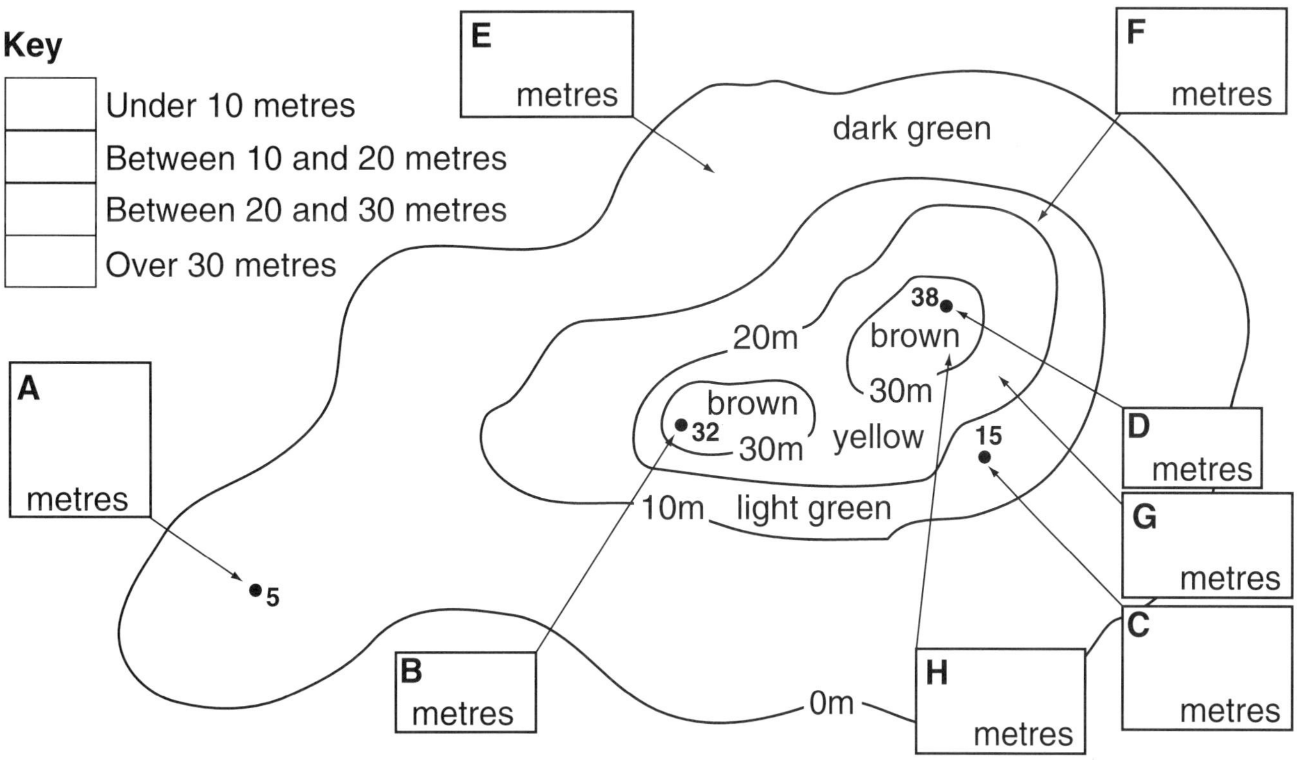

Recap *Height can be shown on maps by s________ h____________,*

or by l__________ c_________________.

In this activity you will learn how height is shown on a map

Height can be shown on a map by using:

- **spot heights**. These show the exact height of a place.
- **contours**. These are lines on a map which join up places which have the same height.
- **layer colouring**. Here areas of different heights are shown by bands of different colours.

Activities

Key

	Below 80m
	80–100m
	100–120m
	120–140m
	Over 140m

1 Study the map below. The solid lines are **contours**.

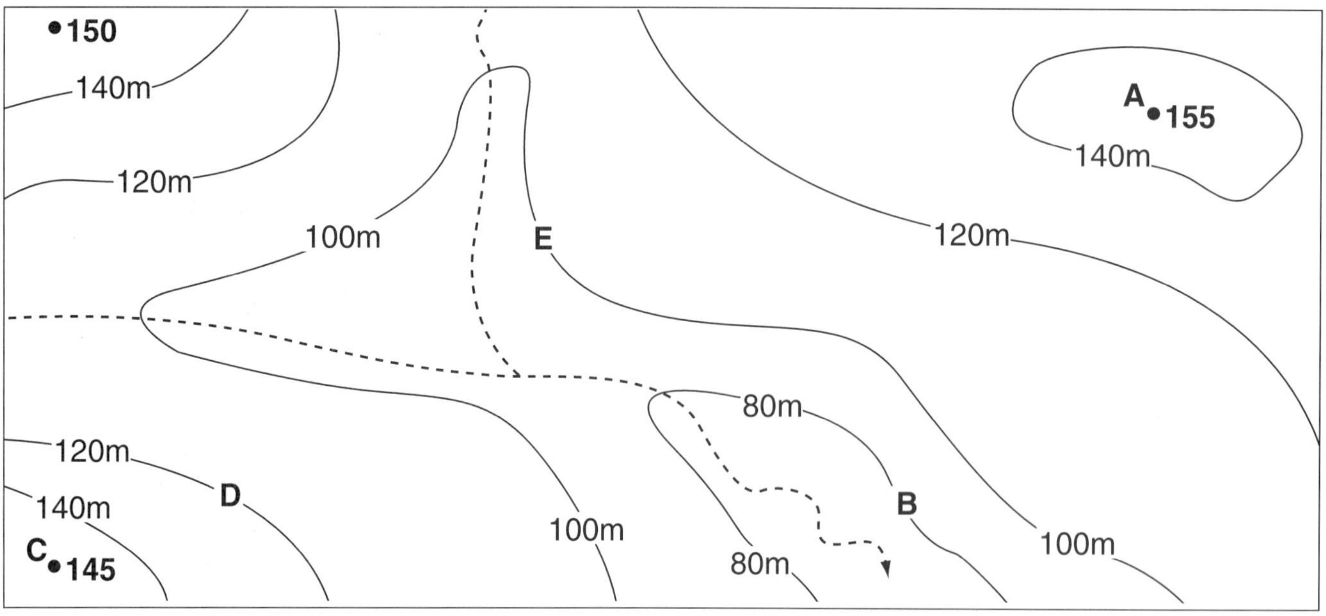

- Go over the dotted lines in **blue** to show the rivers.
- Colour the land **below 80 metres** in **dark green**.
- Colour the land **between 80 metres** and **100 metres** in **light green**.
- Colour the land **between 100 metres** and **120 metres** in **yellow**.
- Colour the land **between 120 metres** and **140 metres** in **orange**.
- Colour the land **over 140 metres** in **brown**.
- Colour in the boxes in the **key** in the same colours.

2 Write down the letters **A** to **E** in order of height, from **highest** to **lowest**.

highest → → → → → → → → → → → → → → **lowest**

_____ _____ _____ _____ _____

Recap *Height can be shown on maps by ____________________,*

________________ or __________ ____________________.

In this activity you will learn how height is shown on a map

Height can be shown on a map by using:

- **spot heights**. These are numbers which show the exact height of a place.
- **contours**. These are lines on a map which join up places which have the same height.
- **layer colouring**. Here areas of different heights are shown by bands of different colours.

Activities

1 Complete your own **contour map** by following the instructions around the diagram below. Start with **Box 1**.

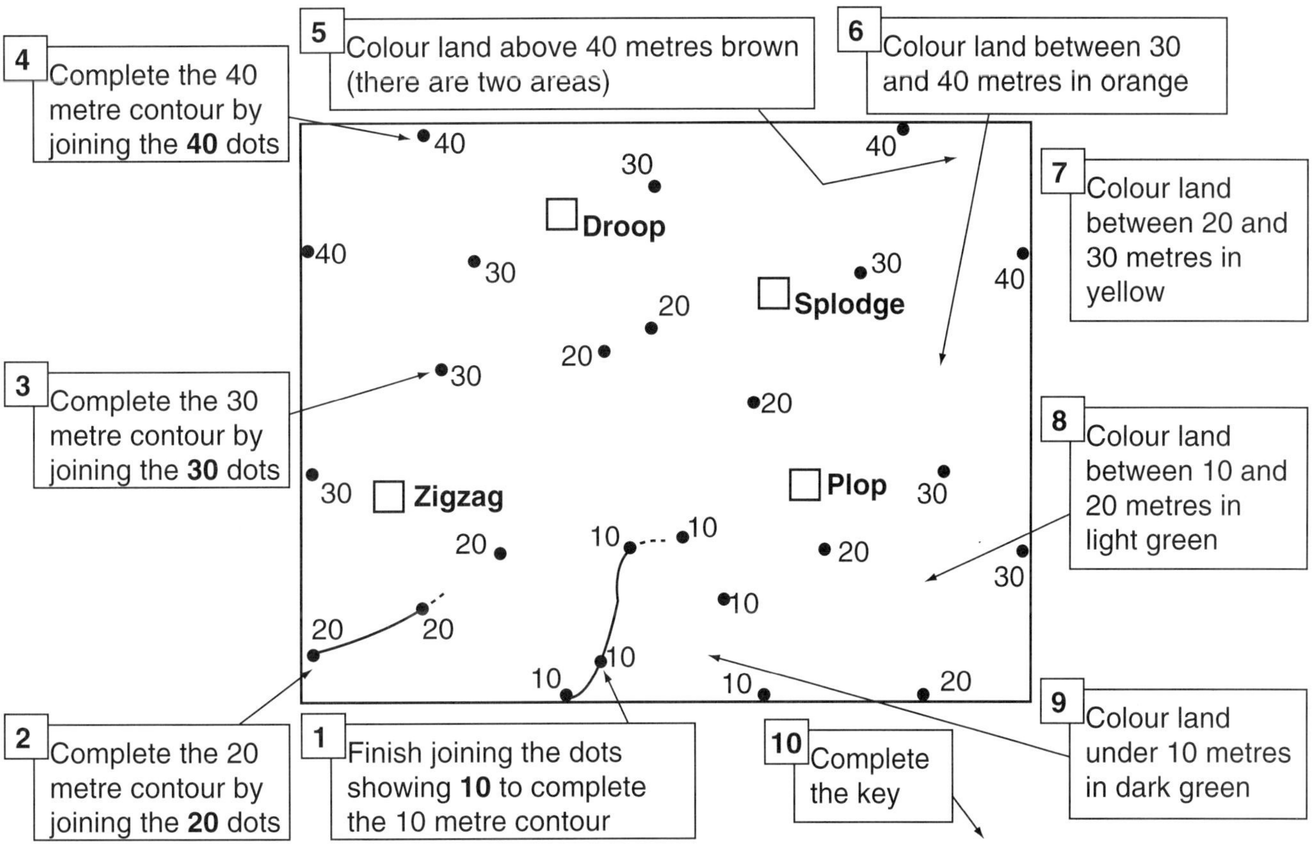

2 Complete the following sentences.

- The height at **Plop** is __________ metres.
- The height at **Droop** is __________ metres.
- The height at **Splodge** is __________ metres.
- The height at **Zigzag** is __________ metres.

Key

	Over 40m
	__________
	20–30m
	__________
	Below 10m

3 Mark the place which you think has the **lowest** height with a ✗.

Recap *Height can be shown on a map by* ______________________________

____.

In this activity you will learn about contours

Relief is the **height** and **shape** of the land.

Contours are lines drawn on a map that can tell us what the relief is like. Contours that are **close together** show **steep** slopes. Contours that are **far apart** show **gentle** slopes.

Activities

1 Look at the diagram below. Complete the paragraphs using the words in the Wordbox.

Word box

flat • steep • gentle
together • contours • apart
contours • far • close

This part of the land has a **g**______slope. The **c**__________
are **f**___ **a**_____ . If there are no contours at all the land is **f**______.

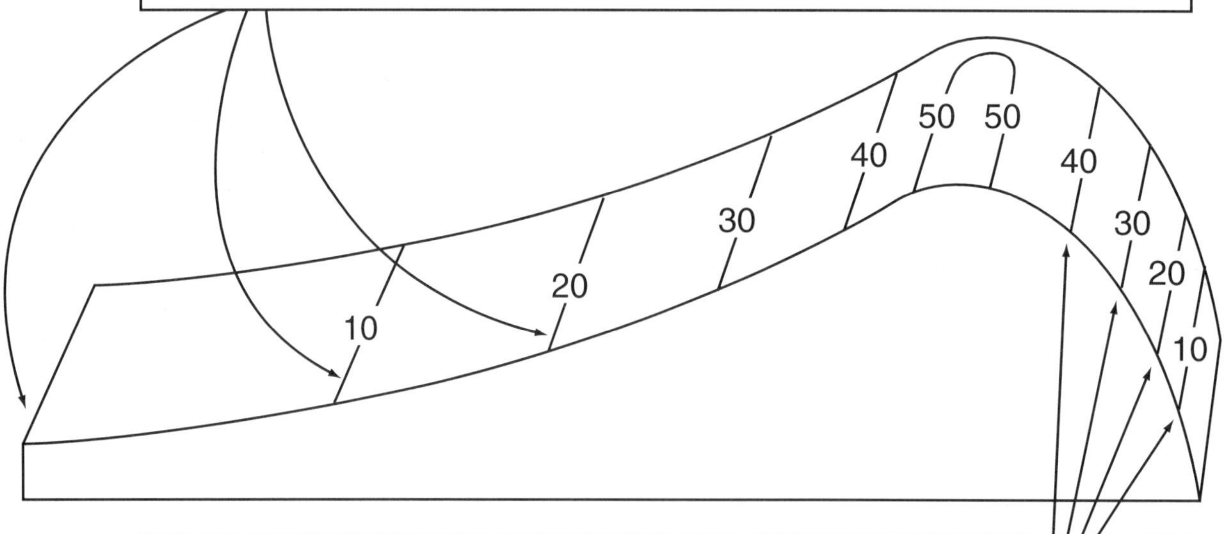

This part of the land has a **s**______slope. The **c**______________
are **c**______ **t**_____________ .

2 Colour the part of the diagram where the land is steep in **dark green**, and the part where the land is gently sloping in **light green**.

Mark the highest point on the diagram with a cross ✗.

Recap *Relief is the* ***h***________________ *and* ***sh***______________ *of the land.*

*C*________________ *l*______________ *show relief on maps.*

In this activity you will learn about contours

Relief is the **height** and **shape** of the land.

Contours are lines drawn on a map that can tell us what the relief is like. Contours that are **close together** show **steep** slopes. Contours that are **far apart** show **gentle** slopes.

Activities

The diagrams below show three different **land-shapes**.

1 Go over the contours on each diagram in **brown**.

2 Cut out the shapes very carefully. Fold along the dotted lines.

3 Stick **Flap A** under **Side A**, and **Flap B** under **Side B** to make three **land-shape models**.

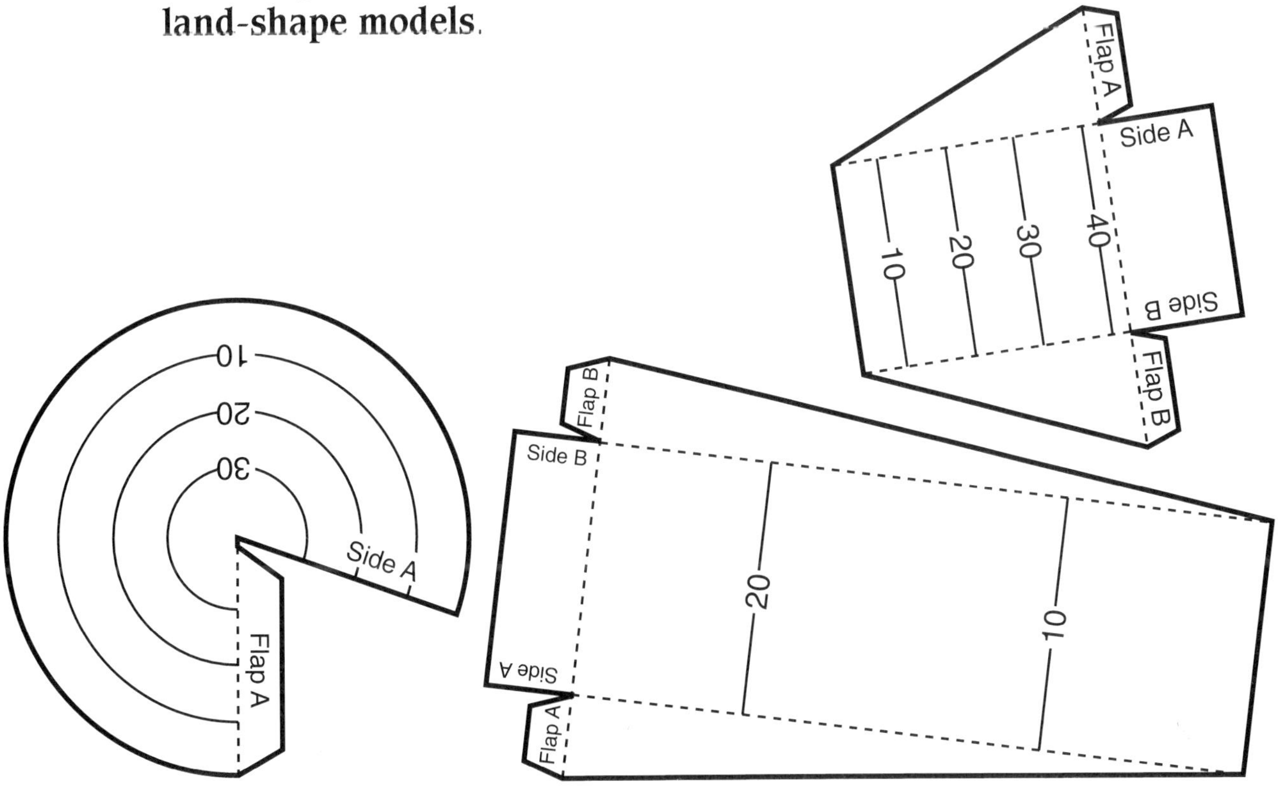

4 Look at your models, and then draw lines to match up the following 'heads' on the left with the 'tails' on the right.

Contour lines are straight and close together on	a round hill
Contour lines are straight and far apart on	a steep, straight slope
Contour lines are in circles on	a gentle, straight slope

Recap **Relief** is the **h**____________ and _____________ of the land.

Relief is shown on maps by _____________________________.

In this activity you will learn about contours

Relief is the **height** and **shape** of the land.

Contours are lines drawn on a map that can tell us what the relief is like. Contours that are **close together** show **steep** slopes. Contours that are **far apart** show **gentle** slopes.

The **pattern** of the contours tells us about the **features** of the land.

Activities

1 Match each of the **land-shape** drawings below to the correct contour pattern by writing the correct letter in the space provided. The first one has been done for you.

Land shape **Letter** **Contour pattern**

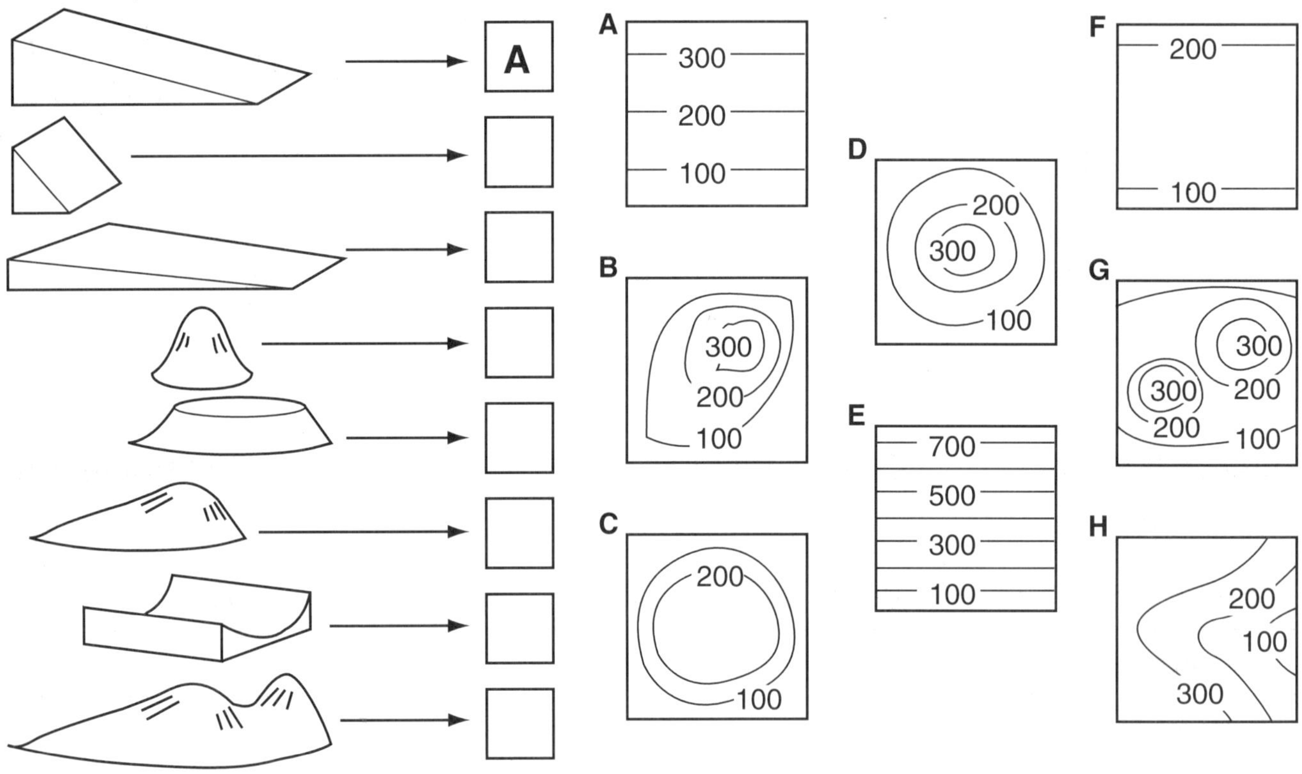

2 Look at the land-shapes below. Decide which contour pattern in the table describes each land-shape, and copy them into the correct space in the table.

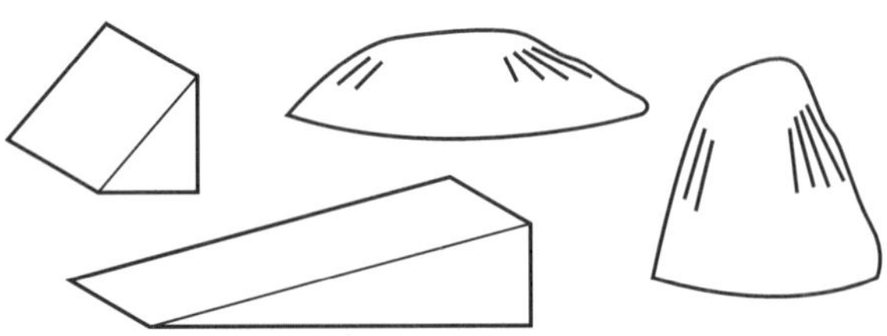

	CONTOUR PATTERNS	
	circles	straight lines
far apart		
close together		

Recap *Relief is* ____.

The ***p***______________ *of contours and their distance* ***a***____________ *tell us about the features of the land.*